# Research Series on the Chinese Dream and China's Development Path

**Project Director**
Xie Shouguang, President, Social Sciences Academic Press

**Series Editors**
Li Yang, Chinese Academy of Social Sciences, Beijing, China
Li Peilin, Chinese Academy of Social Sciences, Beijing, China

**Academic Advisors**
Cai Fang, Gao Peiyong, Li Lin, Li Qiang, Ma Huaide, Pan Jiahua, Pei Changhong, Qi Ye, Wang Lei, Wang Ming, Zhang Yuyan, Zheng Yongnian, Zhou Hong

Drawing on a large body of empirical studies done over the last two decades, this Series provides its readers with in-depth analyses of the past and present and forecasts for the future course of China's development. It contains the latest research results made by members of the Chinese Academy of Social Sciences. This series is an invaluable companion to every researcher who is trying to gain a deeper understanding of the development model, path and experience unique to China. Thanks to the adoption of Socialism with Chinese characteristics, and the implementation of comprehensive reform and opening-up, China has made tremendous achievements in areas such as political reform, economic development, and social construction, and is making great strides towards the realization of the Chinese dream of national rejuvenation. In addition to presenting a detailed account of many of these achievements, the authors also discuss what lessons other countries can learn from China's experience.

More information about this series at http://www.springer.com/series/13571

Guangjin Chen · Jianhua Yang
Editors

# Chinese Dream and Practice in Zhejiang—Society

*Editors*
Guangjin Chen
Institute of Sociology
Chinese Academy of Social Sciences
Beijing, China

Jianhua Yang
Institute of Public Policy Studies
Zhejiang Academy of Social Sciences
Hangzhou, Zhejiang, China

Published with support of Zhejiang People's Publishing House

ISSN 2363-6866                    ISSN 2363-6874   (electronic)
Research Series on the Chinese Dream and China's Development Path
ISBN 978-981-13-7405-0          ISBN 978-981-13-7406-7   (eBook)
https://doi.org/10.1007/978-981-13-7406-7

Jointly published with Social Sciences Academic Press, Beijing, China
The print edition is not for sale in China Mainland. Customers from China Mainland please order the
print book from: Social Sciences Academic Press.

Library of Congress Control Number: 2019935831

This Springer imprint is published by the registered company Springer Nature Singapore Pte Ltd.
The registered company address is: 152 Beach Road, #21-01/04 Gateway East, Singapore 189721,
Singapore

# Series Preface

Since China's reform and opening began in 1978, the country has come a long way on the path of Socialism with Chinese Characteristics, under the leadership of the Communist Party of China. Over thirty years of reform, efforts and sustained spectacular economic growth have turned China into the world's second-largest economy and wrought many profound changes in the Chinese society. These historically significant developments have been garnering increasing attention from scholars, governments, and the general public alike around the world since the 1990s, when the newest wave of China studies began to gather steam. Some of the hottest topics have included the so-called China miracle, Chinese phenomenon, Chinese experience, Chinese path, and the Chinese model. Homegrown researchers have soon followed suit. Already hugely productive, this vibrant field is putting out a large number of books each year, with Social Sciences Academic Press alone having published hundreds of titles on a wide range of subjects.

Because most of these books have been written and published in Chinese; however, readership has been limited outside China—even among many who study China—for whom English is still the lingua franca. This language barrier has been an impediment to efforts by academia, business communities, and policy-makers in other countries to form a thorough understanding of contemporary China, of what is distinct about China's past and present may mean not only for her future but also for the future of the world. The need to remove such an impediment is both real and urgent, and the *Research Series on the Chinese Dream and China's Development Path* is my answer to the call.

This series features some of the most notable achievements from the last 20 years by scholars in China in a variety of research topics related to reform and opening. They include both theoretical explorations and empirical studies and cover economy, society, politics, law, culture, and ecology; the six areas in which reform and opening policies have had the deepest impact and farthest-reaching consequences for the country. Authors for the series have also tried to articulate their visions of the "Chinese Dream" and how the country can realize it in these fields and beyond.

All of the editors and authors for the *Research Series on the Chinese Dream and China's Development Path* are both longtime students of reform and opening and recognized authorities in their respective academic fields. Their credentials and expertise lend credibility to these books, each of which has been subjected to a rigorous peer review process for inclusion in the series. As part of the Reform and Development Program under the State Administration of Press, Publication, Radio, Film, and Television of the People's Republic of China, the series is published by Springer, a Germany-based academic publisher of international repute, and distributed overseas. I am confident that it will help fill a lacuna in studies of China in the era of reform and opening.

Xie Shouguang

# Contents

# Chapter 1
# Introduction: Zhejiang's Social Development and the Chinese Dream

**Guangjin Chen**

The Chinese dream covers the following three basic connotations: China has become a stronger and more prosperous country; the national rejuvenation has been achieved; the people's happiness has been realized. These connotations represent the lofty ideals which have always been pursued by the Chinese people since modern times. Since the reform and opening-up, Zhejiang has unceasingly tapped local resources, especially local social and cultural resources, to strive for common prosperity, Zhejiang has ranked No. 1 among the provinces and autonomous regions (except municipalities directly under the Central Government) across the country in economic aggregate, Zhejiang has stayed ahead nationwide in the per capita income level of urban and rural households and the income gap between urban and rural residents in Zhejiang is the smallest nationwide. In an effort to continuously develop the local economy and incessantly improve the living standard of urban and rural residents, the Party committees and governments at various levels, the primary-level self-governing organizations, enterprises, public institutions, urban and rural residents, and the non-governmental social organizations in Zhejiang have coordinated at different levels, made great experiments and innovations through extensive participation to preliminarily achieve economic modernization, promote social modernization, make remarkable achievements in modern social development, gradually improve the modern social governance system and make sure that it constantly delivers benefits; thus, from the perspective of social development, laying a good foundation for and providing new driving forces for gradually realizing the Chinese dream in Zhejiang, and offering the successful experience from vivid social and living practice for gradually realizing the Chinese dream nationwide.

G. Chen (✉)
Chinese Academy of Social Sciences, Beijing, China

© Social Sciences Academic Press and Springer Nature Singapore Pte Ltd. 2019
G. Chen and J. Yang (eds.), *Chinese Dream and Practice in Zhejiang—Society*,
Research Series on the Chinese Dream and China's Development Path,
https://doi.org/10.1007/978-981-13-7406-7_1

## 1.1 Social Development is an Important Part of Efforts to Realize the Chinese Dream

The substance of the Chinese dream lies in achieving the great rejuvenation of the Chinese nation; the Chinese dream is defined at the following three levels: China has become a stronger and more prosperous country; the national rejuvenation has been achieved; the people's happiness has been realized. "A stronger and more prosperous country" means that China enjoys great comprehensive national strength and has really become one of the major countries and great powers in the world, China, a country with a population of more than 1.3 billion, enjoys a say in an increasingly multipolar world that is commensurate with a country of that size. "The national rejuvenation" means that the Chinese nation has risen again, is restoring its past brilliance, and has even reached a new height, and so once again it stands tall and firm in the world through modernization. "The people's happiness" emphasizes the common interest and coordination among the Chinese people of all ethnic groups and means that common prosperity has been achieved for everyone, and that the Chinese people live more well-off, are safer, have happier lives and have become more confident and vibrant. These three definitions constitute a whole, and the priority and purpose are as follows: The people's happiness has been realized. In particular, as economic development enters an era of new normal, the people's happiness is not only the achievement made through economic development, but also the motive force for boosting further economic development.

The Chinese dream cannot be realized in one stroke. The 18th National Congress of the Communist Party of China vowed to finish building a moderately prosperous society in all respects at the 100th anniversary of the founding of the Communist Party of China. This is the first step towards realizing the Chinese dream. The second step is that, as stressed by Deng Xiaoping since 1987, China will basically achieve modernization and reach the level of the moderately developed countries at the 100th anniversary of the founding of the new China, which means that, as mentioned by the report delivered during the 18th National Congress of the Communist Party of China, China will become a prosperous, democratic, culturally advanced and harmonious modern socialist country. The third step is that after China reaches the level of the moderately developed countries, China will be close to and reach the level of the most developed country in the world by the end of the 21st century through continued hard work. Comrade Xi Jinping pointed out, "The 18th National Congress of the Communist Party of China charted a grand blueprint for finishing the building of a moderately prosperous society in all respects and more rapidly pushing forward socialist modernization, and made the clarion call of the times for moving towards achieving the two centenary goals—to finish building a moderately prosperous society in all respects by the time the Communist Party of China celebrates its centenary in 2021 and to turn China into a modern socialist country that is prosperous, strong, democratic, culturally advanced, and harmonious by the time it celebrates its centenary in 2049". According to the guiding principles adopted during the 18th National Congress of the Communist Party of China, we vow to realize the Chinese Dream of the rejuvenation of the Chinese nation. The Chinese dream is a vivid expression highly acceptable to the people and is the "biggest common denominator".

Therefore, the fundamental connotation of the Chinese dream has formed through a long period of half a century though it is a summary, recently put forward, of a developmental strategy having a vital bearing on China's future and destiny. Now we have the preliminary foundation for realizing it since China ranks No. 2 in the world in economic aggregate, the modern economic structure and social structure have preliminarily taken shape, and the modern political, economic and social systems commensurate with the modern economic and social structures are in the making. With hard work for a century on the basis of the above foundation, China will ultimately become one of the developed countries in the world; this is a glorious and realistic dream. The Chinese dream is shared by the Chinese people; it inherits Chinese history, takes root in China's reality and signifies China's future. The Chinese dream is historical, realistic and future-oriented. The Chinese dream contains the unremitting efforts made by countless dedicated patriots; it carries the common aspirations of the entire Chinese population; it presents the bright future that the country will become stronger and more prosperous, the national rejuvenation will be achieved and the people's happiness will be realized.[1] Based on such an understanding, at the closing ceremony of the 1st Session of 12th National People's Congress, comrade Xi Jinping stressed that we must venture down the Chinese path, carry forward the Chinese spirit and gather Chinese strength. These three aspects stressed by comrade Xi Jinping are the fundamental conditions or principles for realizing the Chinese dream.

The Chinese dream is rich in connotation. The building of a stronger and more prosperous country, the realization of both a national rejuvenation and the people's happiness encapsulate its connotations. According to the 18th National Congress of the Communist Party of China, the overall plan for promoting the cause of socialist modernization with Chinese characteristics consists of making coordinated progress in the political, economic, cultural, social and ecological fields. This systematically sheds light on the Chinese path and Chinese experience resulting from gradual theoretical clarification and continuous practical experiments since the founding of the new China, especially the reform and opening-up; this represents the historical advancement along the fundamental path towards realizing the Chinese dream. Social development has a vitally important status in this framework and plays an extremely important role in it. In the contemporary era, the essence of social development lies in achieving social modernization.[2] A society is not considered a modern society unless it has a modern social structure and social organizational system which are fit for it and serve as its structural foundation, and based on the above foundation, actions are being taken according to the requirements of a modern society to constantly strengthen and improve the people's wellbeing, establish and improve the modern social undertaking and social service system, the modern social security system and the modern social governance system, promote social integration, social fusion, social security and achieve social harmony; this is the main part of efforts to

---

[1]Xi (2013).
[2]Lu (2011).

push forward social development; this is also the social foundation for making the country prosperous and strong and for making sure that the people live happy lives.

Since the reform and opening-up, under the leadership of the Communist Party of China, China has constantly advanced the cause of modern social development and has made tremendous achievements. With an increasing economic aggregate, continuous adjustment of the economic structure and constant improvement of the socialist market economic system, the modern transformation of China's social structure has been expanded continuously, the urban-rural structure has been optimized incessantly and the proportion of the urban population has increased continually; as the social class structure has been adjusted constantly, the proportion of the middle class is on the increase, a modern social structural system has preliminarily taken shape[3]; the ways to organize the members of the society have ceaselessly undergone modern change, a social organizational system dominated by social groups, private non-enterprise units and foundations has developed rapidly, and a modern social organizational structure in which the government, the market and the society support each other has preliminary taken shape; the labor employment system has been improved constantly, labor employment has shown steady growth; the income of urban and rural residents has grown rapidly year by year, the people's living standard has been on the rise; the social undertaking system has been improved gradually, the quality of social public services has been enhanced continually, the level of equal access to basic public services has been increased constantly; a modern social security system has been preliminarily set up, and thus China is steadily moving towards the goal of extending social security to all possible groups and providing moderate security; social governance philosophies keep pace with the times through continuous innovations; China has gradually developed a modern social governance system with Chinese characteristics which is led by the Party committee, spearheaded by the government, features social coordination and public participation and is guaranteed by the rule of law.

When it comes to social development, Zhejiang also shows the same general trend, a more outstanding performance and has made more significant achievements; Zhejiang has gathered a great amount of experience which offers very important inspiration and reference for promoting social development in the rest of the country. Scientifically studying Zhejiang's practice in social development, thoroughly analyzing and fully summarizing Zhejiang's experience in social development is of very significant theoretical and practical value for us in promoting the great cause of realizing the Chinese dream.

---

[3]Lu (2010).

## 1.2 The Adjustments of the Modern Social Structure and the Development of Social Organizations

Social structure has rich connotations; population structure, urban-rural structure, labor employment structure, social class structure, social organizational structure fall within the scope of social structure.[4] From the perspective of social development, the adjustments of the structure of the distribution of the urban-rural populations, labor employment structure, social class structure and social organizational structure are the fundamentals exerting a decisive impact on the modern transformation of the social structure. This section focuses on analyzing the modern transformation of Zhejiang's social structure in these respects.

Zhejiang has stayed far ahead among most provinces and autonomous regions (except municipalities directly under the Central Government) in the adjustment of the structure of its urban-rural population, and Zhejiang's level in this regard is about 10 percentage points higher than the national average level (see Fig.1.1). The time when the rate of Zhejiang's urbanization exceeded 50% was 10 years ahead of the time when the same scenario occurred nationwide. In 2013, Zhejiang ranked No.4 among 28 provinces (autonomous regions, municipalities directly under the Central Government—except Beijing, Tianjin and Shanghai which are the first three municipalities designated directly under the Central Government) in the proportion of urban population, Zhejiang's proportion of urban population was slightly lower than that in Guangdong, Liaoning and Jiangsu. Moreover, internationally, there are four main indicators for measuring the degree of industrialization, including the rate of urbanization. Based on the rate of urbanization, the stage at which the urban population accounts for 40–60% is the stage of industrialization; the stage at which the urban population accounts for more than 60% is the later stage of industrialization. According to such criterion, Zhejiang entered the later stage of industrialization in 2010. Urbanization is not only the structure or manifestation of economic and social development, but it is also a motive force for economic and social development. This is a consensus reached in the academic circles.

The structure of labor employment is the basic part of the social structure. With respect to China's transformation from a traditional social structure to a modern one, it is crucial that the structure of labor employment changes from the traditional one dominated by agricultural employment and manual occupations to the one dominated by non-agricultural employment and semi-manual, non-manual occupations. Since the reform and opening-up, both the industrial structure and the occupational structure in employment have tended to be upgraded in China,[5] showing such a change. The modern transformation of the structure of labor employment in Zhejiang is more apparent than that across the country, and it has become more prominent since the 21st century (see Table 1.1).

---

[4]Lu (2010)
[5]Lu (2004).

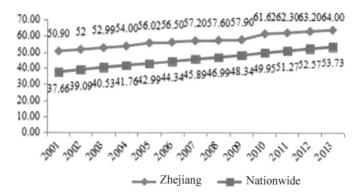

**Fig. 1.1** Comparison of the rate of the urbanization of the population between Zhejiang and the country as a whole. *Source* China Statistical Yearbook (over the years)

**Table 1.1** Comparison of the industrial structure in labor employment between Zhejiang and the country as a whole

|  | Zhejiang | | | Nationwide | | |
|---|---|---|---|---|---|---|
|  | The primary industry | The second industry | The tertiary industry | The primary industry | The second industry | The tertiary industry |
| 窗体顶端 2000 窗体底端 | 35.58 | 35.45 | 28.97 | 50.0 | 22.5 | 27.5 |
| 2001 | 33.44 | 36.10 | 30.46 | 50.0 | 22.3 | 27.7 |
| 2002 | 30.97 | 37.44 | 31.59 | 50.0 | 21.4 | 28.6 |
| 2003 | 28.30 | 41.20 | 30.50 | 49.1 | 21.6 | 29.3 |
| 2004 | 26.06 | 43.61 | 30.33 | 46.9 | 22.5 | 30.6 |
| 2005 | 24.50 | 45.07 | 30.43 | 44.8 | 23.8 | 31.4 |
| 2006 | 22.63 | 45.78 | 31.59 | 42.6 | 25.2 | 32.2 |
| 2007 | 20.07 | 46.78 | 33.15 | 40.8 | 26.8 | 32.4 |
| 2008 | 19.22 | 47.61 | 33.17 | 39.6 | 27.2 | 33.2 |
| 2009 | 18.32 | 48.05 | 33.63 | 38.1 | 27.8 | 34.1 |
| 2010 | 16.00 | 49.79 | 34.21 | 36.7 | 28.7 | 34.6 |
| 2011 | 14.57 | 50.86 | 34.57 | 34.8 | 29.5 | 35.7 |
| 2012 | 14.14 | 50.96 | 34.90 | 33.6 | 30.3 | 36.1 |
| 2013 | 13.67 | 49.97 | 36.36窗体底端 | 31.4 | 30.1 | 38.5 |

*Source* China Statistical Yearbook (2014), Zhejiang Statistical Yearbook (2014)

According to Table 1.1, the industrial structure in labor employment has changed fundamentally in Zhejiang in more than a decade since the beginning of the 21st century; in 2013, the proportion of agricultural employment was less than 14%, being 18 percentage points lower than that across the country; the proportion of non-agricultural employment exceeded 86%, being 18 percentage points higher than that across the country. Of course, in non-agricultural employment, the proportion of employment in the secondary industry approached 50%, being near 20% points higher than that across the country; that in the tertiary industry was more than 2% points lower than that across the country, suggesting a high degree of development of the industrial economy in Zhejiang.

Regarding the occupational structure in labor employment, semi-manual and non-manual occupations developed rapidly and were optimized constantly. According to statistics, in late 2013, the people at and above the undergraduate level and those at the junior college level accounted for 18.6 and 15.5% of the people employed by urban units in Zhejiang, respectively. With wide adoption of the practicing qualification system, vigorous development of vocational education and year-by-year improvement of workers' professional quality in Zhejiang, various types of professional and technical personnel made up an increasing proportion in urban units. In 2013, the ratio of management personnel, technical personnel and workers in the post structure of the employed people became 1:2.4:7.5; in other words, management personnel and technical personnel accounted for nearly 1/3 of the employed people in urban units.

The modern transformation of the social class structure is noticeable in two respects. First, profound social differentiation has arisen from economic and social development and the changes in the pattern of interests, while new social classes have emerged and rapidly developed in this process. The most important change is the growth of two new classes, those of private business owners and individual businesses. Zhejiang has stayed ahead nationwide in the development of individual private economy, resulting in two new social classes on a large scale, those of private business owners and individual businesses. Second, the middle class has expanded continuously. The middle class generally includes two parts: various kinds of small and medium-sized business owners with certain assets (including urban and rural small and medium-sized business owners, individual business owners and agricultural specialized households, and they are classified as the old middle class) and the new middle class including operational management personnel, professional and technical personnel and working staff. According to such a definition, the middle class accounted for about 15% in the Chinese society in the late 1990s, and afterwards, that proportion increased by about 1 percentage point each year; currently it is probably about 30%.[6] In 2013, in Zhejiang, small and medium-sized business owners, individual business owners within the class of private business owners accounted for 12%, while management personnel and technical personnel within the new middle class accounted for more than 1/3; if the personnel in the Party and government departments, white collar workers in enterprises and public institutions and large

---

[6]Lu (2010).

specialized households in rural areas are considered, it is estimated that the proportion of the middle class could exceed 45% in Zhejiang; furthermore, with the further development of the new and hi-tech industries in Zhejiang, that proportion might further increase. In this sense, Zhejiang has the foundation of and conditions for developing a social class structure that is dominated by the middle class.

In Zhejiang, social organizations have developed rapidly and have been highly dense. According to the statistics from the Department of Civil Affairs of Zhejiang Province, in 2013, there were more than 120,000 social organizations registered and put on file, including social groups, private non-enterprise units and foundations in Zhejiang, among which 40,201 social organizations were officially registered. Without regard to the social organizations put on file, there were 8.4 officially registered social organizations for every 10,000 people in Zhejiang. According to the statistics from the Department of Civil Affairs of Zhejiang Province, in the same period, there were 547,245 officially registered social organizations nationwide, with 4 social organizations for every 10,000 people. The density of social organizations in Zhejiang was 2.1 times that of the social organizations across the country. The fast-growing social organizations serve as the new forces for promoting self-service and self-governance in the society in Zhejiang's urban and rural areas.

## 1.3 The Work on Strengthening and Improving the People's Wellbeing

Work should be done to ensure and continuously improve the people's wellbeing, make the people live better material and cultural lives, make sure that the people have access to employment, old-age care, medical services and housing so that they really live and work in peace and contentment. This is the realistic and genuine part of the Chinese dream for every Chinese person. Overall, Zhejiang has also been at the forefront of the country in the development of programs relating to the people's wellbeing, laying a solid foundation for finishing building a moderately prosperous society in all respects in advance.

Employment is fundamental to the people's wellbeing. Since the beginning of the 21st century, Zhejiang's labor employment has grown steadily and the rate of its registered urban unemployment has been significantly lower than the national average level (see Fig.1.2). For the growth of aggregate employment, during the period 2001–2013, employment grew annually by an average of 2.71% in Zhejiang, and before 2009, the growth of labor employment was more prominent; after 2010, the growth of aggregate employment declined, possibly because of such factors as industrial transfer. In the same period, the nation's aggregate employment grew annually by an average of 0.58%, equivalent to 21.4% of Zhejiang's growth. As Zhejiang achieved noticeable growth of employment, on the one hand, Zhejiang guaranteed the employment of local population better. After 2004, the rate of registered urban unemployment declined steadily and was obviously lower than the national average

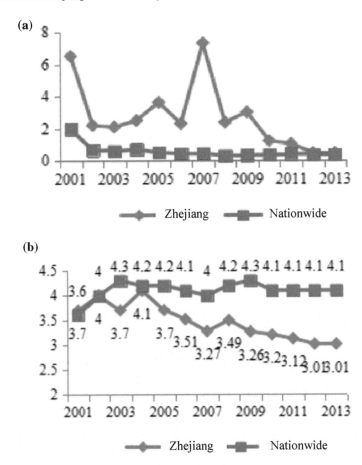

**Fig. 1.2** **a** Comparison of the growth of employment between Zhejiang and the country as a whole. (*Source* China Statistical Yearbook (2014), Zhejiang Statistical Yearbook (2014)), **b** Comparison of the rate of registered urban unemployment between Zhejiang and the country as a whole. *Source* China Statistical Yearbook (2014), Zhejiang Statistical Yearbook (2014)

rate. On the other hand, Zhejiang absorbed the employment of a massive external population. For instance, according to the analysis conducted by the Zhejiang Bureau of Statistics, a population of about 11,824,000 flowed from other provinces into Zhejiang in 2010, accounting for 21.7% of the entire permanent resident population, up 8,135,000 or 220.5% over 2000, an average annual increase of 12.4%. Among the external population, the population working, doing business in Zhejiang or going to Zhejiang due to a job transfer constituted the majority; that population accounted for 84.7% of the entire migrant population in 2010.[7]

---

[7]Zhang (2012).

The increasing income of urban and rural residents is an important material foundation for ensuring and improving the people's wellbeing. In this process, it is also necessary to achieve social fairness. Since the reform and opening-up, like the rest of the country, Zhejiang has always witnessed the rapid growth of the income of urban and rural residents. Since the beginning of the 21st century, the base of the growing income of urban and rural residents has expanded constantly; after the growth effect from the initial reform, especially the rural reform, was unleashed to the greatest extent, the difficulties in realizing a rapid growth of urban and rural residents' income mounted; the Party committees and governments at various levels in Zhejiang attached more and more importance to this problem and made great efforts at raising the income of urban and rural residents, delivering significant outcomes. During the period 2000–2013, the per capita disposable income of urban households increased from 9,279 yuan to 37,851 yuan in Zhejiang, following that in Shanghai and Beijing, an average annual increase of 9.33%; the per capita net income of rural households rose from 4,254 yuan to 16,106 yuan (Zhejiang ranked No. 1 among provinces, municipalities and autonomous regions across the country in this regard for 29 consecutive years, an average annual increase of 8.68%, see Table 1.2); both figures were higher than the national average annual growth rate involving the per capita disposable income of urban households (9.16%) and the national average annual growth rate involving the per capita disposable income of rural households (7.44%). As the income of urban and rural residents increased year by year, their material and cultural level also rose steadily; as from 2000, the Engel coefficient of the per capita living consumption expenditure in urban households was lower than 40% in Zhejiang, suggesting entry into the stage of affluence,[8] basically being in sync with the country as a whole; the Engel coefficient of the per capita living consumption expenditure in rural households was lower than 40% as from 2003, a time being nine years ahead of the time (2012) when that in rural households across the country was lower than 40%. Besides continuous increase in income and the level of consumption expenditure, the per capita housing area of urban and rural households also increased significantly (see Table 1.2). During the period 2000–2013, the per capita housing area of urban households grew by 95.3%, much higher than the national average growth rate in the same period; the per capita housing area of rural households grew by 31%, possibly lower than the national average growth rate, but the per capita housing area was much larger than the national average housing area—in 2012, the national per capita housing area of rural households was 37.1 m$^2$, 60.3% of the per capita housing area of rural households in Zhejiang.

It is worth noting that the resident income gap in Zhejiang was small compared with the national income gap. As from 2000, the ratio of the per capita disposable income of urban households to the per capita net income of rural households in Zhejiang increased and then decreased (see Fig. 1.3), but the ratio of the income of

---

[8]According to the criterion developed by the United Nations Food and Agriculture Organization, the Engel coefficient above 59% means poverty; the Engel coefficient between 50 and 59% means ample food and clothing; the Engel coefficient between 40 and 50% means a well-off life; the Engel coefficient between 30 and 40% means affluence; the Engel coefficient below 30% means the most affluent life.

**Table 1.2**  The growth trends of the income of urban and rural residents, the Engel coefficient and the housing area in Zhejiang

| | Regional GDP growth rate (%) | Per capita income growth rate (%) | | The Engel coefficient (%) | | Per capita housing area of households (m$^2$) | |
|---|---|---|---|---|---|---|---|
| | | Urban areas | Rural areas | Urban areas | Rural areas | Urban areas | Rural areas |
| 2000 | 11.0 | 9.1 | 7.8 | 39.2 | 43.5 | 19.87 | 46.42窗体顶端 |
| 2001 | 10.6 | 13.3 | 6.9 | 36.3 | 41.6 | 20.3 | 47.82 |
| 2002 | 12.6 | 13.4 | 8.4 | 37.9 | 40.8 | 21.12 | 49.53 |
| 2003 | 14.7 | 11.9 | 7.8 | 36.6 | 38.2 | 21.6 | 50.73 |
| 2004 | 14.5 | 7.4 | 7.4 | 36.2 | 39.5 | 23.9 | 51.29 |
| 2005 | 12.8 | 10.4 | 6.4 | 33.8 | 38.6 | 26.1 | 54.98 |
| 2006 | 13.9 | 10.9 | 9.3 | 32.9 | 37.2 | 26.44 | 55.57 |
| 2007 | 14.7 | 8.4 | 8.2 | 34.7 | 36.4 | 34.73 | 57.06 |
| 2008 | 10.1 | 5.4 | 6.2 | 36.4 | 38 | 34.33 | 58.5 |
| 2009 | 8.9 | 9.7 | 9.5 | 33.6 | 37.4 | 35.09 | 59.29 |
| 2010 | 11.9 | 6.9 | 8.6 | 34.3 | 35.5 | 35.29 | 58.53 |
| 2011 | 9.0 | 7.5 | 9.5 | 34.6 | 37.6 | 36.85 | 60.8 |
| 2012 | 8.0 | 9.2 | 8.8 | 35.1 | 37.7 | 37.07 | 61.51 |
| 2013 | 8.2 | 7.1 | 8.1 | 34.4 | 35.6 | 38.8窗体底端 | 60.82 |

*Source* China Statistical Yearbook (2014), Zhejiang Statistical Yearbook (2014)

urban residents to that of rural residents in Zhejiang was apparently lower than the national average ratio, its increase was much smaller and it declined earlier compared with the national situation. For the overall resident income gap in Zhejiang, the Gini coefficient rose, and reached 0.403 in 2005,[9] much lower than the national Gini coefficient 0.485 in the same year. Zhejiang was the province with the lowest Gini coefficient among the provinces across China.

The modern social security system is an important part of security for the people. The development of the modern social security system is conducive to meeting the basic needs, adjusting the income distribution gap and promoting social fairness. Internationally, the role of the social security system in adjusting the income distribution gap even much exceeded that of the tax system in adjustment. For instance, in some OECD countries, if both tax and social security are considered, the public transfer payment mainly aimed at providing social security contributed about 2/3 to the adjustment-induced decrease in the Income distribution Gini coefficient of a country. To fulfill the Chinese dream with the realization of the people's happiness as one of the main goals, it is undoubtedly necessary for China to establish and improve

---

[9]Lu (2006).

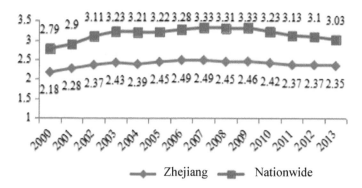

────◆──── Zhejiang  ────■──── Nationwide

**Fig. 1.3** Comparison of the urban and rural resident income ratio between Zhejiang and the country as a whole. *Source* China Statistical Yearbook (2014), Zhejiang Statistical Yearbook (2014)

**Table 1.3** The number of people covered by social insurance in Zhejiang

|      | Endowment insurance | Unemployment insurance | Medical insurance | Work-related injury insurance | Maternity insurance |
|------|--------------------|------------------------|-------------------|-------------------------------|---------------------|
| 2006 | 1052.59 | 504.38 | 730.59 | 603.94 | 382.72 |
| 2007 | 1167.10 | 584.75 | 854.97 | 1002.90 | 504.96 |
| 2008 | 1386.91 | 731.10 | 1053.92 | 1261.84 | 689.98 |
| 2009 | 1527.43 | 784.46 | 1173.73 | 1331.09 | 750.67 |
| 2010 | 1702.22 | 874.95 | 1344.42 | 1475.11 | 863.73 |
| 2011 | 1821.76 | 980.59 | 1514.39 | 1610.76 | 979.79 |
| 2012 | 2083.30 | 1065.56 | 1670.97 | 1731.68 | 1084.78 |
| 2013 | 2272.50 | 1144.53 | 1791.08 | 1826.06 | 1173.17 |

*Source* Zhejiang Statistical Yearbook (2014)

a modern social security system. Since the middle of the 1990s, especially during the 21st century, China has rapidly developed a social security system, and has introduced a number of systems concerning social insurance, social assistance and social welfare. So far, China has preliminarily established a relatively systematic social security system. Zhejiang has carried out extremely solid work on building a modern social security system, continuously made relevant social security systems cover more people and it has endeavored to increase the level of benefit (see Table 1.3).

In the social assistance system, the urban and rural subsistence allowances are the most important assistance programs, designed to provide basic income security for the poor and low-income people in urban and rural areas. Zhejiang has provided security to all possible people in need in this respect. According to the data from the Zhejiang Statistical Yearbook, the rural population covered by subsistence allowances peaked at 623,300 in 2011, excluding the rural childless and infirm population provided with assistance in the form of food, clothing, medical care, housing, and burial expenses; the urban population covered by subsistence allowances peaked at 93,300 in 2009, afterwards, it decreased. More importantly, the level of subsistence allowances was raised. According to statistics, the level of the per capita annual subsistence allowances payments for the urban population covered by subsistence allowances was 2,184 yuan in 2007, it increased to 6,100.3 yuan in 2013, up 1.79 times in nominal terms, an average annual nominal increase of 19%; in the same period, the level of the per capita annual subsistence allowances payments for the rural population covered by subsistence allowances increased from 1,018.9 yuan to 3,387.1 yuan, up 2.32 times in nominal terms, an average annual nominal increase of 22.3%. The average annual nominal growth rate involving the per capita payment from Zhejiang's public finances for urban and rural populations covered by subsistence allowances was much higher than the nominal growth rate involving the per capita annual income of urban and rural residents in the same period. Moreover, the level of subsistence allowances payments for urban and rural populations in Zhejiang was higher than the average national level. According to relevant research, in 2010, the level of the national urban subsistence allowances payments was 267.47 yuan/person/month, while the level of Zhejiang's urban subsistence allowances payments was 366.98 yuan/person/month; in the meantime, Zhejiang ranked No. 4 among 31 provinces across the country in the level of subsistence allowances payments, following Shanghai, Tianjin and Beijing.[10]

## 1.4 The Development of Social Programs and Equal Access to Public Services

The development of social programs, especially educational, medical and health programs, is an important indispensable part of social development. The resource input and allocation for the development of social programs has a direct impact on the realization of equal access to public services. Thus the healthy development of social programs and equal access to public services are essential for realizing the Chinese dream.

Zhejiang has pushed forward the development of the educational programs in an all-round way; educational development at various stages has been relatively balanced and has reached a higher level. As early as 2005, in Zhejiang, 86.5% of 3-5-year-old children with registered permanent residence were enrolled in kindergartens. The enrollment rate at primary schools reached 99.99% in 2002. The rate of admission of primary school graduates into higher schools reached 99.99% in 2005. In Zhejiang, the enrollment rate and consolidation rate at junior middle schools were 99.59 and 99.93; 91.02% of junior middle school graduates entered high schools and secondary vocational schools, the gross enrolment rate in the high school and secondary vocational education reached 86% in 2005. The national gross enrolment

---

[10]Yao (2012).

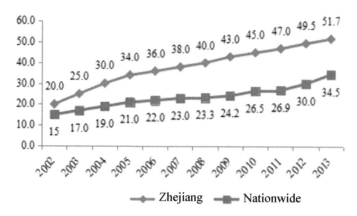

**Fig. 1.4** Comparison of the gross enrolment rate involving the population of the right age for the stage of higher education between Zhejiang and the country as a whole

rate of high school and secondary vocational education did not reach 86% until 2013. As a population of more than 10 million migrated from other areas to Zhejiang, local authorities of Zhejiang generally attached importance to the education of the children of the external population. In 2004, the enrolment rate of the children of the migrant population at the stage of compulsory education reached 96.9% in Zhejiang, more than 60 percentage points higher than the average national level in the same period; about 2/3 of the children of the external population who attended schools in various parts of Zhejiang entered public schools.[11]

Higher education developed very rapidly in Zhejiang. According to statistics, during the period 2000–2013, the number of the institutions of higher learning increased from 35 to 106, and the number of students enrolled rose from 93,500 to 283,400 in Zhejiang. With the development of higher education, the gross enrolment rate involving the population of the right age for the stage of higher education increased rapidly year by year in Zhejiang, it soared from 20% in 2002 to 51.7% in 2013 (see Fig.1.4), Zhejiang really transformed higher education from being elite-oriented to being a kind of widespread education among the entire population. As shown by Fig.1.4, the gross enrolment rate involving the population of the right age for the stage of higher education in Zhejiang was apparently higher than the average national level, and that gap widened year by year before 2011; after 2012, it narrowed to some extent, but it was still large; in 2013, it was 17.2% points.

Zhejiang also made great progress in the development of medical and health programs. The population density of technical personnel relating to medical and health services and that of beds at medical and health institutions are two relatively stable basic indicators for measuring the level of development of medical and health programs. According to statistics, during the period 2002–2013, in Zhejiang, the number of beds at medical and health institutions increased from 119,522 to 230,056,

---

[11]Zhang and Zhu (2004), Xiao (2013).

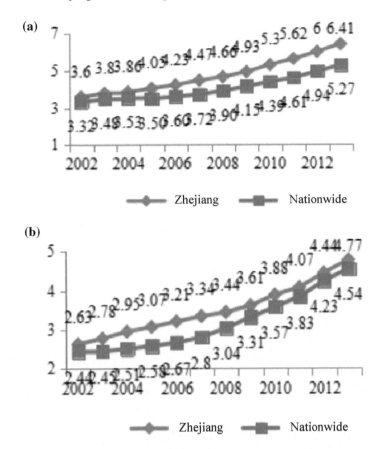

**(a)**

3.6 3.83.86 4.05 4.23 4.47 4.66 4.93 5.3 5.62 6 6.41

3.33 3.48 3.53 3.56 3.60 3.72 3.90 4.15 4.3 4.61 4.94 5.27

2002  2004  2006  2008  2010  2012

⬥ Zhejiang          ■ Nationwide

**(b)**

2.63 2.78 2.95 3.07 3.21 3.34 3.44 3.61 3.88 4.07 4.44 4.77

2.44 2.45 2.51 2.58 2.67 2.8 3.04 3.31 3.57 3.83 4.23 4.54

2002  2004  2006  2008  2010  2012

⬥ Zhejiang          ■ Nationwide

**Fig. 1.5** **a** The number of healthcare-related technical personnel per 1000 people. *Source* China Statistical Yearbook (2014), Zhejiang Statistical Yearbook (2014), **b** The number of beds at medical and health institutions per 1000 people. *Source* China Statistical Yearbook (2014), Zhejiang Statistical Yearbook (2014)

up 92.5%, an average annual increase of 6.15%; the number of beds per 1000 people rose from 2.63 to 4.77. In the same period, the number of healthcare-related technical personnel increased from 163,205 to 352,393, up 1.16 times, an average annual increase of 7.27%; the number of healthcare-related technical personnel per 1000 people rose from 3.6 to 6.4. As indicated by Fig.1.5, the number of healthcare-related technical personnel per 1000 people and the number of medical and health beds per 1000 people in Zhejiang were also apparently larger than the average national levels; in particular, the gap in the number of healthcare-related technical personnel per 1000 people between Zhejiang and the country as a whole tended to widen.

Social programs also cover many other fields, such as culture, sports, social old-age care, social welfare, public transportation and infrastructure. Since the reform and opening-up, especially during the 21st century, Zhejiang has made great efforts and continuous progress in developing social programs in these fields, Zhejiang has achieved rapid development in some fields. For instance, the development of mass sports in Zhejiang is typical. According to *the* Zhejiang Statistical Yearbook (2014), the number of mass sports activities at the provincial, municipal and county levels increased from 7300 to 14,687 and the number of participants rose from 8.39 to 21.67 million during the years 2009–2013.

Zhejiang constantly promoted equal access to basic public services while vigorously developing social programs. In this process, Zhejiang paid particular attention to narrowing the urban-rural gap in the supply of basic public services. Quantitatively, in Zhejiang, the urban-rural gap was not apparent in many fields involving the supply of basic public services. In such a circumstance, the gap in the quality of life and the access to opportunities for development between urban and rural residents narrowed continuously in Zhejiang. As mentioned above, the income gap between urban and rural residents in Zhejiang was smallest nationwide, the Engel coefficient of the living consumption was very close between urban and rural residents; nine-year compulsory education was achieved at a level of almost 100%; Zhejiang basically made high school and secondary vocational education universal, the enrollment rate at the stage of higher education exceeded 50%; the social security system basically fully covered urban and rural areas; the urban-rural gap in social assistance, especially the level of subsistence allowances payments, narrowed year by year, and was much smaller than that in most provinces across the county; Zhejiang basically built a new social security system characterized by urban-rural integration, network-based organization, socialized management, security under the rule of law and commensurate with the level of economic and social development, and a social assistance system covering urban and rural medical assistance, aid for students from the families with financial difficulties, economically affordable housing and low-rent housing security as well as judicial assistance. Zhejiang also continually narrowed the urban-rural gap in the construction of infrastructures. According to the second agricultural census in Zhejiang, as early as 2006, in Zhejiang, 100% of the administrative villages and 99.6% of the natural villages got access to electricity; telephones were made available to 99.4% of the administrative villages and 95.6% the natural villages; cable TV was made available to 91.2% of the administrative villages and 86.8% of the natural villages; roads were built for 97.6% of the administrative villages and 88.6% of the natural villages (91.8% were cement or asphalt roads).

## 1.5   The Innovations in Social Governance and the Development of a Safe Zhejiang

Social governance is an important part of social development. As social development becomes better, the modern changes in the social structure are achieved to a higher degree, and the people's wellbeing is further improved, social inequality can be better controlled within the reasonable range of better reflecting social fairness and justice without affecting economic efficiency and social vitality; as the social security system becomes more sound and the level of equal access to basic public services increases, social contradictions will decrease and the level of social security will become higher. However, no matter how successful the work in these respects may be, social contradictions remain unavoidable. This means that any society needs effective governance at any time; importantly, social governance is necessary to continuously resolve social contradictions, mediate social disputes caused by contradictions, and make sure that social contradictions and disputes will not become antagonistic contradictions and conflicts, thus promoting social harmony and security, and providing a good social environment for social development and for work on other fronts.

Therefore, social governance is also an important part of efforts at building a safe Zhejiang. The building of a safe Zhejiang is an important move made by the Party Committee of Zhejiang Province for carrying out the principles adopted during the 16th National Congress of the Communist Party of China and promoting Zhejiang's social harmony and stability. In 2004, the 6th Plenary (Enlarged) Session of the 11th Party Committee of Zhejiang Province officially put forward the strategy of building a safe Zhejiang, in which comrade Xi Jinping, the then Secretary of the Party Committee of Zhejiang Province, delivered a report *Building a Safe Zhejiang, Promoting Social Harmony and Stability*. In the report, comrade Xi Jinping pointed out that the "safe" in a safe Zhejiang not only meant "safe" in a narrow sense—good public security and few crimes, but also covered the wide-ranging "safe" in a wider scope and at multiple levels in the economic, political, cultural and social fields; its overall plan was as follows: The economy would be further developed, politics would become more stable, culture would become more prosperous, the society would be more harmonious and the people would live better lives. Based on such an understanding, comrade Xi Jinping put forward six specific goals for building a safe Zhejiang, namely, guaranteeing social and political stability, good security, sound economic operations, stable and better work safety, social public security, and making sure that the people live and work in peace and contentment. As the initiative of building a safe Zhejiang was put forward, the discussions about economic and social issues were conducted in a deeper and pragmatic way, and were focused more on the people's life, and the discussions were richer and more complete in content. Except for the goal of ensuring sound economic operations, the remaining five goals are directly related to social governance.

Unlike the traditional social ruling and control, modern social governance is based on its basic philosophy and mode. Regarding modern social governance with Chinese characteristics, as mentioned by comrade Xi Jinping when he served as the Secretary of the Party Committee of Zhejiang Province, equal emphasis is placed on strengthening government administration and promoting social self-governance, and actions are taken to build and improve a pattern of social management in which the Party committee plays the leading role, the government assumes the responsibility, and there is social coordination and public participation.[12] These remarks and thoughts of comrade Xi Jinping's provided enormous guidance for Zhejiang's

---

[12]Xi (2005).

reforms and innovations in modern social governance. In more than a decade, the Party committees at various levels in Zhejiang fully played the leading role, and the governments at various levels maintained a high sense of responsibility in pushing forward social coordination and public participation in Zhejiang's social governance, making tremendous achievements. In particular, with respect to primary-level social governance, the innovative spirit of the society and the people was fully unleashed, many successful social governance modes and much related experience were created.

In the establishment of modern social governance systems and mechanisms, an important aspect lies in proceeding from the philosophy of social governance and correctly handling the relations between the government and the society. At the level of the Party committee and government, the key to conducting good social management and governance is that the leaders fully understand the conditions and opinions of the people, and mobilize the people to actively participate in government decision-making. In this regard, Zhejiang has provided us with many good practices and much practical experience. The innovations drawing special attention are "leaders visiting the areas at lower levels" and "earnest democratic talk". On September 18, 2003, Xi Jinping, the then Secretary of the Party Committee of Zhejiang Province, led some provincial leaders and the people in charge of 15 departments directly under the Party Committee and the People's Government of Zhejiang Province to visit Pujiang County; this was the first time in China that provincial leading cadres visited the areas at lower levels. At present, the practice of "leaders visiting the areas at lower levels" has been consciously, consistently adopted by the leading cadres at various levels in Zhejiang, and has been widely promoted nationwide. The "earnest democratic talk" is a new form of democratic decision-making; it is summarized as "consultative democracy" by the academic circles; it has more substantial democratic connotations compared with Western parliamentary democracy. Zhejiang's "earnest democratic talk" originated in Wenling City, Zhejiang; in 1999, the city held the Agricultural and Rural Modern Education Forum with the original purpose of changing the "traditional practice that cadres preach before the people" to that of a dialogue between cadres and the people; later, it developed into a new primary-level local governance mode with democratic decision-making, democratic management and democratic supervision based on extensive public participation; even the fiscal budget arrangements in towns were made through this kind of "earnest democratic talk". After entry into the 21st century, this innovation has been gradually promoted throughout Zhejiang, and it was granted China Local Government Innovation Award in 2004, an award presented for the second time.

With the establishment of a socialist market economic system, the regulation of labor relations has become an extremely important field in China's social governance. Wages, social security and working conditions are often the factors triggering labor disputes with many employers, especially non-public enterprise units; once disputes occur, they will cause damage to both the employer and the worker. Some areas in Zhejiang became the first to adopt the mode called "social governance" by us today to establish new-type labor relations, while the prominent innovative practice is the "collective consultation on wages" introduced in Wenling City in 2003. Wenling City is a large city of the private economy. The highly developed private economy promoted economic development in Wenling City, but subsequently, labor relations became complicated, labor-capital contradictions were acute, collective work stoppage and collective appeal to higher authorities for resolving contradictions frequently occurred, severely affecting economic development, social harmony and stability in Wenling City. In 2003, with extensive surveys, the Wenling Federation of Trade Unions became the first nationwide to adopt the mechanism of collective consultation on wages in which employees and enterprises hold consultations on an equal footing—with industrial consultations, regional consultations and enterprise consultations focusing on the standard, the bottom line and the extent of increase, respectively—with a view to ensuring a reasonable and stable growth of workers' wages. After collective consultations on wages were held, in Wenling City, workers' wages grew annually by 10–15% on average and labor disputes decreased year by year; there were basically no complaints involving wage disputes in 2006.[13] The collective consultations on wages in Wenling delivered win-win outcomes between labor and capital. Now collective consultations on wages have become an institutional arrangement nationwide.

Primary-level social governance is the foundation for overall social governance. Zhejiang drew fully upon the Fengqiao Experience created in the 1950s and developed a new pattern of primary-level social governance through creative change and development in response to the new situation, new conditions and new problems since the reform and opening-up. Comrade Xi Jinping, the then Secretary of the Party Committee of Zhejiang Province, summarized this pattern as follows: strengthening the basic primary-level work, further summing up, promoting and innovating the Fengqiao Experience, making overall plans and giving all-round considerations, addressing the root causes, reinforcing the foundation, relying on the people, improving systems and placing emphasis on long-term effects.[14] In this regard, Zhejiang also created many new practices and gained much new experience. For instance, in June, 2004, Wuyi County became the first to pilot the establishment of a committee for the supervision of village affairs; Houchen Village in Wuyi County established the first village-level democratic supervision organization nationwide, under which the people elect the committee for the supervision of village affairs and the committee exercises, under the leadership of the village Party committee, supervision over village affairs, especially the village-level financial supervision, in the whole process. At present, all administrative villages in Zhejiang have established a committee for the supervision of village affairs. In 2007, Taohua Town, Putuo District, Zhoushan City initiated a new social management service mode with grid-based management and group-based services, under which the whole town is divided into 32 management service grids, all of the residents are included in the unit grids, each grid is provided with a service team consisting of town cadres, social workers, police

---

[13]Li and Zou (2012).

[14]The speech delivered by the then Secretary of the Party Committee of Zhejiang Province, Xi Jinping, during the National Working Conference on Comprehensive Governance of Social Order on June 11, 2004

officers, teachers and doctors. Currently, this mode has been promoted throughout Zhejiang.

The social coordination and social participation in social governance feature not only mobilization-based participation led by the government and its departments but also the people's participation through self-governance. In particular, the people's self-governance is more effective in coordinating various types of interpersonal relationships and resolving non-governmental social disputes. In this regard, the village-level Harmony Promotion Association in Cixi City, Zhejiang, the Neighborhood Center in Jiangdong District, Ningbo and the Peacemaker Association in Hangzhou are noteworthy innovative practices in social governance. In 2006, the Harmony Promotion Association was established at Wutangxin Village, Cixi City; this practice is very effective, and has been rapidly promoted in 345 villages (communities) across the city. This practice has been given the China Local Government Social Management Innovation Award, an award presented for the sixth time, and it has been adopted nationwide. As from 2008, Jiangdong District, Ningbo City explored the establishment of the Neighborhood Center at communities; the Neighborhood Center is a hub-type social organization mainly responsible for undertaking governmental public services or social affairs programs and managing social organizations dedicated to serving communities. The Neighborhood Center has activated many dormant social organizations and has also incubated more urgently-needed social organizations; it has also played an active role in developing social organizations and socializing social governance. At present, this practice has been promoted throughout Zhejiang and was given the China Social Innovation Award in 2012. The Peacemaker Association, a self-governing organization initiated in Hangzhou, acts as a peacemaker to deal with local affairs and as a grassroots force to resolve contradictions among the people, enabling residents' self-governance and making sure that small matters are handled within villages, large matters are handled within the towns and sub-districts, contradictions are not escalated to higher authorities and are resolved at the local level. Currently, all of the communities (villages) in Hangzhou have established peacemaker associations; more than 20,000 peacemakers are active everywhere, successfully resolving more than 60,000 grassroots contradictions each year. In most communities in Hangzhou, the following has become a reality: The people's contradictions and disputes, residents' appeals in life, the matters among neighbors, large or small, are mostly collected, coordinated and resolved by peacemakers, contradictions and disputes are handled within communities. The peacemaker associations have also extended to specialized sectors, with the establishment of specialized dispute mediation committees involving medical service, accidents and property in Hangzhou, thus bringing about a crisscross mediation organizational network and the first defense line for safeguarding stability. With the efforts of peacemakers across Hangzhou, many disputes among neighbors and family contradictions have been nipped in the bud. In 2009, the Peacemaker Association in Xiacheng District, Hangzhou was granted the China Social Organization Innovation and Development Award, an award presented for the second time.

According to the practical development of social governance, coordination is not only related to the society beyond the government, but also closely associated with the government. In many circumstances, the coordination among government departments is more important. Many local authorities in Zhejiang have an increasingly clear understanding of it, and they have introduced many new measures accordingly. The town-level comprehensive governance centers, county and municipal-level judicial and administrative legal service centers and coordinated emergency response command centers are the innovative measures adopted by local government departments in Zhejiang to carry out social governance in a coordinated way. In early 2004, the first town-level comprehensive governance center in China was established at Qiaosi Town, Yuhang District, Hangzhou. The center integrates the comprehensive governance office, complaint-related letter and visit office, the judicial office, a patrol brigade and a migrant population management office, which all work together to safeguard social stability. At present, comprehensive governance centers have been set up in all towns (sub-districts) across the province. In 2008, Jinhua City became the first nationwide to establish a coordinated emergency response command center, integrating the police calling platforms of multiple departments, including public security 110, fire protection 119, traffic police 122, health 120, industry and commerce 12315, city management 96310 and power supply 95598, into new 110, and thus building an extensive coordinated emergency response system with the coordinated emergency response command center as a hub and with government departments as the backbone. This move has been promoted throughout Zhejiang and was given the National Management Science Innovation Award. In 2009, the Department of Justice of Zhejiang Province became the first nationwide to establish public-benefit-oriented specialized judicial and administrative legal service centers for the people, offering one-stop services to the people, and actively carried out the activity of delivering legal services to communities (villages). At present, legal service centers have been established in all of the counties (cities, districts) across the province, basically all of the villages and communities have been provided with legal advisers, so urban-rural integration in public legal services has been achieved. This practice has been promoted nationwide.

Social governance innovations and the building of a safe Zhejiang have produced marked effects and have promoted social harmony better. During the years 2004–2006, 92.3, 96.4 and 94.8% of the people were satisfied with the state of security, all of these proportions were higher than the national average levels; Zhejiang was considered one of the safest provinces in China.[15] A large number of non-governmental self-governing organizations at the grassroots level have played a huge role in regulating interpersonal relationships and resolving social contradictions and disputes. According to statistics, more and more disputes among the people were mediated and handled in various ways in Zhejiang, with the average annual growth rate reaching 15.83% during the period 2000–2013; now the scale has become very large (see Fig.1.6). With expanded social governance innovations

---

[15]The Zhejiang Bureau of Statistics, Zhejiang's Achievements in Economic and Social Development since the 16th National Congress of the Communist Party of China, in: Zhejiang Association of Regional Economic and Social Development Studies, *Annual Report on Zhejiang's Regional Economic Development (2007)*, China Financial & Economic Publishing House, 2008.

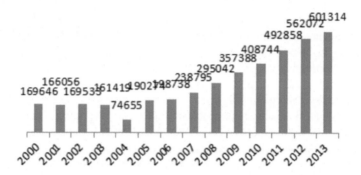

**Fig. 1.6** The growth trend of the mediated disputes among the people in Zhejiang. *Source* Zhejiang Statistical Yearbook (over the years)

and continuous improvement in the coordinated governance mechanism, the public security in Zhejiang's society has improved constantly and the number of criminal cases registered with public security organs has been on the decrease. For instance, according to statistics, during the period January—October, 2008, the registered criminal cases decreased by 2.44% in Zhejiang. Seven types of serious criminal cases, including murder, injury-caused death, arson, explosions, looting, rape and kidnapping, declined by 9.12%.[16] During the period January—October, 2010, the registered criminal cases and eight types of serious criminal cases decreased by 0.48 and 15.88% in Zhejiang.[17] This was contrary to the trend of change in the number of criminal cases registered with public security organs across the country. According to the data from the China Statistical Yearbook, during the period 2000–2013, the number of criminal cases registered with public security organs across the country increased from 3,637,307 to 6,598,247, up 81.4%, an average annual increase of 4.9%.

## 1.6 The Impetus, Path and Mechanism for Zhejiang's Practice of the Chinese Dream

To study the practical experience of the Chinese dream in Zhejiang, it is essential to thoroughly analyze the impetus, path and main mechanism behind it. Historically, Zhejiang achieved rapid economic and social development without a sufficient industrial foundation and a unique location advantage, special national preferential policies or investment support and without many advantages in technology, capital, resources and other factors. Therefore, we must take a holistic and systematic approach to explore the impetus for Zhejiang's development. In summary, the impe-

---

[16]Zhou Changkang, Zhu Zhihua, The Evaluation of and Forecast for the State of Public Security in Zhejiang Province (2008–2009). http://shx.zjss.com.cn/infDetail.asp?id=221&tn=inf
[17]Zhu (2010).

tus for Zhejiang's practical economic and social development mainly comes from three sources. It should be noted that the analysis concerning the sources of impetus for Zhejiang's economic and social development is also an analysis of the path and mechanism for Zhejiang's economic and social development.

### 1.6.1 The Congenitally Weak Foundational Conditions Put Pressure on the Survival and Development of the People of Zhejiang and are also the Sources of Impetus for them to Fully Take the Initiative

Historically, in the era of the planned economy, Zhejiang was on the edge of the planning system, its industrial foundation was fairly weak, and its technical level was low because no large state-owned enterprises were based in Zhejiang; in the days of preparing for wars, Zhejiang was one of the provinces with minimum national investments and construction because Zhejiang was at the frontline of coastal defense. According to statistics, during the years 1952–1978, the Central Government invested 7.7 billion yuan in Zhejiang, with per capita investment of 410 yuan, equivalent to half of the national average level, the lowest among the provinces across the country. Overall, Zhejiang was basically a backward agricultural province before the reform. In 1978, Zhejiang's per capita GDP was only 331 yuan, being 48 yuan lower than the national average level. Zhejiang's total value of industrial output was 13.62 billion yuan, accounting for only 54.38% of the total amount of output value, much lower than the national average level of 61.89%. The urban population accounted for 14.86% of the total population in 1980, lower than the national average level of 19.4%. Zhejiang was also a province with a shortage of natural resources, especially industrial resources, as Zhejiang's per capita quantity of resources was only 11.5% of the national average level; in fact, Zhejiang was the last but two nationwide.

The resources of agricultural production were not abundant in Zhejiang, and its large population and less amount of land constituted an important factor which continuously restricted Zhejiang's rural development. As an agricultural province, Zhejiang was beset by a severe food problem before the reform. In 1978, Zhejiang's per capita cultivated land was only 0.78 mu (one mu = 0.0667 hectares), only 1/2 of the national average level, and so Zhejiang was the last nationwide; the rate of Zhejiang's self-sufficiency in grain was lower than 70%; in the 1960s and 1970s, the people generally allayed their hunger with sweet potatoes, corn and pumpkins in many areas in Zhejiang. In 1978, there were 11 poor counties in Zhejiang.

Over the years, the cadres and people we met during our field surveys in Zhejiang generally believed that the weakness of the foundation and an insufficiency of resources imposed great restrictions and pressure on the survival and development of the people of Zhejiang, and were also the important impetus for the people of Zhejiang to seek new solutions. As long as they were not satisfied with the status quo, we certainly made every endeavor to seize all possible resources, conditions, opportunities and developmental solutions.

### 1.6.2 The Unique Zhejiang Spirit has Provided an Inexhaustible Inherent Driving Source for Zhejiang's Development

Since the emergence of Zhejiang's phenomenon, the people from various sectors of the society have conducted extensive discussions about the traits of the people of Zhejiang, four unique connotations are summarized as follows.[18]

First, the people of Zhejiang are not satisfied with the status quo, they have the burning desire to seek wealth. The people of Zhejiang have an extraordinarily distinctive characteristic—they have the strong desire to shake off poverty and become prosperous, and pursue a well-off life. The Party's policy of reform and opening-up has opened the door that was inhibiting the people's enthusiasm about overcoming poverty to get rich. In order to cast off poverty to become rich, the people of Zhejiang have endured great hardships. Some painstaking jobs despised by urban residents—such as fluffing cotton, repairing shoes, grinding soya beans to make bean curd, producing the exact replica of keys—have become the choices for the people of Zhejiang, especially Zhejiang farmers, to overcome poverty and get rich. Such an intense desire to shake off poverty and change their destiny has constituted the driving source for nurturing the entrepreneurial spirit of the people of Zhejiang and the first impetus for arousing lasting entrepreneurship in Zhejiang.

Second, the people of Zhejiang have the indomitable will to start businesses with continuous self-improvement. In an effort to get rich and change their destiny, the people of Zhejiang always have the strong consciousness to seek self-development. In more than 30 years, the people of Zhejiang vigorously developed township enterprises and an individual private economy, venturing down the road to industrialization with Zhejiang's characteristics. Given a resource shortage and a small market, the people of Zhejiang overcame difficulties by boldly making breakthroughs across the national market even the world market, thus shaping an economic pattern with resources derived from and products sold to the areas outside Zhejiang, and creating developmental modes including "zero resources" and "growing out of nothing"; as a result, Zhejiang has remained within the nationwide norm regarding the development of the market economy. Given the reality that there was dual division between urban and rural areas and the old system restricted farmers from entering cities, Zhejiang farmers relied on their own strength to build "farmer towns", forming an urbanization path with Zhejiang characteristics. The people of Wenzhou demonstrated a spirit of conducting self-reform, taking risks on their own account, making continuous self-improvement and seeking self-development in the 1980s; the people of Zhejiang showed the spirit of taking a long and arduous journey, speaking varied

---

[18]Cheng (2006).

languages, making every effort and overcoming numerous difficulties and dangers in the 1990s; these spirits give expression to the people of Zhejiang's enormous tenacity and resilience in starting businesses.

Third, the people of Zhejiang think diligently and act flexibly in competition and innovation. The people of Zhejiang have adopted highly flexible operational means and countermeasures in starting businesses. At the initial stage of reform and opening-up, the people of Zhejiang started from small commodities, ignored by the people at that time, to seek quick returns and small margins, gradually uncovered vast markets and obtained generous returns, which speeded up Zhejiang's economic and social development.

Fourth, the people of Zhejiang act in a down-to-earth manner and stress practical results. The people of Zhejiang have always placed emphasis on concrete work. At the initial stage of the reform and opening-up, subject to great criticism and pressure, the people of Zhejiang were not impatient to even disdain debating and making self-justification; although they have achieved development and become rich, they are used to concealing their real capacity and refraining from showing off. The style of stressing substantial results can be seen in the whole reform practice in Zhejiang. In the experiments and practice of reform and opening-up, all actions taken by the people of Zhejiang are merely based on this judgment: these actions can bring tangible benefits. The people of Zhejiang have attached importance to drawing upon advanced experience from others, but they never blindly follow that experience; they can unswervingly uphold the paths fit for local conditions and able to deliver tangible benefits, regardless of external opinions and pressure. To seek the entrepreneurial and developmental space under the planning system, the people of Zhejiang took a proactive and sound approach and avoided head-on confrontation with the old system as much as possible, they acted step by step and in a pragmatic way to seek space for survival; in the meantime, they capitalized on the opportunities from the old system to the greatest extent, making substantial progress in promoting economic development and institutional reform.

It should be noted that the booming private economy in Zhejiang has provided great support and a guarantee for Zhejiang's social development. As several million small and medium-sized business owners and individual businesses exist and develop, they are the sources for the rapid growth of the income of urban and rural residents in Zhejiang, and they are also the fundamental factors for ensuring that the income gap between urban and rural residents and the total income gap in Zhejiang are much smaller than the national gap.

### 1.6.3 The Open-Minded Governance and Administration by the Party Committees and Governments at Various Levels have Provided Enormous Impetus for Zhejiang's Economic and Social Development

In China, the Party committees and governments make up one of the most important institutional settings, the behavior of the Party committees and governments make up important conditions of constraint on the behavioral choices of the players in the society. The Party committees and governments at various levels in Zhejiang are part of the whole national governance and administration system, their behavioral choices are inevitably subject to particular conditions of constraint, but the behavior of the Party committees and governments at various levels in Zhejiang is also influenced by Zhejiang's regional cultural traditions. One outstanding feature is that the officials of local governments at various levels are open-minded and stress concrete work and substantial results, they do not adopt administrative means to suppress the innovative experiments, conducted by the people to solve the problems concerning their survival and development, which are in conflict with the old system and old mindsets; they are open-minded and tolerant towards these innovative experiments. This was a crucial factor for ensuring that the entrepreneurial spirit of the people of Zhejiang would be continuously carried forward and would produce huge driving effects since the reform and opening-up.

At the initial stage of reform and opening-up, as Zhejiang faced heavy survival pressure and it was difficult for Zhejiang to push forward industrialization by obtaining massive resources within the system, the people belonging to the lower classes relied on their own strength to set up township enterprises, household industries and specialized markets with a view to seeking spaces for economic development outside the system, while the local Party committees and governments at various levels, especially primary-level Party committees and governments, in Zhejiang mostly gave tacit consent to and did not interfere in these efforts made by the people. When these innovative moves delivered significant growth performance, local governments gradually changed their attitude from sympathy-based acquiescence to rational recognition. When the innovative moves made by the people conflicted with the rigid old system and ideology in Zhejiang so that some conservative people had heated debates on the reform experiments conducted by the people in Zhejiang, the local governments in Zhejiang focused on promoting economic development and protecting the entrepreneurial enthusiasm of the people, introduced the Party's policy of reform and opening-up in light of Zhejiang's reality, assumed responsibilities for the authority at a higher level and the people and organizations at lower levels, successfully built a buffer zone between the top-down political pressure and down-top non-governmental impulse towards innovation, providing a loose and vitally important policy environment for the people's innovative practice.

Since the 1990s, with impetus from Deng Xiaoping's South Talks, the local Party committees and governments at various levels in Zhejiang seized opportunities and actively adjusted roles, gave up the simple hands-off approach, proactively guided and regulated the development of the individual private economy, they no longer directly intervened in the micro economy to help the production and operation activities in enterprises, they established regulations and systems, exercised macro regulation, provided guidance and services, thus offering unprecedented policy incentives for further unleashing the entrepreneurial spirit and triggering a wave of popular entrepreneurship. Since the beginning of the 21st century, the local governments at various levels in Zhejiang have further carried out the reform of the administrative system aimed at improving governmental public services in order to support the entrepreneurial activities conducted by the people. Zhejiang has carried out a series of reforms involving the administrative system—regulating governmental behavior, slashing the items subject to administrative examination and approval, simplifying the examination procedures, universally launching one-stop services with administrative departments as windows and expanding the powers of strong counties—to further optimize the protection and services provided by local governments to entrepreneurial and investment activities, and gradually demonstrate the comparative advantages of local governments in administrative management and public services.

In the field of social development, the Party committees and governments at various levels in Zhejiang have also played the same roles. On the one hand, the Party committees and governments at various levels have generally observed, guided and supported the society and the people's innovative practice in social development and social governance, promptly summed up and promoted the experiences. From the Fengqiao Experience in the 1950s to the social governance innovations in the 21st century, their attitudes have been consistent. When serving as the Secretary of the Party Committee of Zhejiang Province, Xi Jinping provided guidance, on many occasions, for tapping and renovating the Fengqiao Experience, arranging for the work and measures conducive to the building of a safe Zhejiang and social harmony. On the other hand, the local Party committees and governments at various levels in Zhejiang have made active experiments, unswervingly changed government functions, increasingly taken strengthening social development and promoting social development as important work and tasks. Since the beginning of the 21st century, Zhejiang has dedicated tremendous energy to pushing forward the building of a harmonious society, developing social programs, promoting equal access to basic public services, carrying out the construction of a new countryside and vigorously developing social organizations; Zhejiang has also developed many feasible strategic and action plans accordingly, and has incorporated the implementation of these social developmental strategies and plans into the system of evaluating the performance of official duties. In the meantime, Zhejiang has intensified the construction of public finance year by year and has gradually shifted the focus of public financial resources to the field of social development. In recent years, Zhejiang has allocated more than 70% of the annually increased financial resources to improve the people's wellbeing, guarantee social insurance and social assistance, develop social programs and promote equal access to basic public services, providing an important fiscal guarantee and support for Zhejiang's social development. It should be noted that the local Party committees and governments at various levels in Zhejiang have also introduced many policies for actively promoting the social integration of the external population. There are 10 million rural migrant workers from other areas in Zhejiang, but large-scale sharp conflicts between the external population and the local population, between employers and rural migrant workers, have seldom occurred, and this is closely associated with the efforts made by the local Party committees and governments at various levels in Zhejiang in promoting the social integration of the external population.

## 1.6.4   Local Knowledge and Experience from Zhejiang's Practice of the Chinese Dream

Local knowledge is an extremely innovative, inclusive and explanatory concept developed and expounded by U.S. scholar Clifford Geertz. He defined "local" as follows: "local" here refers to not only space, time, class and various issues, but also unique features; in other words, it associates the local knowledge about the events which have happened with the local imagination about the events which may happen.[19] Given the concept and theory of local knowledge, we should focus on the specific situation and conditions for generating Zhejiang's experience when summing up Zhejiang's experience. Only when we understand the local situation and conditions can we summarize the connotation of the general knowledge and creatively transform it into the general knowledge which can be absorbed and utilized. If the authorities in other areas want to draw upon Zhejiang's experience, they cannot mechanically copy Zhejiang's experience; it is essential for them to profoundly understand its inherent mechanism and value orientation, and then consider the local situation and conditions to creatively apply it.

To completely and profoundly grasp the intrinsic quality of the Zhejiang Spirit, it is necessary to thoroughly analyze the impact of Zhejiang's regional cultural traditions and their modern transformation on the behavior of the people of Zhejiang. Overall, Zhejiang's regional cultural traditions have distinctive features, especially the strong trait of independence and the intense character of the commercial culture. The most concentrated theoretical embodiment of this cultural tradition is the pragmatist school in eastern Zhejiang which is unique in the cultural tradition of the Chinese nation. The basic theoretical characteristics of this school are the learning style of stressing practical application, the spirit of autonomy, the utilitarian orientation of placing equal emphasis on righteousness and benefit, the business-friendly consciousness of developing both industry and commerce and the value standpoint of recognizing private interests. These theoretical propositions have been gradually incorporated into the cultural spirit of the people of Zhejiang in a long historical process and have exerted a nonnegligible impact on their behavioral pattern.[20] Based on this theoretical perspective of local knowledge, some scholars have summarized Zhejiang's economic organizational forms and production modes as socialized small production. Under this mode, as the main force in Zhejiang's economic and social development, small enterprises are mostly available with families as the basic production organizations, and they are dominated by individual workshops and household industries and commerce; the structure of their property rights is relatively closed, most enterprises are controlled by individuals or families and have strong kindred or regional traits. Such an economic organizational form and production mode, which is neither small production nor socialized mass production, are creations of the people of Zhejiang in 30 years of reform and opening- up. Such a form of production

---

[19]Geertz (1998).
[20]Cheng (2006).

practice is a production mode under which families are the basic production units and connection is built by social division of labor and the market. Such a form of production practice has not only the characteristics of the small production mode in the traditional society, but also the main characteristics of the socialized mass production mode in the modern society under which families are the basic production units and the main production network relies on kinship, geographical relationship and business contact—it is based on social division of labor, relies on the market as the bond and takes the form of specialized production. This is a unique modern mode and a modern mode especially suitable for Zhejiang's situation and conditions.[21]

Although the theory of local knowledge can offer inspiration and reference for us to understand Zhejiang's experience in modernization, it is still necessary for us to draw upon Zhejiang's experience profoundly and also go beyond Zhejiang's experience to summarize Zhejiang's experience. In summary, we believe that Zhejiang's experience in economic and social development presents the following outstanding features, while these features can provide the general guidance and reference for us to achieve the ambitious goals for the Chinese dream.

First, putting the people's wellbeing first. The philosophy of putting the people's wellbeing first has been adopted throughout Zhejiang's practice in social development. Developing the private economy epitomizes putting the people's wellbeing first. As millions of individual private enterprises develop, the employment issue concerning urban and rural residents in Zhejiang is addressed better, and more than 10 million jobs have been created for the workers from other provinces. The growth of urban and rural residents' income in Zhejiang largely relies on the development of the private economy.

Second, ensuring coordination among and participation by multiple actors. A fundamental experience from Zhejiang's social development is that social development and social governance are considered a cause undertaken by the whole people and with active participation by multiple actors; the Party committees and governments, enterprises, public institutions, primary-level organizations, non-governmental social organizations and citizens serve as the actors in social development and social governance, they play different but indispensable roles in social development and social governance.

Third, always persevering in reform and innovation. Zhejiang's economic and social development is a process of continuous reform and innovation. Reform and innovation not only involve the institutional level, but also mean renewal of mindsets and advancing with the times. They mean reform and innovation in relevant systems, the establishment of a spirit of reform and innovation, and continuous experimentation of new developmental thoughts and developmental measures. It is necessary to proceed from the demands of the times to creatively tap and transform the existing experience which has been widely recognized. Since the reform and opening-up, Zhejiang has rediscovered and renovated, again and again, the Fengqiao Experience promoted nationwide for decades, making it play a new role in the new era.[22]

---

[21] Yang (2008).
[22] Chen (2009).

Fourth, carrying out work in a systematic, coordinated, scientific and consistent way. Zhejiang's economic and social development, especially social development, is undoubtedly based on the participation of multiple actors, but this does not mean that there is no macro plan. On the contrary, with careful analysis and summarization of Zhejiang's development for more than 30 years, we can find that the macro plan and guidance of the Party committees and governments are essential. Importantly, such a plan is highly systematic, coordinated and scientific. The "Eight-Eight Strategies", six action plans for finishing the building of a moderately prosperous society and the system of five goals for building a safe Zhejiang, developed through efforts led by comrade Xi Jinping when serving as the Secretary of the Party Committee of Zhejiang Province, are systematic, coordinated and scientific. The *Action Plan for Ensuring Equal Access to Basic Public Services* (2008–2012) developed and initiated in 2008, the first one in China, called for building and improving a multilevel social security system with full coverage, extending basic public services to both urban and rural areas, making them balanced among regions and shared by everyone, and promoting social fairness and justice, as well as the well-rounded development of the people. Thus, these major developmental strategies, plans and action plans of Zhejiang Province are highly consistent, while the successive Party committees and governments have always persisted in these strategies, plans and action plans and have relentlessly moved towards their goals. This experience has played a crucial role in propelling Zhejiang to make tremendous achievements in many respects and to remain ahead nationwide.

Fifth, continuously changing government functions to make the government assume the responsibility for promoting social development more. This can be measured by the structure of allocating Zhejiang's public financial expenditure in the people's wellbeing and social development (see Table 1.4). According to Table 1.4,[23] from the perspective of absolute quantity, Zhejiang increased the general budget expenditure in the people's wellbeing and social development year by year while this expenditure accounted for more than 40% of the total general budget expenditure; in particular, its proportion exceeded 45% after 2011, apparently higher than the national average level. In Zhejiang, the expenditure in the people's wellbeing and social development has made up the largest proportion of the general budget expenditure.

Sixth, strengthening the quantitative monitoring of social development. In the book *China: A Macro History*, historian Huang Renyu holds that a problem in traditional Chinese governance is a lack of "mathematically manageable".[24] This view makes sense. Almost all of the major developmental strategies, plans and action plans developed by Zhejiang since the beginning of the 21st century are accompanied by the corresponding monitoring systems. These monitoring systems consist of several monitoring indicators and can quantitatively reflect the progress in implementing strategies, plans and action plans, their drawbacks and lackings; they include the index of the people's wellbeing and the system of indicators for the evaluation of

---

[23]This table does not include the statistical data before 2006 due to different statistical calibers.
[24]Huang (2007).

**Table 1.4** The allocation of Zhejiang's fiscal expenditure on the people's wellbeing and social development

| | 窗体顶端 Education 窗体底端 | 窗体顶端 Social security and employment 窗体底端 | Medical and health services | Environmental protection | 窗体顶端Urban and rural community affairs窗体底端 | Proportion in the general fiscal budget expenditure |
|---|---|---|---|---|---|---|
| 2006 | 窗体顶端 310.77 窗体底端 | 88.3 | 88.23 | 20.32 | 127.37 | 43.1 |
| 2007 | 383.89 | 107.98 | 112.28 | 29.75 | 154.63 | 43.6 |
| 2008 | 453.99 窗体底端 | 141.52 | 142.87 | 46.52 | 193.95窗体底端 | 44.3 |
| 窗体顶端 2009 窗体底端 | 519.33 | 153.08 | 177.05 | 55.42 | 224.61 | 42.6 |
| 2010 | 606.54 | 206.39 | 224.53 | 82.07 | 272.3 | 43.4 |
| 2011 | 751.42 | 291.82 | 278.98 | 78.11 | 338.43 | 45.2 |
| 2012 | 877.86 | 345.44 | 305.91 | 77.7 | 307.82 | 46.0 |
| 2013 窗体底端 | 950.07 窗体底端 | 397.06 | 350.73 | 98.14窗体底端 | 332.93窗体底端 | 45.0 |

*Source* Zhejiang Statistical Yearbook (over the years)

the people's wellbeing, the annual targets specified in the *Action Plan for Ensuring Equal Access to Basic Public Services*, the evaluation system for the degree of realizing equal access to basic public services in Zhejiang, the system of monitoring indicators for finishing the building of a moderately prosperous society, the system of indicators of the comprehensive evaluation for the level of social development, the system of indicators for the evaluation of the monitoring for the progress in new-type urbanization, the comprehensive evaluation system for the level of coordinated urban and rural development, and the annual special evaluation reports on other fields concerning social development. All of these systems of the indicators of evaluation and evaluation reports are the important basis for achieving "mathematically manageable".

Overall, since the reform and opening-up, Zhejiang has made significant achievements in social development and has acquired rich experience. The analysis and summarization conducted here are still very preliminary. Many other things in Zhejiang's practice in social development deserve our in-depth research and careful summarization. That research is of very important theoretical and practical value for us in understanding and realizing the Chinese dream.

# References

Clifford Geertz, Local Knowledge: Fact and Law in Comparative Perspective, trans. by Deng Zhenglai, in: Liang Zhiping (editor-in-chief), *Cultural Interpretation of Law* (revised and enlarged edition) (U.S.), SDX Joint Publishing Company, 1998, p. 126.

Chen Hongguo, The Fengqiao Experience and the Generation Mode Involving the Rule of Law with Chinese Characteristics, *Science of Law (Journal of Northwest University of Political Science and Law)*, 2009(1).

Cheng Lixu (editor-in-chief), *Zhejiang's Phenomenon: Improving the Cultural Soft Power*, Party School of the CPC Central Committee Press, 2006.

Huang Renyu, China: A Macro History, SDX Joint Publishing Company, 2007

Li Gangyin, Zou Tiran, Wenling City, Zhejiang Adopts the Mode of Collective Consultation on Wages, Delivering Win-win Outcomes between Labor and Capital, Workers Daily, July 26, 2012.

Lu Xueyi (editor-in-chief), *A Research Report on the Social Classes in Contemporary China*, Social Sciences Academic Press, 2002.

Lu Xueyi (editor-in-chief), *Social Mobility in Contemporary China*, Social Sciences Academic Press, 2004.

Lu Xueyi (editor-in-chief), *The Social Structure in Contemporary China*, Social Sciences Academic Press, 2010.

Lu Xueyi, Social Development Is Aimed at Achieving Social Modernization, *Sociological Study*, 2011(4).

Lu Yunhang, A Comparative Analysis of the Resident Income Gap in Zhejiang, *Zhejiang Economy*, 2006(22).

Xi Jinping, A Speech at the Symposium with the Outstanding Youth Representatives from Various Sectors, *People's Daily*, May 5, 2013.

Xi Jinping, Developing the Philosophy of Building a Harmonious Society, Zhejiang Daily (Zhijiang Xinyu), April 4, 2005. The 18th National Congress of the Communist Party of China further improved this mode and added "security under the rule of law". The 3rd Plenary Session of the 18th Central Committee of the Communist Party of China changed "social management" to "social governance" which better reflects comrade Xi Jinping's thought and philosophy of combining government administration with social self-governance.

Xiao Qinghua, The Evolution, Dilemmas and Trends of the Education Policy for the Children of Rural Migrant Workers, *Academic Forum*, 2013(12).

Yang Jianhua, *Socialized Small Production – The Endogenous Logic of Zhejiang's Modernization*, Zhejiang University Press, 2008.

Yao Jianping, An Analysis of the Subsistence Allowances Standards in Chinese Cities (I), *China Soft Science*, 2012(11).

Zhang Dongsu, Zhu Genhua, 96.9% of the Children of the Migrant Population at the Stage of Compulsory Education Reached 96.9% in Zhejiang Province, Zhejiang Daily, October 7, 2004. Nationally, the proportion of the children of the external population entering public schools did not reach 2/3 until 2010. See Xiao Qinghua, The Evolution, Dilemmas and Trends of the Education Policy for the Children of Rural Migrant Workers, Academic Forum, 2013(12)

Zhang Jianwei, A Study and Analysis of the External Population in Zhejiang Province, *Statistics Science & Practice*, 2012(2).

Zhu Zhihua, The Evaluation of and Forecast for the State of Stability Safeguarding and Public Security in Zhejiang Province (2010-2011), in: Zhejiang Association of Regional Economic and Social Development Studies, *Annual Report on Zhejiang's Regional Economic Development (2011)*, Zhejiang Education Publishing House, 2011.

# Chapter 2
# The Change in Social Structure

**Feng Tian**

Since the reform and opening-up, Zhejiang has fully leveraged its advantage of a unique location and followed the trend, derived the driving forces from institutional innovation and made use of the mercantilist culture to invigorate the private economy, thus Zhejiang has made great progress in the economic and social fields. In particular, since the beginning of the 21st century, Zhejiang has followed the law of the market economy and urbanization to intensify the reform of the economic system and inter-regional and international opening-up, and Zhejiang has focused on more rapidly adjusting the structure and changing the growth mode and government functions, moving faster to promote social development and improve the people's well-being; Zhejiang has promoted sound and rapid economic development, correctly handled the relations between the pace of economic growth and its quality; Zhejiang has also accelerated social development through economic development, speeded up the improvement of the basic public service system, strengthened and innovated social management, safeguarded social stability and rationalized the relations between fairness and efficiency in social development. Economic development has provided favorable conditions for strengthening social development and optimizing the social structure, so the capacity for social management has been enhanced gradually, the society has become increasingly harmonious and the social structure has been optimized continuously amidst rapid and sound economic and social development.

F. Tian (✉)
Chinese Academy of Social Sciences, Beijing, China

© Social Sciences Academic Press and Springer Nature Singapore Pte Ltd. 2019
G. Chen and J. Yang (eds.), *Chinese Dream and Practice in Zhejiang—Society*,
Research Series on the Chinese Dream and China's Development Path,
https://doi.org/10.1007/978-981-13-7406-7_2

## 2.1   Social Structure and Social Development

### 2.1.1   *Optimizing the Social Structure Is the Objective Requirement for Zhejiang's Economic and Social Development*

Since the late 1970s, Zhejiang has entered a long period of rapid economic and social development. During the period 1978–2012, Zhejiang's GDP grew annually by an average of 12.7%; Zhejiang was at the forefront nationwide in rate of growth and economic aggregate. From the perspective of economic growth, Zhejiang is one of the benchmark provinces nationwide. In particular, Zhejiang can follow the economic law to carry out institutional innovations during economic marketization, which is of great referential and guiding significance for the whole country.

Although Zhejiang was in a long period of economic growth, several great fluctuations occurred. For instance, according to the annual statistical data, Zhejiang's fastest economic growth occurred in 1995 and 1996 at the initial stage of the market-oriented reform in the 1990s, with an average annual growth rate of nearly 40%; afterwards, great fluctuations took place in 1998 and 1999, the economic growth rate decreased to about 7%. The main cause for fluctuation in economic growth was the impact from the Asian financial crisis in 1997. That crisis directly affected Zhejiang's enterprises with a high degree of dependence on exports, thus Zhejiang's economic growth rate declined. A similar situation also occurred after the global financial crisis broke out in 2007. Therefore, in terms of fluctuation in economic growth, if there is not a vast domestic consumer market and a large number of consumers, an export-oriented economy is vulnerable to fluctuation. In order to ensure stable economic growth, it is urgently necessary to optimize the social structure to generate a middle class with a high capacity for consumption and a strong desire to consume, reduce the middle and low-income population and the people employed in the low-end industries.

With long-term rapid economic growth, in 2013, Zhejiang's per capita GDP exceeded USD 10,000, much higher than the average national level. According to the law of modern social development, generally, once the per capita GDP in a country or territory exceeds USD 2,000, the country or territory reaches the turning point from the stage of economic take-off to the stage of accelerated growth. When the per capita GDP in a country exceeds USD 4,000, the country basically becomes one of the middle-income countries. When the per capita GDP in a country exceeds USD 10,000, the country enters the stage of the high-income countries and developed countries from the stage of the middle-income countries. In 2013, Zhejiang's per capita GDP exceeded USD 10,000. Thus, Zhejiang can be considered to be generally in the process of transition from the stage of the middle-income countries to the stage of the high-income countries and developed countries. According to the developmental experience of the developed countries, after the per capita GDP exceeds USD 10,000, economic growth and social development will be subject to more uncertainties, while strengthening social development and optimizing the social structure is the key to maintaining stable economic growth at this stage. The social policies at this stage should proceed from safeguarding the fundamental interests of the people and focus on intensifying social development to achieve the balance between efficiency and fairness while promoting economic development, providing a good social environment for the growth of the middle-income groups, thus boosting domestic consumer demand for driving stable economic growth.

### 2.1.2 Expanding the Middle-Income Group Is Essential for Achieving Sound Economic and Social Development in Zhejiang

Zhejiang's economic development cannot be separated from economic globalization. With international division of labor, Zhejiang has fully utilized comparative advantages—including low labor cost—and the advantage of its location due to its proximity to the coast in order to seize the historical opportunities brought about by the transfer of the international production manufacturing industry to the developing countries, so Zhejiang has not only successfully completed industrialization, but has also become an important part of the world's factory under the product-related international division of labor. According to W. Arthur Lewis' dual economy theory, at the initial stage of industrialization, the surplus labor from rural areas and the agricultural sector supplies massive cheap labor to the society, while this labor supply is essential precisely for the development of the industrial sector, thus the most important characteristic in the change of social structure is that the labor force transfers from the agricultural sector to the industrial sector and from rural areas to urban areas. Such a labor transfer across spaces and across industrial sectors is the basic part and main characteristic of the change in the social structure during industrialization. Industrialization and the change in the social structure are correlated and influence each other; in fact, economic development and the change in the social structure are two aspects of the same process. In 2012, the rate of urbanization of Zhejiang's population exceeded 60%; Zhejiang basically finished the stage of transition from an agricultural society to an industrial society.

With the disappearance of China's demographic dividend, the costs of such resource factors as labor and land have increased, the existing comparative advantage from low cost will fade away, the industrial developmental mode which relies on export trade and is labor-intensive has become unsustainable, the traditional growth mode depending on resource consumption and low-cost labor has restricted industrial structural adjustment, upgrading and change in Zhejiang, while the advantage from low-cost labor is a characteristic of the stage of transition from a traditional agricultural society to an industrial society; this means that it is impossible to merely rely on the comparative advantage from low-cost labor to achieve economic growth. After becoming an industrial society, industrial structural adjustment, upgrading and transformation do not merely mean recombination of such production factors as traditional resources, energy and labor; more importantly, it is necessary to attract the technically competent talents with knowledge so as to improve the enterprises' production efficiency and their capability for innovation, while these talents are mostly part of the middle-income group in a modern society. According to historical experience, the size of the middle-income group represented by these talents is closely associated with the success in industrial structural adjustment, transformation and upgrading. In the meantime, industrial structural adjustment, upgrading and transformation also have a direct bearing on the employment of the low-end working population, producing the crowding-out effect on the low-end labor force and decreasing the proportion of the low-end working population. Therefore, in an effort to promote industrial structural adjustment, upgrading and transformation, it is essential to constantly optimize the social structure, continuously improve the quality of the labor force and increase the income, shaping a social structure dominated by the middle-income group.

Furthermore, the ability to achieve the optimization of the social structure is also an important factor affecting the capacity to resist risks of a country or territory during industrial structural adjustment, upgrading and transformation. During the Asian financial crisis, which broke out in 1997, South Korea and Indonesia showed totally different performances and had different consequences; except economic differences, the biggest difference between the two countries consisted of social structure. South Korea had a huge middle-income group with knowledge and skills before the financial crisis, while Indonesia had a social structure which featured a huge wealth gap and was dominated by a low-end labor force. After the occurrence of the financial crisis, South Korea swiftly got out of the trouble through a series of policy adjustments, while Indonesia struggled to recover slowly. As indicated, in order to enhance Zhejiang's capacity to resist risks during industrial structural adjustment, upgrading and transformation, it is urgently necessary to have a social structure dominated by a middle-income group. Therefore, strengthening social development and optimizing the social structure is one of the necessary conditions for sound economic and social development in Zhejiang.

### 2.1.3 The Optimization of the Social Structure Is an Important Achievement Made by the Role of Zhejiang's Unique Social Culture in Guiding the Self-development of the Society

After the initiation of the reform and opening-up, Zhejiang became the first to preliminarily establish and improve the market economic system. The development of the private economy is closely associated with the mercantilist social culture peculiar to Zhejiang. In the mercantilist social cultural environment, Zhejiang has always been a vibrant and competitive province, and it has a huge group of entrepreneurs and people starting businesses, and their unique entrepreneurial spirit is closely related to the mercantilist social culture. Guidance by social culture means that it internalizes the people's values and behavioral criteria into individual goals and motives, thus driving individuals to act in the ways guided by a particular culture. From the perspective of motivation of individuals by culture, a particular culture can give rise to the ability to self-develop peculiar to a society. The ability to self-develop is defined as compared with the guidance consciously provided by a country and government through particular policies and measures; the ability to self-develop is the result of the actions without particular intention taken by individuals according to their cultural acquisition and internalized behavioral patterns without specific government order in a society.

The mercantilist culture peculiar to Zhejiang has generated the Zhejiang Phenomenon. The Zhejiang Phenomenon means that the people of Zhejiang have relied on their own strength to boldly start businesses and blaze new trails subject to a lack of natural resources and without national input and special preferential policies, so Zhejiang has changed from a small province of resources to an economically strong province with a unique pattern has taken shape in which the people get rich and the province becomes strong. Obviously, such a kind of development results from the important role of the mercantilist culture in guiding the self-development of the society.

For Zhejiang, an important achievement that made the role of the unique mercantilist culture in guiding self-development of the society is continuous optimization of the social structure. According to an economic census, as of late 2008, the capital owned by individuals in the secondary and tertiary industries accounted for 53.5% in Zhejiang, while that proportion in the coastal provinces of Jiangsu and Guangdong was only 29.9 and 18.9%. If objective conditions, including an economic foundation and the geographical location, are considered as similar, the most crucial factor is the role of the social culture in guiding the self-development of the society. According to the theory of social stratification, the owners and shareholders of large enterprises are generally among the upper class of the society, while the owners of small and medium-sized enterprises are mostly among the middle-upper and middle classes of the society, the owners of some small private enterprises belong to the middle-low classes of the society. The unique feature of Zhejiang's social culture lies in guiding the development of the entrepreneurs of small and medium-sized enterprises and the people starting businesses and providing the favorable prerequisite for building a social structure dominated by a middle-income class.

Social development is a process which calls for participation of multiple actors; it is aimed at promoting self-management, autonomous and coordinated management of the society. Therefore, in Zhejiang's social development, the self-development of the middle-income group generated by the social culture peculiar to Zhejiang is conducive to cultivating social forces, improving the mechanism of social participation and conscientiously pushing forward the orderly participation of citizens and social coordination. Thus, from the perspective of optimizing the social structure, in Zhejiang, there are a large number of entrepreneurs and people starting businesses, fostering a favorable cultural environment, conducive to self-development of the society, for building a huge middle-income group in the whole society and shaping a social structure dominated by the middle class.

## 2.2 The Changes in the Structure of the Population in Zhejiang

The changes in the structure of the population—including the changes in the structure of the urban-rural population, the regional distribution of the population, the industrial structure of the population and the structure of the cultural quality of the population—are the most closely related social indicators in economic and social development. After the reform and opening-up was initiated, the structure of Zhejiang's population showed an obvious change conducive to economic and social development, while that process of change has laid a solid foundation for speeding up social development at present.

### 2.2.1 New-Type Urbanization Has Been Promoted Continuously, the Urbanization of the Population Has Been Accelerated

Generally, the distribution of the population between urban and rural areas is most vulnerable to change during economic and social development since the rural labor force enters cities or becomes industrial workers at the local level; this process is generally called the urbanization of the population. As the most economically developed province in China, Zhejiang has made continuous experiments and innovations during the reform and opening-up, venturing down a new type of road towards the urbanization of the population, one with Zhejiang's characteristics, so the rate of the urbanization of the population has increased continuously, the pattern of urban-rural integration has gradually emerged. According to statistical data, the rate of the urbanization of Zhejiang's population was only 31.2% in 1990 and it soared to 48.7% in 2000; afterwards, it exceeded 50%, and reached 56.0% in 2005; it exceeded 60% in 2010, and reached 63.2% in 2012, up nearly 11 percentage points over the average national level (see Fig. 2.1).

The continuous optimization of the structure of the urban-rural population in Zhejiang has, to a great extent, to do with the following fact: The government has sought truth from facts, tailored measures to suit local conditions and made the best use of the circumstances. In the middle and later periods of the 1990s, Zhejiang took the optimization of the structure of the urban-rural population as the endogenous impetus for driving economic growth, and introduced the policies for actively promoting urbanization. In late 1998, Zhejiang became the first nationwide to put forward and implement the strategy of urbanization, so Zhejiang entered the stage of urbanization

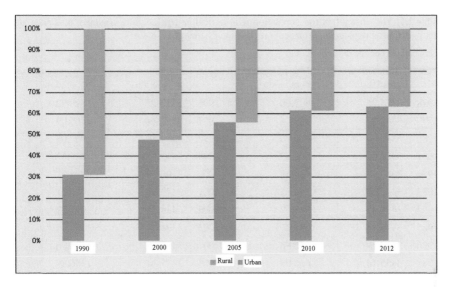

**Fig. 2.1**   The urbanization rate in Zhejiang in the main years

promoted by policy from the stage of urbanization solely regulated by the market. "Urban-rural integration is a fundamental issue and is the fundamental way to address the issues relating to agriculture, rural areas and farmers." After 2003, with urban-rural integration as the means, Zhejiang endeavored to promote all-round coordinated urban and rural development, venturing down a rapid new-type road towards urbanization; in 2004, Zhejiang developed the first urban-rural integration plan nationwide. In 2005, Zhejiang unveiled the *Plan of Zhejiang Province for Fostering Coordinated Urban-Rural Development and Promoting Urban-Rural Integration*, specifying the guiding line of thought, its main tasks and strategic measures for promoting coordinated urban and rural development and the urban-rural integration in a certain period of time to come. In 2006, Zhejiang became the first nationwide to put forward and implement the new-type strategy for urbanization, and issued the *Opinions on Further Strengthening Urban Work and Venturing down the New-type Road towards Urbanization*. After the urbanization route was determined, continuous institutional innovations and policy orientation led Zhejiang's efforts to optimize the structure of the urban-rural population, thus urbanization entered a period of rapid growth.

In 2010, the rate of Zhejiang's urbanization exceeded 60%, the issues concerning population urbanization and non-agricultural employment of the labor force form rural areas had been basically addressed, and the optimization of the structure of the urban-rural population entered the stage of making breakthroughs in key areas and conducting joint construction. In 2011 and 2012, Zhejiang unveiled the *12*th *Five-Year Plan of Zhejiang Province for the New-type Urbanization* and the *Plan of Zhejiang Province for Thoroughly Pushing Forward the New-type Urbanization*,

**Table 2.1** The changes in the population with agricultural registered permanent residence and non-agricultural registered permanent residence in Zhejiang, 1978–2014

Unit: 10,000 people

| Year | Agricultural population | Non-agricultural population | Year | Agricultural population | Non-agricultural population |
|---|---|---|---|---|---|
| 1978 | 3321.96 | 429.00 | 1996 | 3570.17 | 829.92 |
| 1979 | 3332.57 | 459.76 | 1997 | 3557.19 | 865.09 |
| 1980 | 3346.40 | 480.18 | 1998 | 3539.78 | 907.08 |
| 1981 | 3362.04 | 509.47 | 1999 | 3519.79 | 947.67 |
| 1982 | 3387.79 | 536.53 | 2000 | 3506.20 | 995.02 |
| 1983 | 3413.05 | 550.05 | 2001 | 3473.63 | 1046.21 |
| 1984 | 3425.47 | 567.62 | 2002 | 3438.76 | 1097.22 |
| 1985 | 3395.35 | 634.21 | 2003 | 3394.08 | 1157.50 |
| 1986 | 3417.19 | 652.88 | 2004 | 3353.16 | 1224.06 |
| 1987 | 3455.14 | 666.05 | 2005 | 3335.30 | 1266.81 |
| 1988 | 3487.61 | 682.24 | 2006 | 3317.26 | 1312.17 |
| 1989 | 3515.46 | 693.42 | 2007 | 3308.21 | 1351.13 |
| 1990 | 3538.13 | 696.78 | 2008 | 3292.37 | 1395.48 |
| 1991 | 3555.37 | 706.00 | 2009 | 3282.23 | 1433.95 |
| 1992 | 3560.13 | 725.78 | 2010 | 3279.06 | 1468.90 |
| 1993 | 3563.24 | 750.06 | 2011 | 3279.43 | 1501.88 |
| 1994 | 3565.19 | 776.01 | 2012 | 3277.74 | – |
| 1995 | 3567.14 | 802.49 | | | |

making comprehensive arrangements for promoting that kind of urbanization in a profound way in a certain period of time to come.

As shown by the course of Zhejiang's optimization of the structure of the urban-rural population, Zhejiang started with the construction of small towns to foster coordinated urban-rural development, and improving equal access to basic public services in urban and rural areas is the most distinctive part of Zhejiang's efforts at promoting rapid new-type urbanization. According to statistical data, in 2012, the rate of urbanization of Zhejiang's population exceeded 63.2%, the population with agricultural registered permanent residence was more than 30 million for a long time, while the population with urban registered permanent residence exceeded 15 million in 2011. This means that 2/3 of the people of Zhejiang remained in the state of agricultural registered permanent residence, but in fact this population with agricultural registered permanent residence had been employed on a non-agricultural basis through coordinated urban-rural development during the new type of urbanization, and the integration of public services had broken the segmentation caused by the household registration system, so new urban residents emerged (see Table 2.1).

Besides effective policy guidance and institutional design, Zhejiang's optimization of the structure of the urban-rural population is also closely associated with the growth of small and medium-sized enterprises. That growth has provided endogenous impetus for the urbanization of the population – on the one hand, it has helped address the issues concerning the transfer of the surplus rural labor force and non-agricultural employment of the labor force form rural areas; on the other hand, it has narrowed the income gap between urban and rural areas, and increased the level of coordinated urban-rural development, providing industrial and employment support for optimizing the structure of the urban-rural population and ensuring sustainable rubanization of the population.

## 2.2.2 The Management Mechanism Has Undergone Continuous Innovations, Population Distribution and Economic Development Have Tended to Become Coordinated

The distribution of the population is closely associated with economic development. The distribution of the population among and within regions is often strongly correlated with the geographical location, natural conditions, resource distribution and economic aggregation in the regions. Generally, the distribution of the population is most closely related to industrial development. As Zhejiang is at the forefront of China's reform and opening-up and most active in economic development, Zhejiang is greatly attractive to the population; however, the population is excessively concentrated, it will put more resource and environmental pressure on a region and is unfavorable for sound economic and social development; if the population is excessively dispersive, it is not beneficial to meeting the demand for the industrial agglomeration for labor. Therefore, optimizing the distribution of the population, promoting a rational flow of the population and achieving coordinated population and economic development is conducive to driving economic development and accelerating social development.

The changes in the distribution of the population mainly resulted from the following two factors: the natural growth of the population—mainly births and deaths—and the mechanical growth of the population—mainly population migration and flow. Since the natural growth of the population was relatively stable for a long time, the optimal distribution of the population in Zhejiang was mainly attributable to the mechanical growth of the population. According to statistical data, in the fourth population census in 1990, Zhejiang was a net population exporter, population outflow from Zhejiang exceeded population inflow to Zhejiang, and the net population outflow was about 700,000 people. As shown in the fifth population census in late 2000, Zhejiang became a net population importer, population inflow to Zhejiang exceeded population outflow from Zhejiang, and the net population inflow was about 910,000 people. As indicated by the sixth population census in 2010, population inflow to Zhejiang greatly exceeded population outflow from Zhejiang, and the population inflow was 9.97 million people. During the period 2000–2014, 2,755,000 people with registered permanent residence migrated from other areas to Zhejiang, 1,562,400 people migrated from Zhejiang to other areas, and the mechanical growth was a population of 1,192,600 within 15 years. This suggests that Zhejiang's economic growth produced a significant effect on population absorption and aggregation; there was continuous improvement in economic vitality and industrial development; massive population inflow and aggregation provided ample labor resources for Zhejiang's economic development and was beneficial to coordinated population and economic development.

The optimal distribution of the population in Zhejiang was attributable to innovations to the mechanism of the management of the migrant population in recent years; the prefecture-level cities established special bodies for the coordination of the management of migrant population services, and such cities as Hangzhou, Ningbo, Wenzhou, Shaoxing, Jiaxing, Huzhou, Zhoushan and Taizhou also set up special permanent bodies. In order to guide the scientific flow and the rational distribution of the population, Zhejiang has also made active progress in promoting the education of the children of the migrant population, optimizing the employment environment for the external population and establishing a social security system involving the migrant population suited to the reality.

According to the law which governs the changes in regional economy and the distribution of the population, the adjustment and optimization of population's spatial distribution in Zhejiang were consistent with the spatial distribution of industries. During the period 2000–2010, economic growth generated massive regional population inflow to Zhejiang as a whole, and the distribution of the population was optimized and adjusted greatly within regions in Zhejiang. Compared with 2000, the five fastest-growing prefecture-level cities are Ningbo, Hangzhou, Jiaxing, Wenzhou and Jinhua where the growth rates were 25.1%, 24.1%, 23.2%, 18.7% and 15.2%, respectively (see Table 2.2). These five cities are the prefecture-level cities which were most active in the economic field, showed the greatest economic strength and the fastest economic growth in the past several decades. Quzhou and Lishui saw negative growth of their total population. Therefore, the distribution of the population among prefecture-level cities within Zhejiang was also optimized continuously in the past 10–20 years; the areas with a large economic aggregate and rapid growth also showed the most significant population growth, while the economically underdeveloped areas were the areas where the advantage of location was not obvious and the natural environment was relatively weak; the population basically tended to be stable. This proves that the distribution of Zhejiang's population and its economic development tended to be coordinated.

**Table 2.2** Distribution of the Population and its growth in cities in 2010

|  | Year-end population (10,000 people) | Proportion in Zhejiang's population (%) | Cumulative growth rate in ten years (%) | Proportion of external population in Zhejiang (%) | Proportion of external population in city (%) |
|---|---|---|---|---|---|
| Hangzhou | 870.54 | 16 | 24.1 | 14.7 | 20 |
| Ningbo | 761.08 | 14 | 25.1 | 16.8 | 26.1 |
| Wenzhou | 913.45 | 16.8 | 18.7 | 23 | 29.8 |
| Jiaxing | 450.46 | 8.3 | 23.2 | 9.5 | 24.9 |
| Huzhou | 289.42 | 5.3 | 8.1 | 3.8 | 15.7 |
| Shaoxing | 491.29 | 9 | 12.1 | 7.7 | 18.5 |
| Jinhua | 536.64 | 9.9 | 15.2 | 10.4 | 22.8 |
| Quzhou | 212.32 | 3.9 | −2 | 0.7 | 3.8 |
| Zhoushan | 112.14 | 2.1 | 11.9 | 1.8 | 19.1 |
| Taizhou | 597.38 | 11 | 13.9 | 10.3 | 20.4 |
| Lishui | 211.79 | 3.9 | −2.9 | 1.3 | 7.1 |

## 2.2.3   The Relations between Population and Industries Have Become Increasingly Close

During the initial stage of market-oriented reform, Zhejiang successfully seized opportunities to rapidly complete industrialization as a large number of private enterprises stood out. With further economic and social development in Zhejiang, the secondary industry was increasingly subject to constraints from the labor, energy and resource environment, and the ability of the secondary industry to stimulate economic growth and absorb the working population weakened gradually; therefore, as Zhejiang has entered the middle and later periods of industrialization thanks to rapid development, it is urgently necessary to achieve industrial structural adjustment, upgrading and transformation, while the previous progress in industrialization has created favorable preconditions for the development of the tertiary industry in Zhejiang.

In 2002, Zhejiang unveiled the developmental plan for the tertiary industry, calling for transforming the industrial structure of the national economy from the "secondary-tertiary-primary" one to the "tertiary-secondary-primary" one and gradually shaping a modern tertiary industrial system suitable for economic and social development. According to the plan, by the end of the period of the 10th Five-Year Plan, the total number of people employed in the tertiary industry will exceed 10 million, and by 2010, a "tertiary-secondary-primary" industrial structure will have been achieved throughout the province. The people employed in the tertiary industry will account for about 45% of all the people employed in the society.

In 2008, Zhejiang issued the *Implementation Opinions on Further Accelerating the Development of the Service Industry*, identifying developing the service industry

**Table 2.3** The development of the primary, secondary and tertiary industries in Zhejiang 2004–2014

Unit: 100 million yuan

| Year | The primary industry | The secondary industry | The tertiary industry |
|------|---------------------|------------------------|----------------------|
| 2004 | 814.10 | 6250.38 | 4584.22 |
| 2005 | 892.83 | 7166.15 | 5378.87 |
| 2006 | 925.10 | 8509.57 | 6307.85 |
| 2007 | 986.02 | 10148.45 | 7645.97 |
| 2008 | 1095.96 | 11567.42 | 8799.31 |
| 2009 | 1163.08 | 11908.49 | 9918.78 |
| 2010 | 1360.56 | 14297.93 | 12063.82 |
| 2011 | 1583.04 | 16555.58 | 14180.23 |
| 2012 | 1667.88 | 17316.32 | 15681.13 |

as an important way to more rapidly promote industrial structural adjustment and change the economic developmental mode. In 2009, Zhejiang issued the *Several Opinions on Promoting the Development of the Tertiary Industry*, introducing preferential policies—including reduction and exemption of corporate income tax, house property tax and land use tax—for the emerging sectors of the tertiary industry such as cultural, financial, intermediary, logistics, exhibition and convention and tourism sectors. In 2011, Zhejiang issued the *Several Policy Opinions on Further Accelerating the Development of the Service Industry*, calling for continuously promoting the rapid development of that industry.

Compared with the secondary industry, the tertiary industry enjoys the following greatest advantage: the dependence upon energy resources is slight, while it is highly flexible in absorbing employment and promoting economic growth. Therefore, Zhejiang vigorously pushed forward the development of the tertiary industry, and saw increasingly close relations between population and industry amidst the adjustment and optimization of the economic structure. In 2002, the tertiary industry had become the main channel for population employment in Zhejiang. According to statistics in 2002, the workers employed in the tertiary industry accounted for 67.49%, while those employed in the secondary industry accounted for 29.95% (see Table 2.3). According to the statistical analysis of the past several decades, as Zhejiang underwent industrial structural adjustment, upgrading and transformation, the proportion of people employed in the primary industry declined, the agricultural surplus labor continuously migrated to the secondary and tertiary industries, the proportion of people employed in the secondary industry fluctuated slightly, while that in the tertiary industry increased significantly. This suggests increasingly close relations between population and the tertiary industry in Zhejiang.

## 2.2.4 The Cultural Quality of the Population Has Improved Constantly

In the modern society, science and technology is the No. 1 productive force, while scientific advancement and technical innovation mainly rely on human capital rather than material resources. Therefore, the cultural quality of the population exerts a decisive impact on the post-industrialization society, and the continuous progress in productive forces depends upon constant improvement in the cultural quality of the population. The ability to make constant improvements in the cultural quality of the population is an important indicator for judging the ability of a region to maintain long-term competitiveness and economic vitality in the future.

Since the reform and opening-up, Zhejiang has witnessed constant improvement in the cultural quality of the population; in particular, since the 21st century, high-caliber talents above the level of university education have shown an explosive rate of growth. According to statistical data, in 1982, a year during the initial stage of the reform and opening-up, there were only 182,100 people above the level of university education in Zhejiang; the number soared to 485,000, 1,467,900 and 5,077,800 in 1990, 2000 and 2010, respectively. In the meantime, the illiterate and semiliterate population was on the decrease, it declined from 9,306,700 in 1982 to 3,061,000 in 2010. In more than 30 years, the cultural quality of the population improved significantly in Zhejiang.

The improvement in the cultural quality of the population is closely related to rapid economic and social development in Zhejiang. Since economic marketization, Zhejiang has achieved superfast economic growth and has made marked improvements in economic foundation and economic aggregate under the condition that Zhejiang has not enjoyed special reform and opening-up policies, a unique geographical location and an advantageous economic foundation. Generally, if a region enjoys a high level of economic and social development, the level of its industrial development and its rate of return on human capital are higher, and it is more capable of attracting talents. Zhejiang is a typical example of attracting outstanding talents with good economic conditions and a developmental foundation on the basis of economic development. For the main indictors concerning the cultural quality of the population, after a round of economic development during the initial stage of reform and opening-up, the proportion of illiterate and semiliterate people and the proportion of the people above the level of university education among every 100,000 people in Zhejiang were lower than the average national levels, which was in striking contrast to Zhejiang's position in the economic level. Therefore, Zhejiang introduced a number of policies for attracting talents, playing a very active role. In 2004, Zhejiang adopted ten policies, including that for the chief worker system, involving experts, scholars, enterprise operation management talents, professional and technical talents, high-skilled talents and the talents adept in the non-public sectors of the economy. As from March 1, 2005, Zhejiang carried out the talent residence permit system throughout the province, mainly aimed at encouraging domestic and foreign high-level talents to work and serve in Zhejiang through a flexible policy of flow. In

**Table 2.4** The educational level of Zhejiang's population in the main years

Unit: 10,000 people

| Year | University | Senior middle school | Junior middle school | Primary school | Illiterate, semiliterate |
|------|-----------|---------------------|---------------------|----------------|--------------------------|
| 1982 | 18.21 | 202.19 | 691.55 | 1531.44 | 930.67 |
| 1990 | 48.5 | 290.37 | 983.98 | 1643.92 | 723.64 |
| 2000 | 146.79 | 495.36 | 1531.94 | 1683.34 | 321.85 |
| 2010 | 507.78 | 738.12 | 1996.41 | 1568.54 | 306.1 |

2011, Zhejiang initiated the Seagull Program for the overseas high-level innovative talents working in Zhejiang for more than 2 months but not more than 6 months in a year and for more than 3 consecutive years. Under the Seagull Program, the eligible people will be provided with 500,000 yuan in scientific and technological talent incentives by the provincial government on a one-time basis, and they will also be provided with favorable conditions and conveniences in exit and entry, medical service and insurance in light of actual needs. These policies have offered very convenient conditions for Zhejiang's enterprises to attract external talents, and they have also laid a good institutional foundation for external talents to enter and serve Zhejiang. Therefore, as shown, with the introduction of these systems, the decade from 2000 to 2010 witnessed the fastest improvement in the cultural quality of the population in Zhejiang in the past 30 years (see Table 2.4).

## 2.3 The Transformation of the Employment Structure in Zhejiang

The transformation of the employment structure is one of the important parts of economic transformation and upgrading. With rapid economic and social development in Zhejiang, the transformation of the employment structure has become an important part of efforts in supporting Zhejiang's industrial structural adjustment, transformation and upgrading in recent years. In particular, in the process of economic and social development, in an effort to transform the economic growth mode, achieve coordinated economic and social development and optimize the social structure in Zhejiang, it is important to better coordinate the steps for developing the industrial structure and the employment structure, and enabling concurrent upgrading and transformation of the industrial structure and the employment structure.

### 2.3.1  Employment and Industries Have Promoted Each Other, the Employment Pattern Has Become Increasingly Optimal

The industrial structure and the employment structure complement and restrain each other. According to the statistical data on Zhejiang since the reform and opening-up, during the initial stage of reform and opening-up launched in 1978, the output value of the primary industry accounted for more than 1/3 of the total output value, while that of the secondary industry accounted for about 40%, and that of the tertiary industry less than 20%. In the early 1990s, in Zhejiang, the proportion of the primary industry decreased to about 20%, while that of the secondary industry exceeded 50% and that of the tertiary industry was only about 1/3; Zhejiang had basically just entered an industrial society (see Table 2.5). However, the acute contradiction in this period was that industrial development was less able to promote labor transfer, while the main cause was that Zhejiang's private economy consisted of small and micro enterprises and family workshops to a great extent, the surplus labor in rural areas can be employed at the local level, while the secondary and tertiary industries, capable of massively absorbing the working population and the labor force from rural areas, had not yet produced a scale effect.

The main characteristic of the change in Zhejiang's industrial structural since the market-oriented reform, especially during the 21st century, is a continued decrease in the proportion of the primary industry. The proportion of the primary industry was 4.4% in 2014, while that of the secondary industry rose and then declined, it was lower than 50% in 2014; that of the tertiary industry increased continuously, it was 47.9% in 2014. From the perspective of output value, Zhejiang had a "secondary-tertiary-primary" industrial structure in the middle and later periods of industrialization; the proportion of the primary industry has decreased rapidly, that of the secondary industry has started to decline and that of the tertiary industry has been on the rise.

With rapid change in the industrial structure, Zhejiang has introduced a number of policies for guiding the transformation and upgrading of the structure of the employment of the population, with a focus on removing the policy barriers to the change and upgrading of the employment structure, enhancing the quality of workers, promoting the role of scientific and technological innovation and capital input in the quantity of the labor force and rationalizing the labor market. On the one hand, in order to accelerate coordinated economic and social development and promote benign interaction between economic growth and employment expansion, Zhejiang has concurrently worked on intensifying the reforms, promoting development, adjusting the structure and expanding employment, and has established an economic structure and growth mode conducive to expanding employment while stressing efforts to enhance competitiveness. On the other hand, Zhejiang has fostered coordinated economic development between urban and rural areas and among regions, and has made efforts to speed up the construction of small towns and the adjustment of the rural economic structure, improve the urban and rural employment

**Table 2.5** The output value of the primary, secondary and tertiary industries, 1978–2014

Unit: 100 million yuan

| Year | The primary industry | The secondary industry | The tertiary industry | Year | The primary industry | The secondary industry | The tertiary industry |
|------|------|------|------|------|------|------|------|
| 1978 | 47.09 | 53.52 | 23.11 | 1996 | 594.94 | 2232.17 | 1361.43 |
| 1979 | 67.56 | 64.07 | 26.12 | 1997 | 618.90 | 2554.57 | 1512.64 |
| 1980 | 64.61 | 84.07 | 31.24 | 1998 | 609.30 | 2766.95 | 1676.38 |
| 1981 | 69.06 | 94.68 | 41.12 | 1999 | 606.31 | 2974.74 | 1862.87 |
| 1982 | 84.88 | 98.44 | 50.69 | 2000 | 630.98 | 3273.93 | 2236.12 |
| 1983 | 82.89 | 113.12 | 61.08 | 2001 | 659.78 | 3572.88 | 2665.68 |
| 1984 | 104.40 | 141.48 | 77.37 | 2002 | 685.20 | 4090.48 | 3227.99 |
| 1985 | 123.88 | 198.91 | 106.37 | 2003 | 717.85 | 5096.38 | 3890.79 |
| 1986 | 136.29 | 230.89 | 135.29 | 2004 | 814.10 | 6250.38 | 4584.22 |
| 1987 | 159.41 | 281.47 | 166.11 | 2005 | 892.83 | 7164.75 | 5360.10 |
| 1988 | 195.68 | 354.39 | 220.18 | 2006 | 925.10 | 8511.51 | 6281.86 |
| 1989 | 210.95 | 386.25 | 252.24 | 2007 | 986.02 | 10154.25 | 7613.46 |
| 1990 | 225.04 | 408.18 | 271.47 | 2008 | 1095.96 | 11567.42 | 8799.31 |
| 1991 | 245.22 | 494.11 | 350.00 | 2009 | 1163.08 | 11908.49 | 9918.78 |
| 1992 | 262.67 | 653.43 | 459.60 | 2010 | 1360.56 | 14297.93 | 12063.82 |
| 1993 | 315.97 | 983.96 | 625.99 | 2011 | 1583.04 | 16555.58 | 14180.23 |
| 1994 | 438.65 | 1398.12 | 852.52 | 2012 | 1667.88 | 17316.32 | 15681.13 |
| 1995 | 549.96 | 1854.52 | 1153.07 | | | | |

service system, guide the orderly flow of the rural labor force and enhance the ability of urban areas to absorb the labor force.

According to statistical data, the degree of coordination between the structure of the employment of the population and the industrial structure was on the rise and the degree of structural deviation was on the decline in Zhejiang. In 2000, 9,699,700 people were employed in the primary industry, accounting for 35.58% of all the employed people; 9,663,000 people were employed in the secondary industry, accounting for 35.45% of all the employed people; 7,898,200 people were employed in the tertiary industry, accounting for 28.97% of all the employed people; the employed population featured a "primary-secondary-tertiary" structure. In 2012, the employed population in the primary industry decreased to 5,220,100, accounting for 14.14% of the total employed population; the employed population in the secondary industry was 18,809,200, accounting for 50.96% of the total employed population; the employed population in the tertiary industry was 12,883,100, accounting for 34.90% of the total employed population. The employment structure became relatively consistent with the industrial structure—a "secondary-tertiary-primary" structure, and the degree of coordination between the structure of the employment of the population

**Table 2.6** The proportions of the employed population in the primary, secondary and tertiary industries in Zhejiang, 2000–2012

Unit: %

| Year | The primary industry | The secondary industry | The tertiary industry | Year | The primary industry | The secondary industry | The tertiary industry |
|------|------|------|------|------|------|------|------|
| 2000 | 35.58 | 35.45 | 28.97 | 2007 | 20.07 | 46.78 | 33.15 |
| 2001 | 33.44 | 36.10 | 30.46 | 2008 | 19.22 | 47.61 | 33.17 |
| 2002 | 30.97 | 37.44 | 31.59 | 2009 | 18.32 | 48.05 | 33.63 |
| 2003 | 28.30 | 41.20 | 30.50 | 2010 | 16.00 | 49.79 | 34.21 |
| 2004 | 26.06 | 43.61 | 30.33 | 2011 | 14.57 | 50.86 | 34.57 |
| 2005 | 24.50 | 45.07 | 30.43 | 2012 | 14.14 | 50.96 | 34.90 |
| 2006 | 22.63 | 45.78 | 31.59 | | | | |

and the industrial structure increased significantly. Of course, there is still a great amount of room for Zhejiang to improve the structure of the employment of the population as compared with the developed countries where the employed population in the primary industry accounted for less than 10% and that in the tertiary industry accounted for more than 60% (see Table 2.6).

## 2.3.2 Coordinated Urban-Rural Development Has Been Fostered, the Employed Population Has More Rapidly Transferred to the Secondary and Tertiary Industries

During the initial stage of the market economy's transformation, Zhejiang seized opportunities to make great progress in economic and social development, the rural surplus labor started transferring to urban areas, generally there was a great amount of room for improving the allocation of labor resources, the employed population in the primary industry made up a relatively high proportion; in 2000, the employed population in the primary industry still accounted for more than 1/3; this affected the efficiency of the utilization of labor resources and led to a slow improvement in the productivity of agricultural laborers. In order to ensure coordinated urban and rural development and guide the transfer of rural surplus labor, as from 2003, Zhejiang earnestly adjusted the agricultural structure, rationally developed and allocated rural labor resources, guided and served rural labor, addressed the issues concerning the employment and the social security of the farmers whose land had been expropriated, and incorporated rural employment into the overall plan for economic and social development. The experience mainly covers the following two aspects: First, carrying out the reform involving the expansion of the powers of strong counties, focusing on improving the ability for development and aggregation of the county economy, guid-

**Table 2.7** The changes in the size of the population employed in the primary, secondary and tertiary industries in Zhejiang, 2000–2012

Unit: 10,000 people

| Year | The primary industry | The secondary industry | The tertiary industry | Year | The primary industry | The secondary industry | The tertiary industry |
|------|------|------|------|------|------|------|------|
| 2000 | 969.97 | 966.3 | 789.82 | 2007 | 683.32 | 1592.84 | 1128.85 |
| 2001 | 935.24 | 1009.55 | 851.86 | 2008 | 670.16 | 1660.04 | 1156.3 |
| 2002 | 885.29 | 1070.13 | 903.14 | 2009 | 657.95 | 1726.06 | 1207.97 |
| 2003 | 826.03 | 1201.3 | 891.41 | 2010 | 581.87 | 1810.36 | 1243.79 |
| 2004 | 779.65 | 1304.94 | 907.36 | 2011 | 535.27 | 1868.83 | 1270.01 |
| 2005 | 759.53 | 1397.69 | 943.54 | 2012 | 522.01 | 1880.92 | 1288.31 |
| 2006 | 717.81 | 1452.29 | 1002.28 | | | | |

ing the rural surplus labor force capable of seeking employment in non-agricultural industries to urban areas. Second, vigorously developing small towns, giving priority to developing central towns. For a long time, the spontaneous organization by the market economy gave birth to a large number of small towns with a certain economic strength and regional economic functions in Zhejiang. From the perspective of the urbanization of the population, the costs for transferring the rural population to the surrounding small towns are much lower than those for transferring them to large and medium-sized cities, the rising small towns provide low-cost opportunities for transferring rural surplus labor. In terms of employment, small towns have the functions of some regional centers and can give rise to the secondary and tertiary industries, and provide ample job opportunities for rural labor transferring to the secondary and tertiary industries, thus stimulating the transfer of the employed population from the primary industry to the secondary and tertiary industries.

According to statistical data, Zhejiang saw benign development of the structure of the employment of the population, with the transfer of the employed population from the primary industry to the secondary and tertiary industries. During the period 2000–2012, the population employed in the primary industry decreased by nearly 4,480,000 from 9,699,700 to 5,220,100; that in the secondary industry increased by nearly 9,150,000 from 9,663,000 to 18,809,200; that in the tertiary industry increased by nearly 4,990,000 from 7,898,200 to 12,883,100. As the population employed in the primary industry decreased rapidly, that in the secondary and tertiary industries increased rapidly (see Table 2.7).

The benign development of the employed population in Zhejiang is closely associated with its full-fledged labor market system which is unified between urban and rural areas. Since the beginning of the 21st century, Zhejiang has basically established a market-oriented employment system which has been integrated between urban and rural areas, and Zhejiang has completely removed the restrictive policies for the employment of rural laborers in urban areas in terms of geography, identity and registered permanent residence; Zhejiang has also introduced the policy for making sure that workers choose jobs independently, that the market regulates employment and that the government promotes employment, so that employers recruit workers independently and workers seek employment through fair competition, thus providing a good institutional guarantee for promoting the coordinated development of employment between urban and rural areas.

### 2.3.3 The New and Hi-tech Industries Have Maintained a Good Momentum of Development, Talent Aggregation Has Increased

Since the beginning of the 21st century, Zhejiang has devoted great energy to developing new and hi-tech industries, it has optimized and upgraded the traditional industrial structure, so that the capacity for technical innovation of the enterprises has improved significantly, the traditional industrial level has increased markedly, and the competitiveness of the products on the market has been enhanced noticeably. Subsequently, talents have gathered continually in Zhejiang's new and hi-tech industries.

In 2003, Zhejiang convened the first working conference on talents, making the *Decision on Actively Implementing the Strategy of Building a Strong Province through Talents*, which marked Zhejiang's entry into the stage of rapid talent development. Zhejiang also vowed to give priority to promoting the development of talents for enterprises, making sure that the government plays the leading role, that enterprises serve as the main players and that the market allocates resources; with policy guidance and platform construction, Zhejiang has guided enterprises to give priority to developing talents, and has let the enterprises play the leading role in talent development, and it has promoted connection between capital and talents. As of late 2008, Zhejiang had boasted various types of talents whose number reached 6,248,500, accounting for 17.9% of all of the employed people. The talent aggregation effect emerged. During the period 2002–2008, the professional and technical personnel in Zhejiang were granted 24 national awards for technical inventions, 106 national awards for scientific and technological progress and 6 national awards for natural science; Zhejiang was at the forefront nationwide in the number of national awards for many consecutive years.

Attracting high-level talents at home and abroad is a strategic measure for improving and upgrading Zhejiang's talent structure and participating in international talent competitions. After the national Recruitment Program of Global Experts was initiated, Zhejiang carried out the *Plan of Zhejiang Province for Introducing Overseas High-level Talents*, and adopted a number of policies designed to encourage the personnel studying abroad to work in Zhejiang, actively introduce talents at home and abroad, bringing in the high-level talents studying abroad, and the Qianjiang Talent Program, with a view to encouraging and supporting domestic and foreign high-level talents to start businesses and carry out innovations in Zhejiang. As of late 2009, more than 9,400 people studying abroad had been working in and had started businesses in

Zhejiang, 87 people were included in the provincial Recruitment Program of Global Experts, including 46 people included in the national Recruitment Program of Global Experts.

In order to meet the needs of the enterprises for high-skilled talents during the transformation and upgrading of the enterprises, Zhejiang developed and introduced a number of policy measures, established some measures for management of the appraisal and selection for the Qianjiang Skill Award and Chief Technician; Zhejiang sent the gold-collar and blue-collar outstanding high-skilled talents to foreign countries for receiving training, conducted free training to develop urgently-needed high-skilled talents and it drafted the implementation opinions on strengthening the building of skilled talents in enterprises with a view to intensifying that building in terms of cultivation, introduction, evaluation and incentives; moreover, it stepped up efforts to cultivate high-skilled talents in traditional industries, and drafted the *Administrative Measures of Zhejiang Province for the Appraisal and Selection of Skill Masters in Traditional Industries*. In 2012, Zhejiang generated 148,000 additional high-skilled talents, up 31% over the same period of the previous year, accounting for 20.1% of the skilled workers; policies produced the institutional effect continuously, and so high-skilled talents were on the increase.

The positive effect from the aggregation of new and hi-tech talents increasingly became prominent. According to relevant statistical data, since 2008, the information transmission, computer service and software sectors based on new and hi-tech talents had developed at rates apparently higher than those of other sectors; their output value increased by 15.4% in 2010 over 2009, it rose by 27.2% and 21.5% in 2011 and 2012, respectively (see Fig. 2.2). The superfast growth of new and hi-tech industries stimulated the development of the secondary and tertiary industries, injecting endless innovation impetus for rapid and sound economic and social development in Zhejiang.

## 2.4   The Development of the Middle-Income Group

Economic development will certainly bring about a change in social structure. As shown by the course of modern national development, workers arise during the initial stage of industrialization; with the transformation of the economic growth mode and the industrial structure as well as an increasing level of education of the people, the income rises, jobs become increasingly skills-oriented, so blue-collar workers decrease in the modern society, and they are replaced by the massive middle-income group with decent jobs, a stable income, a good education, peace of mind and high consumption ability. The structure of the Western society is dominated by the middle-income group and is olive-shaped, it solves the problem concerning social fairness caused by widening the wealth gap and also helps eliminate the excessive potential destabilizing factors among the people belonging to the lower classes with extreme views. Therefore, it is necessary to increase the proportion of the middle-income group so that the structure of the social income changes from a pyramid-shaped one

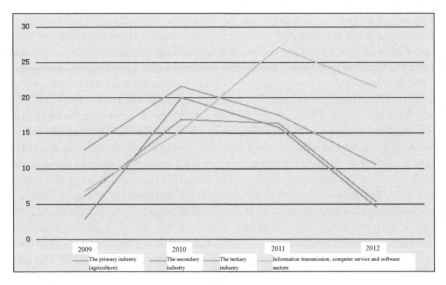

**Fig. 2.2** The growth rates in the primary, secondary and tertiary industries, the information transmission, computer service and software sectors, 2009–2012

with few high income earners and many low income earners into the olive-shaped one dominated by the middle-income group and with high income earners as the minority; this represents the main trend of historical development.

The middle-income group in modern society is mainly the social group with certain assets or certain skills. In Zhejiang, the middle-income group mainly consists of three parts: First, the small and medium-sized business owners with certain assets; second, the white-collar class with new knowledge and new skills; third, the blue-collar workers with high technical competence.

## 2.4.1   Zhejiang Ranks No. 1 in the Development of the Small and Medium-Sized Enterprises, the Traditional Middle-Income Group Has Maintained a Good Momentum of Growth

Zhejiang is one of the areas where the private economy developed at the earliest in China. As a large province famous for the private economy nationwide, Zhejiang is reputed as the Kingdom of Small and Medium-sized Private Enterprises. The small and medium-sized private enterprises account for more than 99% of all the private enterprises, indicating their importance in Zhejiang's private economy.

With the intensification of the reform and opening-up, rapid economic and social development, small and medium-sized enterprises have played an increasingly important role in Zhejiang's national economic and social development; even with the impact of the financial crisis, small and medium-sized enterprises in Zhejiang have still maintained the momentum of rapid development, thus the rise and decline of small and medium-sized enterprises determines Zhejiang's economic and social development. As of the middle of 2011, there were more than 3.08 million market players in Zhejiang, including 830,000 registered enterprises and 2,213,000 individual businesses. Small and medium-sized enterprises accounted for more than 99% of all the enterprises in Zhejiang, their total industrial output value and industrial added value accounted for more than 80% in the province, their fiscal and tax revenue and total amount of exports accounted for more than 60% of those in the entire province, and the people employed by them in urban areas accounted for more than 90%. The *Several Opinions of the People's Government of Zhejiang Province on Promoting the Development of Small and Medium-sized Enterprises and Accelerating Entrepreneurial and Innovative Development*, issued in 2010, focuses on the small enterprises with an annual sales revenue below 10 million yuan and calls for concentrating assistance efforts on the small and micro enterprises and start-ups with an annual sales revenue below 5 million yuan, and identifies small and micro enterprises and start-ups as one of the developmental priorities for a certain period of time to come.

Against such a background, the scale and proportion of small and medium-sized enterprise owners and micro enterprise owners in Zhejiang are large compared with other provinces across the country. In Zhejiang, small and medium-sized enterprise owners and individual businesses generally have obvious kinship, affinity and geographical characteristics; this means that the number of small and medium-sized enterprise owners is much larger than that of small and medium-sized enterprises. Among the middle-income group in Zhejiang, small and medium-sized enterprise owners and micro enterprise owners will enjoy a good developmental prospect in the future, and they will certainly become an important part of the middle-income group in Zhejiang. However, it must become obvious that small and medium-sized enterprise owners are part of the traditional old middle-income group, they are large in number and enjoy a stable position during the early stage of industrialization; with expanding industrialization, it is likely that the development of global enterprises and large enterprises will endanger the survival of small and medium-sized enterprises, thus threatening the social status of small and medium-sized enterprise owners. Therefore, as Zhejiang endeavors to optimize its social structure and build a society dominated by the middle class, it is necessary to value and guide small and medium-sized enterprise owners.

## 2.4.2 The Emerging Industries Have Developed Rapidly, the Emerging Middle Class Dominated by Professional and Technical White-collar Workers Has Thrived

With accelerated global industrial reorganization, it is urgently necessary to change the situation: China has been at the low added value end of the global industrial chain for a long time. As the frontier of China's economic development, Zhejiang actively seized opportunities during the previous round of global transfer of the manufacturing industry to finish the stage of economic take-off. Zhejiang has closely followed the times to proactively carry out industrial structural adjustment, transformation and upgrading, and to gradually speed up the development of new and hi-tech industries. Therefore, the emerging middle-income class dominated by professional and technical personnel, scientific and technological talents will certainly arise.

The new and hi-tech industries have played a very important role in accelerating industrial structural adjustment and upgrading in Zhejiang. The new and hi-tech industries have continuously expanded, and their proportion and status in Zhejiang's economy have been on the increase. During the period of the 11th Five-Year Plan, Zhejiang fully realized that in order to occupy a favorable position in global competition, and in the domestic and international division of labor, it is essential to give priority to developing the new and hi-tech industries in the development of the national economy, while speeding up the development of the new and hi-tech industries is the key to adjusting and optimizing the industrial structure and is also the priority in cultivating new economic growth points and enhancing regional competitiveness in a certain period of time to come. According to statistical data, the output value of Zhejiang's new and hi-tech industries grew annually by an average of 27.5% during the period of the 11th Five-Year Plan. According to the statistics on the industrial enterprises above the designated size, the added value of the new and hi-tech industries reached 239.6 billion yuan, accounting for 23% of the total output value of those industries. As of 2010, the output value of the new and hi-tech industries in Zhejiang surpassed one trillion yuan for the first time to reach 1,166.8 billion yuan, up 1.64 times compared with 2006. In the meantime, the main participants in the new and hi-tech industries grew rapidly, the number of enterprises was on the rise; as of 2010, there were 3,586 enterprises identified and recognized as part of the new and hi-tech industries, and they employed nearly 1.16 million people in Zhejiang (see Table 2.8).

The biggest difference between the new and hi-tech industries and the traditional manufacturing industry lies in the degree of dependence upon talents; the new and hi-tech industries cannot develop without a fairly large number of talents. The white-collar class with the corresponding knowledge and skills is the production factor that is indispensable for the development of the new and hi-tech industries; that class is also the most important part of the middle-income group in the modern social structure. In particular, as shown by the course of modern social development, as the society changes from an industrial society into a post-industrialization society and an information society, the emerging white-collar class replaces the traditional class

**Table 2.8** The changes in the quantity of talent resources in Zhejiang, 2000–2006

Unit: 10,000 people

|                | 2000   | 2001   | 2002   | 2003   | 2004   | 2005   | 2006   |
|----------------|--------|--------|--------|--------|--------|--------|--------|
| Total          | 152.07 | 158.96 | 162.73 | 173.33 | 198.17 | 232.64 | 259.25 |
| Hangzhou City  | 36.36  | 37.22  | 37.09  | 38.93  | 43.88  | 59.42  | 63.48  |
| Ningbo City    | 21.44  | 22.24  | 23.5   | 25.61  | 28.2   | 31.9   | 38.62  |
| Wenzhou City   | 19.55  | 21.85  | 21.96  | 24.47  | 29.75  | 32.81  | 35.31  |
| Jiaxing City   | 10.74  | 10.93  | 11.8   | 12.54  | 14.96  | 18.44  | 22.61  |
| Huzhou City    | 7.56   | 7.2    | 7.37   | 7.5    | 8.98   | 9.74   | 10.29  |
| Shaoxing City  | 12.63  | 13.57  | 14.13  | 14.93  | 16.95  | 19.86  | 24.01  |
| Jinhua City    | 11.94  | 12.39  | 13.4   | 14.03  | 14.21  | 17.97  | 18.58  |
| Quzhou City    | 6.61   | 6.96   | 6.61   | 7.02   | 8.47   | 8.62   | 9.26   |
| Zhoushan City  | 4.54   | 4.67   | 4.58   | 4.68   | 6.09   | 5.64   | 6.45   |
| Taizhou City   | 13.33  | 14.13  | 14.5   | 15.16  | 17.5   | 18.72  | 19.4   |
| Lishui City    | 7.32   | 7.63   | 7.74   | 8.09   | 8.73   | 9.52   | 9.84   |

**Table 2.9** The changes in the number of professional and technical personnel in Zhejiang, 2000–2006

Unit: 10,000 people

|                | 2000   | 2001   | 2002   | 2003   | 2004   | 2005   | 2006   |
|----------------|--------|--------|--------|--------|--------|--------|--------|
| Total          | 109.95 | 109.65 | 111.52 | 114.57 | 120.65 | 135.69 | 141.37 |
| Hangzhou City  | 25.99  | 25.99  | 25.68  | 26.2   | 26.07  | 29.34  | 33.64  |
| Ningbo City    | 15.58  | 15.7   | 16.1   | 16.96  | 17.16  | 24.31  | 19.55  |
| Wenzhou City   | 13.68  | 13.93  | 14.45  | 15.28  | 17.37  | 18.08  | 20.55  |
| Jiaxing City   | 7.99   | 7.48   | 7.93   | 8.06   | 8.95   | 10.18  | 10.96  |
| Huzhou City    | 5.35   | 4.95   | 5.15   | 5.03   | 5.43   | 5.76   | 6.33   |
| Shaoxing City  | 9.61   | 9.77   | 10.06  | 10.29  | 11.53  | 12.39  | 12.68  |
| Jinhua City    | 9.17   | 8.91   | 9.42   | 9.37   | 9.75   | 10.74  | 11.48  |
| Quzhou City    | 4.43   | 4.53   | 4.29   | 4.35   | 4.57   | 4.24   | 4.4    |
| Zhoushan City  | 3.05   | 3.17   | 3.02   | 3.02   | 3.13   | 3.15   | 3.2    |
| Taizhou City   | 9.96   | 9.93   | 9.98   | 10.34  | 10.93  | 11.6   | 11.94  |
| Lishui City    | 5.1    | 5.27   | 5.4    | 5.57   | 5.64   | 5.77   | 5.93   |

of small and medium-sized enterprise owners to become the main part of the middle-income group in the modern society. According to the statistical data from relevant departments, the quantity of talent resources increased by more than 1 million from 1,520,700 to 2,592,500 during the 6 years from 2000 to 2006 (see Table 2.9). Talent resources were mainly concentrated in the cities with a large economic aggregate such as Hangzhou, Ningbo and Wenzhou.

### 2.4.3   Innovations Have Been Made in the Manner of Cultivation, the Status of the Marginalized Middle and Low Classes Dominated by the Blue-Collar Technical Workers Has Been Improved

In the developed countries, as the society changes from an industrial society into a post-industrialization society, the economic structure changes from the one dominated by the secondary industry to the one dominated by the tertiary industry, the blue-collar workers mainly engaged in manual labor experience a decline in their position in the social structure, and they gradually become the social class with a low social status. However, China's overall condition is different from that of the developed countries to some extent, China is a populous country with great regional differences, a relative scarcity of talents and a high degree of dependence upon industry for economic growth, and China's modern service industry is still at the initial stage of development; therefore, even in Zhejiang, an economically developed area, the blue-collar technical workers with certain skills remain within the marginalized class in the middle-income group; in particular, with respect to some industries and work which suffer a shortage of talents, the income of blue-collar technical workers is much higher than that of the ordinary white-collar workers in enterprises. It is difficult to recruit the blue-collar technical workers, and it is harder to recruit the outstanding blue-collar workers with high technical competence; this problem has affected Zhejiang's economic development for a long time.

As the demographic dividend fades away, subject to the pressure from industrial adjustment, transformation and upgrading, the labor-intensive enterprises in Zhejiang have to undergo change, and it is imperative to increase the technological content in enterprise production; in this process, blue-collar technical workers with certain working skills become the essential talents in enterprises. In recent years, in order to address the shortage of blue-collar technical workers during enterprise production and operation, Zhejiang has explored a gold-collar and blue-collar high-skilled talent cultivation mode under which enterprises play the leading role in talent cultivation based on institutions and supplemented by social training. Take Ningbo as an example; as of 2012, the total number of high-skilled talents had reached 210,000, and the proportion of high-skilled talents in skilled talents had increased from 19% in 2009 to 22.8% in 2012.

Given the widespread shortage of high-level technical talents, during the period 2001–2010, Zhejiang organized 10 provincial skills contests involving more than 30 industries and 120 types of work and jobs and more than 800 municipal skills contests, with the participation of more than 6 million workers, including rural migrant workers. With these contests, more than 2,200 workers obtained the qualification of technician and senior technician and more than 500 workers were granted the title of Provincial Technical Master in Zhejiang. More than 30,000 workers obtained the qualification of senior worker through various types of contests. In order to arouse the learning and innovation capability of blue-collar workers, Zhejiang also extensively promoted the advanced operations approaches named after workers, and established such systems as Occupational Skill Leader, Chief Worker and Chief Technician. Moreover, Zhejiang sent 100 outstanding technical workers to foreign countries to receive training each year during the period 2011–2013. As indicated, blue-collar technical workers can further improve their economic income, developmental prospect and social status, and they are also an important part of the middle-income group.

## 2.5   The Overall Trend of the Change in Social Structure

### 2.5.1   The Mechanism of Optimizing Social Structure Has Preliminarily Taken Shape, the Path and Elements for Building a Society that is Dominated by the Middle Class Have Emerged

Zhejiang's rapid economic and social development has been successively driven by marketization, industrialization and urbanization; the social structure changes amidst economic and social development. According to the result concerning the change in the social structure, the basic mechanism and elements for building a social structure dominated by the middle-income group in the modern society have preliminarily taken shape. As shown by the history of social development, there was not a huge middle-income group in the agricultural society before industrialization and urbanization; the emergence of the middle-income group complements the road towards industrialization and urbanization, while the market mechanism is most crucial for the formation of the middle-income group.

According to the course of modern social development, there was not a society dominated by the middle class in the agricultural society before industrialization, while with economic and social development arising out of industrialization, the income in the industrial sector and urban areas is higher than that in the agricultural sector and rural areas; with the role of the market mechanism, the population gradually gathers in industrial towns, the people's jobs gradually transfer from the agricultural sector to the industrial sector, the economic structure shifts to the service industry. Why can a huge middle-income group arise and why can a society emerge that is dominated by the middle class? The key lies in giving full scope to the role of the market mechanism and going down the road towards industrialization and urbanization; as the industrial structure becomes optimized, transformed and upgraded continuously, the social structure is improved constantly. This is extremely similar to Zhejiang's developmental path.

Zhejiang's economic and social development is achieved basically under the market mechanism; population continuously transfers to urban areas during industrialization, the developmental path for the industrial structure and the structure of the employment of the population features a transition from the primary industry to the secondary industry and aggregation from the secondary industry to the tertiary industry; in particular, the process of industrialization has basically been completed, the new and hi-tech industries and the modern service industry develop rapidly, and this is fully consistent with the characteristics of modern social development. The change in the social structure brought about by economic and social development is also very apparent; the middle-income class—represented by small and medium-sized enterprise owners, new and hi-tech talents and blue-collar technical workers—and the managers of the traditional government departments, state-owned enterprises and public institutions become the basic elements of the middle-income group.

Therefore, according to the course and status quo of Zhejiang's development, the path, mechanism and elements for building a social structure dominated by the middle class have preliminarily taken shape, all parts of the middle-income class in the modern developed countries have basically arisen and the middle-income class is huge in Zhejiang. In the meantime, the trend of changes in the middle-income group is basically consistent with the historical changes in the social structure of the developed countries.

## 2.5.2  The Income Structure Has Been Improved Constantly, the Middle and High-Income Classes Have Been on the Rise

As one of the most economically developed provinces in China, Zhejiang has stayed ahead nationwide in the level of its residents' income. According to statistical data, during the years 2004-2010, in Zhejiang, the per capita disposable income of urban households increased from 14,546.4 yuan to 27,359 yuan, the per capita net income of rural households rose from 5,944.1 yuan to 11,302.6 yuan, much higher than the national average levels. As of 2013, in Zhejiang, the per capita disposable income of urban residents was 37,851 yuan, and the per capita consumption expenditure was 23,257 yuan; the per capita net income of rural residents was 16,106 yuan, the per capita living consumption expenditure was 11,760 yuan. Therefore, the average income level of residents in Zhejiang was high nationwide.

Zhejiang has been far ahead nationwide in the proportion of the middle and high-income groups. According to the analytical data on the disposable income of urban residents in 2013 from the survey conducted by the National Bureau of Statistics, as urban residents are grouped by their income in 2013, the per capita disposable income of the low-income group, the middle-low-income group, the middle-income group, the middle-high-income group and the high-income group was 11,434 yuan, 18,483 yuan, 24,518 yuan, 32,415 yuan and 56,389 yuan, respectively. According to the survey on Zhejiang in 2012, in Zhejiang, the average annual personal income of the low-income group, the middle-low-income group, the middle-income group, the middle-high-income group and the high-income group was 9,193 yuan, 20,216 yuan, 30,704 yuan, 49,429 yuan and 156,207 yuan, respectively (see Table 2.10). These data also suggest that the proportion and number of the middle and high-income

**Table 2.10** Comparison of urban and rural resident income between Zhejiang and the country as a whole, 2004–2010

Unit: yuan

|  | 2004 | 2005 | 2006 | 2007 | 2008 | 2009 | 2010 |
|---|---|---|---|---|---|---|---|
| Per capita disposable income of urban households (nationwide) | 9421.6 | 10493 | 11759.5 | 13785.8 | 15780.8 | 17174.7 | 19109.4 |
| Per capita disposable income of urban households (Zhejiang) | 14546.4 | 16293.8 | 18265.1 | 20573.8 | 22726.7 | 24610.8 | 27359 |
| Per capita net income of rural households (nationwide) | 2936.4 | 3254.9 | 3587 | 4140.4 | 4760.6 | 5153.2 | 5919 |
| Per capita net income of rural households (Zhejiang) | 5944.1 | 6660 | 7334.8 | 8265.2 | 9257.9 | 10007.3 | 11302.6 |

groups in Zhejiang were much larger than the average national levels. Therefore, as shown by the current resident income, Zhejiang enjoys certain advantages.

According to the developmental trend of resident income, Zhejiang's resident income will continue to grow in the future. On the one hand, as the Lewis turning point, in an economic sense, generated by population transformation has arrived, the price of labor will be on the increase. In recent years, Zhejiang has continuously suffered a shortage of rural migrant workers, and this means that the relationship between labor supply and demand has been readjusted, the labor market has started to favor workers, workers' income will grow substantially. According to statistical data, in recent years, the wage income of urban and rural residents has grown markedly in Zhejiang, and the wage income among rural residents' income has grown faster than that of urban residents in Zhejiang; this also proves that after the Lewis turning point arrives, the price of labor increases, resulting in an increase in resident income, thus it can be judged that the number and proportion of the middle and high-income groups will increase in Zhejiang in a certain period of time to come.

On the other hand, continuous improvement in the cultural quality of thew population and significant optimization of the occupational structure and employment structure in Zhejiang have also provided the necessary conditions for the growth of the middle and high-income groups. According to the course of modern social development, as the highly educated talents increase within the society and the occupational structure and employment structure improve, the middle and high-income groups will certainly be on the increase, and a social structure dominated by the middle-income group will ultimately take shape.

### 2.5.3 The Function of Social Security in Meeting the Basic Needs Has Basically Formed, the Low-Income Population Has Decreased Significantly

The formation of the modern society dominated by the middle class is mainly driven by industrialization; industrialization has transferred a massive labor force from the primary industry to the secondary and tertiary industries; with the transfer of labor and the formation of a modern social structure, the traditional social units which perform the function of social security, such as families and communities, have seen weakening functions, so it is essential to develop the socialized social security system for meeting the basic needs; otherwise, there is the possibility of falling into the middle-income trap with a widening wealth gap during development.

In recent years, Zhejiang has accelerated the building of social security and has improved the people's well-being while ensuring sound and rapid economic growth. According to the latest data released by the government, in 2013 alone, an additional 2.70 million and 1.61 million people were covered by endowment insurance and medical insurance, construction began with respect to 194,000 government-sponsored houses and 111,000 government-sponsored houses were completed in Zhejiang. In the meantime, Zhejiang paid attention to addressing the issues concerning the employment and life of the households with difficulties in finding jobs and the low-income groups. In 2013, 1,043,000 people were newly employed in urban areas, the monthly standards for subsistence allowances for urban and rural residents increased to 526 yuan and 406 yuan, respectively. The social function of social security for meeting the basic needs in the society dominated by the middle class has basically taken shape.

The society dominated by the middle class features an olive-shaped social structure. To build such a social structure, it is essential to reduce the size of the population belonging to the lowest class of the society, while that reduction covers the following two levels: On the one hand, from the perspective of the type of occupation, the reduction in the size of the employed population in traditional employment sectors, such as agriculture; on the other hand, from the perspective of income, the reduction of the low-income population and of the poor population. The optimization of the low class in Zhejiang's social structure is also reflected in the continued reduction of the low-income population and of the poor population.

In 2001, Zhejiang started to pilot coordinated employment between urban and rural areas, and developed the unified labor resource management system between urban and rural areas, Zhejiang initiated the policy of ensuring equal employment of workers between urban and rural areas. Since 2004, in order to speed up labor transfer and intensify training concerning farmers' occupational skills and entrepreneurial ability, Zhejiang has carried out such programs as the Program for Improving the Quality of 10 Million Farmers, and has gradually established a uniform, open, competitive and orderly labor market between urban and rural areas, the unified labor and social security system between urban and rural areas has been increasingly improved and the market mechanism has become the basic system for allocating labor forces between urban and rural areas. In 2013 alone, 228,000 rural working people were trained, 79% of whom were involved in transfer employment. The size of the employed population in the primary industry declined greatly; in late 2013, there were 5,070,000 people employed in the primary industry, accounting for 13.7% of the total employed population; the proportion of the population employed in agriculture decreased by 59.9 percentage points compared with that at the time of initiating the reform and opening-up.

Since 2000, Zhejiang has successfully carried out the 100-Town Poverty Alleviation Program and the Project for Making the Underdeveloped Towns Become Well-to-do, which focus on mitigating regional poverty; Zhejiang completed the Project for Making the Low-income Rural Households Become Well-to-do which focused on mitigating the class-induced poverty during the period 2008–2012. As of 2012, the low-income rural households with the per capita net income equal to and above 4,000 yuan accounted for 79.4% in Zhejiang. In 2013, Zhejiang started to initiate a new round of rural poverty alleviation projects with the Program for Doubling the Income of the Low-income Rural Households as the main part. During the period 2009–2012, the per capita net income of the low-income rural households increased annually by an average of 20%; the relative gap in the per capita net income between the low-income rural households and rural residents decreased from 1:2.76 in 2009, 1:2.67 in 2010, 1:2.47 in 2011 to 1:2.32 in 2012, so the relative gap in income narrowed year by year.

In 2012, the Party Committee of Zhejiang Province put forward the new poverty alleviation standard, identified the rural households with the per capita net income lower than 5,500 yuan in 2010 as the low-income rural households defined by the provincial standard. This is a high starting point for poverty alleviation and development as determined under the condition that the level of economic development is relatively high in Zhejiang; this poverty alleviation standard is 100% higher than the national standard. Such a measure shifts poverty alleviation efforts from absolute poverty to relative poverty—the traditional poverty alleviation efforts focused on absolute poverty. Zhejiang has carried out the more targeted poverty alleviation work at a high starting point.

For the above two considerations, Zhejiang has constantly improved its social security system, building a safety net for effectively meeting the basic needs in the society dominated by the middle class; in the meantime, Zhejiang has made continued progress in the transfer of rural labor and poverty alleviation, and has reduced the size and proportion of the population employed in agriculture and the low-income population in terms of occupational structure and level of income, thus cutting down the size of the population belonging to the low class of the society and providing active support for optimizing the social structure.

## 2.5.4 The Social Institutions Have Been Increasingly Full-Fledged, the Middle-Income Group Has Become More Stable

Since the reform and opening-up, Zhejiang has witnessed rapid economic development, drastic social transformation and a swift change in the structure of the population, the emerging social classes have emerged. The middle-income class is the most stable and most responsible social class among the emerging social classes. As shown by the course of social development, a stable society is a society dominated by the middle-income group whose proportion often reaches 60%. According to the above analysis, in recent years, Zhejiang has continuously optimized its social structure, the middle-income class is the most important social class among the emerging social classes in Zhejiang, and the stable growth of the middle-income group is one of the important changes in Zhejiang's social structure.

The stable growth of the middle-income class in Zhejiang is attributable to economic development and the achievements arising out of increasing social institutional improvements. The social institutional improvements are relative to substantive development and they involve the establishment and improvement of social institutions relating to the adjustment and building up of the social structure. These social institutions can be defined at two levels: First, the social institutions, in a narrow sense, directly related to social development, such as the social security system and the social management system; second, the aggregate of economic and social policies and systems, in a broad sense, conducive to shaping a middle-class-dominated social structure, such as the industrial policies and talent systems beneficial to the growth of the middle-income group, the poverty alleviation policies and labor transfer systems conducive to eliminating the low-income population within the low class.

At present, Zhejiang has entered the crucial period for building a middle-class-dominated social structure and has made outstanding achievements in economic and social institutional improvement. From the macro perspective, Zhejiang has maintained rapid economic and social development, and has achieved industrial structural optimization, upgrading and transformation, the per capita level of income has been on the rise, the people live more affluent lives, thus providing a good economic and social environment for continued development, expansion and growth of the middle-income group. At the micro level, the class of the small and medium-sized enterprise owners with certain assets—a class forming an important part of the middle-income group and the basic element of a society dominated by the middle class—and the white-collar class with a certain amount of knowledge and the senior blue-collar class with high skills show a good momentum of development. In particular, in the recent development, Zhejiang has paid special attention to the development of new and hi-tech industries and the building and introduction of talents, and Zhejiang has valued the roles of knowledge, skills and the talents with knowledge and skills in competition in the modern society, Zhejiang has placed emphasis on the fundamental role of the market economy. These mechanisms are fundamental to the operation of and competition in the modern society. The optimization of Zhejiang's social structure has entered a crucial period of integration and reconstruction; the adjust-ment of the social structure and the stable development of the middle-income group is closely associated with social institutional development. In particular, in recent years, Zhejiang has effectively pushed forward social institutional improvement to continually strengthen social security and social management, and has carried out social institutional optimization and integration to build up the social institutions and construction mechanisms conducive to the formation of a society dominated by the middle class.

# Chapter 3
# Urban-Rural Integration

**Chunguang Wang**

Ten years ago, the Research Group for "The Zhejiang Experience and Its Implication for the Development of China" conducted surveys and research on Zhejiang's urban-rural integration, and found that Zhejiang had initiated the process of urban-rural integration at that time, but it had just begun and still faced many problems; Ten years later, what progress has been made in Zhejiang's urban-rural integration? Is Zhejiang still ahead nationwide? Which experience can be drawn upon by other areas? What problems and dilemmas exist in Zhejiang's urban-rural integration? These issues are discussed and studied in this chapter.

## 3.1 The Urban-Rural Integration and New-Type Urbanization

Urban-rural integration and new-type urbanization have become important developmental strategies for China's modernization; however, the relations between urban-rural integration and new-type urbanization are not clear. This chapter presents an in-depth analysis of Zhejiang's practice to gain a clearer understanding of their relations.

### 3.1.1 The Basic Connotation of Urban-Rural Integration

The concept of urban-rural integration does not exist in the drive for modernization in others countries; it is just a concept with Chinese characteristics; however, this does not mean that the problems and phenomena involving urban-rural integration

C. Wang (✉)
Chinese Academy of Social Sciences, Beijing, People's Republic of China

© Social Sciences Academic Press and Springer Nature Singapore Pte Ltd. 2019          65
G. Chen and J. Yang (eds.), *Chinese Dream and Practice in Zhejiang—Society*,
Research Series on the Chinese Dream and China's Development Path,
https://doi.org/10.1007/978-981-13-7406-7_3

do not occur in the drive for modernization in other countries. Relevant problems and phenomena in other countries are not as obvious as they are in China. According to economist W. Arthur Lewis, a dual economy once existed between urban and rural areas during industrialization in European countries and in the U.S., but later, it faded away. Undeniably, the developed countries experienced a process that went from an urban-rural gap to urban-rural integration and balanced urban-rural development in the drive for modernization. In China, there are not only a dual economy but also a dual society, a dual system and dual administration between urban and rural areas. At present, as China endeavours to achieve modernization and overall development, it is necessary for China to work on the developmental task and goal of breaking that dual society, dual system and dual administration between urban and rural areas to achieve urban-rural integration.

The definitions and understanding of urban-rural integration vary with different periods and different areas. So far, no general consensus has been reached in this regard. Some research equates urban-rural integration with urbanization; some research holds that urban-rural integration is aimed at building close industrial connections, complete infrastructure and the corresponding organizational system between urban and rural areas; some research focuses on the rational layout of urban and rural spaces. Currently, relevant views are mostly expressed in documents of the Party and of the government and in much of the media. In 2003, the 3rd Plenary Session of the 16th Central Committee of the Communist Party of China vowed to foster coordinated urban-rural development. The *Decision of the Central Committee of the Communist Party of China on Several Issues Concerning the Improvement of the Socialist Market Economic System* stressed coordinated development in five aspects—coordinated urban-rural development, coordinated regional development, coordinated economic and social development, coordinated harmonious development of the people and nature, coordinated domestic development and opening-up—and put coordinated urban-rural development above the coordinated development in the other four aspects. This was the first time that the Central Committee of the Communist Party of China had envisioned coordinated urban-rural development; however, the report did not expound how to foster coordinated urban-rural development nor what it is. During the 4th Plenary Session of the 16th Central Committee of the Communist Party of China, convened in September, 2004, Hu Jintao made the judgment of "two general trends": agriculture supports industry and provides accumulation for industry at the initial stage of industrialization; industry re-feeds agriculture, urban areas support rural areas to achieve the coordinated development of industry and agriculture, urban and rural areas after industrialization reaches a certain high level. Such a judgment is of important significance in guiding the policies of the Central Government and the governments at various levels to adjust their policies. The *Decision of the Central Committee of the Communist Party of China on Some Major Issues Concerning Building a Socialist Harmonious Society*, adopted during the 6th Plenary Session of the 16th Central Committee of the Communist Party of China in 2006, identified the construction of a new countryside and coordinated urban-rural development as important parts of the strategic goal of building a harmonious society, and stated that one of the main tasks for building a harmonious socialist society in the future consisted of gradually reversing the widening developmental gap between urban and rural areas and among regions and basically establishing a social security system covering urban and rural residents. The report delivered in the 3rd Plenary Session of the 18th Central Committee of the Communist Party of China mentioned, many times, urban-rural integration in such respects as the reform of the fiscal and tax system and the building-up of land, and pointed out, "The dual urban-rural structure is the main barrier to urban-rural integration, it is essential to improve systems and mechanisms, establish new-type industrial-agricultural, urban-rural relations—in which industry promotes agricultural development, urban areas stimulate rural development, agriculture and industry deliver mutual benefits, and urban-rural integration is achieved—so that farmers can participate in the drive towards modernization on an equal footing, and share the achievements of modernization". According to the documents and reports issued by the Central Committee of the Communist Party of China, urban-rural integration has at least the following four connotations: First, making sure that policies and institutions are consistent and similar, removing the differences in policies and systems between urban and rural areas; second, ensuring equal access to resources through allocation; third, narrowing the income gap between urban and rural areas; fourth, achieving urban-rural coordination in economic development and making sure that cities support rural areas.

Zhejiang is one of the first provinces to introduce the policy of urban-rural integration. As early as 2004, when serving as the Secretary of the Party Committee of Zhejiang Province, comrade Xi Jinping put forward the "Eight-Eight Strategies" which included the important strategy of urban-rural integration, and held that urban-rural integration was the fundamental way to address the issues relating to agriculture, rural areas and farmers. Urban-rural integration, raised by Xi Jinping, has three implications: First, encouraging farmers to enter cities, making farmers non-agricultural; second, nurturing small towns, building a new countryside; third, promoting agricultural industrialization, developing the rural economy.[1] The first implication is urbanization and non-agriculturization; in fact, like the rest of the country, Zhejiang has not yet completed urbanization, thus urbanization and non-agriculturization remains one of the important tasks in urban-rural integration. The second implication is a combination of building small towns and rural development; the third implication is agricultural industrialization and rural modernization.

New-type urbanization, currently put forward by the Central Committee of the Communist Party of China, and urban-rural integration are not mutually exclusive; on the contrary, the former is an important part of the latter. This means that new-type urbanization is essential for urban-rural integration, so promoting new-type urbanization does not mean that efforts are not being made to develop rural areas and agriculture and let all farmers enter cities. In the future drive towards modernization, farmers, rural areas and agriculture will not disappear; instead, they will become more affluent, prosperous and competitive. In other words, new-type urbanization and the construction of a new countryside, and rural modernization are two impor-

---

[1] Xi (2006), p. 159–160.

tant interrelated parts, which are mutually reinforcing, of urban-rural integration. New-type urbanization is the people-oriented type of urbanization and is relative to physical urbanization. "New-type" means that the rural people who frequently migrate to cities for working are granted permanent urban residency and given the same treatment as urban residents, so that they are able to integrate into the urban society. In the past long-time drive towards modernization, China did not attach importance to the people's urbanization, China paid more attention to urban expansion and economic development, a large number of rural migrant workers working, doing business in cities and making enormous contributions to urban development were excluded from the urban society, they were not provided with the same resident and citizen treatments, so they were in a migrant state for a long time, causing severe social unfairness and other social problems.

However, new-type urbanization cannot be completed in one stroke and in a short time. China has developed certain plans for new-type urbanization, calling for urbanizing 100 million people by 2020. Obviously, this is still greatly different from the current reality that more than 200 million rural people are migrant in urban areas. From another perspective, as new-type urbanization is promoted, some rural migrant workers will return to rural areas, rural areas remain home for them. Therefore, the construction of a new countryside, and rural modernization are as important as new-type urbanization. The recently unveiled *National Plan for Urbanization* dedicates Chap. 7 to discussing the issue of promoting urban-rural integration; it calls for improving the systems and mechanisms for urban-rural integration; promoting the construction of the urban and rural factor markets; pushing forward urban-rural integration in planning, infrastructure and public services; speeding up agricultural modernization; building a new socialist countryside, etc.

## 3.1.2 The Essence of Urban-Rural Integration

Urban-rural integration does not mean that there is no difference between urban and rural areas. In fact, as long as there are urban and rural areas, some differences cannot and should not be removed; otherwise, there is urban-rural unification or sameness rather than urban-rural integration. Urban and rural areas feature symbiosis and coexistence. If rural areas disappear, urban areas will no longer exist, urban-rural differences will disappear.

In China's practice, urban-rural integration first focuses on resolving the differences in systems and policies between urban and rural areas, and then is aimed at addressing the developmental imbalance between urban and rural areas. Of course, both aspects are closely related. Essentially, these differences and imbalance involve not only the quantity but also rights, equality of opportunity and other fronts. When delivering a speech in the working conference of Zhejiang Province on rural areas in 2005, comrade Xi Jinping pointed out, "It is necessary to intensify reforms to really remove the barriers between urban and rural areas, resolve the urban and rural contradictions, provide farmers with fair national treatments, complete property rights and equal developmental opportunities; many arduous tasks still need to be finished in order to carve out the ways to narrow the urban-rural gap."[2] Apparently, unequal rights and opportunities still exist between urban and rural areas; they are largely caused by the existing systems and policies; in order to achieve urban-rural integration, priority should be given to addressing the following issue: intensifying the reform of urban and rural systems, adjusting urban and rural policies, and allocating public resources in a more balanced way, so as to narrow, even eliminate, the differences in rights and opportunities between urban and rural areas. Only in this way can conditions and a foundation be provided for really achieving balanced development between urban and rural areas.

If rights and opportunities are unequal, that inequality will affect the ability to balance the development between urban and rural areas, between urban residents and the rural population; this poses challenges to and pressure on China's sustainable development. As early as 2005, the *China Human Development Report 2005*, released by the United Nations Development Programme, clearly stated that with rapid economic development, it was urgently necessary for China to cope with the following challenge in social justice: ensuring equality for its massive population in opportunity and capability. The rural population makes up the majority of that massive population. As mentioned by Amartya Sen, an Indian American Nobel laureate in economics, development does not merely mean GDP growth or the increase in personal income, technical progress, which represent a narrow outlook on development; development is a process of expanding real freedom for the people, while freedom refers to the capability for enjoying the life which the people have reason to treasure. In his opinion, capability is a freedom, namely, various combinations of all the listed feasible activities. Such an outlook on freedom covers the "opportunities" which an individual enjoys and also involves the "process" of personal selection. He analyzed five types of instrumental freedom: political freedom, economic facilities, social opportunities, guarantees of transparency and protective security. In his view, these freedoms promote each other. He can put forward such a development theory largely because he came from India, a large developing country. His theory is also of important referential significance for China as China is promoting urban-rural integration. In the past 30 years of reform and opening-up, as farmers enjoyed unprecedented opportunities or freedoms, they unleashed enormous developmental energy and impetus, significant development was achieved in the economic and social fields in the society; however, as there has been severe opportunity inequality, rural areas have lagged behind urban areas, so the urban-rural gap has increasingly widened. Of course, Amartya Sen's views did not contain such a consideration: merely opportunities and freedoms are not enough, various resources are also necessary; for instance, the efforts to develop education and increase the educational level certainly entail massive input of educational resources, while social opportunities and guarantees of transparency also need to be supported by various resources. At present, the urban-rural differences in China exist in not only opportunity but also in

---

[2]Xi 2006, p. 152.

resources. This is the fundamental cause for its being difficult to curb the widening urban-rural gap in China.

Equality in rights and opportunities means that equal rights and opportunities are available in both urban and rural areas, and to both urban and rural residents, both local and non-local Chinese citizens. Therefore, under the vision of urban-rural integration, the differences in system and policy will not and should not exist between urban and rural residents, between local and non-local people in China, all of them should fall within the scope of Chinese citizens. Hence, the people can move, migrate and work freely. Of course, urban-rural integration also contains a very strong orientation: developmental opportunities can also be provided in rural areas, so the scenario that the people flock to urban areas should not arise, but this should not be restricted by systems and policies; the developmental strategy of urban-rural integration should be carried out to ensure that rural areas are livable and also suitable for pursuing development or provide opportunities for seeking employment and starting business. Therefore, urban-rural integration certainly calls for promoting rural modernization, agricultural industrialization and achieving industrial coordination between urban and rural areas.

Given the above understanding about the essence of urban-rural integration, the process of and issues concerning urban-rural integration in Zhejiang are discussed at two levels: new-type urbanization and the construction of a new countryside or rural modernization (see Table 3.1). The work at both levels is aimed at addressing equality in rights and opportunities between urban and rural areas. it is necessary for us to analyze, from the perspectives of policy and system, the realization of equal rights and opportunities, and to conduct an evaluation of the effects against specific goals, discuss the connection and interaction between new-type urbanization and the construction of a new countryside and rural modernization. New-type urbanization is designed to overcome underdevelopment and low quality in urbanization, but this does not mean that all of the rural population should be forced to gather in urban areas. New-type urbanization should be promoted by building a new countryside, pushing forward rural modernization, tapping rural developmental potential and space so that rural areas are the same as urban areas in the suitability for living, working and starting businesses, both urban and rural areas really become the areas and spaces for being freely selected by the people to live and work, in other words, two-way free movement and migration between urban and rural areas is achieved.

## 3.2  The Reform of the Urban and Rural Systems and Urban-Rural Integration

Zhejiang has stayed ahead nationwide in the reform of urban and rural systems and in urban-rural integration. Zhejiang's development is attributable to its efforts, and it drives Zhejiang to go farther and deeper in this regard.

**Table 3.1** The framework for analysis of urban-rural integration

| Two aspects of urban-rural integration | Policy and system | Specific goals and effects |
|---|---|---|
| 1. New-type urbanization | Equal rights and opportunities; Social integration | The realization of urbanization: 70% of the population lives in towns |
| 2. The construction of a new countryside and rural modernization | Access to the rights and opportunities which are the same as those in urban areas; The policy and institutional system of urban-rural integration; No institutional and policy barriers to movement between urban and rural areas | The economic and social gap between urban and rural areas is narrowed, and even eliminated; Infrastructure and public services are as developed as they are in urban areas; Urban-rural integration is achieved, it is difficult to draw a distinction between urban and rural areas |

### 3.2.1 The Trajectory of the Reform of Urban and Rural Systems

Zhejiang was not the first to put forward the initiative of urban-rural integration, but Zhejiang became the first to unveil the plan of urban-rural integration, and carry out reforms and innovations in system and policy. Objectively, Zhejiang has the conditions for promoting urban-rural integration. Nationally, Zhejiang was the first province where farmers spontaneously promoted urbanization. The development in Longgang Town in Cangnan County, Qiaotou Town in Yongjia County, Liushi Town in Yueqing City, Keqiao in Shaoxing County, Luqiao in Huangyan County, and even Yiwu, was spontaneously pushed forward by farmers. In the meantime, Zhejiang farmers developed industry at the local level, bringing about a great impact and value, which cannot be underestimated, in terms of balanced development of urban and rural areas in Zhejiang. At present, the urban-rural difference and regional difference in Zhejiang are the smallest nationwide; in other words, Zhejiang is at the forefront nationwide in balanced development between urban and rural areas and among regions in Zhejiang; this lays an important economic foundation for the reform of urban and rural systems in Zhejiang. From another perspective, early on, Zhejiang's leaders realized the importance of urban-rural integration. Zhejiang cannot develop well without urban-rural integration.

In 2002, Zhejiang reached an important node in promoting urban-rural integration and coordinated urban-rural development; coordinated urban-rural development and the construction of a new countryside were identified as important developmental strategies. In 2004, Zhejiang issued Document No.393—the *Plan of Zhejiang Province for Promoting Coordinated Urban-Rural Development and Urban-Rural Integration*, the first plan of this kind in China. Although Chengdu City also unveiled a similar plan in the same year, Zhejiang was the first province to do so in China. The plan specified the overall requirement for urban-rural integration, and identified six tasks and seven measures. It called for carrying out institutional reform and establishing the systems for urban-rural integration, and stressed that it was most crucial to achieve urban-rural integration in public services.

In order to build the system of urban-rural integration, it was necessary to first reform the household registration system. In the early 1980s, Zhejiang was the first province permitting farmers to work and do business in urban areas by means of self-sufficiency of grains. Longgang Town in Cangnan County, Wenzhou City was a model where rural population entered urban areas by means of self-sufficiency of grains and farmers carried out urban construction by themselves. In the 1990s, Zhejiang reformed the household registration system in 120 towns. In 1997, Zhejiang introduced the policy of granting permanent urban residency on the basis of house purchase nationwide, and carried out the policy of registered permanent residence whose booklet was affixed with a blue seal. As from 1998, Zhejiang abolished the control indicators concerning entry into urban areas. In 2003, Zhejiang initiated the household registration reform aimed at abolishing the classification of agricultural and non-agricultural registered permanent residence. In fact, registered permanent residence is one of the urban and rural carriers of interest, and merely reforming the household registration system is not enough to promote urban-rural integration; land is the most valuable resource in rural areas, while public services are the advantages of urban areas; rural areas lack public services, while urban areas lack land. Against such a background, based on the reform of the household registration system, the subsequent reform of urban and rural systems in Zhejiang focused on reforming the rural land system and ensuring equal access to public services in urban and rural areas. This was proved by the practice in Jiaxing City.

Jiaxing City, Zhejiang is the city which became the first among the prefecture-level cities in Zhejiang to promote urban-rural integration and has performed well in this respect; it has become the model of urban-rural integration. With respect to coordinated urban-rural development, Jiaxing City focused its efforts on reforming the household registration system and the land system. As early as the late 1990s, Jiaxing City planned rural and agricultural modernization, and took some concrete actions. For instance, in 1999, Jiaxing City unveiled the *Plan of Jiaxing City for Rural and Agricultural Modernization*; in 2000, Jiaxing City issued the *Implementation Issues on Pushing Forward the Five-Ones Project*; in 2003, Jiaxing City unveiled five action plans[3] and five strategies.[4] In 2004, Jiaxing City released the *Plan of Jiaxing City for Urban-Rural Integration*, comprehensively carried out a strategy for urban-rural integration and set the overall goal for promoting urban-rural integration. Jiaxing City became the first prefecture-level city in Zhejiang to develop the plan for the

---

[3]Five action plans cover agricultural industrialization, rural industrialization, rural urbanization, cultivation of farmers with knowledge, environmental ecologicalization.

[4]Five strategies cover alignment with Shanghai and promotion of development through opening-up, industry-based establishment of the foundation for city development, rejuvenation of the city through science and education, urban-rural integration, sustainable development.

urban-rural integration. In the same year, based on the plan, Jiaxing City developed six special plans and carried out integration in six respects.[5] The most crucial effort in Jiaxing City is the implementation of comprehensive reform, while the reform centers on "two separations and two exchanges". "Two separations" refer to separation between homestead and contracted land, and separation between relocation of rural houses and land circulation; "two exchanges" means that exchange of contracted land for shares and rental for the purpose of increasing the security, promoting intensive operations and transforming the manner of production, and the exchange of homestead for money, houses and spaces with the aim of promoting centralized living and changing lifestyle. "Two separations and two exchanges" are designed to reach the following three goals: First, promote land circulation and large-scale agricultural operations, which is conducive to agricultural industrialization and modernization; second, exchange homesteads to make farmers live in a centralized way even in urban areas so as to achieve urbanization; third, circulate rural land resources to increase the value of land, let farmers share land appreciation in industrialization and urbanization.

In the meantime, at the institutional level, Jiaxing City carried out reform measures which featured "one reform for conducting nine coordinated reforms" and "five coordinated reforms for promoting the work on five fronts". "One reform for conducting nine coordinated reforms" means the land system is reformed to push forward coordinated reforms in nine respects including full employment, social security, the household registration system, new resident services, agriculture-related management, town construction, the financial system, public services and regional coordinated development. "Five coordinated reforms for promoting the work on five fronts" means that coordinated reforms in five respects—including land, registered permanent residence, public services, government management, investment and financing systems—are carried out to make farmers become urban residents, enable the marketization of collective land, ensure equal access to public services, make government functions people-oriented and diversify investment and financing, so as to gradually shape the systems and mechanisms conducive to urban-rural economic and social integration.

Jiaxing's practice provides an important model for other prefecture-level cities in Zhejiang for promoting urban-rural integration. The authorities of other prefecture-level cities visited Jiaxing to draw upon Zhejiang's experience with a view to promoting their own urban-rural integration. The important experience acquired by Jiaxing City in urban-rural integration covers the following two aspects: First, land resources are put to good use through the market mechanism; second, besides land utilization, Jiaxing City is also dedicated to improving the work relating to public services and social security for integrating public services and social security between urban and rural areas, so that farmers can enjoy the same social welfare as urban residents, participate in urbanization and become urban residents.

---

[5]Six special plans are developed to promote urban-rural integration in the following six respects: spatial layout, infrastructure construction, industrial development, labour employment and social security, social development, ecological environmental improvement and protection.

Urban-rural integration in public services is an important part of urban-rural integration in Zhejiang. According to the previous practice, there were huge differences in public services between urban and rural areas, while Zhejiang is the province which early on put forward the initiative of urban-rural integration in public services nationwide. With the construction of public infrastructures, Zhejiang is building transportation, information, water and power supply, sewage and garbage collection and treatment networks covering both urban and rural areas. In the meantime, Zhejiang has witnessed the preliminary establishment of a public service system covering both urban and rural areas throughout the province, which involves social security, social assistance, educational, medical and cultural development, disaster relief, planning, employment training and services, thus removing the dual system in public services between urban and rural areas. At present, Jiaxing has incorporated farmers into the employment training system; in particular, the government has established a free training mechanism for the female farmers above the age of 40 and the male farmers above the age of 50 who meet with difficulties in finding jobs due to land circulation and centralized living, under which free training is provided to these farmers; the government has also required each town to set up a labor service cooperative for addressing their employment issue. Large administrative villages or several villages work together to establish a cooperative through industrial and commercial registration, which is under enterprise-oriented operations. The labor service cooperatives are mostly headed by chairmen of village committees or secretaries of village Party committees. In the meantime, Jiaxing City carried out the social endowment insurance system covering both urban and rural areas as from 2007; Jiaxing became the first prefecture-level city nationwide to achieve full coverage of social endowment insurance at the institutional level. It is worth noting that Jiaxing has carried out the unemployment insurance system covering both urban and rural areas which breaks through the provision, specified in the unemployment insurance regulations, of limiting unemployment insurance coverage to enterprise workers and incorporates farmers into the scope of unemployment insurance.

Conducting institutional reform and policy adjustment, building new systems and mechanisms are of important value for promoting urban-rural integration. From the Central Government to local governments, urban-rural integration has been no longer a trouble in philosophy. As early as 2004, the Central Government put forward the philosophy of coordinated urban-rural development. Recently, the Central Government has developed the plans for building an old-age care security system covering both urban and rural areas and promoting equal access to basic public services, and Zhejiang has stayed ahead nationwide in this regard, Zhejiang has basically established social security and public service systems and mechanisms covering both urban and rural areas. With the impact of the national land system, Zhejiang is not greatly reforming the land system; however, Zhejiang has made great efforts with regard to the land resource allocation mechanism, and some local authorities have become the channels and reform core for promoting urban-rural integration, so the market mechanism has been increasingly given a more important status and roles in urban and rural land allocation, so that rural land circulation in Zhejiang has occurred more frequently and easily than in the rest of the country.

**Table 3.2** The ranking of cities in Zhejiang in the overall level of coordinated urban-rural development

| Region | 2007 | 2008 | 2009 | 2010 | 2011 | 2012 |
|---|---|---|---|---|---|---|
| Hangzhou City | 2 | 3 | 4 | 4 | 4 | 3 |
| Ningbo City | 1 | 1 | 1 | 2 | 1 | 1 |
| Wenzhou City | 8 | 8 | 9 | 9 | 9 | 9 |
| Jiaxing City | 3 | 4 | 3 | 3 | 2 | 2 |
| Huzhou City | 6 | 5 | 5 | 5 | 5 | 4 |
| Shaoxing City | 5 | 6 | 6 | 6 | 6 | 6 |
| Jinhua City | 9 | 9 | 8 | 7 | 8 | 7 |
| Quzhou City | 10 | 10 | 10 | 10 | 10 | 11 |
| Zhoushan City | 4 | 2 | 2 | 1 | 3 | 5 |
| Taizhou City | 7 | 7 | 7 | 8 | 7 | 8 |
| Lishui City | 11 | 11 | 11 | 11 | 11 | 10 |

Note: China Academy for Rural Development, Zhejiang University: *The Report on Performance Evaluation Concerning Comprehensive Reform in Coordinated Urban-Rural Development in Jiaxing City (2008–2012)*

## 3.2.2 The Reform Involving Urban-Rural Integration and Practice Effect

The year 2002 was the year of initiating the reform involving urban-rural integration in Zhejiang. So far, Zhejiang has carried out practical work in promoting urban-rural integration for more than a decade. As mentioned above, Zhejiang has preliminarily built a social security and public service system covering both urban and rural areas, and its effects have gradually emerged. Zhejiang has developed composite indicators concerning coordinated urban-rural development. Table 3.2 shows the ranking of the prefecture-level cities in Zhejiang in coordinated urban-rural development. Ningbo City basically ranked No.1 across the province during the period 2007–2012, while Jiaxing, Hangzhou and Zhoushan ranked neck and neck.

The composite indicators concerning the level of coordinated urban-rural development in Zhejiang consist of 4 primary indicators and 20 secondary indicators. These 4 primary indicators are economic development, social programs, the people's life and ecological environment. According to Table 3.3, Jiaxing City was given 91.27 points in the overall level of coordinated urban-rural development in 2012. If this indicator system really represents or reflects the level of urban-rural integration, such prefecture-level cities as Jiaxing, Ningbo, Zhoushan and Hangzhou appear to achieve urban-rural integration soon.

During the past decade, Zhejiang moved faster to promote urban-rural integration across the province. According to the composite evaluation indicator system for coordinated urban-rural development established by the Zhejiang Provincial Development and Reform Commission, the score given to Zhejiang was 57.59 points in

**Table 3.3** The scores given to Jiaxing in comprehensive evaluation concerning the level of coordinated urban-rural development (2007–2012)

| Field | No. | Indicator name | Score in comprehensive evaluation concerning the level of coordinated urban-rural development | | | | | | |
|---|---|---|---|---|---|---|---|---|---|
| | | | Full score | 2007 | 2008 | 2009 | 2010 | 2011 | 2012 |
| Coordinated urban-rural economic development | 1 | Proportion of the employed people in the secondary and tertiary industries | 6 | 5.31 | 5.47 | 5.54 | 5.64 | 5.73 | 5.75 |
| | 2 | Labor productivity in the primary industry | 5 | 4.58 | 4.79 | 4.79 | 4.79 | 4.79 | 4.79 |
| | 3 | Per capita GDP | 6 | 4.49 | 4.75 | 4.85 | 5.27 | 5.68 | 5.75 |
| | 4 | Per capita local fiscal revenue | 7 | 4.89 | 5.25 | 5.47 | 6.01 | 6.69 | 6.71 |
| | | Score in economic development | 24 | 19.27 | 20.25 | 20.65 | 21.72 | 22.90 | 23.01 |
| Coordinated urban-rural development in social programs | 5 | Proportion of fiscal expenditure in agriculture, rural areas and farmers and its increase | 6 | 3.15 | 3.48 | 4.99 | 5.21 | 5.33 | 5.57 |
| | 6 | Proportion of administrative villages connected by standard roads | 4 | 3.84 | 3.84 | 3.84 | 3.84 | 3.84 | 3.84 |
| | 7 | Rate of coverage of safe drinking water in rural areas | 4 | 3.78 | 3.84 | 3.84 | 3.84 | 3.84 | 3.84 |
| | 8 | Ratio of educational fund per student in urban areas to that in rural areas | 5 | 4.21 | 4.33 | 4.54 | 4.79 | 4.79 | 4.79 |
| | 9 | Number of medical personnel per 1,000 people | 5 | 3.18 | 3.16 | 3.48 | 3.75 | 3.99 | 4.06 |
| | 10 | Ratio of agricultural technicians to the people engaged in agriculture | 4 | 1.33 | 1.37 | 1.33 | 1.33 | 1.81 | 2.47 |
| | | Score in social programs | 28 | 19.48 | 20.02 | 22.01 | 22.75 | 23.60 | 24.57 |

(continued)

**Table 3.3** (continued)

| Field | No. | Indicator name | Full score | Score in comprehensive evaluation concerning the level of coordinated urban-rural development | | | | | |
|---|---|---|---|---|---|---|---|---|---|
| | | | | 2007 | 2008 | 2009 | 2010 | 2011 | 2012 |
| Coordinated urban-rural development in the people's life | 11 | Per capita resident income gap between urban and rural areas (times) | 10 | 8.76 | 8.86 | 8.87 | 9.02 | 9.56 | 9.59 |
| | 12 | Ratio of per capita domestic expenditures on electricity consumption in urban areas to those in rural areas | 3 | 1.76 | 1.92 | 2.05 | 2.22 | 2.43 | 2.63 |
| | 13 | Ratio of per capita cultural, entertainment, educational, medical and health expenditures in urban areas to those in rural areas | 3 | 2.14 | 2.22 | 2.28 | 2.51 | 2.82 | 2.88 |
| | 14 | Ratio of the level of IT application in urban areas to that in rural areas | 3 | 2.76 | 2.88 | 2.88 | 2.88 | 2.88 | 2.88 |
| | 15 | Degree of difference in the level of subsistence allowances between urban and rural areas | 3 | 2.51 | 2.86 | 2.88 | 2.88 | 2.88 | 2.88 |
| | 16 | Proportion of the people covered by social insurance among all employed people | 10 | 5.43 | 5.71 | 6.14 | 7.57 | 7.93 | 8.98 |
| Score in the people's life | | | 32 | 23.37 | 24.44 | 25.09 | 27.07 | 28.49 | 29.82 |
| Coordinated urban-rural development in ecological environment | 17 | Comprehensive score in environmental quality | 5 | 2.32 | 2.45 | 2.68 | 2.70 | 3.03 | 3.37 |
| | 18 | Proportion of rural garbage collected and disposed of | 3 | 2.77 | 2.88 | 2.88 | 2.88 | 2.88 | 2.88 |

(continued)

**Table 3.3** (continued)

| Field | No. | Indicator name | Score in comprehensive evaluation concerning the level of coordinated urban-rural development | | | | | | | |
|---|---|---|---|---|---|---|---|---|---|---|
| | | | Full score | 2007 | 2008 | 2009 | 2010 | 2011 | 2012 |
| | 19 | Rate of popularization of sanitary toilets in rural areas | 4 | 3.67 | 3.73 | 3.84 | 3.84 | 3.84 | 3.84 |
| | 20 | Proportion of villages improved | 4 | 3.42 | 3.50 | 3.66 | 3.68 | 3.76 | 3.79 |
| | | Score in ecological environment | 16 | 12.19 | 12.55 | 13.06 | 13.10 | 13.50 | 13.87 |
| Total score | | | 100 | 74.31 | 77.19 | 80.81 | 84.64 | 88.49 | 91.27 |

*Source* China Academy for Rural Development, Zhejiang University: *The Report on Performance Evaluation Concerning Comprehensive Reform in Coordinated Urban-Rural Development in Jiaxing City (2008–2012)*

**Table 3.4** The changes in the income gap between urban and rural areas in Zhejiang

|  | 2007 | 2010 | 2011 | 2012 | 2013 |
|---|---|---|---|---|---|
| Disposable income of urban residents (yuan) | 20574 | 27359 | 30971 | 34550 | 37851 |
| Rural resident income (yuan) | 8265 | 11303 | 13071 | 14552 | 16106 |
| Ratio | 2.49:1 | 2.42:1 | 2.37:1 | 2.37:1 | 2.35:1 |

2004, and it increased to 87.3 points in 2012. Zhejiang divides coordinated urban-rural development into four stages: the stage of preliminarily coordinated urban-rural development (the extent to which coordinated urban-rural development is achieved is 45–60 points), the stage of basically coordinated urban-rural development (60–75 points), the stage of holistically coordinated urban-rural development (75–90 points) and the stage of full integration (above 90 points). Zhejiang was at the stage of preliminarily coordinated urban-rural development in 2004, but it reached the stage of holistically coordinated urban-rural development in 2012. Of course, the level of coordinated urban-rural development varied with different indicators and different areas. In 2012, Zhejiang grew rapidly in general in the degree of realizing 33 indicators. Zhejiang had the degree of realization above 90% and reached the stage of full integration in 14 indicators, accounting for 42.4%, an increase of 5 indicators compared with the previous year; Zhejiang had the degree of realization at 75–90% and reached the stage of holistically coordinated urban-rural development in 12 indicators, accounting for 36.4%; Zhejiang had the degree of realization at 60–75% and was at the stage of basically coordinated urban-rural development in 4 indicators, accounting for 12.1%; Zhejiang had the degree of realization below 60% and was at the stage of preliminarily coordinated urban-rural development in 3 indicators, accounting for 9.1%.

From the perspective of income (see Table 3.4), Zhejiang stayed ahead among the provinces across the country in urban and rural resident income for a long time; the income gap between urban and rural areas in Zhejiang was much smaller than the average national level (33:1) and it narrowed year by year; it narrowed by 0.14 units from 2.49:1 in 2007 to 2.35:1 in 2013. This was obviously an effect of Zhejiang's efforts in promoting coordinated urban-rural development.

In terms of the gap in the level of coordinated urban-rural development, different areas can be divided into three echelons (see Table 3.5): The first echelon includes the areas which reached the highest level of coordinated urban-rural development and were in the state of full integration; in other words, they were given a score above 90 points in the degree of realizing coordinated urban-rural development; these areas are three prefecture-level cities including Hangzhou, Ningbo and Jiaxing—Ningbo was at the highest level. The second echelon includes the areas which entered the stage of holistically coordinated urban-rural development and they are Wenzhou, Huzhou, Shaoxing, Zhoushan, Jinhua, Taizhou—Zhoushan and Huzhou were at the highest level and were very close to the level of full integration, while Wenzhou, Taizhou and Jinhua were at relatively low levels and were slightly better than the stage of basically coordinated urban-rural development. The third echelon includes the areas which were at the level of basically coordinated urban-rural development, and they are Quzhou and Lishui. Most prefecture-level cities (mode) were at the level of holistically coordinated urban-rural development; this reflects the overall situation of coordinated urban-rural development in Zhejiang. To which extent can coordinated urban-rural development reflect urban-rural integration? Generally, they are often considered to have the same meaning. However, in fact, there are certain differences among them. Coordinated urban-rural development is considered merely from the perspective of the government, while the main players in urban-rural integration include not only the government, but also enterprises, social organizations and individual businesses. Both coordinated urban-rural development and urban-rural integration are processes, but the former places more emphasis on the means, while the latter stresses objectives more; means and objectives are not completely the same; sometimes coordinated urban-rural development does not necessarily bring about urban-rural integration. In terms of the above self-evaluation made by Zhejiang, the overall level of coordinated urban-rural development is just a perspective for measuring the process of urban-rural integration, so it is necessary to conduct in-depth analysis and discussions. The evaluation system developed by the Zhejiang Provincial Development and Reform Commission consists of indicators on four fronts including economic development, public services, the people's life and the ecological environment. These four fronts basically represent the issues concerning urban-rural integration, and they also reflect the feasibility and sensitivity of the evaluation system in measurement. However, it should be noted that all of the indicators adopted in the evaluation system are objective ones without subjective indicators, while subjective indicators are very important; if the people's subjective views on their satisfaction with and their needs for urban-rural integration are not considered, the legitimacy and rationality of coordinated urban-rural development will be compromised. In the meantime, the objective indicators on these four fronts do not take into consideration urban-rural integration phenomena in some important respects, such as social organizations and social participation.

As shown by the evaluation of coordinated urban-rural development and the data from our field surveys, Zhejiang really made great efforts in promoting coordinated urban-rural development in more than a decade in the past, and has made significant achievements in urban-rural integration. However, both coordinated urban-rural development and urban-rural integration are processes, and cannot be achieved in a short time.

## 3.3 Urban-Rural Economic Integration

Urban-rural economic integration is the important foundation and condition for urban-rural development in Zhejiang. Since the reform and opening-up, Zhejiang has promoted economic development in both urban and rural areas, and even Zhejiang's economic development started in towns; the township economy has played a crucial role and enjoys an important status in Zhejiang's economy. However, in

**Table 3.5** Scores in the indicators concerning the level of the coordinated urban-rural development in Zhejiang and 11 cities in 2012*

| Region | Scores of the coordinated urban-rural development |
|---|---|
| Weight | 100 |
| Zhejiang Province | 87.30 |
| Hangzhou City | 90.42 |
| Ningbo City | 91.59 |
| Wenzhou City | 78.98 |
| Jiaxing City | 90.99 |
| Huzhou City | 89.86 |
| Shaoxing City | 86.40 |
| Jinhua City | 82.28 |
| Quzhou City | 72.91 |
| Zhoushan City | 89.08 |
| Taizhou City | 81.32 |
| Lishui City | 72.92 |

*Source*The Zhejiang Provincial Development and Reform Commission, Zhejiang Provincial Bureau of Statistics: *The Evaluation Report on the Level of the Coordinated Urban-Rural Development in Zhejiang Province 2012*, http://www.zjdpc.gov.cn/art/2014/1/3/art_7_619070.html

the late 1990s, the township economy lost some of its previous advantages, while the urban economy enjoyed more advantages in knowledge, technical revolution and market competition, thus promoting coordinated urban-rural economic development became an important task.

### 3.3.1 Urban-Rural Industrial Structural Planning and Change

Urban-rural industrial planning enjoys an important status in Zhejiang's coordinated urban-rural development. Among the main tasks specified in the second part of the *Plan of Zhejiang Province for Promoting Coordinated Urban-Rural Development and Urban-Rural Integration*, the first main task lies in promoting coordinated urban-rural industrial development, and ecological agriculture, the advanced manufacturing industry and the modern service industry become the main industries in coordinated urban-rural development. The advanced manufacturing industry is concentrated in urban areas, while the modern service industry extends to rural areas, resulting in an interactive and coordinated industrial pattern; ecological agriculture represents the main direction for rural development. When discussing the issues concerning coordinated urban-rural development in the special workshop on the main leading cadres at the ministerial and provincial levels in February, 2004, comrade Xi Jinping said, "First, holistically pushing forward the strategic adjustment of the urban-rural industrial structure, shaping a new pattern of coordinated development of the primary, secondary and tertiary industries… following the requirements of optimizing the urban-rural industrial layout to combine the optimization and upgrading of the urban industrial structure with rural development of the secondary and tertiary industries give full scope to the role of central cities in simulating the development of rural areas, so as to promote the enhancement of agricultural efficiency and the increase of farmers' income and rural development."[6]

Zhejiang has certain characteristics in regional, urban-rural development: regionally, Zhejiang is relatively balanced in the economic field; in 2013, Zhejiang's per capita GDP was much higher than the average national level and reached 68,593.06 yuan, the per capita GDP in the prefecture-level cities in Zhejiang was higher than the average national level, the per capita GDP in Hangzhou City with the highest per capita GDP was 51,063 yuan more than that in Wenzhou City with the lowest per capita GDP, a gap of more than 100%. In the meantime, the urban-rural income gap in Zhejiang was much lower than the average national level, Zhejiang ranked No.3 nationwide for 11 consecutive years since 2001 in the level of the per capita disposable income of urban residents, only second to Shanghai and Beijing; Zhejiang ranked No.1 among various provinces for 27 consecutive years since 1985 in the level of per capita net income of rural residents in Zhejiang; the urban-rural income gap in Zhejiang narrowed from 2.42 in 2010 to 2.37 in 2011, while the national urban-rural income gap was 3.13.

Zhejiang has witnessed coordinated urban-rural economic development thanks to the following factor: since the reform and opening-up, Zhejiang has started and expanded economic development from the areas below the county level, with one product in one village, one industry in one town, thus giving birth to a massive economy. The main players in economic development are mostly individual households, private enterprises and collective enterprises, with a dominance of farmers as participants. After the initiation of the reform and opening-up, Zhejiang early on carried out a contract system with remuneration linked to output in agriculture, and also early on initiated and rapidly developed the town, village and county economy, which was largely attributable to a relatively balanced economic development between urban and rural areas and among regions. However, in the middle and later periods of the 1990s, with town reform and urbanization, Zhejiang's industrial economy and service economy was concentrated in cities; in particular, with the development of new and hi-tech industries and the service industry, the scale effect and good infrastructure in cities became the competitive advantages in development, so large cities such as Hangzhou and Ningbo started to be far ahead of other cities in economic development. Nevertheless, the urban-rural income gap in Zhejiang fluctuated between 2.4 and 2.5—below 3—in the past decade. This is because Zhejiang's urban economy was not completely decoupled from the rural economy, and many farmers who

---

[6]Xi 2006, p. 157.

became rich early on remained passionate about and still strongly supported rural development though they entered cities.

The most ideal urban-rural income gap should be lower than 1.5, while Zhejiang's urban-rural income gap fluctuated around 2.4 for many years, thus Zhejiang's urban-rural income gap was still large, so great efforts should be made to narrow it through the coordinated urban-rural development and urban-rural integration. Although urban-rural integration does not merely mean the narrowing of the urban-rural income gap, its narrowing is crucial. The current urban-rural income gap reveals many weaknesses in rural economic and industrial development; at least, it can not provide a solid foundation for increasing farmers' income. In the current plan for promoting coordinated urban-rural development and urban-rural integration, Zhejiang gives priority to pushing forward agricultural industrialization, developing ecological agriculture to increase rural and farmers' income. Zhejiang has made a certain degree of progress in agricultural industrialization and the development of ecological agriculture. However, it is not enough to reverse and narrow the urban-rural income gap due to the following factors: On the one hand, agricultural industrialization is a process and cannot be achieved in a short time; on the other hand, agriculture has not yet enjoyed a high degree of competitiveness, making it difficult to attract talents and capital. One key point in urban-rural economic integration lies in connecting the services between urban and rural areas, especially extending the urban service industry to rural areas, making rural areas become the important direction for and targets of urban life and consumption.

## 3.3.2  The Transformation of the Urban-Rural Employment Structure and Agricultural Modernization

Urban-rural economic integration should be first reflected in employment integration. Zhejiang's economy has entered the later period of industrialization or the post-industrialization stage, suggesting a marked decrease in the number of employed people in agriculture and rural areas. In Zhejiang, the ratio of the number of the people employed in urban areas to that in rural areas was adjusted from 23.53:76.47% in 2003 to 51.54:48.46% in 2011, the proportion of the people employed in rural areas decreased by nearly 28 percentage points, while that in urban areas increased by 28 percentage points and exceeded that in rural areas. This means that from the perspective of the structure of employment, the urban-rural economic pattern had become more rational than before. A massive rural labor force migrated to and worked in urban areas, easing the employment pressure in rural areas, contributing to increasing rural and farmers' incomes and offering a certain social space for agricultural industrialization. However, a large part of the people employed in rural areas did not work in the agricultural field, they worked in the non-agricultural fields; the structure of employment in the primary, secondary and tertiary industries was 20.1:46.8:33.1 in 2007 and 14.6:50.8:34.6 in 2011. In the past 5 years, the proportion of employment in the primary industry declined by 5.5 percentage points, while that in the secondary and tertiary industries increased to some extent; in particular, that in the secondary industry showed the fastest growth and increased by 4 percentage points. Obviously, with regard to the people employed in rural areas, who accounted for 48.46% of the employed people in Zhejiang, only 14.6% of them were engaged in the primary industry, while 34.6% worked in the non-agricultural sectors. In other words, only 30.13% of the workers in rural areas were engaged in the primary industry, while 69.87% were engaged in the secondary and tertiary industries. This also suggests that the secondary and tertiary industries in Zhejiang's rural areas are relatively developed.

In the meantime, Zhejiang has built a unified policy and public service system for coordinated urban-rural development in employment. Zhejiang has carried out a unified unemployment registration management system in urban and rural areas, extending its employment policy to cover all eligible urban and rural workers. Zhejiang has also encouraged the development of the secondary and tertiary industries in rural areas, supported and promoted the processing of materials supplied by clients, intensified training in occupational skills and improved the social security policy to promote local transfer employment of rural labor and further stabilize the employment of rural migrant labor. Zhejiang has moved faster to extend the urban public service system to rural areas, enabling public employment services to fully cover both urban and rural areas. The grassroots service platforms for human resources and social security have been built in 96% of the sub-districts, 98% of the towns, 98% of the communities and 97% of the administrative villages throughout the province.

The proportion of the labor force engaged in the secondary and tertiary industries in Zhejiang has been higher than the average national level, while the working people engaged in agricultural production make up a low proportion and are mostly older, they are low-quality, not young and dominated by women. As rural labor transfers to industry and urban areas, agricultural operations have increasingly suffered a shortage of high-quality labor, a seasonal and regional shortage of labor. This presents opportunities and challenges for agricultural modernization and industrialization. Within such an employment structure, Zhejiang has increased input in agricultural production in terms of policy, capital and technology. Although Zhejiang is a small agricultural province, it has remained ahead nationwide in the level of agricultural modernization. On July 30, 2014, the Department of Agriculture of Zhejiang Province released the *Annual Report on Comprehensive Evaluation of the Progress in Agricultural Modernization in Zhejiang Province 2013*, showing that the overall score concerning Zhejiang's agricultural modernization in the level of agricultural output, the level of factor input and the level of sustainable development reached 73.22 points, the rural households driven by agricultural industrialization organizations accounted for 54.2% in Zhejiang, being 31 percentage points higher than the national level of 23.2%. In 2013, the value of the per capita agricultural labor output in Zhejiang was 30,296 yuan, being 8,902 yuan more than the national level of 21,394 yuan; the agricultural added value per unit of cultivated area was 5,765 yuan, more than two times the national level of 2,805 yuan; the per capita net income of rural residents was 16,106 yuan, being 7,210 yuan more than the average national level of 8,896 yuan.

In Zhejiang's agricultural modernization, land circulation is an important aspect. The rural land circulation service centers have been established in some counties and cities; in Zhejiang, the land circulated in rural areas has made up a high proportion, and the proportion has reached 95% in some towns. With massive circulation of rural land, Jiaxing City has promoted the development of family farms, while family farms have served as importation operational mechanisms and platforms for agricultural modernization in Zhejiang. According to statistics, currently there are 425 family farms in Jiaxing City, covering an area of 71,100 mu, with the average operation area of approximately 167 mu. This suggests that land circulation is the prerequisite for the establishment of family farms. Jiaxing City has introduced various policies to vigorously promote rural land circulation.

Zhejiang has made great efforts to promote the construction of modern agricultural parks. Zhejiang has identified the land circulation rate as an important indicator for evaluating and accepting modern provincial agricultural parks, and requires the rate of cultivated land circulation and the forest land circulation rate to be higher than 40 and 30%. Thus local governments have taken a number of policy measures for promoting land circulation; for instance, Jiande City has made the measures concerning a special fiscal fund subsidy for circulating the contractual right of land, providing a certain fund subsidy to the rural households circulating the contractual right of land to others and the town and village-level circulation service organizations.

Rural land circulation takes various forms, but it is certain that the workers engaged in agricultural production are willing to circulate it. In Zhejiang, the people engaged in agriculture are older and agriculture suffers a shortage of labor, thus circulation is profitable for many agricultural land contractors. The family farm policy is conducive to attracting social capital and some production operational personnel to the agricultural field and boosting agricultural modernization and industrialization. In the meantime, as Zhejiang is one of the most economically developed provinces in China, in order to lay a better foundation for promoting agricultural modernization, the governments at various levels in Zhejiang have increased agricultural input in the construction of infrastructures, the promotion of technology, technical innovation, market-oriented development and the construction of information platforms, thus creating good policy conditions for agricultural modernization. In turn, agricultural modernization can effectively promote urban-rural integration.

## 3.4 Urban-Rural Social Integration

Besides economic integration, social integration is also part of urban-rural integration. What is urban-rural social integration? It should be noted that urban-rural social integration does not mean that social differences completely disappear between urban and rural areas; on the contrary, there are some social differences between urban and rural areas, while these differences will and should not disappear; otherwise, the rural society would no longer exist, and the diversity in social life would be harmed. However, urban-rural social integration also means that some existing differences need to be removed. What are these differences? They are the differences in the social security system, public services and the social governance system. Urban-rural social integration means that the differences in the social system, public services and the social governance system are removed, and practices and mechanisms are unified so that both urban and rural residents enjoy the same social rights. Zhejiang has made significant progress in urban-rural social integration. The progress in Zhejiang has been introduced and discussed from the perspective of social security, public services and social governance.

### 3.4.1  Urban-Rural Integration in Social Security

At present, Zhejiang has made social security cover both urban and rural areas. Like the rest of the country, currently Zhejiang has provided different levels of security for civil servants of state organs, the personnel in public institutions and other groups; however, there are no differences between urban and rural residents in medical insurance, endowment insurance, social assistance and subsistence allowances. Zhejiang has some highlights in urban-rural integration in endowment insurance for residents. As early as September, 2009, Zhejiang established unified endowment insurance for urban and rural residents, filling a gap in the endowment insurance system and achieving a change from "raising children as a guarantee against old age" and "seeking old-age care through land" into "enjoying old-age care from social security". On this basis, Zhejiang has gradually increased the level of basic old-age care for urban and rural residents. So far, in Zhejiang, the average pension standard and the pension payment rate reach 120 yuan and 100%, higher than the average national levels. In the meantime, Zhejiang has introduced some policies to encourage residents across the province to actively participate in contributory endowment insurance. In 2011, Zhejiang issued the *Opinions of the People's Government of Zhejiang Province on Accelerating the Implementation of the Social Endowment Insurance System for Urban and Rural Residents*, stimulating and guiding the people to seek insurance coverage early on and make more insurance contributions for enjoying more benefits, and specifying the measures for the adjustment of the basic pension and raising explicit requirements for adding the pension with a limit to the years of making insurance contributions. Zhejiang has also introduced the measures for building connections between the endowment insurance for urban and rural residents and the family planning policy, and a series of documents concerning the requirements for verification of demographic data on the endowment insurance for urban and rural residents and concerning the verification of personal information on survival, so that Zhejiang's system of endowment insurance for urban and rural residents functions better.

Zhejiang built the subsistence allowances system early on. Zhejiang explored the subsistence allowances system as from 1996 and fully implemented it in 1998, providing insurance coverage for all insurable scenarios; Zhejiang is the third province for establishing the subsistence allowances system covering both urban and rural areas across the province, following Guangdong and Shanghai, and Zhejiang's standard for subsistence allowances is higher than the average national level. For instance, in 2013, Hangzhou City adjusted the level of subsistence allowances in urban areas by increasing the standard for subsistence allowances for urban residents in urban areas from 525 yuan/person/month to 588 yuan/person/month; the standard for subsistence allowances for rural residents in urban areas from 450 yuan/person/month to 588 yuan/person/month. In the same year, in Beijing, the levels of subsistence allowances of urban residents and rural residents were 580 yuan/person/month and 480 yuan/person/month. As indicated, Hangzhou's standards for subsistence allowances have exceeded those in Beijing, and Hangzhou has also truly achieved urban-rural integration.

Besides the population with registered permanent residence in Zhejiang, the institutional design does not exclude external population from social security. This is also the requirement raised by the Central Government. However, the policies and practices for the external population vary in different areas. Generally, in terms of policy and system, migrant workers are entitled to seek coverage from the social insurance for enterprise workers in urban areas, but they enjoy neither the policy of endowment insurance for urban and rural residents nor the subsistence allowances system. Ningbo City and Wenzhou City have many policy differences in allowing migrant workers to seek coverage from endowment insurance. Ningbo City has adopted the social insurance policy of keeping a low level and full coverage, and issued the *Interim Measures of Ningbo City for Social Insurance for Migrant Workers* and the *Detailed Rules of Ningbo City for the Implementation of Social Insurance for Migrant Workers* in light of the characteristics of migrant workers' employment and Ningbo City's reality of the social insurance system as from 2007; according to these stipulations, the standard social insurance contribution for migrant workers is about 2,200 yuan/person/year with respect to five insurances, it is fully borne by enterprises without contributions from individuals; enterprises shall seek insurance coverage for each migrant worker. Therefore, the social insurance practice for migrant workers is obviously different from that for urban residents. Wenzhou City has adopted the practice of keeping a high level and low coverage: the contributions involving social insurances—including endowment insurance, medical insurance, work-related injury insurance, unemployment insurance, maternity insurance ("five insurances")—are made according to the unified standards for enterprise workers with urban registered permanent residence in Wenzhou City, while the minimum contributions involving social insurances (five insurances) for the general migrant workers amount to about 6,350 yuan/person/year, including 4,850 yuan from enterprises and 1,500 yuan from individuals. Of course, different practices exert different impacts on the enthusiasm of migrant workers about seeking coverage from social insurance. The practice adopted by Ningbo City is more able to stimulate migrant workers to seek coverage from local social insurance, while Wenzhou City's practice is not so conducive to attracting migrant workers to seek coverage from social insurance. Migrant workers cannot work and live in the areas to which they migrate for a long time, and they can seek coverage from social insurance in their home-towns, thus not all of them are interested in seeking coverage from social insurance in the areas to which they migrate, while enterprises try to reduce pressure on social insurance as much as possible. As shown, even in Zhejiang, a developed province, migrant workers do not fully seek social security. This leaves room for improvement in urban-rural integration.

### 3.4.2   Equal Access to Public Services in Urban and Rural Areas

As early as 2008, Zhejiang started to carry out the action plan for ensuring equal access to basic public services. In 2003, Zhejiang unveiled the *12th Five-Year Plan of Zhejiang Province for the Basic Public Service System*, calling for establishing a well-functioning basic public service system covering both urban and rural residents across the province and basically achieving equal access to basic public services by 2015.

Public services refer to the general, non-exclusive, mandatory, unpaid and non-competitive public goods and services, while equal access to public services means the same opportunities and rights in public goods and services between urban and rural areas, among regions and among groups. According to Zhejiang's regulations, basic public services include basic living services, basic development services, basic environmental services and basic safety services. The basic living services cover employment promotion, social security and housing security and are aimed at safe-guarding the right to survive. The basic development services cover education, med-ical and health service, population and family planning, culture and sports and are designed to safeguard citizens' basic developmental rights. The basic environmental services cover living infrastructures, the construction of public information infras-tructures and are aimed at protecting the environment and creating a clean, conve-nient and comfortable environment for citizens' survival and development. The basic safety services cover such basic public services as living and work safety, disaster prevention and mitigation and emergency management and they are aimed at creating a safe and harmonious environment for citizens' survival and development.

In the past several years, Zhejiang's public services showed a certain amount of progress and effects in these four aspects. Besides the social security system with full coverage, Zhejiang has also made important achievements in employment services, employment training, social welfare, services for the handicapped, rural dilapidated housing rehabilitation, free urban and rural compulsory education, integrated health service in urban and rural communities, the construction of urban and rural public cultural and sports facilities, postal, communication and other facilities and improve-ment in ecological safety. The average number of years during which the new labor force receives education has reached 12.8, the average life expectancy has increased steadily, and Zhejiang has basically ensured access to education, labor remuneration, medical service, old-age care and housing.

Since the beginning of the 21st century, Zhejiang has carried out the campaign of "100-village demonstrations and 1,000-village improvements" across the province with a view to replanning the rural layout, promoting rural road improvements, garbage disposal, sewage treatment, the construction of drinking water and lighting facilities, thus greatly improving the rural environment and infrastructure and enhancing the living quality. Take Ningbo as an example, in 2004 alone, Ningbo allocated 6,191 million yuan to dismantling 3,139,300 $m^2$ of old houses, building 4,933,500 $m^2$ of new houses and 885.9 km of village roads, adding 7,918,200 $m^2$ of green space, improving 1,395.28 km of riverways, providing an additional 338,000 people with access to drinking water, adding 4,685 public toilets and 15,823 garbage cans. In late 2004, Ningbo City finished the task of improving 305 villages as compared with the plan of improving 850 villages. During the period 2008–2012, the Party Committee of Zhejiang Province provided 200,000 yuan and 100,000 yuan subsidies to each village which had been improved and had treated domestic sewage, while the governments of the prefecture-level cities and counties also offered subsidies accordingly. With more than a decade of efforts, the rural infrastructure has improved greatly and the appearance of villages has changed significantly; villages have become more suitable for living and working than before, thus stimulating the development of village tourism and other industries.

During the period of the 12th Five-Year Plan, Zhejiang carried out the "Eight-Eight Strategies" in an all-round way, pushed forward six actions for building a moderately prosperous society in all respects and established higher requirements for promoting urban-rural integration in public services. Overall, Zhejiang improved the public services greatly in the past 10–20 years, but the level of equal access to public services still needs to be further increased, some villages are still underdeveloped in public services, and have greatly lagged behind urban areas, whether in quantity or quality, in public services; some systems lack connections, the public service resources are basically concentrated in cities. The 12th Five-Year Plan of Zhejiang Province specifies concrete indicators concerning equal access to basic public services; for instance, the rate of employment service coverage is expected to reach 100%, entrepreneurial training is expected to be provided for 50,000 people, various types of occupational skills training will be conducted for 5 million person-times, about 14 million urban and rural residents will be covered by social endowment insurance, the people covered by insurance should account for more than 95%, the rate of coverage from new rural cooperative medical insurance is expected to be higher than 95, 100% of the target groups should be covered by subsistence allowances, natural disaster relief, medical assistance, support of the rural people enjoying five guarantees (food, clothing, medical care, housing, and burial expenses) and the urban people without identification papers, normal residence permit, and source of income, old-age care service subsidies, funeral and interment subsidies, benefits for the entitled groups, centralized support of key entitled groups, settlement of demobilized service personnel, basic social medical insurance rehabilitation programs, raising (foster) service, emergency rehabilitation of disabled children, free compulsory education, nutritional improvement in rural compulsory education, free secondary vocational education and state stipends for regular senior high school students. Regarding public cultural services, Zhejiang has planned to focus on building cultural facilities in central towns, communities and villages, provide complete cultural centers, libraries, museums in counties (county-level cities, districts), and cultural activity centers or cultural activity rooms in towns (sub-districts), and establish a system of a public library network covering the whole province.

As indicated, with further development during the period of the 12th Five-Year Plan, Zhejiang will significantly improve equal access to basic public services in urban and rural areas, urban-rural integration will become more apparent, the urban-rural gap will further narrow, and regional balanced development will become more hopeful.

### 3.4.3   Urban-Rural Integration in Social Governance

The equal access to basic public services in urban and rural areas and urban-rural integration in basic public services include urban-rural integration in social governance. This is because the equal access to public services entails changes in the reform of and innovations to institutions and mechanisms, personnel allocation and the manner of implementation. Of course, the most striking difference in social governance between urban and rural areas is the difference in the degree of organization of primary-level organizations: rural primary-level organizations are villages and village committees, while urban primary-level organizations are neighborhood committees; although all of them are self-governing organizations, village committees centralize the political and economic resources of the villages; in particular, village committees in many villages serve as the agents of village collectives; many villages have their own collective income and collective assets, while neighborhood committees have no such economic foundation. In order to promote urban-rural integration, Zhejiang has changed the previous practice of basically seldom putting public resources into the social governance of villages; Zhejiang has increasingly provided financial resources for the social governance of villages and has also increasingly changed the organizational mode in the rural society; for instance, as village committees perform an increasing number of public services, the government evaluates village committees by adopting more indicators in an increasingly concrete way, more and more villages have introduced electronic equipment for exercising control. Therefore, villages are administered in an increasingly administrative, technical and information-based way. The grid-based management and group-based services in Zhoushan City originated in rural areas and have been promoted throughout the city. This mode typically reflects urban-rural integration in social governance.

Local authorities in Zhejiang have, to varying degrees, learnt and adopted Zhoushan City's practice of grid-based management and group-based services. Of course, other areas also have some innovative practices in social governance. After Jiaxing City abolished the classification of agricultural and non-agricultural registered permanent residence, Jiaxing City first merged villages and made such improvements as centralized living, and then introduced community neighborhood committees and property management; Jiaxing City promoted, to some extent, the urban social governance mode to rural areas, so that urban and rural areas tend to be the same in management. From the perspective of services, urban social governance has advantages and is conducive to boosting equal access to basic public services in urban and rural areas; however, the self-governance function of the rural society has been weakened to a certain degree. As we know, in the traditional rural society, besides village committees, there are also the rules and mechanisms which govern social operations, which have operated for one thousand years, so they are highly effective in stabilizing the order of social governance in rural areas, but they have become very weak—and may even disappear—amidst urban-rural integration in social governance, so undoubtedly, the social governance in rural areas will become more administrative and will face many challenges and meet with contradictions. Therefore, in an effort to promote urban-rural integration in social governance, it is necessary to provide more spaces for the self-governance of villages instead of reducing its spaces; it is essential to give more choices to villagers while increasing rural social services and public services, and urban citizens also have such needs.

### 3.4.4 The Citizenization of Farmers and the Localization of the External Population

The 3rd Plenary Session of the 18th Central Committee of the Communist Party of China put forward the strategy of new-type urbanization. The difference between new-type urbanization and the original urbanization consists in putting the people first or being people-centered. In other words, the previous kind of urbanization placed excessive emphasis on material and physical urbanization and did not center on the people. The people in the new-type urbanization include at least three parts: the urban residents living in shanty towns and the villages in cities, the migrant population without local registered permanent residence and the rural population with local registered permanent residence. Apparently, all of these people exist in Zhejiang and should be key targets in Zhejiang's new-type urbanization and urban-rural integration. Zhejiang has stayed ahead nationwide, to some extent, in new-type urbanization; for instance, on November 1, 2011, the residence permit came into force in Zhejiang; this permit gives more social rights to the new residents (external population without local registered permanent residence) in Zhejiang.

In Zhejiang's urban-rural integration, the citizenization of farmers presents two states: First, all of the farmers with local registered permanent residence can become urban residents, as Zhejiang has abolished the classification of agricultural and non-agricultural registered permanent residence, with the aim of encouraging farmers to move to urban areas; second, the farmers who still live in rural areas or still engage in agricultural production and labor have more and more enjoyed citizen treatment or the treatment that is increasingly close to that given to citizens. As shown by the above public services and social security, social governance, Zhejiang's farmers have been increasingly citizenized or have begun to enjoy the social rights that are increasingly close to those given to citizens. Regarding actions, Zhejiang has also moved faster regarding the transfer of farmers to urban areas, making them citizenized. The *Plan of Zhejiang Province for Promoting Coordinated Urban-Rural Development and Urban-Rural Integration*, unveiled by Zhejiang in 2005, called for more rapidly cultivating central towns and turning them into the nodes connecting urban and rural areas and the important carriers for making rural areas prosperous, serving agriculture and gathering farmers together. The *Plan of Zhejiang Province for the Development of Central Towns (2006–2020)*, issued by the People's Government of Zhejiang Province in 2007, gave priority to supporting the development of about 200 central towns. In 2010, the Party Committee and the People's Government of Zhejiang Province issued the *Several Opinions on Further Accelerating the Development and Reform of Central Towns*, calling for building up, by 2015, 200 central towns across the province into the county centers or subcenters with distinctive industrial characteristics, a good ecological environment, social progress and complete functional facilities. With these efforts, Zhejiang's urbanization was promoted at a rate apparently higher than the average national level. In 2012, Zhejiang's level of urbanization reached 63.2%, being 10.3 percentage points higher than the average national level.

How to give equal treatment to the external population, called "new residents" by Zhejiang, and local residents in public services, social security and social governance while advancing urban-rural integration is an issue which has not yet been addressed and which is also the biggest challenge for China's new-type urbanization at present. Zhejiang has made some new attempts and acquired a certain amount of new experience in this regard. As from 2011, Zhejiang adopted the residence permit policy for the external population, dividing residence permits into ordinary and special residence permits. Applying for a residence permit is conditional. A special residence permit is issued to the people, as part of the external population, who have gained honors, have been elected deputies to the people's congress or CPPCC members in their places of residence, have made investments and started businesses or have been introduced as talents; these people are the elites among the external population, making up a very small proportion. An ordinary residence permit is issued to the majority of the external population, but the applicants have to meet the following conditions before they are granted it: they must hold one of Zhejiang's temporary residence permits and they must have lived there for three consecutive years; they have to have a fixed domicile, a stable job. have received education above the senior high school level, have made social insurance contributions for more than three years, they must not have violated the family planning policy and they must not have broken laws or committed crimes.

A residence permit provides the external population with access to more public services, but the public services accessible to the external population are fewer than those to which the local population can get access. According to Zhejiang's policy, all of the residence permit holders can enjoy at least several public services and policy treatment as follows: If enterprises or units have made contributions involving provident funds, residence permit holders terminate labor relations with units and plan to leave the areas to which they migrate, the residence permit holders can withdraw the balance from individual accounts, including the equal part contributed by units, on a one-time basis; residence permit holders can enjoy the family planning assistance policy; if residence permit holders suffer from infectious diseases, including tuberculosis, schistosomiasis and AIDS, the residence permit holders can enjoy free examination and treatment stipulated by the state; residence permit holders can participate in the local appraisal and selection activities concerning honorary titles and enjoy treatment accordingly; the residence permit holders who meet relevant policy conditions can apply for renting and living in government-sponsored houses or the houses in the places where the migrant population lives in a centralized way (a specific policy is separately made).

Obviously, Zhejiang's residence permit policy specifies application conditions and benefits; there is a certain threshold for obtaining a residence permit, and not all of the external population can unconditionally enjoy the benefits from a residence permit. This seems to help attract part of the external population to become residents of Zhejiang; however, in fact, the existing system fails to arouse the enthusiasm of the external population, especially the rural migrant population, about being localized and urbanized. Nevertheless, the residence permit policy at least provides many of the external population working and living in Zhejiang with access to some public services which are better than before, and this is conducive to resolving some contradictions between the external population and the local population and the local society.

In a broad sense, urban-rural integration ensures that both urban and rural residents with local registered permanent residence enjoy the same basic public services and more of the external population enjoys the same basic public services as local residents.

## 3.5   The Practice in Urban-Rural Integration and the Chinese Dream

Zhejiang started the process of the urban-rural integration early on, producing a good effect. Zhejiang has built a relatively complete policy and management system for urban-rural integration. In the meantime, the philosophy of urban-rural integration has been deeply rooted among the leaders and cadres of the governments at various levels, and serves as a guide for their practical actions. Zhejiang initiated the process of the urban-rural integration early on nationwide largely because Zhejiang was economically and socially developed to some extent and the governments at various levels in Zhejiang were some of the first to foster the philosophy of social governance of urban-rural integration. Zhejiang's practice in urban-rural integration has provided some hard-earned, valuable experience for national modernization, new-type urbanization and urban-rural integration. This issue is discussed here at the national and social levels.

### 3.5.1  The Value and Significance of Urban-Rural Integration for the Country

In the past more than 30 years, China witnessed tremendous, leapfrog development, creating a new miracle in the world. So far, China has entered the stage of building a moderately prosperous society in all respects. However, China's current social gap is larger than before. The Central Committee of the Communist Party of China maintains that China is currently well-off in an unbalanced state and at a low level, and the goal of building a moderately prosperous society in all respects will be achieved by 2020. An important requirement for building a moderately prosperous society in all respects is relatively balanced economic and social development which is reflected between urban and rural areas, among regions, among groups and among classes. Compared with other provinces across the country, Zhejiang has achieved relatively balanced development between urban and rural areas and among regions; for instance, the urban-rural income gap is 0.8 times smaller than the national average; the highest per capita GDP is about 1.3 times higher than the lowest one in the prefecture level in Zhejiang; Zhejiang's level of urbanization is about 10 percentage points higher than the national average level; the level of urban-rural balanced development in various areas exceeds 80% in many indicators. Such relatively balanced development is a good reference for the whole country. Why can Zhejiang have developed so well? This epitomizes urban-rural integration and is also the result of practice in urban-rural integration.

Zhejiang's achievements in urban-rural integration can offer at least the following experience for the country: First, planning comes first. Zhejiang has specially developed plans for urban-rural integration, presenting careful plans for social, economic development, public services and ecological environment in urban and rural areas and providing a policy guide for promoting urban-rural integration. Zhejiang has made overall plans for province-wide urban-rural integration; Zhejiang is a frontrunner nationwide in this regard. Second, Zhejiang has, according to plans, introduced a slew of policy measures for carrying out relevant plans. Third, Zhejiang has established a system of indicators for evaluation of urban-rural integration, playing an important role in supervising and promoting the efforts of the governments at various levels in pushing forward urban-rural integration. Fourth, Zhejiang has pressed ahead with urban-rural integration on a step-by-step basis, it has first built model villages and towns to demonstrate the significance and effect of urban-rural integration to other villages and towns, thus arousing the enthusiasm in different areas. Fifth, the People's Government of Zhejiang Province has channeled more resources into urban-rural integration to arouse the enthusiasm of local governments and villages, thus tapping various local resources for promoting urban-rural integration.

Some people may believe that Zhejiang's urban-rural integration is based on a very good economic foundation, while many other provinces in the country have no such conditions. Urban-rural integration really entails a certain amount of economic input, but it does not completely depend upon the economic foundation. Urban-rural integration is a philosophy and a developmental philosophy; under the same economic conditions, different philosophies may produce different developmental effects. Thus urban-rural integration can be promoted nationwide, the key lies in adjusting the developmental philosophy and designing the corresponding institutional policies and measures. Promoting urban-rural integration nationwide is not impossible. At present, as long as China combines urban-rural integration with the new-type urbanization it can be more conducive to pushing forward the building of a moderately prosperous society in all respects in China in a better and faster way.

### 3.5.2 The Value and Significance of Urban-Rural Integration for the Society

The urban-rural income gap and the difference in social status between the rural population and urban residents have been escalated into great social problems in China, or that gap and difference have caused many social problems, especially the problems in social solidarity and fusion. The urban-rural income gap has narrowed to some extent in recent years, and its impact on China's Gini coefficient has declined, but it remains an important factor affecting China's income gap. As the urban-rural income gap exists, a massive number of the rural population has flowed to urban areas for working and doing business, bringing the urban-rural gap to the urban society, generating two huge groups with very obvious differences, and even certain tensions—urban residents and the rural migrant population. As a large number of young people have emerged in rural areas, the rural society has declined, bringing about new issues relating to agriculture, rural areas and farmers.

Zhejiang's practice in urban-rural integration can solve many social problems China is facing, especially the problems concerning the urban-rural income gap and the difference in social status between urban and rural residents. Urban-rural integration has largely improved the situation in Zhejiang that cities are not like cities, villages are not like villages. Thanks to urban-rural integration, cities have become more livable for the people, and rural areas have become more beautiful as infrastructure has improved, thus attracting more urban residents to rural areas for enjoying leisure, and even living there. An important sign of urban-rural integration is that urban and rural residents can move and migrate with each other; in other words, urban residents can live and work in rural areas, while rural residents can live and work in urban areas, so that the differences between urban and rural residents disappear. In the meantime, with the introduction of the residence permit policy, Zhejiang has attempted to narrow the gap between local residents and the external population, ease the tension between the two groups, and make sure that more of the external population is integrated into Zhejiang's society.

Overall, urban-rural integration is an important way to promote social harmony. If the urban-rural gap and the gap between local people and the external population can be effectively bridged, China's developmental achievements can be shared by the majority of the people, social harmony and solidarity can be promoted. Are these endeavors the intrinsic requirements for building a moderately prosperous society in all respects and realizing the Chinese dream?

# Reference

Xi Jinping, *Carrying out Solid Work to Stay Ahead—Line of Thought and Practice in Promoting New Development in Zhejiang*, The Party School of the CPC Central Committee Press, 2006.

# Chapter 4
# The Social Programs and Equal Access to Public Services

Jinjun Wang

Modern society is a high-risk society. In the modern society, it is difficult for individuals to bear the high risks incurred to them by a high division of labor based on specialization, thus it is necessary for the government to build a public service system covering the entire population. Generally, the public services provided by a modern government mainly include the basic services involving the people's well-being such as employment and basic social security, public utility services such as education, medical services and public culture, the basic services relating to public benefits such as environmental protection and infrastructure construction and public security services such as production, consumption and public order.

Since the beginning of the 21st century, the Chinese Government has started to break the previous welfare system based on registered permanent residence and the unit system, and has been dedicated to building a system of equal access to public services covering the entire population, the Chinese Government has also made efforts to achieve equal access to basic public services by enhancing the government's public service responsibility, increasing fiscal expenditure on public services, establishing and improving a minimum public service system covering the whole society. The *Decision of the Central Committee of the Communist Party of China on Some Major Issues Concerning Building a Harmonious Socialist Society*, adopted during the 6th Plenary Session of the 16th Central Committee of the Communist Party of China, called for gradually achieving equal access to basic public services, and increasing fiscal input in education, health, culture, employment, reemployment services, social security, the ecological environment, public infrastructure and public order; the document also presented major decisions and arrangements on establishing and improving a basic public service system, and identified "promoting equal access to basic public services" as the major policy orientation for national economic

J. Wang (✉)
Party School of the Party Committee of Zhejiang Province, Hangzhou, China

© Social Sciences Academic Press and Springer Nature Singapore Pte Ltd. 2019
G. Chen and J. Yang (eds.), *Chinese Dream and Practice in Zhejiang—Society*,
Research Series on the Chinese Dream and China's Development Path,
https://doi.org/10.1007/978-981-13-7406-7_4

and social development during the period of the 12th Five-Year Plan. Since the 18th National Congress of the Communist Party of China, the Party and government have continued to stress that institutional reforms should be intensified to improve public services. When delivering a speech at the press conference attended by the members of the Standing Committee of the new Political Bureau in 2012, Xi Jinping pointed out, "The Chinese people love life, and hope to have better education, more stable jobs, more satisfactory income, more reliable social security, better medical and health services, more comfortable living conditions and a more beautiful environment, and they hope that their children can grow up, work and live better; the aspiration of the people to live a better life is the focus of our efforts."[1] The 3rd Plenary Session of the 18th Central Committee of the Communist Party of China vowed to provide a better guarantee and improve the people's well-being, promote social fairness and justice by intensifying the social institutional reform, reforming the income distribution system to promote common prosperity.

## 4.1 The Overall Vision of Social Programs and Public Services

Public services can be defined in a broad sense and in a narrow sense. The public services in a broad sense include all goods and services provided by the government. The public services in a narrow sense mainly refer to various social services—involving culture, education, medical services, social security, science and technology, sports—provided to the people by utilizing public resources. Social programs refer to the social construction and social service programs led by the governments at various levels and are the activities which are in parallel to the actions of administrative departments and enterprises including financial institutions. Specifically, social programs refer to the social services—involving educational, scientific and technological, cultural and health activities—initiated by the state for social benefit and carried out by state organs or other organizations. In relevant documents released by the governments at various levels in China, social programs cover education, medical and health services, labor employment, social security, science and technology, culture, sports, community, tourism, population and family planning. Therefore, social programs fall within the scope of the public services in a narrow sense; however, generally, public services are more extensive than social programs; besides social programs, public services also include various services for the disadvantaged groups, such as disaster relief and assistance. In the policy for equal access to public services, that equal access generally refers to equal access to the services concerning social programs, excluding disaster relief and assistance.

---

[1] The Group of Compilation of the Learning Materials Concerning the Principles from General Secretary Xi Jinping's Major Addresses: *Learning Materials Concerning the Principles from General Secretary Xi Jinping's Major Addresses*, China Fangzheng Press, 2014, p.180.

### 4.1.1   Zhejiang's Overall Line of Thought and Major Strategies for Building a Basic Public Service System

Since 2003, with the goal of achieving equal access to public services, Zhejiang has actively adjusted the structure of fiscal expenditures by allocating more fiscal funds to support the public service fields and favor rural areas, the underdeveloped areas and the low-income groups. During the period 2003–2013, Zhejiang's fiscal expenditure on education increased from 16.4 billion yuan to 95 billion yuan, an average annual increase of 19%; the expenditure on medical and health services increased from 4.5 billion yuan to 35.1 billion yuan, an average annual increase of 23%. With the growth of fiscal expenditures, the public service policies were adjusted, relevant policy adjustments started from the new rural cooperative medical services; the new rural cooperative medical system was piloted as from 2003; 22 million people had been covered by the new rural cooperative medical insurance and the per capita pooled fund reached 665.9 yuan in 2013. As from 2005, Zhejiang conducted biennial free physical examinations among the farmers covered by the new rural cooperative medical insurance. On the educational front, during the years 2005–2007, 1.76 million students from families with financial difficulties received financial aid, loving-care nutritional meals were provided to 900,000 poverty-stricken students without charge, 2,787,000 m$^2$ board and lodging renovation projects were completed, and 210,000 teachers were trained. The system of supporting education on a voluntary basis in the underdeveloped areas was carried out; each year as from 2005, 50 educationally advanced counties sent 100 backbone teachers to 25 underdeveloped counties and 2 island counties for one-year voluntary teaching, thus institutionally promoting balanced development of teachers. Zhejiang actively promoted the building of a social security system covering both urban and rural areas, the input from the finance at various levels increased from 11 billion yuan in 2003 to 30.1 billion yuan in 2007.

In October, 2004, Zhejiang issued the *Several Opinions on Establishing and Improving the Long-term Mechanism for Doing Substantive Work for the People*, calling for establishing and improving the mechanism for providing information on the conditions of the people, a democratic decision-making mechanism, a mechanism for the distribution of responsibilities, a mechanism to guarantee input and a mechanism for supervision and evaluation. In light of local reality, the cities, counties (county-level cities, districts) issued the implementation opinions on the selection of projects for doing substantive work for the people, work requirements and the distribution of responsibilities. In particular, since 2005, the annual government work reports have presented the commitments to the people across the province with respect to the substantive work relating to the immediate interests of the people in employment, social security, medical services, education, housing, environmental protection and rural facilities, and have specified the clear quantitative goal for each substantive task, and these have been well received by the people.

In recent years, as Zhejiang has entered a new stage at which the per capita GDP exceeds USD 10,000, coordinated urban-rural and regional development has reached a new height, the quality of life and the level of urban and rural residents have been on the rise, sustained, healthy and rapid economic development has laid a solid foundation for building a system for promoting equal access to basic public services. During the 12th Party Congress of Zhejiang Province in June, 2007, the Party Committee of Zhejiang Province put forward, for the first time, the developmental line of thought of making progress in the economic, political, social and cultural fields, they stated that social development should center on improving the people's well-being and called for building a moderately prosperous society for the people across the province. In early 2008, the Party Committee and the People's Government of Zhejiang Province officially unveiled six action plans for promoting the building of a moderately prosperous society in all respects, made arrangements on the action plans for promoting the improvement of the capability for independent innovation, the construction of major projects, resource conservation and environmental protection, equal access to basic public services, the increase in the income of low-income groups and the law-based safeguarding of citizens' rights and interests. In the same year, Zhejiang initiated the first action plan in China for promoting equal access to basic public services; the plan stated that Zhejiang would take five years to establish and improve a multilevel social security system with full coverage, a system of social programs with equitable allocation and balanced development and a system of rationally distributed public facilities shared by both urban and rural areas, so as to ensure that basic public services cover both urban and rural areas, are regionally balanced and shared by everyone and that they promote social fairness and justice and the well-rounded development of the people.

According to the *12th Five-Year Plan of Zhejiang Province for National Economic and Social Development* and the *12th Five-Year Plan of Zhejiang Province for the Basic Public Service System*, Zhejiang's overall line of thought of promoting equal access to basic public services is as follows: Following the overall strategy of comprehensively carrying out the "Eight-Eight Strategies" and making the people rich by starting businesses and of building a strong province through innovation, working on the requirement of building a moderately prosperous society for the people across the province, improving the basic public service system and taking it as public goods to be provided to the people, establishing and improving a convenient, efficient and sustainable basic public service system which satisfies the conditions of the province, is well-functioning and covers both urban and rural areas with a view to promoting equal access to basic public services in Zhejiang. In the meantime, Zhejiang endeavored to narrow the gap in basic public services between urban and rural areas, among regions and among different groups, allocated more public resources to rural areas, the poverty-stricken areas and the disadvantaged groups to ensure public service resources are shared by everyone. Zhejiang established and improved the extensive and multilevel social security system and public facility system to provide residents across the province with equal access to basic public services, including education, medical services, culture, sports, social security, infrastructure and ecological environmental protection. Zhejiang stressed the leading role of the government in providing basic public services, improved the fiscal guarantee mechanism, established a long-term mechanism for the government's provision of public services, gave full scope to the active roles of the market and social forces, made innovations to the mode of providing basic public services, further shaping a pattern of basic public service provision characterized by fair competition and extensive participation, making sure that the basic public service system with equal access benefits all urban and rural residents across the province.

With the establishment and improvement of the basic public service system, Zhejiang has further safeguarded and improved the people's well-being, and has continuously moved towards the overall requirement of building a moderately prosperous society for the people across the province. By 2015, Zhejiang will achieve equal access to basic public services and finish building a well-functioning sustainable basic public service system covering both urban and rural areas. Zhejiang's main goals of building a basic public service system are as follows: (1) a well-functioning institutional system. The basic living system, basic security system and basic safety service system fully cover both urban and rural areas; the mechanisms involving supervision, management, resource allocation and service provision are established in an all-round way, and dynamic adjustments are made according to the national standard for the provision of basic public services. (2) Balanced development of urban and rural areas. As Zhejiang works on building a basic public service system, it should strive to narrow the gap in the per capita fiscal expenditure in basic public services between urban and rural areas and among regions, give overall considerations, allocate more resources to part of the rural areas and the underdeveloped areas, achieve balanced coverage by public resources, further standardize the public service facilities in different areas and develop basic public services between urban and rural areas in a balanced way. (3) Effective expansion of provision. Zhejiang substantially increases the input in basic public services, carries out the public service improvement projects, expands the resource aggregate involving basic public services, broadens the channels for public service provision, and actively guides the market and social forces, giving rise to a diversified pattern of basic public service provision. (4) Enhance the satisfaction of the people. Zhejiang should build a basic public service system by proceeding from the developmental aspirations and fundamental interests of the people, making sure that all urban and rural residents can get equal access to public service resources, and comprehensively establishing a basic public service network focusing on the primary-level areas. In the meantime, Zhejiang should establish effective mechanisms and channels for expressing the people's needs, improve the provision of basic public services and social satisfaction on the basis of soliciting opinions from the people.

## 4.1.2 Zhejiang's Main Goals of Building a Public Service System

### 4.1.2.1 More Rapidly Establishing a High-level Social Security System With Full Coverage

Efforts are being made to speed up the building of a multilevel, sustainable social security system which provides full coverage, meets the basic needs and covers all urban and rural residents. First, improving a social security system including endowment, medical, work-related injury, unemployment and maternity insurances, focusing social insurance on rural migrant workers, the handicapped, the flexibly employed personnel and the personnel at non-public economic organizations. Second, improving the new urban-rural social assistance system and the social assistance policy, comprehensively legalizing and standardizing social assistance, enriching the primary-level social assistance forces, coordinating the standards of subsistence allowances and medical assistance between urban and rural areas, providing legal aid to the people with difficulties. Third, establishing a new welfare system commensurate with Zhejiang's level of economic and social development and for all of the people in urban and rural areas, with a focus on the elderly people, the disabled children, the abandoned babies, vagrants and beggars, temporarily homeless people and psychiatric patients, pushing forward social benefit services and community welfare services. Fourth, comprehensively carrying out the safeguard policy for the entitled groups, improving the mechanism of increasing the standard of benefit subsidies for the key entitled groups, building a new safeguard mechanism for the entitled groups which combines preferential treatment with universal treatment. Fifth, giving priority to employment, improving employment security, adopting the proactive employment policy to expand employment platforms and opportunities, increase the number of employed people, and further protecting the legitimate rights and interests of workers, fully carrying out the labor contract system and improving the working environment.

### 4.1.2.2 Promoting Balanced Development of Basic Public Education in Urban and Rural Areas

In an effort to improve equal access to basic education, it is necessary to make sure that everyone gets equal access to public educational resources, especially safeguarding the right of the disadvantaged groups to receive compulsory education, focusing on addressing the issues concerning rural education and the education of the migrant population. It is essential to first promote balanced development of rural compulsory education. Actions are being taken to allocate the compulsory educational resources between urban and rural areas in a coordinated way, establish a mechanism for the development of compulsory education with equal access in both urban and rural areas; the mechanism involving regular movement of headmasters and teachers during the stage of compulsory education has been established and improved to promote IT application in rural middle and primary schools and gradually achieve a basically balanced development of compulsory education schools in urban and rural areas in facility improvements, fund input and the introduction of teachers. Rural preschool education is being strengthened, certain financial aid is being provided to help rural poverty-stricken children and disabled children enter kindergartens. Second, the work on the education relating to the children of rural migrant workers has improved. Relevant work is being carried out to make sure that the children of eligible rural migrant workers receive compulsory education; actions are being taken to establish and improve a mechanism for making sure that the children of rural migrant workers receive compulsory education.

### 4.1.2.3   Speeding up the Building of the Urban-Rural Basic Medical and Health System

(1) Optimizing the medical services in urban and rural areas. Giving full play to the fundamental role of community health service institutions, improving the primary-level medical service network, setting up shared medical resource centers to provide local residents with equal access to medical resource services. Intensifying the development of the primary-level medical and health talents, cultivating general practitioners, encouraging the medical and health personnel to serve the people at the primary level, promoting rational movement of medical personnel. Pushing forward the reform of public hospitals, improving the hospital management systems to really guarantee the quality of medical care. Increasing financial input into rural medical and health services and the support for rural medical and health programs.

(2) Improving public health services in urban and rural areas. Establishing and improving the system involving the adjustment of public health service items, incorporating food safety, the hygiene of drinking water, occupational health and health emergency response into public health service items, making greater efforts to guarantee the public health of key groups, enhancing the capability of dealing with major public health emergencies.

(3) Improving drug supply and the guarantee of safety. Standardizing the drug procurement system, improving the system that guarantees a supply of drugs based on the national system for essential drugs, pushing forward the building of the network of drug distribution. Strengthening the supervision of drug safety focusing on essential drugs, strictly putting in place the responsibility for the safe manufacturing of drugs and standardizing the market order.

#### 4.1.2.4 Improving the Urban-Rural Public Cultural and Sports Service System

(1) Building a coordinated system for urban-rural basic public cultural services. Carrying out the project for improving the quality of rural cultural talents, conducting cultural service training among the backbone and management personnel in the field of mass culture, enhancing the working ability and professional quality, broadening the channels for the exchange of rural cultural and artistic talents. Pushing forward the co-building and sharing of the basic public cultural service resources in urban and rural areas, carrying out the activities of enhancing friendship through culture and spreading culture in rural areas. Reinforcing the construction of central cultural villages. Encouraging farmers to conduct cultural activities by themselves, building the brands of rural cultural activities.

(2) Accelerating the construction of cultural infrastructures. Improving the conditions of necessary equipment at the public cultural service venues including county-level libraries and town-level cultural stations, enhancing the functions of cultural services, strengthening IT application in and digital development of cultural infrastructures to narrow the urban-rural gap in public cultural facilities, improving the supporting policies for rural cultural facilities.

(3) Promoting the development of mass sports programs. Improving the primary-level public sports facilities, especially increasing the fund guarantee and input for the construction of public sports facilities in the poor areas, achieving equal access to public sports facilities in urban and rural areas. Optimizing the policy regarding public sports services, making more sports facilities open to the general public, establishing and improving the modern public sports service systems and enhancing the quality of public sports services.

#### 4.1.2.5 Strengthening the Construction of the Living Infrastructures in Urban and Rural Areas

(1) Improving the rural water and electricity supply infrastructures. Thoroughly carrying out the project for keeping rural drinking water safe, improving the conditions of rural drinking water, reinforcing the construction of the safety guarantee for the water supply infrastructures and emergency response system, promoting urban-rural integration of the water supply. Further pushing forward the construction of rural electricity supply facilities, speeding up the renovation of the rural power grid, making sure that the electricity demand of rural residents and enterprises is met.

(2) Promoting the development of coordinated urban-rural transportation. Strengthening the construction of rural roads and their maintenance management, expanding the coverage by urban buses, building the urban-rural transportation safety net. Achieving urban-rural integration in passenger transportation. Push-

ing forward urban-rural integration in transportation and logistics to increase the level of transportation services.

(3) Further extending urban postal and communication services to rural areas. Strengthening the construction of the postal service facilities in urban and rural areas, fully leveraging the advantages of the postal network, increasing the level of rural postal service. Intensifying the construction of the rural communication network to achieve urban-rural integration in information technology.

### 4.1.2.6    Promoting Coordinated Urban-Rural Ecological Environmental Protection

(1) Improving environmental quality and safety. Thoroughly carrying out the actions for keeping the source of water, air and soil clean, intensifying the prevention and control of environmental pollution. Improving the quality of emission reduction in industrial, agricultural and living-related projects to effectively reduce the emissions of pollutants. Strengthening the control of various environmental risks, the prevention and control of such pollutants as heavy metals and hazardous chemicals, increasing the level of the safe disposal of domestic garbage.

(2) Making complete overall improvements of the environment in urban and rural areas. Strengthening rural environmental protection, carrying out the project of "1,000-village demonstrations and 10,000-village improvements", comprehensively implementing the action plans for building green towns and a beautiful countryside, enhancing the quality of the ecological environment in rural areas. Strengthening the protection and management of key ecological areas as well as organizing and mobilizing the people to participate in ecological protection.

(3) Making further efforts in effective environmental monitoring, controlling and statistics. Strengthening the construction of the system of environmental monitoring, environmental law enforcement and emergency response, especially enhancing the capability for rural environmental monitoring and that for guaranteeing environmental safety. Further standardizing the statistical method for rural environmental information, reinforcing the improvement of relevant systems involving data processing and reporting.

## 4.2 The Mechanism of Ensuring Equal Access to Public Services

### 4.2.1 Zhejiang's Policy Guarantee for Promoting Equal Access to Basic Public Services

#### 4.2.1.1 Specifying Goals and Tasks, Being the First Nationwide to Develop the Master Action Plan

Since the reform and opening-up, Zhejiang has witnessed sustained, rapid and healthy economic and social development, Zhejiang has accelerated the adjustment of government functions, made active innovations in the governmental administrative system, strengthened the social management and public service functions and optimized the structure of public fiscal expenditures, thus laying a solid foundation for further promoting equal access to basic public services in Zhejiang. In 2008, Zhejiang carried out the *Action Plan for Ensuring Equal Access to Basic Public Services (2008–2012)*, the first one in China, making innovations to the public service system, optimizing the quality of public services and continuously enhancing the capability for public services, so that Zhejiang has made continuous improvements in equal access to basic public services. In 2012, Zhejiang unveiled the *12th Five-Year Plan of Zhejiang Province for the Basic Public Service System*, providing clear guidance on continuing to improve the basic public service system in Zhejiang during the period of the 12th Five-Year Plan.

The *12th Five-Year Plan of Zhejiang Province for the Basic Public Service System* specified the following guiding thought: guaranteeing the basic needs of urban and rural residents for survival and development, enhancing the capability for the provision of primary-level services and improving the systems and mechanisms. The plan stressed a rational and effective allocation of resources in the basic public service provision system to make sure that urban and rural residents share basic public services, and build a sustainable basic public service system suited to the province's reality; the plan was dedicated to strengthening and improving the mechanism of a financial guarantee, a service provision mechanism and a mechanism for the evaluation of supervision to ensure the establishment and improvement of the basic public service system (see Table 4.1).

#### 4.2.1.2 Increasing Fiscal Support, Improving the Mechanism of Fiscal Guarantee for Public Services

When working in Zhejiang, Xi Jinping expressed many guiding opinions on improving public services and building a service-oriented government. Regarding fiscal guarantee, Xi Jinping pointed out, "It is necessary to follow the requirement of building a service-oriented government, strengthen the public service functions, improve

**Table 4.1** The goals specified in the 12th Five-Year Plan of Zhejiang Province for ensuring equal access to the basic public services

| Basic living services | Labor service | Provide full employment service to workers without charge |
| --- | --- | --- |
| | | Improve the system of occupational skills training for all workers |
| | | Safeguard the legitimate rights and interests of workers |
| | Social security | Expand the coverage of endowment, medical, unemployment, work-related injury and maternity insurances |
| | | Expand and improve the coordinated urban-rural social assistance system, comprehensively promote the rule of law in social assistance and standardize it |
| | | Establish and improve the appropriate universal new social welfare system for all residents |
| | | Comprehensively carry out the policy for safeguarding the entitled groups, build a new safeguard system for the entitled groups which combines preferential treatment with universal treatment |
| | Basic housing security | Strengthen basic housing security in urban areas |
| | | Renovate the dilapidated houses of rural households in difficulty |
| Basic developmental services | Basic public education | Promote balanced development of nine-year compulsory education |
| | | Consolidate the popularization of preschool education |
| | | Improve the layout of regular senior high schools, develop secondary vocational education |

(continued)

**Table 4.1** (continued)

| | | Improve the quality of special education |
|---|---|---|
| | Basic medical and health care | Gradually incorporate such key tasks as food safety, occupational health, mental health, the hygiene of drinking water and health emergency response into public health service items |
| | | Improve the primary-level health service network according to the circle of 20 min medical and health services |
| | | Improve the drug supply and safety guarantee systems |
| | Family planning | Strengthen the services relating to good birth, care and education to improve the quality of the population |
| | | Uphold and improve the existing family planning policy to stabilize the low fertility level |
| | Public culture and sports | More rapidly build a coordinated urban-rural public cultural service system covering the whole province and benefiting the entire population |
| | | Increase the actual effect of radio and television, film and television on benefiting and serving the people, give prominence to the attribute of public benefit |
| | | Actively carry out the activity of fostering a love of reading in the people, vigorously carry out the key publication programs focusing on agriculture, rural areas and farmers |
| | | Strengthen the construction of the primary-level public sports facilities, achieve equal access to public sports facilities in urban and rural areas |

(continued)

**Table 4.1** (continued)

| | | |
|---|---|---|
| Basic environmental services | Living infrastructures | Establish the strategy of giving priority to developing public transportation |
| | | Strengthen the guarantee of the supply of water and electricity in urban and rural areas |
| | | Focus on resident needs to more rapidly build the community-level public service platforms in urban and rural areas, promote one-stop services |
| | | Improve the layout of farmer's markets and the supporting facilities |
| | Public information infrastructures | Strengthen the construction of universal postal services and communication network facilities |
| | | Reinforce the construction of weather service workstations |
| | | More rapidly build an extensive, highly functional and technically advanced public place name service system |
| | Environmental protection | Improve the environmental quality and the people's living quality |
| | | Enhance the capability for a guarantee of environmental safety |
| | | Build green towns and a beautiful countryside |
| Basic safety services | Life services | Strengthen food safety supervision |
| | | Improve the transportation safety system |
| | | Strengthen comprehensive governance of public security |
| | | Push forward the construction of the fire protection system |
| | | Improve the system for guaranteeing the safety of consumption |

(continued)

**Table 4.1** (continued)

| | | |
|---|---|---|
| | Work safety | Improve the working and production environment to ensure work safety |
| | | Improve the occupational hazard prevention and control system |
| | | Strengthen safety education and training |
| | Disaster prevention and reduction and the management of emergency responses | Improve disaster prevention and reduction, and the emergency response mechanism |
| | | Improve the emergency response system to enhance the capability for dealing with emergencies |

the public fiscal system, optimize the structure of fiscal expenditures, increase public fiscal input and transfer payment".[2] In order to promote the transformation of government functions, put the people first in finance, optimize the government's structure of fiscal expenditures, increase the fiscal expenditure on public services and the fields of social security and safeguards for the people's well-being, gradually increase the publicness of government finance, establish a long-term mechanism for increasing fiscal expenditure in basic public services and enhance the capability of finance at various levels for guaranteeing basic public services, Zhejiang has carried out a number of fiscal guarantee mechanisms: First, improving the public fiscal system, deepening the reform of the budget system; second, optimizing the structure of fiscal expenditures, arranging more fiscal expenditures on the fields relating to the people's well-being, making sure that more than 2/3 of incremental financial resources are utilized for improving the people's well-being and carrying out social programs; third, establishing a well-regulated and transparent fiscal transfer payment system, especially intensifying transfer payment to rural areas and the underdeveloped areas; fourth, improving the division of the responsibilities and the powers over financial affairs among the governments at various levels, establishing a rational hierarchical mechanism for guarantees, so that local governments continuously intensify the reform of the public fiscal system and enhance the fiscal capability for providing basic public services.

According to the data from the Zhejiang Provincial Bureau of Statistics, during the period of the 11th Five-Year Plan, Zhejiang's fiscal expenditure on the people's well-being reached 759.5 billion yuan, an average annual increase of 21.1%, more than 2/3 of the incremental fiscal expenditure focused on the people's well-being for

---

[2]Xi (2007).

4 The Social Programs and Equal Access to Public Services

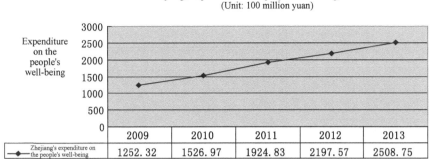

**Fig. 4.1**   Zhejiang's expenditure on public services, 2004–2013

5 consecutive years, and that proportion reached 75% in 2010.[3] During the period of the 12th Five-Year Plan, the government's fiscal expenditure on public services was on the increase. In 2011, Zhejiang's executed fiscal expenditure was 384.24 billion yuan, among which 192,483 million yuan were utilized in the programs relating to the people's well-being, including education, medical and health care, social security, culture, sports, agricultural, forestry and water affairs, science and technology, accounting for about 50.09% of the total fiscal expenditure. In 2012, Zhejiang's executed fiscal expenditure was 416,188 million yuan, among which 219,757 million focused on the people's well-being, accounting for about 52.80% of the total fiscal expenditure. In 2013, Zhejiang's executed fiscal expenditure was 473,078 million yuan, among which 250,875 million yuan focused on the people's well-being, accounting for about 53.03% of the total fiscal expenditure.[4] In recent years, in order to expedite the building of a coordinated urban-rural public service system, Zhejiang has actively increased the fiscal transfer payment to the islands and underdeveloped cities and counties, greatly improving the insufficient and unbalanced provision of basic public services in remote areas and underdeveloped areas, further increasing the degree of equal access to basic public services in Zhejiang (see Figs. 4.1 and 4.2).

Note: As budget items were adjusted as from 2007, the public service items in and before 2006 mainly included culture, sports and radio, education, science, health, benefits for the entitled groups, social welfare, retirement from administrative organs, social security allowances, armed police, public security organs, procuratorial organs, courts and judicial organs. The public service items during the period 2007–2008 mainly included public security, education, science and technology, culture, sports and media, social security and employment, medical and health care, environmental protection.

---

[3] Yu et al. (2012).
[4] www.tjj.zj.gov.cn.

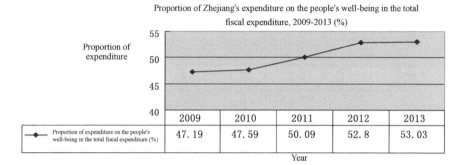

**Fig. 4.2** The proportion of Zhejiang's expenditure on the people's well-being in the total fiscal expenditure, 2004–2013

Note: In Figs. 4.1 and 4.2, the data for the period of 2004–2008 come from Yu Jianxing, Xu Yueqian, Zhejiang's Experience in Building a Service-oriented Government, *Chinese Public Administration*, 2012(2); the data on the period of 2009–2013 come from www.tjj.zj.gov.cn.

## 4.2.2  Zhejiang's Current Overall Implementation of the Work on Promoting Equal Access to Basic Public Services

After Zhejiang developed the *Action Plan for Ensuring Equal Access to Basic Public Services* in 2008, the People's Government of Zhejiang Province established the working group for implementing that action plan in late 2008 to lead and coordinate the work on promoting equal access to basic public services, and Zhejiang further clarified the corresponding working mechanisms in the annual implementation plans developed in the subsequent years so as to make sure that the work on promoting equal access to basic public services can be carried out smoothly; Zhejiang also defined the responsibilities of the main players and improved the evaluation system, thus making significant progress in public services.

### 4.2.2.1  Promoting Coordinated Urban-Rural Development of the Social Security System to Achieve Urban-Rural Integration in Social Security

In order to build a coordinated urban-rural employment and social security system, Zhejiang thoroughly carried out the social endowment insurance system for urban and rural residents, improved the mechanism involving the adjustment of the endowment insurance benefits and the system of cross-regional transfer and continuance of endowment insurance, piloted the building of the national system for basic old-age care services, improved the system of policies concerning cross-institutional and cross-regional transfer and continuance of such basic medical insurances as medical insurance for urban workers and urban residents and the new rural cooperative medical care, launched the all-in-one medical insurance card across the province, continued to push forward the unemployment, work-related injury and maternity insurance systems and improved the urban-rural housing security system and the diversified housing security system covering low-rent housing, public rental housing and economically affordable housing; moreover, it persevered in stimulating employment though entrepreneurship and promoting coordinated employment in urban and rural areas, improved the mechanism of building entrepreneurship-oriented cities and full employment communities (villages), improved the systems and mechanism conducive to achieving full employment of university graduates, transfer employment of rural migrant workers and assistance-based employment of the groups with difficulties.

As from 2009, Zhejiang issued the opinions on the implementation of the social endowment insurance system for urban and rural residents, the plan for provincial pooling of funds for the basic endowment insurance for enterprise workers, developed policy documents on more rapidly stimulating university students to seek coverage from the basic medical insurance for urban residents, carrying out municipal and outpatient pooling of funds for basic medical insurance, and strengthening the management of basic medical insurance funds, thus promoting the work on ensuring universal social security across the province to a new height. Zhejiang also integrated the urban and rural medical insurance systems, built a new-type urban-rural social assistance system, explored the connection between the basic living security for the farmers whose land has been expropriated and the systems involving basic endowment insurance for workers and social endowment insurance for urban and rural residents, gradually carried out provincial pooling of funds for unemployment insurance, basically built the urban-rural housing security system and explored and established a social insurance registration system covering urban and rural residents. At the end of the period of the 11th Five-Year Plan, in Zhejiang, there were 16.06 million, 13.44 million, 29.70 million, 8.75 million, 14.75 million, 8.64 million, and 12.14 million people covered by basic endowment insurance for enterprise workers, basic medical insurance for urban workers, the new rural cooperative medical care, unemployment insurance, work-related injury insurance, maternity insurance and social endowment insurance for urban and rural residents, respectively; 4.22 million farmers whose land has been expropriated were covered by social security. In 2014, the People's Government of Zhejiang Province vowed to continue expanding the universal coverage of social security, make sure that an additional 800,000 people would be covered by endowment insurance, 600,000 people by medical insurance, 500,000 by work-related injury insurance, 500,000 by unemployment insurance and 500,000 by maternity insurance throughout the year. In the meantime, Zhejiang relied on communities to build a universal system for the management of information for insurance coverage registration, and 50% of the people with Zhejiang's registered permanent residence who were covered by insurance were registered at the end of

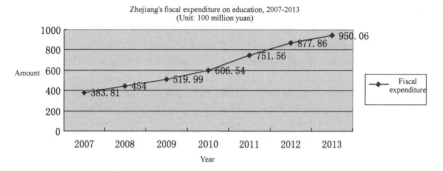

**Fig. 4.3** Fiscal expenditure on education, 2003–2013

the year. Zhejiang steadily increased the standard for basic pension benefits for urban and rural residents from 80 yuan to 100 yuan.

### 4.2.2.2 Intensifying Support for Rural Education to Achieve Balanced Development of Education in Urban and Rural Areas

In recent years, Zhejiang has increased fiscal funds in education. According to the fiscal statistical data on Zhejiang, during the ten-year period of 2003–2013, Zhejiang's fiscal expenditure on education increased from 16,421 million yuan to 95,006 million yuan, an increase of 4.8 times (see Fig. 4.3).

(1) Improving the mechanism of a fund guarantee for compulsory education. As from the autumn of 2006, Zhejiang fully waived all tuition and miscellaneous fees for compulsory education in urban and rural areas; as from 2007, Zhejiang officially, fully incorporated rural compulsory education into the scope of public financial security; as from the spring of 2010, Zhejiang waived the accommodation fee item at public schools in rural compulsory education which was an administrative and institutional fee item; as from 2014, Zhejiang increased the minimum standards for an annual daily public fund per student at schools during the stage of compulsory education, with the minimum standards at primary schools and junior middle schools being 610–810 yuan.

(2) Enhancing the overall quality of rural teachers, carrying out the voluntary teaching system to promote rational movement of teacher resources. As from 2008, Zhejiang carried out the Lingyan Project among rural primary and middle school teachers; as of 2011, Zhejiang trained 39,000 rural backbone teachers under the Lingyan Project, improving the capability of rural teachers. The voluntary teaching system was implemented to promote balanced development of teachers.

(3) Carrying out the project of loving-care nutritional meals at rural primary and middle schools. During the period of 2005–2011, Zhejiang allocated 680 million yuan to provide the rural primary and middle school students from low-income

families with 2–3 nutritionally rational meals which balance a portion of vegetables and meat each week, ensuring loving-care nutritional meals for 2.59 million students. In 2012, Zhejiang increased the lowest standard of loving-care nutritional meals for the rural primary and middle school students from low-income families—the standard increased from 350 yuan/student/year to 750 yuan/student/year, so that students can enjoy one meal each day, and the students who were the beneficiaries accounted for 7% of all of the students in compulsory education.

(4) Actively improving the running and accommodation conditions of rural schools. As from 2008, Zhejiang carried out the project for renovating small schools in rural areas, effectively improving the conditions of the schools in remote mountainous areas. Besides the improvement of school conditions, Zhejiang carried out a project to repair and renovate the dormitories of rural primary and middle school teachers as from 2009; these dormitories generally became functionally complete and structurally safe and can now meet the daily needs of teachers.

### 4.2.2.3 Promoting Urban-Rural Integration in Medical and Health Care

In recent years, Zhejiang has established and improved the basic medical security system, endeavored to make sure that everyone was covered by insurance and increase the security level; Zhejiang also improved the primary-level medical and health service system, pushed forward the building of the primary-level medical and health talents with a focus on general practitioners and comprehensively carried out the reform involving coordinated allocation of rural medical and health resources at the county level.

(1) Further improving the new rural cooperative medical system, increasing the level of basic medical security. As of 2012, in Zhejiang, the coverage of the new rural cooperative medical care reached 97.7%, the per capita fund pooling standard stood at 482.5 yuan, including 342.2 yuan in fiscal subsidies, and both figures increased to some extent compared with the previous years. The maximum payment limit in all areas exceeded 6 times the per capita net income of local farmers, the reimbursement ratio of hospitalization expenses within the scope of policy in the areas involved in social pooling of funds exceeded 72%, the actual compensation rate for general outpatients reached 27.8%. The medical security for such diseases as childhood leukemia, congenital heart disease and uremia was comprehensively piloted with the county as the unit, while the actual compensation rate was not lower than 70% of the prescribed expense. The payment mode concerning the new rural cooperative medical care was reformed and the unified service platform for reimbursement and medical assistance involving the new rural cooperative medical care was built in 78 counties (county-level cities, districts). In 2013, Zhejiang increased the minimum stan-

dard of fiscal subsidies involving basic medical security for urban and rural residents to 290 yuan. Zhejiang intensified and improved the reform of the public hospital input and compensation mechanism, pooled together 200 million yuan for promoting urban medical resources to the lower levels; 15 provincial hospitals and 27 hospitals in 24 counties, county-level cities and districts have run medical institutions through trusteeship-based cooperation, so that local people can conveniently enjoy high-quality medical services.

(2) Improving the primary-level medical and health system to enhance the capability for medical and health services. In 2011, Zhejiang sought an investment of 251.8 million yuan from central finance and arranged 190 million yuan in special provincial subsidies to support the construction of special-purpose houses at 9 county hospitals, 6 mental health hospitals, 12 county-level health supervision bodies, 86 health centers in central towns, more than 2,900 village clinics (community health service stations) and the building up of the capacity in 28 county hospitals. All counties (county-level cities) have achieved the goal of building at least one Second-level Grade A medical institution, and the village-level medical and health services have ensured full coverage. In the building of the primary-level medical teams, Zhejiang cultivated 1,062 rural community doctors in a directed way, arranged for 1,200 general practitioners and 1,000 community nurses to receive on-the-job training and developed 170 inter-disciplinary public health backbone talents. In 2012, 23 counties in 8 cities carried out the work on signing service concerning general practitioners, making health management service more effective and comprehensive. Zhejiang pushed forward integration in rural health, and the compact integrated management rate reached 65.1%.

(3) Achieving full coverage of the national essential drug system. Zhejiang has made sure that the essential drug system fully covers the government-sponsored primary-level medical and health institutions, the selling prices of drugs have decreased by an average of 30% and the people's spending on drugs has decreased by more than 3 billion yuan. Zhejiang has further consolidated the implementation of the essential drug system at the government-sponsored primary-level medical and health institutions, extended the essential drug system to the village clinics under integrated management, non-governmental primary-level medical institutions and public hospitals, 64.88% of village clinics (community health service stations) have been governed by the essential drug system in Zhejiang. In the meantime, Zhejiang has strengthened training in essential drug knowledge among the primary-level medical personnel to guide medical personnel to use drugs in a standardized and scientific way.

(4) Energetically exploring and pushing forward the reform of county-level public hospitals. In 2011, Zhejiang identified 29 counties (county-level cities, districts) to first pilot the comprehensive reform of county-level public hospitals with a focus on the construction of 55 county-level leading medical disciplines; 30 projects for the construction of county-level leading medical disciplines were added in the same year. The long-term partner assistance relationship was established between 18 provincial hospitals and 38 county hospitals in the under-developed areas, between 73 third-level hospitals and 250 medical institutions

including town health centers, improving the capability for comprehensive medical services of county hospitals. In 2014, all county-level public hospitals in Zhejiang carried out a comprehensive reform by putting a stop to the practice of charging more for medicines to make up for low prices for medical services. The reform of county-level public hospitals was carried out together with the reforms involving the policy of markups on pharmaceuticals, the policy regarding medical service charges, the policy on medical insurance settlement and payment and the policy on fiscal input. The power to develop the plan for the adjustment of the prices of medical services was delegated to the pilot counties (county-level cities, districts). Besides implementation of the zero markup measure and other reform measures, the pilot counties also established new mechanisms involving the economical operation of hospitals, internal management of hospitals and hospital personnel management and incentives, making improvement in the capability for services of county-level public hospitals, their level of management, the people's satisfaction and the enthusiasm of the medical personnel.

### 4.2.2.4   Enabling Public Cultural and Sports Services to Fully Cover Urban and Rural Areas Under the Principle of Making them Universal and Shared

Zhejiang has actively improved the public cultural service system, intensified the reform involving the administrative system and operational mechanism of non-profit cultural public institutions, moved towards the goal of comprehensively improving the people's well-being in the cultural field and benefiting the people through culture, correctly managed the direction and focus of cultural program development, effectively provided public cultural goods, expanded the coverage of basic public cultural services and endeavored to ensure equal access to basic public cultural services in urban and rural areas.

(1) Strengthening the construction of the primary-level cultural infrastructure, building a network of cultural facilities covering the provincial, municipal, county, town and village levels. A number of municipal and county-level key cultural facilities have been completed and put into operation or are under construction. The county-level libraries, county-level cultural centers, town-level integrated cultural stations and cultural information and resource-sharing projects have basically provided full coverage; the plan for achieving full coverage by the village-level cultural activity rooms has been carried out. As of late 2013, the coverage rate reached 97.8%. Zhejiang became the first to allow free admission to museums, libraries, art galleries, cultural centers (stations) across the province, and provide free library cards, and the province-wide online library; Zhejiang has actively built a public library service system covering both urban and rural areas.

(2) Innovating the cultural service mode, increasing cultural provision and continuously carrying out cultural activities for the people. The public cultural service system has shown a good momentum of all-round improvement; with a focus on rural areas, Zhejiang has carried out the project for cultural development of the new countryside and the project for providing a minimum of cultural security; Zhejiang has encouraged the activity of enhancing friendship through culture among counties (county-level cities, districts). Moreover, each year Zhejiang arranges the special fund for the minimum amount of cultural security, offering directed cultural services to the disadvantaged groups.

(3) Carrying out the project for improving the quality of the primary-level cultural personnel, cultivating the primary-level key cultural and artistic personnel. In 2012, the primary-level cultural personnel were trained for more than 150,000 person-times at the provincial, municipal and county levels; more than 30,000 cultural and sports teams and more than 500,000 people as amateur cultural and artistic backbone across the province were integrated to set up the Zhejiang Federation of Cultural Volunteers for actively carrying out the activities of cultural volunteer services.

(4) Speeding up equal access to public services involving sports in urban and rural areas. Zhejiang has effectively carried out a popular fitness project and it has energetically pushed forward the popular fitness programs. Zhejiang has provided financial aid to build well-off sports villages, provincial-level town (subdistrict) popular fitness centers, central village popular fitness squares, further improving the fitness environment for the people. Zhejiang has vigorously carried out the mass sports activities. Zhejiang has deeply conducted the popular fitness activities with local characteristics which integrate sports, leisure, tourism and culture and are coordinated among areas across the province. The mass sports organizations and backbone teams have been improved continuously; Zhejiang has established relevant training bases for improving the overall quality of the primary-level sports personnel, training social sports instructors and the primary-level sports backbone including sports program coaches and referees.

### 4.2.2.5 Promoting Coordinated Urban-Rural Construction of Public Service Infrastructures

First, steadily pushing forward housing construction in urban and rural areas. After Zhejiang carried out the project for renovating the dilapidated houses in rural areas in 2006, the dilapidated houses of 243,000 rural households in difficulty were renovated. On this basis, in 2012, the People's Government of Zhejiang Province launched the project of model villages for renovating rural houses; 342 villages were improved in two years, greatly enhancing the rural living environment. Regarding government-subsidized housing, during the period of the 11th Five-Year Plan, the governments at various levels intensified the construction of government-subsidized housing; in late 2010, Zhejiang resolved the housing difficulties for 770,100 urban middle and low-income households, the housing security benefited 13.8% of urban households. Zhejiang has made sure that low-rent housing fully covers the urban households with housing difficulties at the levels below two times the standard of subsistence allowances. In recent years, Zhejiang has continued to raise funds for the construction of government-subsidized housing to support the construction of government-subsidized housing including public rental housing, so the housing conditions of the households in difficulty across the province have been further improved.

Second, improving the construction of infrastructures covering both urban and rural areas. Zhejiang has taken the construction of a new countryside as an opportunity, increased the support for agriculture, rural areas and farmers, promoted coordinated urban-rural regional development and actively pushed forward the construction of urban and rural infrastructures. The input from the finance at various levels in agriculture, rural areas and farmers increased year by year; with a focus on the project of "1,000-village demonstrations and 10,000-village improvements", the 10-Million Farmers' Drinking Water Project, the Village Broad Road Project, Zhejiang has intensified the construction of rural public infrastructures, gradually improved the infrastructures in the underdeveloped areas, further promoted urban-rural integration in infrastructures. In an effort to actively promote new-type urbanization, Zhejiang has vigorously supported the accelerated development of the underdeveloped areas, and made development more balanced between urban and rural areas.

## 4.3   The Mechanism for the Purchase of Public Services

The government's purchase of public services means that the government hands over the public service functions originally undertaken by the government to social organizations, enterprises and public institutions through open tendering, directional entrustment and invitations for bids with a view to enhancing the quality of public service provision and the efficiency of fiscal fund utilization, improving the structure of social governance and meeting the public's diverse and individual needs.[5] Since the reform and opening-up, with economic development and social progress in Zhejiang, the people have growing needs for the services provided by the government and have increasingly high requirements for the quality and efficiency of public service provision, thus it is necessary to cope with challenges by making institutional innovations. The government hands over part of public services to be provided by the enterprises and social organizations which meet certain conditions; this is of important significance for transforming the functions of the governments at various levels, cultivating social organizations, promoting marketization, innovating the mechanism through which the government provides public services, making improvements in the level and efficiency of the provision of public services. In 2014, the General Office of the People's Government of Zhejiang Province issued the *Implementation Opinions on the Government's Purchase of Services from Social Forces*, bringing

---

[5]Xu and Zhaoting (2013).

experimental innovations to the diversified provision of public services, actively carrying out the activities concerning the government's purchase of public services,
increasing the support from government finance for the cultivation of social organizations, constantly enhancing the capability of social organizations for undertaking
the transferred government functions and making improvements in the level and
efficiency of the provision of public services.

Since the 18th National Congress of the Communist Party of China, especially
the 3rd Plenary Session of the 18th Central Committee of the Communist Party
of China, the innovations to the government's purchase of services from the society
have been accelerated. In particular, regarding the government's purchase of services
from social organizations, the central finance offered 200 million yuan for social
organizations' participation in social service programs for three consecutive years;
in 2013, 9 social organizations in Zhejiang were included and received 3.25 million
yuan in financial aid; in 2014, 9 social organizations in Zhejiang were included and
received 3.65 million yuan in financial aid. According to preliminary statistics, the
fiscal funds at the provincial, municipal and county levels for supporting the public
welfare programs of social organizations totaled 168 million yuan in 2013.

The government's purchase of services from the society takes a number of innovative forms. As shown by Zhejiang's practice in recent years, the government purchases services mainly in the following three ways: direct purchase, indirect purchase
through a platform and purchase with welfare lottery funds.

### 4.3.1   The Government's Direct Purchase of Public Services

In September, 2013, the General Office of the State Council issued the *Guiding
Opinions on the Government's Purchase of Services from Social Forces*, specifying
detailed rules for various parts of the work on the government's purchase of public services and specially listing the players eligible for undertaking the services purchased
by the government, including such social forces as the social organizations registered
with the department of civil affairs according to laws or exempted from being registered as approved by the State Council, the enterprises and organizations registered
with the administration of industry and commerce or competent departments for
industries according to laws. Regarding fund management, the document stressed,
"the funds necessary for the government's purchase of services from social forces
are considered to be within the existing fiscal budget arrangements; the increased
funds necessary for the development of public services provided by the government
shall be included in the fiscal budget according to the requirements of budget management". Therefore, the institutional framework for using special fiscal funds to
support social organizations has been preliminarily established. In recent years, as
local governments at various levels in Zhejiang have promoted the purchase of public
services, they have generated many cases of innovation, while relevant innovations
are represented by two types: the government's purchase of home-based elderly care

services from social organizations first carried out in Haishu District, Ningbo and the innovations in the government's purchase of cultural services in Zhoushan.

#### 4.3.1.1   The Government's Purchase of Home-Based Elderly Care Services from Social Organizations in Ningbo

With economic and social development and increasing ageing, there are new tasks and requirements for the socialized home-based elderly care services. In order to further expand the work on the home-based elderly care services and better adapt to population ageing, in 2004, Haishu District, Ningbo became the first to experiment with the government's purchase of home-based elderly care services and carried out the pilot work on the home-based elderly care services in 17 communities; in 2005, Haishu District practiced the mode of the government's purchase of home-based elderly care services from social organizations which is characterized by government support, operation by social organizations and social participation. The innovation and experimentation program of the government's purchase of home-based elderly care services in Haishu District was given the China Local Government Innovation Award, an award presented for the fourth time, in 2008; it became a unique national service brand.

Xingguang Senior Service Association in Haishu District, Ningbo mainly undertakes the government-related home-based elderly care service program in Haishu District. The association was established as advocated by the district government amidst the implementation of the policy involving the socialized home-based elderly care services in June, 2003. With government support, the association leverages its professional advantages in old-age care, integrates the old-age care resources in the society to the greatest extent, actively carries out various service activities for the elderly people living alone, with difficulties and of an advanced age, constantly enriches old-age care service forces, and effectively achieves extensive social participation.

In order to ensure the long-term operation of the home-based elderly care service program in Haishu District and guarantee the funds for the program, the government of Haishu District included the funds for purchasing the home-based elderly care services into the government's fiscal budget. In 2004, after the first batch of more than 600 elderly people of an advanced age living alone were identified as the targets of the home-based elderly care services, the government of Haishu District allocated 1.50 million yuan from the district's annual fiscal budget according to the cost of the service, 2,000 yuan/person/year, to support the government's purchase of services from social organizations.[6] The work relating to the elderly care services undertaken by the Xingguang Senior Service Association mainly includes: First, identifying the elderly people (including the handicapped) living alone and without any income above the age of 60 as the targets of the home-based elderly care services; ascertaining, through examination, about 600 elderly people eligible for obtaining the

---

[6]Wang (2007).

services purchased by the government in Haishu District; second, determining the content of the home-based elderly care services according to the needs of the home-based elderly care personnel and the elderly people; third, training the home-based elderly care personnel and recruiting volunteers; fourth, inspecting and supervising the quality of the work relating to the home-based elderly care services.

The most characteristic institutional arrangement in the home-based elderly care service program of Haishu District is the incentive mechanism in various forms. As one of the incentive mechanisms, the Haishu Senior Service Award, established in 2009, is the highest award for Haishu District to promote the work relating to elderly care services; this award has produced the most active effect in that it has fostered a good social trend in respecting and loving the elderly people in the whole society, further pushing forward the work relating to the home-based elderly care services in Haishu District.

### 4.3.1.2 The Government's Purchase Of Public Cultural Service in Zhoushan

Zhoushan has fully mobilized and organized various forces to participate in the construction of the modern public cultural service system, so that public cultural services are deeply rooted in the soil of social culture. Zhoushan Municipal Bureau of Culture, Radio, TV, Film, Press and Publications has started with socialized operations to innovate the primary-level public cultural service mode, launch www.taowenhua. cn—Zhoushan's socialized operational platform for cultural and sports products and services; this is a concrete measure for carrying out the government's purchase of public cultural services, building a cultural co-building incubation platform and maximizing the effects of public cultural services and funds. As from the second half of 2013, the Zhoushan Municipal Bureau of Culture, Radio, TV, Film, Press and Publications has considered how to incorporate then non-governmental cultural and artistic groups with potential for development into the government's agenda for standardized operations. With repeated surveys and solicitation of opinions, the *Administrative Measures of Zhoushan City for the Socialized Operation of Public Cultural Products and Services* was issued in early 2014. Since 2014, except for a small number of performance tasks, Zhoushan has handed over a great many non-profit cultural and sports activities to the society and the people, and has reshaped and cultivated the providers of public cultural services; moreover, Zhoushan has adopted the mode under which the government purchases services and it has experimented with a fiscal supply mode conducive to maximizing the effects of funds and public interests. On the morning of April 14, 2014, Zhoushan's socialized operational platform for cultural and sports products and services—www.taowenhua.cn—was officially launched. According to relevant information, this is the first cultural trading platform nationwide, on which the people can choose the cultural and artistic groups and cultural and sports programs according to their preferences like on Taobao, and they can even evaluate programs and performances after viewing them, so the people's satisfaction becomes an important indicator for evaluating public cultural services and also serves as the reference for other buyers who wish to purchase services. The columns "The Most Popular Program" and "The Most Popular Group" will also further stimulate groups to bring about innovations.

(1) Providing smooth channels for social participation. This platform allows entry of social organizations and groups at a low threshold; after registration, social organizations and groups can upload their introduction and program lists according to the agreement of the competent department; as long as they are chosen by the cultural centers in communities, military camps, schools, nursing homes and other service recipients, the two sides can independently reach an agreement, they will stage performances, once the service recipients confirm and are satisfied with their performances, the government will allocate performance subsidies according to the standard of 3,000–8,000 yuan/performance. Since operations began, 43 social organizations, cultural and artistic groups have been registered, 1,436 people have participated in providing services, 337 programs have been provided, and 93 service recipients have been registered, giving full expression to the appeals of the whole society for culture.

(2) Strengthening the connection between demand and supply. This platform provides the people with more options and initiative. In the previous campaign of bringing culture to the countryside, what the people can view was nothing but the cultural programs delivered by the government. Now the government no longer leads the delivery of cultural programs, the people can independently choose cultural programs, the mode has been changed from "bringing culture" to "choosing culture", thus meeting the diverse cultural needs of the people at various levels.

(3) Making sure that program operations are transparent. The Zhoushan Municipal Bureau of Culture, Radio, TV, Film, Press and Publications has overcome covert deals, power rent-seeking and other dilemmas in offline transactions; a series of operating procedures, including the provision of cultural products and services, their sales, after-sales services, evaluation and payment, can be completed online, all of the programs which can be handed over to the society and the market are handed over to the society and the market. At present, this platform has released 9 cultural programs, including directional service programs, the programs for competitive bidding and the programs purchased by the government and social forces. The Internet is fully leveraged to build the platform for cultural products and service demand and supply information and the mechanism for receiving feedback from the people, thus effectively connecting cultural programs with the people's needs and making sure that the public cultural transactions are open and transparent.

(4) Placing emphasis on ensuring that management is transparent and well-regulated. Program release, user demand, qualification examination, program scheme, ordering (reviewing, bidding), contract filing, pictures showing activity completion, the people's evaluation on satisfaction and the performance evaluation are presented through this online platform, indicating that public cultural and sports products are purchased in an open, fair, just and transparent way and

are managed in a well-regulated way. The fund payment is made according to the contract agreement between the two sides, the activity pictures, program lists, the evaluation of service recipients and the follow-up rating by the department of culture; various parts are indispensable.

### 4.3.2 The Government's Indirect Purchase of Public Services

Indirect purchase of public services is mainly reflected in the innovations to public service purchasing which have been made on the platform-oriented social organizations in recent years. Specifically, private non-enterprise units or foundations turn funds into a development-oriented platform for supporting, by means of funds, the development of relevant social organizations, and leverage these non-profit social organizations to promote institutional innovations in the government's purchase of public services and to improve the public service provision mode.

At present, the indirect purchase mode can be divided, by the difference in the government's roles, into the platform-oriented organizations established by the government and non-governmental platform-oriented organizations. Both types of innovations are closely associated with social development and the development of social organizations. In recent years, the authorities in many areas, including Beijing, Shanghai, Guangzhou, Shenzhen and Chengdu, have actively made innovations involving platform-oriented organizations to promote institutional innovations such as the government's purchase of services from social organizations. With respect to the innovations involving the platform-oriented organizations led by the government or administrative departments, the Taizhou Social Organization Development Foundation in Taizhou City, Zhejiang and the Hangzhou Jianggan Social Organization Development Foundation in Jianggan District, Hangzhou City are the platform-oriented foundations led by the government which have emerged in recent years. They are aimed at indirectly promoting the development of public services by supporting the development of non-profit social organizations rather than directly providing public services. Sixty-eight cities and counties in Zhejiang have been home to different types of social organization service platforms (including public institutions and social organizations), 52 social organization service centers, 38 social organization promotion societies and 7 social organization development foundations.

Registered in 2009, the Taizhou Social Organization Development Foundation is a non-profit organization which is in the charge of and registered with the Department of Civil Affairs of Zhejiang Province and serves the social organizations throughout the city; it is also the first platform-oriented foundation specially designed to serve the development of social organizations in China. The purpose of the foundation is to cultivate and support the development of social organizations, guide social organizations in serving the society. The foundation is mainly responsible for supporting, within a certain scope, various types of non-profit charity social organizations, urban-rural primary-level social organizations, industry associations, assisting organizations to conduct the publicity of public benefit activities, providing financial aid to organizations for carrying out public benefit activities, supporting the theoretical research and innovations in the field of social organizations, and receiving the government's entrustment to purchase services from social organizations. The foundation is dedicated to integrating high-quality public benefit resources for crossover cooperation, creating more conditions for the people to participate in public benefit programs.

In 2013, the government of Jianggan District, Hangzhou planned to allocate 5 million yuan each year for supporting social organizations in undertaking public service programs and other expenditures on cultivation and incubation of social organizations, thus the Hangzhou Jianggan Social Organization Development Foundation, the first one in the city, was established in May, 2013. In the first year of operation, more than 2 million yuan were allocated from the finance of Jianggan District as the initial fund; subsequently, each year the government will continue to inject funds and other social bodies are encouraged to actively inject funds. The foundation extensively serves the construction of social organization public service platforms, public welfare program bidding and tendering, the cultivation and incubation of social organizations, the introduction of professional talents and rewards for outstanding social organizations. Where community-level social organization service centers are established in sub-districts (towns), the foundation will provide 300,000 yuan-500,000 yuan in subsidies on a one-time basis. The public benefit service programs declared by social organizations are reviewed and determined by the review committee consisting of the departments of supervision, auditing, finance and civil affairs; the public benefit service programs in each year are determined through open review and disclosure to the public, while the foundation allocates the special fund to support social organizations in performing public benefit services. The social organizations provided with financial aid extensively carry out public benefit services for the aged, disabled and infirm within Jianggan District. Since the foundation was established, with fierce competition, the first batch of 17 public benefit service programs supported by the foundation have been accepted by social organizations, they have become active throughout the district and these programs will be provided with 50,000 yuan–150,000 yuan in financial support.

The platform-oriented innovations in Taizhou City and Jianggan District, Hangzhou, Zhejiang are the typical platform-oriented organization innovations led by the government and also the new forms of promoting the development of public benefit programs in recent years. They are aimed at pushing forward the development of non-profit social organizations. The government provides financial support to advocate and integrate them, contributing to promoting the cultivation of social organizations and stimulating the institutional innovations to and the development of the government's purchase of public services.

### 4.3.3   Purchase of Public Services with Welfare Lottery Funds

Issuing a welfare lottery to promote the development of public benefit programs is a unique and effective mode under which the government actively cultivates social forces and achieves diversified provision of public services; the welfare lottery has developed in China for many years and has become an important force for developing public social programs. According to statistics, since Zhejiang issued the welfare lottery in 1987, 40 billion yuan in welfare lottery has been issued to raise more than 12 billion yuan in public welfare funds, including the public welfare fund from lotteries turned over to central finance. In more than two decades, with the goal of issuing a welfare lottery aimed at supporting the aged, disabled, poor and orphans, the departments of civil affairs at various levels allocated more than 4 billion yuan in public welfare funds from lotteries to support more than 40,000 programs, including welfare houses, nursing homes, homes for the members of revolutionary martyrs' families, community service units, old-age care service centers (stations), refuges, open universities for the aged, rural Starlight Program for Old-age Welfare Service, the units for honoring martyrs, funeral and interment facilities, the Tomorrow Program for Surgical Rehabilitation of the Disabled Orphans, emergency rehabilitation of poverty-stricken disabled children, the Welfare Lottery Helps Me Walk, medical assistance for children with serious diseases. In the 27 years since 1987, Hangzhou has issued welfare lotteries to raise more than 9 billion yuan, providing more than 2,000 jobs in the society; Hangzhou has continuously ranked No.1 across the province in the quantity of issued welfare lotteries and was at the forefront among the top four provincial capitals nationwide. According to incomplete statistics, in more than two decades, Hangzhou has raised more than 2.8 billion yuan in public welfare funds from lotteries for the country, Hangzhou newly built and reconstructed many social welfare facilities, and Hangzhou has used the public welfare funds from lotteries for the construction of social welfare programs, including social welfare houses, children's welfare houses, Starlight Home for the Aged, senior apartments, the stations for centralized support of rural childless and infirm people and home-based elderly care service stations. In 2012, Hangzhou issued 1.78 billion yuan in welfare lotteries to raise 519 million yuan in public welfare funds, and thus conducted a series of public benefit assistance and image building activities to deliver tangible benefits for the public good according to the goal of issuing welfare lotteries aimed at supporting the aged, disabled, poor and orphans and the cultural philosophy of stressing public benefit, charity, health, happiness and innovation.

With many years of development, Zhejiang has actively promoted the development of public benefit programs through the welfare lottery funds, and Zhejiang has brought innovations to the purchase of public services in order to ensure the efficiency and quality of public service provision to some extent and ease the financial pressure on the government in providing public services.

## 4.4  A New System for the Urban-Rural Social Programs

### 4.4.1  Promoting Urban-Rural Integration by Starting with Reforming the Land System and the Household Registration System

Actively and steadily pushing forward urbanization and placing emphasis on developing small and medium-sized cities and small towns is the major strategic decision made in light of China's basic conditions and reality. Zhejiang has actively proceeded from reforming the land system and the household registration system to promote urban-rural integration in a coordinated way, providing a strong guarantee for promoting county urbanization and equal access to basic county-level public services.

In recent years, Zhejiang has steadily improved the state of its rural land, brought innovations to and reformed the rural land system; it has continued to press ahead with the reform of the land expropriation system, has gradually standardized the scope of land expropriation, explored and established the mechanism involving the sharing of land appreciation revenue, and it has improved the compensation and settlement mechanism for land expropriation; moreover, it has built and improved the markets for circulation of the contractual right of land and rural property rights exchange platforms, improved the rural land rights confirmation and registration system, steadily promoted pilot circulation of rural collectively-owned profit-oriented construction land, actively explored the mechanism for the exiting and circulation of rural homesteads, more rapidly established a unified construction land market in urban and rural areas, intensified the reform of the system of forestry property rights, improved the forestry property right circulation mechanism, promoted the reform of state-owned forest farms and explored and established the cultivated land protection compensation mechanism. The reform of the land system has provided the basic guarantee for safeguarding farmers' rights and interests and developing towns in a scientific way.

In order to further promote urban-rural integration, Zhejiang has energetically experimented with and developed a unified household registration policy in urban and rural areas. The *12th Five-Year Plan of Zhejiang Province for Institutional Reform* called for intensifying the institutional reform for the sake of coordinated urban-rural development and the reform of the household registration system. For local farmers migrating to urban areas, a household registration system was established within the scope of counties and cities to ensure that the original rights and interests can be retained, the basic public services for local urban residents can be enjoyed and the original economic and property rights and interests can be circulated and traded; this household registration system was first piloted in the pilot towns in small cities. Zhejiang steadily pushed forward the localized management of the population mainly through residence permits, conducted the pilot reform of points-based household registration system for migrant workers to gradually turn the rural migrant workers with stable labor relations and living in urban areas for a certain number of years into urban residents. The reform of the household registration system is aimed at gradually removing the different treatments attached to registered permanent residence, including those in medical services, employment and housing security, thus really making sure that basic public services fully cover urban and rural areas.

At present, Jiaxing City and Deqing County in Huzhou City, Zhejiang have adopted a unified household registration system in urban and rural areas, while 9 other cities are also choosing 1 county (county-level city, district) to initiate this work. Take Deqing County as an example; according to the principle of promoting this work in an active and steady way, the county identified 33 policies involving treatment differences between urban and rural areas in this reform of the household registration system, adjusted 17 policies, out of these 33 policies, whose time was ripe and had satisfied the conditions, to become unified between urban and rural areas. As from September 30, 2013, Deqing County officially conducted conversion of the household registration information and data on residents across the county and comprehensively carried out the reform of the household registration system; it is the first pilot county for the reform of the household registration system in Zhejiang. The reform of the household registration system in Deqing County has ensured that urban and rural residents equally enjoy various rights and has provided new impetus for local economic and social development; the county has, amidst urbanization, gradually given shape to a pattern of bringing win-win outcomes to the government, the market and the people; the county has offered feasible practical experience for gradually removing the restrictions on registered permanent residence, achieving urban-rural integration in registered permanent residence and equal access to basic public services in urban and rural areas; the county has also provided a new choice of a pathway for China's urbanization. The county's experience in the reform of the household registration system has produced a strong demonstration effect and deserves to be promoted.

The reform of the household registration system has been facilitated by the orderly and rapid construction of small towns. Zhejiang is the region with the fastest and most distinctive construction of small towns in China. There are more than 330 towns officially identified and recognized as part of the Top 1,000 Towns in China; unlike other provinces and municipalities, Zhejiang has developed small towns with local characteristics—each town, and even each village, has an industrial cluster, many central towns can be considered modern small cities, such as Zhouxiang Town in Cixi City, famous for the developed household appliances industry, and Hengdian Town in Dongyang City, famous as a film and television city, towns of buttons, zippers and ties. Zhejiang has actively promoted industrial and urban integrative development while cultivating and developing small cities, and has carved out a new path for exploring the road towards new-type urbanization that is characterized by local urbanization. In an effort to promote the construction of small towns, Zhejiang has endeavored to extend the high-quality resources in large and medium-sized cities to central towns, even to central villages, Zhejiang has encouraged farmers to gather in small towns, adopted the rural local urbanization path suited to the province's conditions so that most farmers can start businesses and settle down at the local level. This has also helped the rural economy to grow, it has also helped to increase farmers' income, improve rural infrastructures and develop rural social programs; this is of important significance for narrowing the urban-rural gap, achieving coordinated urban-rural development and building a harmonious socialist society. As Zhejiang has placed emphasis on developing small cities on the basis of cultivating central towns, it has promoted urban-rural integration and has also achieved local urbanization, which presents distinctive characteristics. The experiment carried out in Haiyan County, Jiaxing City offers a typical model for local urbanization. Haiyan County has experimented the local urbanization path of achieving non-agricultural employment and citizenization at the local level; with emphasis placed on putting the people first, pursuing green, low-carbon, compact and intensive development as well as city-industry integration, based on continuing to intensify comprehensive reform for coordinated urban-rural development, the county has, with the county as the unit, designed two ways for different groups to achieve citizenship: entering urban areas or staying in villages; the county has actively carried out the strategy of "small county and large city", and has stepped up to make the county large and strong, towns exquisite and well-rounded, villages excellent and beautiful, so that farmers can seek employment, achieve transfer and obtain security at the local level, and thus Haiyan can become a beautiful county where industries are superior, the environment is picturesque and the people live an elegant life.

## 4.4.2   The Reform of Public Institutions and the New System for the Provision of Public Services

As an important part of the public sector, public institutions play an important role in the government's public services. With all-round progress in the reforms of government institutions, enterprises, the scientific and technological, cultural, health and educational systems, further intensifying the reform of public institutions is essential for building a new public service system. Since the beginning of the 21st century, Zhejiang has introduced a number of policy documents concerning the reform of public institutions, including the *Opinions on Intensifying the Reform of Public Institutions*, the *Several Policy Opinions on Promoting the Restructuring of Provincial Public Institutions* and the *Interim Measures of Zhejiang Province for Open Recruitment of Personnel for Public Institutions*; the guiding thought behind the reform is as follows: Following the principles of separating public service units from the government, of providing classified guidance, of acting in a market-oriented way and according to local conditions, and proceeding from the requirement of adapting to the development of a socialist market economy to establish the management system and operational mechanism which are conducive to optimal allocation of resources, define government affairs and responsibilities, and conform to the characteristics of public institutions and their developmental law, thus promoting coordinated development of Zhejiang's national economy and social programs.

Zhejiang has divided the existing public institutions into public benefit-oriented public institutions, public institutions engaged in intermediary services, public institutions responsible for supervision and management and public institutions involved in production operations according to the classification standard covering fund source, degree of marketization, social function and future development. The public benefit-oriented public institutions are funded by public finances on the premise of adjusting the layout, improving the structure and optimizing resource allocation, and should strive to intensify the reform of their internal operational mechanism and strengthen their internal management to ensure that the quality of their services is improved and public benefit is delivered. The eligible public institutions responsible for supervision and management will be gradually turned into administrative organizations or managed by making reference to the civil servant law. The public institutions engaged in intermediary services are restructured, in light of their industrial characteristics, into social intermediary organizations which make their own management decisions and independently assume economic and legal responsibilities. The existing public institutions involved in production operations are more rapidly restructured into enterprises, put under the scientific legal person governance structure and turned into the market players which are responsible for their own management decisions, profits and losses.

Based on the classified reform of public institutions, Zhejiang has, by means of reforms and innovations, gradually combined the reform of public institutions with the building of a public service system with equal access, and has created a level playing field for public service providers by reforming public institutions. In recent years, Zhejiang has actively leveled the playing field, and has accorded equal treatment to private institutions and public institutions in establishing the conditions, the authentication of qualifications and the appraisal of occupational qualifications and professional titles. In recent years, as the reform pioneer in this regard, Wenzhou City has accelerated the reform of public institutions to innovate the public service provision system, gradually establish an institutional framework for ensuring fair competition between public institutions and social organizations in the field of public services, and progressively shape a pattern in which public institutions and social organizations compete for providing public services. Wenzhou's reforms and innovations exhibit distinctive characteristics: The government not only supports the development of social organizations, but it also ensures that the social organizations which have developed or enjoy potential for development engage in fair competition with other social organizations and public institutions in a competitive environment, so multiple players provide relevant public services at the same time and the service performance is enhanced through competition. In this regard, Wenzhou has made a number of policy innovations: regarding the development of industry associations, breaking the monopoly of industrial organizations, introducing multiple associations to an industry for competition. Under the principle that access is allowed to the fields which do not fall within the scope of prohibition in terms of access, Wenzhou has further relaxed the restrictions on the entry of social organizations into the fields of social management and services, and has created conditions in land use, project and taxation for the entry of social organizations, and has followed the principle of ensuring equal participation to foster an environment in which government departments, enterprises and social organizations share public resources equally.

Wenzhou's reform is a policy of coordinated innovation in fair competition. With policy innovations, Wenzhou has ensured that social organizations can equally engage in competition, and Wenzhou has introduced a series of policies in the educational, medical and community service fields, thus leveling the playing field for social organizations and public institutions as much as possible; this can further promote the development and growth of social organizations, speed up the reform of Wenzhou's public institutions, and also broaden the channels for providing public services and establish a new system of providing public services.

## 4.5 The Achievements in Social Programs and Equal Access to Public Social Services

Zhejiang has accelerated the overall development of the urban and rural social programs, improved the systems and mechanisms conducive to urban-rural integration, intensified the coordinated development of the programs in education, medical service, culture and registered permanent residence, social security and infrastructure in urban and rural areas; Zhejiang has also more rapidly established the systems and mechanisms for ensuring equal access to basic public services, including social security, social programs and public facilities, in urban and rural areas, Zhejiang has also moved faster to carry out coordinated urban-rural institutional reform, so a new pattern of urban-rural integration in social programs and public service provision has preliminarily taken shape in Zhejiang.

### 4.5.1 A Comparatively Perfect Basic Public Service System has Preliminarily Taken Shape

Since Zhejiang became the first to carry out the action plan for ensuring equal access to basic public services in 2008, it has effectively promoted coordinated urban-rural, regionally balanced provision of basic public services, and the sharing of basic public services by everyone; Zhejiang has made continuous improvements in the basic public service system, and has witnessed the preliminary formation of a comparatively perfect basic public service system. Relevant systems have basically covered all of the four large categories of public services, including basic life services, basic developmental services, basic environmental services and basic safety services. Zhejiang has basically established the social security system, labor employment public service system, basic public education system and public health service system covering both urban and rural areas; Zhejiang has comprehensively increased the level of such infrastructures as transportation, communication, water and supply of electricity; Zhejiang has established and improved the universal postal service system, public weather service system and place name public service system. Zhejiang has gradually established and implemented the provincial standards for basic public services and the mechanism for their dynamic adjustment.

Zhejiang has established and improved the mechanism of financial guarantees, built the long-term mechanism for increasing fiscal expenditures on basic public services, optimized the structure of fiscal expenditures, and ensured that more than 2/3 of Zhejiang's incremental financial resources are used for the people's well-being. Zhejiang has improved the capability of county finance for guaranteeing basic public services. Zhejiang has expedited the formation of the unified, standardized and transparent system of financial transfer payments. Zhejiang has brought innovations to the mechanism for the provision of services and has gradually established the mechanism for ensuring orderly competition and diversified participation in providing basic public services, thus enhancing the efficiency of services. Zhejiang has given full play to the active role of social organizations in the expression of the demand for basic public services, the provision, evaluation and supervision of services. Zhejiang has improved the evaluation and supervision mechanism, established the mechanism for the evaluation and supervision of basic public service performance, and has incorporated basic public service performance into the government evaluation and accountability system. Zhejiang has encouraged multiple parties to participate in evaluation, thus actively introducing third-party evaluation. Zhejiang has gradually established and improved the mechanisms for the guarantee of basic public service development, including financial guarantee, service provision, evaluation and supervision, thus ensuring high quality and efficiency of the provision of basic public services.

### 4.5.2   Equal Access to Public Services has Improved Significantly

With the continuous improvement in the basic public service system in Zhejiang, equal access to public services has improved markedly. Under the principle of ensuring that everyone equally shares basic public services, Zhejiang has practically safeguarded the rights and interests of the disadvantaged groups in basic public services, strengthened the basic public services for special groups, and gradually narrowed the gap in social security benefits among groups; Zhejiang has reinforced the basic public services for the migrant population, and progressively narrowed the gap in the per capita fiscal expenditure on basic public services among counties (county-level cities, districts); Zhejiang has further increased the proportion of the input in the basic public services in rural areas and the underdeveloped areas, and has gradually narrowed the gap in the benefits involving basic public services among groups; Zhejiang has made significant improvements in standardizing basic public service facilities in counties (county-level cities, districts), towns (sub-districts), villages (communities). The degree of realizing equal access to basic public services has exceeded 90%, and the balanced development of basic public services within the scope of counties has been basically achieved. Zhejiang has become the first to establish a social endowment insurance system covering both urban and rural residents, and social insurances have more rapidly shifted from full institutional coverage to full coverage of enterprises and personnel.

According to the government work report of Zhejiang Province in 2014, new progress was made in Zhejiang's urban and rural social programs in 2013. In Zhejiang, the per capita disposable income of urban residents was 37,851 yuan, up 9.6%; the per capita net income of rural residents was 16,106 yuan, up 10.7%; the minimum monthly standards of living security for urban and rural residents were raised to 526 yuan and 406 yuan, respectively; Zhejiang improved the system of the government's responsibility for employment promotion and strengthened the building of the employment service system, and an additional 1,043,000 people were employed in urban areas; a fairer and more sustainable social security system was established, an additional 2.70 million people were covered by endowment insurance, an additional 1.61 million people were covered by medical insurance, construction began with respect to 194,000 units of government-subsidized housing, and 111,000 units of government-subsidized housing were completed; Zhejiang comprehensively promoted the development of educational programs, finished the three-year action plan for preschool education, accelerated the development of compulsory education, vocational education and higher education; Zhejiang vigorously developed medical and health programs and reinforced the building of the public health service system in urban and rural areas.

### 4.5.3  The Accessibility and Diversity of the Provision of Public Services have Increased Continuously

With innovations to the mechanism for the provision of public services, Zhejiang has actively carried out the public service improvement project, increased the total provision of public services, and constantly improved the accessibility and diversity of the provision of public services.

Regarding the basic public services, Zhejiang has basically achieved full coverage of provision of services. With regard to the construction of public service facilities, based on the standard of the area of an integrated service venue in central urban areas and that at the county level not smaller than $1,000\,\text{m}^2$ and $500\,\text{m}^2$, Zhejiang has created primary-level platforms that are more normalized and standardized, and has ensured that towns (sub-districts) and villages (communities) are fully covered. Regarding the standardization of the compulsory education schools, Zhejiang has made all-round improvements in the quality and level of senior middle, junior middle and primary schools by revising the measures of Zhejiang Province for the evaluation of schools in the standardization of nine-year compulsory education. With regard to the primary-level health services, Zhejiang has further enhanced the rural three-level medical and health service network to improve the primary-level health infrastructures and comprehensively strengthen the primary-level integrated health service functions. Zhejiang has allocated more equipment to urban and rural integrated cultural stations by promoting the development of the libraries in counties and towns, county-level cultural centers and integrated cultural stations in towns (sub-districts). Regarding the press and publication services for the people, a love of reading in the people has been advocated and Zhejiang has fostered an environment of an ardent love for reading. Regarding equal access to public services relating to sports, Zhejiang has gradually built popular fitness facilities covering both urban and rural areas.

With regard to the diversity of public services, institutional innovations have been brought to continuously meet the ever-growing diverse service needs of the people. As mentioned by comrade Xi Jinping, "Under the conditions of the market economy, some things can be done not directly by the government... encouraging and supporting the development of social organizations to relieve the people's anxieties is essentially conducive to sharing burdens for the Party committee and government".[7] Zhejiang has actively guided social forces to participate in the provision of public services, and a pattern of diversified provision of public services has basically formed. Zhejiang has increased its support for social organizations, and has handed over the basic public service items fit for being undertaken by the society to social organizations through service purchase and by other means; Zhejiang has also given scope to the role of charity in raising funds for basic public services and providing services. In the meantime, Zhejiang has actively pushed forward the reform of public institutions. According to the requirements of keeping a separation between public service units and the government, between public institutions and enterprises and between government regulation and management, Zhejiang has really turned public institutions into independent institutional legal persons and public service providers. Moreover, Zhejiang has expanded the fields of basic public services open to social capital, encouraged and guided social capital to build up old-age care centers and foster service institutions and the institutions for rehabilitation of the handicapped as well as public cultural and sports facilities.

### 4.5.4   The Mechanism for Expressing and Responding to the Need of Public Services has Improved Gradually

As Zhejiang promotes equal access to basic public services in an all-round way, it has developed the line of thought of putting the people first, established the mechanism for smoothly expressing and responding to the needs for basic public services and has effectively improved the structure of the provision of public services. Zhejiang has improved the Party and government-led mechanism for safeguarding the people's rights and interests; Zhejiang has established the mechanisms for the coordination

---

[7]Xi 2007.

of scientific and effective interests, for the expression of appeal, for the mediation and handling of contradictions, and for the safeguarding of rights and interests. Zhejiang has improved the primary-level community governance pattern, basically built a community governance system with Zhejiang's characteristics. Zhejiang has actively pushed forward the project for the construction of community-level public service platforms. Zhejiang has established the system for dynamic tracking of public services and activities, fully leveraged the resources available in sub-districts and communities in urban and rural areas to publicize the policies of basic public services and the performance of public services to local people through bulletin boards, posters, manuals, WeChat and microblog and by other means, thus making sure that the people get more relative information and have further participation opportunities. Zhejiang has introduced an electronic system for the evaluation of satisfaction, statistics regarding regular satisfaction questionnaire surveys and online satisfaction surveys in order to extensively solicit the people's opinions on public services, and has enabled a real-time connection between the quality of public services and the performance evaluation and linked the people's evaluation of service quality to the evaluation of performance in public services. "The people really make choices and become stakeholders; furthermore, the people serve as the main players and investors in some things".[8]

# References

Xi Jinping, *Zhijiang Xinyu*, Zhejiang People's Publishing House, 2007, p. 246.
Yu Jianxing, Xu Yueqian, Zhejiang's Experience in Building a Service-oriented Government, *Chinese Public Administration*, 2012(2).
Xu Jialiang, Zhaoting, The Realistic Dilemmas and Route Innovations in the Government's Purchase of Public Services: Shanghai's Practice, *Chinese Public Administration*, 2013(8).
Wang Shizong, The Applicability of Local Governance in China and Its Limitations—Take the Policy of Haishu District, Ningbo for the Government's Purchase of the Home-based Elderly Care Services as an Example, *Journal of Public Management*, 2007(4).

[8]Xi (2007).

# Chapter 5
# Ensuring and Improving the People's Well-Being

**Zhijun Liu and Huanhong Ying**

The issue of the people's well-being is the issue of the people's life. The report delivered during the 17th National Congress of the Communist Party of China summarized the people's well-being as the people's access to education, employment, medical services, elderly care, and housing. In the past, the people mainly held that the issue of the people's well-being was the issue of survival, livelihood, ample food and clothing. At present, as China enters the new stage of building a moderately prosperous society in all respects, the issue of the people's well-being has become richer in connotation, wider in scope and more complicated in level; it has become the focus of the people's attention.[1] Therefore, since the beginning of the 21st century, based on relatively abundant materials, Zhejiang's policy of the people's well-being has focused on making all-round improvements in the people's well-being with the aim of safeguarding the people's economic, political, cultural and social rights and interests. Zhejiang has comprehensively put into practice the philosophy of putting the people first, and has vowed to promote the people's well-rounded development, earnestly solve the most pressing and real problems of the greatest concern to the people; the comprehensive policies concerning the people's well-being have been introduced, Zhejiang has placed more emphasis on the political, economic, social and cultural rights and interests when making the systematic and comprehensive policies and measures for improving the people's well-being; the strategy of urban-rural integration has been implemented steadily, Zhejiang has become the first to develop and implement the plan for promoting urban-rural integration.[2]

---

[1] Ye (2008).

[2] Liu and Xia (2012).

---

Z. Liu (✉)
Zhejiang University, Hangzhou, China

H. Ying
Zhejiang Academy of Social Sciences, Hangzhou, China

© Social Sciences Academic Press and Springer Nature Singapore Pte Ltd. 2019
G. Chen and J. Yang (eds.), *Chinese Dream and Practice in Zhejiang—Society*,
Research Series on the Chinese Dream and China's Development Path,
https://doi.org/10.1007/978-981-13-7406-7_5

"Under no circumstance can the people's interests be treated lightly." The people may not pay attention to the GDP, but they are concerned about food, clothing, shelter, transportation, employment, their children's education, medical services, old-age care and other issues; given these issues, it is essential to turn the outlook on development into the scientific outlook on development and shift the focus to putting the people first and sincerely carry out substantive and better work and overcome difficulties for the people.[3] As early as 2004, Zhejiang became the first nationwide to make the great decision of establishing a long-term mechanism conducive to doing substantive work for the people, which required the governments at various levels to address the most pressing, most immediate issues that concern the people the most, do better, meticulous and substantive work relating to the people's production and life, so that the people really enjoy the tangible benefits from sound and rapid economic and social development. Paying attention to the people's well-being and doing substantive work for the people is the important commitment made by the successive Party committees and people's governments of Zhejiang Province, while the overall line of thought of addressing the issue of the people's well-being is as follows: guiding the cadres at various levels to really focus on the people's well-being, wholeheartedly serve the people, practically solve the problems relating to their well-being, about which the people have great concern, including those involving employment, social security, education, medical services and housing, actively foster a good atmosphere and environment for building a harmonious socialist society.[4]

## 5.1 Ensuring and Improving the People's Well-Being

Based on the work carried out by the successive Party committees and people's governments of Zhejiang Province, Zhejiang initiated the *Action Plan for Ensuring Equal Access to Basic Public Services (2008–2012)*, the first one in China, in 2008. The action plan called for establishing and improving a multilevel social security system with full coverage, making sure that basic public services cover both urban and rural areas, are regionally balanced and shared by everyone, promoting social fairness and justice and well-rounded development of the people.[5] In order to achieve this goal, the action plan stressed an investment of more than 217 billion yuan in carrying out ten major projects within five years since 2008, including the employment promotion project, the social security project, the educational equality project, the Health for All project, the cultural and sports popularization project, the social welfare project, the community service project, the comfortable housing project for the people, the public facilities project and the project of loving care for rural migrant workers, with 81 tasks arranged.[6] These tasks involve coordinated work relating to the people's

---

[3]Xi (2013), p. 26.
[4]Zhong and Xie (2007).
[5]Su (2008).
[6]Su (2008).

well-being between urban and rural areas, between the developed and underdeveloped areas; they represent the consistent goal of successive collective leadership of Zhejiang Province.

### 5.1.1  Addressing the Weaknesses in the Underdeveloped Areas

As Zhejiang speeds up the building of a moderately prosperous society in all respects and strives to basically achieve modernization in advance, a comparatively salient problem is wide regional disparity.[7] The successive governments of Zhejiang Province have realized that the people throughout the province cannot become well-off if the people in the underdeveloped areas do not become well-off; modernization cannot be achieved throughout the province if the underdeveloped areas are not modernized. Zhejiang's ability to build a moderately prosperous society in all respects and basically achieve modernization in advance largely depends upon narrowing regional disparity. This requires accelerated development of the developed areas and leapfrog development of the underdeveloped areas.[8]

With such a philosophy, Zhejiang has consistently worked on overcoming the weaknesses in the underdeveloped areas; Zhejiang has further adjusted policies, made relevant measures, especially adopting such means as increasing transfer payments, to enhance the consumption ability of the underdeveloped areas so that the people in various parts of the province can share the achievements in economic and social development.[9] Take fiscal input as an example, Zhejiang's fiscal expenditure on social security reached 24,435 million yuan in 2006, up 21.8% compared with 2005. Zhejiang has adopted more preferential policies for the underdeveloped areas while increasing the overall input in social programs. Zhejiang has also arranged special funds from finance, introduced a slew of preferential tax policies, made efforts to promote employment and reemployment, and supported such projects as the Project for Training Ten Million Rural People as Labor Forces.

### 5.1.2  Building an Urban-Rural Social Security System

Since 1996, the departments of finance at various levels in Zhejiang have focused on increasing input, intensifying reforms and strengthening management, proceeded from the province's conditions to build an institutionally unified, coordinated new urban-urban social security system with different standards, so Zhejiang has preliminarily established a system of coordinated urban-rural subsistence allowances, a

---

[7]Xi (2013).
[8]Xi (2013).
[9]Xi (2013).

system of social security for the farmers whose land has been expropriated, the new rural cooperative medical care system and the medical assistance system; Zhejiang has continuously extended the social security system to rural areas.[10]

As early as 1995, Zhejiang initiated the system of coordinated urban-rural subsistence allowances to provide assistance for the people with difficulties in urban and rural areas below the standard of local subsistence allowances. In late 1997, Zhejiang became the third province where a system of coordinated urban-rural subsistence allowances was established nationwide, following Guangdong and Shanghai. In 2001, the People's Government of Zhejiang Province issued the *Measures of Zhejiang Province for Subsistence Allowances*, establishing this system in the form of government regulations. In order to provide security for all of the people possible, the departments of finance at various levels have strictly carried out the requirement of incorporating a sufficient amount of subsistence allowances funds into the fiscal budget. In 2003, Zhejiang set the goal of establishing the system of social security for the farmers whose land has been expropriated, and has introduced relevant policy measures, required local authorities to establish the living security risk reserves for the people whose land has been expropriated, so as to mitigate the future payment pressure and the fiscal risks. Zhejiang is also one of the four provinces for piloting the new rural cooperative medical care nationwide. In 2003, 27 counties carried out the preliminary pilot work; in 2005, Zhejiang entered the stage of full implementation; in 2007, the following basic goal was achieved: the rural coordinated cooperative medical system for serious diseases with county (county-level city, district) was established throughout the province, and more than 80% of the farmers participate in the system.

Zhejiang has always attached importance to social assistance. In 2003, the Party Committee and the People's Government of Zhejiang Province focused on establishing a long-term mechanism for helping the poor, and issued policy opinions on building a new social assistance system covering urban and rural areas. With three years of experiments and efforts, Zhejiang has basically built a government-led, a framework for a system of coordinated urban-rural social assistance with social mutual assistance, so that the basic life of most people with difficulties has been really guaranteed; Zhejiang has been at the forefront nationwide on many fronts.[11]

First, Zhejiang was the first to carry out the system involving centralized support of the rural people enjoying five guarantees (food, clothing, medical care, housing, and burial expenses) and the urban people without identification papers, a normal residence permit, and a source of income. Second, Zhejiang was the first to carry out the urban-rural medical assistance system. Third, Zhejiang was the first to introduce the "education voucher" system for financially aiding the children from families in difficulty. Third, Zhejiang has comprehensively carried out the housing assistance system for urban and rural families with difficulties. Finally, Zhejiang has promoted the building of an urban and a rural legal aid system in an all-round way. Local authorities in Zhejiang have universally established legal aid agencies, incorporated

---

[10]Chen (2005).
[11]Liu and Chen (2007).

special funds for legal aid in the fiscal budget, offering free legal aid to the people in difficulty, including the targets of subsistence allowances, the rural people enjoying five guarantees and the urban people without identification papers, a normal residence permit, and a source of income, as well as the handicapped. On this basis, in 2007, Zhejiang issued the *Opinions on Strengthening the Work on Rural Legal Aid*, further extending legal aid to rural areas and rural migrant workers. Moreover, Zhejiang has also constantly intensified the work on assistance for disaster victims, employment assistance, assistance for urban vagrants and beggars,[12] social mutual assistance and the building of the social assistance management service system; Zhejiang has acquired a great amount of good experience and practices, and has made significant achievements on these fronts.[13]

### 5.1.3 Promoting Coordinated Urban-Rural Development to Address the Issues Relating to Agriculture, Rural Areas and Farmers

Properly addressing the issues relating to agriculture, rural areas and farmers is the top priority of the whole Party's work,[14] while the successive collective leadership of Zhejiang Province has been unwavering, at all times, in upholding the guiding principle of giving top priority to the issues relating to agriculture, rural areas and farmers, taking the construction of a new countryside as the number one priority, and making addressing the issues relating to agriculture, rural areas and farmers the top priority in the whole Party's work; it is necessary to take the strategic perspective of governing and rejuvenating the country, give full play to the role of the farmers in the development of agriculture, rural areas and farmers and the leading role of the Party committee and the government, and constantly enhance the capability for addressing issues relating to agriculture, rural areas and farmers; it is essential to make the main leaders of the Party and the government directly responsible for the work on agriculture, rural areas and farmers, consciously carry out the requirement of "giving top priority to relevant issues" in leadership decisions, strategic planning, fiscal input, work arrangement and the evaluation of officials' performance, and create a strong synergy of and good atmosphere in the whole society for supporting agriculture, loving farmers and serving rural areas.[15]

The specific operational strategy lies in overcoming the line of thought of pursuing rural and agricultural development merely from rural and agricultural perspectives, adopting the line of thought and philosophy of "enriching villages, flourishing agriculture and benefiting the people by means of re-feeding to achieve coordinated urban-rural development" to make healthy progress in industrialization, urbaniza-

---

[12]Liu and Chen (2011).
[13]Liu and Chen (2007).
[14]Xi (2013), p. 190.
[15]Xi (2013), p. 100.

tion and marketization, and meanwhile promote coordinated urban-rural development, give full play to the roles of industrialization, urbanization and marketization in driving the development of agriculture, rural areas and farmers.[16] It is necessary to remove the institutional restrictions on enhancing agricultural efficiency, increasing farmers' income and promoting rural development, to fundamentally overcome the difficulties concerning agriculture, rural areas and farmers, further emancipate and develop the rural productive forces to speed up agricultural and rural modernization.[17] It is also necessary to more rapidly adjust the pattern of the distribution of the national income, channel more public funds to rural areas, strengthen the construction of rural infrastructure and the development of social programs, and extend public services to more rural areas.[18]

In recent decades, Zhejiang has vigorously carried out the strategy of promoting coordinated urban-rural development, more quickly pushed forward the building of advanced manufacturing bases and urbanization, Zhejiang has developed the central cities, central towns and massive characteristic economy to stimulate industrial and population agglomeration, so that 3/4 of the rural labor forces across the province have transferred to and worked in the secondary and tertiary industries, and they have become the new forces for boosting industrialization and urbanization; Zhejiang has promoted new-type urbanization to drive agricultural modernization, adopted the philosophy of modern industrial development to operate agriculture, and it has armed agriculture with advanced equipment and facilities; Zhejiang has fostered the leading enterprises in the processing and circulation of agricultural products to stimulate agricultural development, actively encouraged and guided industrial and commercial enterprises, especially private enterprises, to invest in agriculture, and has given birth to a large number of leading agricultural enterprises; Zhejiang has proactively adjusted the pattern of the distribution of the national income, allocated more public financial resources to rural areas, more rapidly extended urban infrastructures to rural areas, more expeditiously made public services available in rural areas, shaped a mechanism in which urban and rural areas interact and promote each other, thus vigorously promoting urban-rural integration.[19]

---

[16]Xi (2013), p. 168.
[17]Xi (2013), p. 43.
[18]Xi (2013), p. 169.
[19]Xi (2013), p. 168.

## 5.2 Increasing the Income of Urban and Rural Residents

### 5.2.1 The Characteristics of the Increase in the Income of Urban and Rural Residents

#### 5.2.1.1 The Overall Income of Urban and Rural Residents has Increased Rapidly

"In recent years, Zhejiang has witnessed rapid economic development, its GDP has grown annually by an average of more than 13%, profound changes have taken place in urban and rural areas, and the life of urban and rural residents has improved greatly."[20] In 2007, Zhejiang's GDP was 1,863.84 billion yuan, up 14.5%. The per capita GDP was USD 4883 on the basis of the average annual exchange rate of 7.604 in 2007, up 12.7% compared with the previous year. The per capita disposable income of Zhejiang's urban residents was 20,574 yuan in 2007, up 12.6% compared with the previous year. The per capita disposable income of the urban low-income households accounting for 20% was 7924 yuan, up 12.5% compared with the previous year. The per capita net income of rural residents was 8265 yuan, up 12.7% compared with the previous year; the proportion of the households with the per capita net income above 8000 yuan increased from 37.9 to 45.1%. The per capita disposable income of Zhejiang's urban residents increased from 27,359 yuan in 2010 to 37,851 yuan in 2013, an average annual nominal increase of 11.4%, while the per capita net income of rural residents increased from 11,303 yuan in 2010 to 16,106 yuan in 2013, an average annual nominal increase of 12.5%, which were 1.4 times and 1.8 times the national levels, respectively; Zhejiang ranked No.3 among 31 provinces (autonomous regions, municipalities) across the country, following Shanghai and Beijing, and ranked No.1 among provinces (autonomous regions) in the per capita disposable income of urban residents for 13 consecutive years; Zhejiang ranked No.1 among provinces (autonomous regions) in the per capita net income of rural residents for 29 consecutive years.

#### 5.2.1.2 The Operating Income of Urban Residents and the Transfer Income of Rural Residents have Grown Rapidly

Property income has become an important part of the income of urban households and a new growth point for the income of urban residents. In 2007, the per capita property income of Zhejiang's urban residents was 1080 yuan, the proportion of the per capita property income in the total income of households increased from 1.6% in 2002 to 4.8% in 2007. In 2013, the trend by which the income structure of urban residents shifted from a wage income-dominated one to a diversified one was further strengthened, and the proportion of the operating income increased greatly.

---

[20] Xi (2013), p. 45.

In the per capita disposable income of urban residents, the wage income was 24,453 yuan, up 9.2%; the operating income, property income and transfer income grew by 9.1%, 1.4% and 7.1%, respectively. In 2013, the per capita transfer income of Zhejiang's urban residents was 10,179 yuan, among which old-age pensions and retirement pensions were 8622 yuan, up 4.2 times compared with 2000. In 2013, the income structure of rural residents was optimized to some extent; in the per capita income of rural residents, the wage income was 8577 yuan, up 11.7%; the income from household operations was 5757 yuan, up 8.8%; the property income and transfer income grew by 9.8% and 13.3%, respectively. The non-agricultural income continued to be the main source of the increase in farmers' income, while the transfer and property income from land expropriation compensation, old-age subsidies and rentals accounted for about 10%.

### 5.2.1.3 Industrial Development has Promoted the Rapid Growth of the Income of Urban and Rural Residents

During the period 2001–2012, industry contributed 38.6% to the growth of the total income of urban households on average in Zhejiang. Except 2002, 2009 and 2012, industry contributed more than 30% to the growth of the total income of urban households in Zhejiang. The proportion of industrial income in the total income of urban households in Zhejiang was relatively stable and fluctuated at about 38% (see Table 5.1).

As new-type urban-rural relations—in which industry promotes agricultural development, urban development drives rural development, industry and agriculture benefit each other and urban-rural integration arises—has gradually taken shape, rural residents have shared the achievements in modernization and industrialization, industry has contributed more than 50% to the growth of rural residents' income. According to Table 5.2, the proportion of rural residents' income from industrial economic development in the net income of rural residents in Zhejiang increased steadily from 41.5% in 2001 to 45.0% in 2004, 46.0% in 2008 and 47.4% in 2012. During the period 2001–2012, industry contributed 50.4% to the growth of rural residents' net income on average in Zhejiang.

### 5.2.1.4 The Proportion of Fiscal Expenditure on the People's Well-Being has Increased

Since 2008, 2/3 of the annual incremental fiscal expenditure has been used for the people's well-being, noticeably higher than the national average. The fiscal expenditure on the people's well-being has focused on employment, old-age care, medical services and basic security in other respects, housing security, culture and sports, rural environmental improvement, poverty alleviation, pollution prevention and control and public security. In 2012, Zhejiang's fiscal expenditure on poverty alleviation

**Table 5.1** The rate of contribution from industry to the growth of urban residents' total income in Zhejiang Unit: yuan, %

| Year | Total income of urban households | Industrial income in the total income of households | Proportion of industrial income in the total income of households | The rate of contribution from industry to the growth of the income of urban residents |
|------|------|------|------|------|
| 2001 | 10519 | 3832 | 36.4 | 33.7 |
| 2002 | 12682 | 4464 | 35.2 | 29.2 |
| 2003 | 14295 | 5372 | 37.6 | 56.3 |
| 2004 | 15882 | 6226 | 39.2 | 53.8 |
| 2005 | 17877 | 7049 | 39.4 | 41.3 |
| 2006 | 19954 | 8006 | 40.1 | 46.1 |
| 2007 | 22584 | 8865 | 39.3 | 32.7 |
| 2008 | 24981 | 9719 | 38.9 | 35.6 |
| 2009 | 27119 | 10293 | 38.0 | 26.8 |
| 2010 | 30135 | 11491 | 38.1 | 39.7 |
| 2011 | 34264 | 13229 | 38.6 | 42.1 |
| 2012 | 37995 | 14217 | 37.4 | 26.5 |

**Table 5.2** The rate of contribution from industry to the per capita net income of rural residents in Zhejiang Unit: yuan, %

| Year | Per capita net income of rural residents | Industrial income in the per capita net income of rural residents | Proportion of industrial income in the per capita net income | The rate of contribution from industry to the growth of the income of rural residents |
|------|------|------|------|------|
| 2001 | 4582 | 1901 | 41.5 | 48.8 |
| 2002 | 4940 | 2098 | 42.5 | 55.1 |
| 2003 | 5431 | 2402 | 44.2 | 61.9 |
| 2004 | 6096 | 2744 | 45.0 | 51.4 |
| 2005 | 6660 | 2989 | 44.9 | 43.5 |
| 2006 | 7335 | 3295 | 44.9 | 45.3 |
| 2007 | 8265 | 3707 | 44.9 | 44.3 |
| 2008 | 9258 | 4256 | 46.0 | 55.3 |
| 2009 | 10007 | 4626 | 46.2 | 49.4 |
| 2010 | 11303 | 5296 | 46.9 | 51.7 |
| 2011 | 13071 | 6196 | 47.4 | 50.9 |
| 2012 | 14552 | 6903 | 47.4 | 47.7 |

was 406.3 billion yuan, the fiscal expenditure on medical services and health grew by 9.7%, while that on social security and employment grew by 18.4%, and that on education grew by 16.8%. In 2013, the level of Zhejiang's per capita pension benefits was 2300 yuan, the minimum standard of the basic pension for urban residents reached 80 yuan and the reimbursement ratio of hospitalization expenses within the scope of the policy involving new rural cooperative medical care reached 75%. Thanks to a growing wage income and the policy of supporting and benefiting agriculture, the income of Zhejiang's rural residents grew more rapidly, so the income gap between urban and rural residents further narrowed.

## 5.2.2 The Effects from the Increase in the Income of Urban and Rural Residents

The ultimate goal of promoting material well-being and raising cultural-ethical standards is to promote the well-rounded development of the people, including improving the people's material life, enriching the people's cultural life, enhancing the people's quality of survival, the cultural-ethical, scientific and cultural fields.[21] Since the reform and opening-up, the people of Zhejiang have become the first to push forward the market-oriented reform, they have stayed ahead in economic development, achieved diversified cultural development and coordinated development of social programs, the income of Zhejiang's urban and rural residents has increased rapidly and the people of Zhejiang have achieved a huge leap from a poverty-stricken society to a moderately prosperous society in all respects.

### 5.2.2.1 Material Life has Improved Immensely

1. The Engel's Coefficient has declined continually

The consumption mindset of urban and rural residents has been constantly adjusted and changed along with growing income, the consumption mode has undergone qualitative changes and consumption has tended to become increasingly diversified. During the period 1979–2007, the overall level of consumption of urban and rural residents grew rapidly, the per capita consumption expenditure of urban residents increased from 301 yuan in 1978 to 14,091 yuan, up 45.8 times; the per capita living consumption expenditure of rural residents rose from 157 yuan to 6442 yuan, up 40 times. In 2013, the per capita consumption expenditure of urban and rural residents was 23,257 yuan and 11,760 yuan, respectively, up 7.9% and 10.4% compared with the previous year. In 2013, the total retail sales of consumer goods was 1,513.8 billion yuan, up 11.8% compared with the previous year. As consumption expenditure increased markedly, the Engel's Coefficient of urban and rural residents was on the

---

[21] Xi (2013), p. 297.

decrease; in the early 1980s, the Engel's Coefficient of urban residents was higher than 55%, while that of rural residents was higher than 60%; in 2007, the Engel's Coefficient of urban residents and that of rural residents were 34.7% and 36.4%; in 2013, both figures were 34.4 and 35.6%.

2.  The levels of clothing, housing and nutrition have increased significantly

When it comes to clothing, urban and rural residents have paid attention to texture, style and color combinations. The people have pursued clothing brands, fashion and individuality. The per capita expenditure on clothing consumption of urban residents was 1406 yuan in 2007, 20.4 times that in 1981; that per capita expenditure of rural residents was 399 yuan in 2007, while that in 1978 was only 17 yuan. The per capita expenditure on clothing consumption of urban residents was 2235 yuan in 2013, 11.9 times and 33.6 times that in 1990 and 1981.

In late 2007, 50% of the urban households owned commercial housing. In late 2011, the per capita building area of urban residents' housing was 36.9 m$^2$ in Zhejiang, and 59.8% of the urban households owned commercial housing. In 2013, the per capita area of urban residents' housing was 38.8 m$^2$, up 45.8% compared with 2002. With the improvement in the housing conditions of Zhejiang's urban residents, some wealthy households have started to invest in real estate, and more and more households have owned multiple housing units. About 20% of the urban residents owned two or more housing units in 2007. The house decoration has tended to become high-quality and the living environment has improved. Rural houses have been generally upgraded from shabby old houses into new houses which are large, tall and spacious; in particular, a considerable part of the rural houses built since the beginning of the 21st century can be comparable to beautiful and comfortable urban houses with complete supporting facilities. The per capita housing expenditure of Zhejiang's rural residents was 1934 yuan in 2013, 74.4 times what it was in 1980.

The structure of the food consumption of urban and rural residents has changed from simple quantitative expansion to all-round qualitative improvement. From the perspective of the trend in food consumption, the residents' mindset regarding consumption has been renewed constantly, more and more residents have dined out. In 2007, the per capita expenditure of urban and rural residents on dining out was 1356 yuan, accounting for 27.7% of the food expenditure. In 2013, the per capita grain expenditure of urban residents was 494 yuan, its proportion decreased from 18.2% in 1981 to 6.2%. The structure of the food consumption of rural residents has changed from the staple food-dominated one to the non-staple food-dominated one; with gradual adjustment of the structure of the diet, the nutritional level of rural residents has become rational and scientific.

3.  A large number of high-end consumer durables have entered households

New-type household appliances have been gradually adopted by households; resident consumption is shifting to a type aimed at enjoyment and learning; cars, computers and mobile phones have become important consumer durables for urban residents. In 2013, every 100 urban residents in Zhejiang owned 44.28 cars, 101.56 home computers and 217.43 mobile phones, up 91.3 times, 6.2 times and 5.9 times compared with 2000. At present, the mindset regarding the people's consumption habits has changed from meeting the demand in life to improving the quality of life. Accord-ing to statistical data, the consumption of electronic products and cars has exceeded house improvement and decoration, and they have become the main choices in mass consumption.

Consumer durables have also rapidly become popular among rural residents. In recent years, such emerging consumer goods as cameras, motorcycles, and combined acoustic equipment, air-conditioners, telephones and computers have entered rural households. In 2013, every 100 rural households in Zhejiang owned 169.3 color TV sets, 96.5 refrigerators, 101.3 air-conditioners and 57.6 kitchen ventilators. Thanks to road construction and the increase in resident income, the number of motorcy-cles owned by rural residents has soared. In 2007, every 100 households owned 58 motorcycles on average; every 100 households owned 4 private cars.

### 5.2.2.2  Cultural and Ethical Life has Become Increasingly Rich

1. Tourism and fitness have become the new growth points in the consumption habits of urban and rural residents

With the steady growth of incomes, urban and rural residents have increasingly high demands for the quality of life, and tourism and fitness have become the ways for the people to relax after work and learning. Expenditure on tourism of urban and rural residents has grown year by year, and the tourists have increased continuously in terms of person-time. The per capita group tourism and sightseeing expenditure of Zhejiang's urban residents was 844 yuan in 2013, up 3.4 times and 31 times compared with 2002 and 1992.

2. The cultural facilities have been on the increase, the entertainment modes have become diverse

With the increasing material level of urban and rural residents, the people have started to pursue a better ethical and cultural life, their consumption habits relating to culture and entertainment have become increasingly popular among residents. The leisure life of the people has become richer. In 2012, expenditure on cultural and entertainment services by urban and rural residents accounted for 6.0% of the entire household consumption expenditure—that of urban residents and that of rural residents accounted for 7.15% and 4.01%, respectively. There has been great input in public cultural development, the provision of cultural services has increased con-stantly, cultural venues and facilities have become available to the people without charge, and the effectiveness of the network of public cultural facilities has increased. Households have incessantly enhanced their philosophy of educational investments, and resident educational expenditure has grown substantially.

3. Service-related consumption habits have shown a momentum of rapid growth, the trend of socializing domestic services has become evident

The per capita expenditure on service-related consumption habits on culture, education, entertainment, leisure, tourism, medical services, healthcare and other aspects was 5639 yuan in 2011, up 47.0% compared with 2006. Regarding service-related consumption, the housekeeping service expenditure grew by 1.2 times compared with 2006, the residential service expenditure grew by 100% compared with 2006, indicating an increasingly evident trend of socializing the domestic services. The expenditure on dining out, medical services, transportation, and on cultural and entertainment services grew by 55.4%, 96.9%, 42.8% and 44.7% compared with 2006, respectively. In 2013, the per capita service-related consumption of Zhejiang's rural residents was 3493 yuan, accounting for 29.7% of their consumption expenditure, suggesting that the mode of rural residents' consumption has gradually changed to a development and enjoyment-oriented one, and the structure of their consumption has been optimized and upgraded continuously.

4. The expenditure of online consumption has grown rapidly, the degree of IT applications has been on the rise

In 2011, every 100 urban households in Zhejiang owned 103.6 computers—every 100 households owned 91.8 home computers based on Internet access; in other words, 88.6% of the home computers had access to the Internet. In 2011, every 100 urban households owned 44.4 mobile phones based on Internet access. With the increasing number of IT applications, online consumption has grown rapidly, and the people can enjoy convenient online shopping at home. The per capita consumption expenditure of Zhejiang's urban residents was 23,257 yuan in 2013, up 7.9% compared with the previous year. The per capita expenditure on online shopping relating to goods and services was 343 yuan, up 48.9% compared with the previous year. In 2013, every 100 rural households in Zhejiang owned 221.6 mobile phones and 49.6 computers, 11 times and 55.7 times that in 2000. In recent years, the IT application-related consumption and online shopping with computer and smartphone as the media have been gradually conducted in rural households, and have become popular among young villagers; the expenditure in online shopping of rural residents has surged, and IT applications in consumption have become one of the highlights in the consumption habits of rural residents regarding their lifestyle.

## 5.3 Social Security and Social Assistance

"Social security is essential for the people and can help the people overcome difficulties"[22]; working better on social security for the people has been the pressing task for the successive collective leadership of Zhejiang Province. This is because social security directly sustains the people's life. It is necessary to affix the social "safety rope" to the people, improve the work on social security, further consolidate the achievements in ensuring that the laid-off personnel from state-owned enterprises receive the basic living subsidy on schedule and that the basic pension for enterprise retirees is provided in full on time; it is necessary to build connections among "three

---

[22]Xi (2013), p. 240.

security lines", expand the coverage of social insurance according to laws, actively promote the building of the "new five-guarantee" system covering both urban and rural areas, including the subsistence allowances, basic endowment insurance for the unemployed workers and unemployment insurance, basic living security for the farmers whose land has been lost, public health development and centralized support of elderly people with no family, and gradually increase the level of social security along with economic development.[23] With the above philosophy, Zhejiang has finished fruitful experiments and practical work in building an extensive social security system, steadily pushing forward social security programs and gradually intensifying social assistance.

### 5.3.1 Building an Extensive Social Security System

In an effort to expand the institutional reform involving social security, Zhejiang has always kept to a main line: promoting social security at the three levels in a coordinated way, including employment, social insurance and social assistance. With respect to the building of an extensive social security system, Zhejiang has made overall arrangements for more rapidly building a coordinated urban-rural employment system, becoming the first to establish a relatively perfect urban social insurance system and to more quickly build a new social assistance system covering both urban and rural areas.[24]

So far, Zhejiang has made significant achievements in building an extensive social security system; the coverage of social security has been expanded continuously, so Zhejiang has further moved towards the goal of making sure that everyone enjoys benefits under the social security system. Zhejiang has become the first nationwide to establish a social security system covering both urban and rural residents. On the one hand, Zhejiang has actively made institutional innovations, introduced the endowment insurance policy in which both insurance contributions and benefits are based on low standards; Zhejiang has promoted work-related injury insurance in an all-round way, and has endeavored to expand the coverage of social security; on the other hand, Zhejiang has adopted the basic line of thought of promoting coordinated urban-rural development, it has speeded up the building of a rural social security system, and Zhejiang has become the first nationwide to establish a coordinated urban-rural subsistence allowances system and the basic living security system for the farmers whose land has been expropriated; moreover, Zhejiang has established the new rural cooperative medical care system, the medical insurance system for urban residents and the social endowment insurance system for urban and rural resi-

---

[23] Xi (2013), p. 241.

[24] The Survey Group of the Provincial and Ministerial Class for Advanced Studies at the Party School of the Central Committee of the CPC, There Is No Harmonious Society If There Is No Social Security – Survey Report on Zhejiang's Accelerated Efforts in Building an Extensive Social Security System, *Zhejiang Today*, 2005(7).

dents, thus, Zhejiang has ushered in an era during which everyone is covered by social security.[25] So far, universal coverage of social security has begun to take shape, the "3+1" medical security system consisting of basic medical insurance for urban workers, basic medical insurance for urban residents, new rural cooperative medical care and a system for urban-rural medical assistance has been basically established and promoted in an orderly way. The coverage of work-related injuries, unemployment and maternity insurances has also been expanded greatly, Zhejiang has proceeded from work-related injury and medical insurances which rural migrant workers need most to gradually put them under the "umbrella" of the social security system. Breakthroughs have been made in new rural cooperative medical care. The new system of rural cooperative medical care has been carried out in all counties (county-level cities, districts) across the province; the proportion of the people covered by the new system of rural cooperative medical care has continued to be higher than 95%. The urban-rural old-age security system has also been basically established, the people below the age of 60 who satisfy the conditions, are covered by it and make contributions to it have accounted for more than 90%.[26] Zhejiang can be considered to have preliminarily established a multilevel social security system which covers both urban and rural areas and is commensurate with the level of economic and social development.

## 5.3.2 Promoting the Development of Social Security Programs

Zhejiang has become the first to push forward the "3+1" medical security system, including basic medical insurance for urban workers, basic medical insurance for urban residents, new rural cooperative medical care and urban-rural medical assistance system[27]; Zhejiang has achieved the basic goal of making sure that medical insurance fully covers urban and rural residents.

Full coverage of endowment insurance has been achieved. In 2008, Zhejiang amended the *Regulations on the Basic Endowment Insurance for Workers* to ensure that the endowment insurance covers the entire society. According to the draft amendment, the workers having established labor relations with enterprises, individual economic organizations and private non-enterprise units and the staff having established labor relations with state organs, public institutions and social groups but not incorporated into the scope of designated staffing are eligible for being covered by insurance as stipulated by laws. Urban individual businesses, flexibly employed personnel and other personnel voluntarily seeking insurance coverage are also incorporated into the scope of insurance coverage.[28]

---

[25]Sun (2011).

[26]Yang (2012).

[27]Yue (2008).

[28]Zhang (2008).

The difficulties in the policy-oriented system of agricultural insurance have been overcome. In 2006, Zhejiang became the first to pilot the policy-oriented system of agricultural insurance. Under the principle of combining government-driven development with market-oriented operations, Zhejiang has adopted the mode of coinsurance operations, and has overcome three difficulties in agricultural security, including building the agricultural risk prevention system, improving the efficiency of disaster relief resource allocation and aligning agricultural subsidies with international rules, which is of great demonstration significance for institutional improvement in the construction of the new socialist countryside.[29]

A provincial-level system of assistance management has been built. In 2004, with the 1st anniversary of the implementation of the *Measures for the Administration of Relief for Vagrants and Beggars without an Assured Living Source* promulgated by the State Council, the first provincial relief management information system in China was put into operation in Zhejiang; the system enables networking and centralized management of 45 stations across the province, real-time updating and storage of information data, it presents information through both pictures and text and is flexible in statistics; it can also perform the functions of access control, automatic early-warning and intelligent searching. The system is designed for the actual operation and management of relief stations in Zhejiang; it digitalizes Zhejiang's relief management and makes great improvements in the internal management of relief stations and the software level of the work on various fronts.[30]

The system of subsistence allowances for farmers has been established. The system incorporates farmers into the scope of security and shows the government's awareness of responsibility and the requirement of functional transformation; it makes sure that both urban and rural farmers enjoy the subsistence allowances; it caters to the needs of coordinated urban-rural development, narrows the income gap between urban and rural areas and among farmers, and it creates the relatively favorable conditions for building a moderately prosperous society in all respects.[31]

The social security system for the farmers whose land has been expropriated has been established and improved. With respect to the basic living security for the farmers whose land has been expropriated, Zhejiang has achieved this goal: Once land has been lost, security must be provided; security is available upon land expropriation. In 2007, 2.91 million farmers whose land had been expropriated were incorporated into the scope of social security, among whom 1.09 million eligible people covered by security received the basic living security benefits or basic endowment insurance benefits on a monthly basis, 31.6 billion yuan in security funds were raised, the farmers whose land had been expropriated and covered by security and the total raised security funds in Zhejiang accounted for 1/3 of the national funds.[32]

---

[29]Hu (2006).

[30]Xu (2004).

[31]Fu (2005).

[32]Zhejiang's Social Security System Has Become Increasingly Perfect, *China Information News*, February 28, 2008, Page 3.

The social security policy for rural migrant workers has been introduced. "Rural migrant workers are important forces for economic development and the building of a harmonious society"[33]; based on this understanding, the successive Party committees and people's governments of Zhejiang Province have stressed that with the increasing level of economic and social development, it is necessary to gradually address the issues concerning full employment of rural migrant workers, their wages, social security, their children's education, medical services, housing, cultural life and political status, and progressively grant permanent urban residency to the eligible rural migrant workers. One of the important tasks lies in gradually opening the social security policy to rural migrant workers, expanding the coverage of rural migrant workers with social insurance and provident funds.[34] Regarding medical services, the local authorities have tried every means to reduce the medical expenses for rural migrant workers, they have issued the "Love Card" to rural migrant workers, and offered medical assistance to them so that they can receive medical services at less cost. With regard to social security, the authorities in some economically developed areas have expanded the coverage of social endowment insurance, and incorporated rural migrant workers into the scope of insurance.[35] With more than 10 years of experiments, the Zhejiang Model of social security for rural migrant workers mainly characterized by "two standards" has taken shape; it proceeds from the actual needs of rural migrant workers to develop types of insurance in the priority order of work-related injury insurance, medical insurance and endowment insurance, supplemented by the reform of the household registration system, employment service and management, producing a good effect.[36]

Furthermore, with the establishment and improvement of social security programs, Zhejiang has continuously, promptly adjusted and increased the social security benefits and levels in various social security programs, established the mechanism for the adjustment of pension benefits, the mechanism involving dynamic adjustment of the standard of subsistence allowances and the level-based subsidy mechanism; Zhejiang has also steadily increased the level of medical security for urban and rural residents, increased the minimum payment limits for medical insurance for urban workers, medical insurance for urban residents and the new rural cooperative medical insurance from 4 times the average wage of local workers, average disposable income of residents and per capita net income of farmers to 6 times.[37]

---

[33] Xi (2013), p. 250.

[34] Xi (2013), p. 252.

[35] Xi (2013), p. 255.

[36] Liu and Chen (2010).

[37] Sun (2011).

### 5.3.3 Intensifying Social Assistance

Social assistance is the most fundamental part of social security. The Party Committee and the People's Government of Zhejiang Province have always attached importance to building up a basic assistance system based on the minimum living security line and covering education, medical services and housing.

**Hierarchical and classified assistance is provided**. With regard to many people in difficulty belonging to the "sandwich layer", Zhejiang has become the first nationwide to adopt the system of hierarchical and classified assistance in response to different degrees of difficulties and assistance needs, so as to improve the new social assistance system. According to the *Circular Concerning Further Improving the New Social Assistance System* issued by the People's Government of Zhejiang Province, the households with an income higher than the subsistence allowances standard but still facing difficulties in life are incorporated into the social assistance system across the province. Local authorities have, based on the level of economic and social development and the capability for security, rationally determined the assistance levels and thus developed assistance standards accordingly, and have provided classified assistance to the people in difficulty according to different circumstances under which poverty and difficulties arise.[38]

**The "threshold" in medical assistance has been gradually removed**. Zhejiang's medical assistance system started in September, 2004; there was a certain threshold in medical assistance during the initial stage; only when the medical expenses for assistance applicants exceeded a certain amount could they apply to the department of civil affairs for assistance. The daily medical expenses of a small amount were not included into the scope of assistance. In 2007, Zhejiang issued the *Circular Concerning Further Improving the Work on Subsistence Allowances and Medical Assistance*, comprehensively introducing the "zero starting point" medical assistance and improving the mechanism for immediate assistance covering various groups in difficulty.[39]

**The households with the per capita net income slightly lower than the minimum living security line have been incorporated into the scope of social assistance**. Zhejiang has stayed ahead nationwide regarding various aspects of social assistance. In July, 2014, the 11th Session of the Standing Committee of the 12th People's Congress of Zhejiang Province deliberated and adopted the *Regulations of Zhejiang Province on Social Assistance*, incorporating the households with a per capita net income slightly lower than the minimum living security line into the scope of social assistance for the first time, so as to reflect the principle of hierarchical and classified assistance and weaken the Cliff Effect. According to the regulations, the households not incorporated into the scope of subsistence allowances and with the per capita monthly income of household members below 1.5 times the standard subsistence allowances and whose property conditions comply with the regulations of the governments above the county level are identified as the households with the

---

[38]Jiang (2006).
[39]Liu (2007).

per capita net income slightly lower than the minimum living security line which are eligible for enjoying assistance. Moreover, the regulations also extended medical assistance to the personnel from the households whose actual living standard is lower than the standard for households at levels slightly lower than the local subsistence allowances because the self-paid portion in excess of the specified medical expenses for serious diseases exceeds the bearing capability of households; under the regulations, educational assistance covers the stages from preschool education to higher education, and basic living assistance is provided to the households which suffer expenditure-induced poverty for special causes, including serious diseases.[40]

**The rule of law has been continuously promoted in the development of a program relating to the handicapped**. The successive collective leadership of Zhejiang Province has taken developing the programs for the handicapped as the glorious mission of the Party committees and governments at various levels and the bounden duty of the whole society; the successive collective leadership of Zhejiang Province has attached great importance to the programs for the handicapped and has taken the implementation of the *Law of the People's Republic of China on Safeguarding the Handicapped* as an important part of efforts in governing the country under the rule of law, institutionalizing and standardizing the programs for the handicapped and promoting the programs for the handicapped under the rule of law, and moving towards the goal, set by the Party Committee and the People's Government of Zhejiang Province, of synchronizing the development of the programs for the handicapped with economic and social development in Zhejiang Province and making Zhejiang Province stay ahead nationwide.[41] According to the household survey conducted by the Zhejiang Provincial Disabled Persons' Federation and the Zhejiang Provincial Bureau of Statistics in 2013, the degree of making the handicapped become well-off was 88.6%, the degree of making the handicapped become well-off in survival, development and environment was 97.8%, 81.8% and 80.0%, respectively; the survival environment for and developmental conditions of the handicapped improved continuously, and steady progress was made in achieving the goal of being well-off in Zhejiang in 2013.

## 5.4 Social Welfare and Social Charity

The development of the social welfare and social charity programs is the main means for effectively supplementing institutional social security; it is of great significance for meeting the basic living needs of the people in difficulty, and practically overcoming the difficulties, in production and life, for those people, including laid-off workers and the poor rural population.

---

[40] Wang and Xu (2014).
[41] Xi (2013), p. 245.

### 5.4.1 Building a Social Welfare System Focusing on the Elderly People

Zhejiang has endeavored to develop social welfare programs in an all-round way on the one hand and has focused social welfare programs on particular aspects in light of the society's realty on the other hand. Against the general background of population ageing, emphasis has been placed on developing the welfare for the elderly people in the near term, including improving the system of home-based elderly care services, enhancing the communities' care function and ameliorating the mechanism of socialized services. Zhejiang has really made sure that public welfare institutions meet the needs of the rural people enjoying five guarantees and the urban people without identification papers, normal residence permits, and sources of income, the needs involving support of the elderly people in difficulty and centralized support of the people with severe disabilities; Zhejiang has encouraged and supported social forces to run old-age care service institutions.[42] Over the years, Zhejiang has carried out the cataract-related sight rehabilitating project for the elderly people enjoying five guarantees in rural areas and the elderly people without identification papers, normal residence permits, and a source of income in urban areas as well as the elderly people from households supported by subsistence allowances in urban and rural areas, the project for renovating the dilapidated and old houses of rural households supported by subsistence allowances and the rural Starlight Program for Old-age Welfare Service. Zhejiang has established a mechanism for the participation of non-governmental organizations in services, and has gradually built a new social welfare system covering both urban and rural areas and benefiting the external population.[43] As of late 2012, the coverage of primary-level sports and fitness facilities had reached 85% in Zhejiang; there were 225 provincial elderly sports activity centers (clubs); the elderly cultural activity venues were built in an all-round way; as of June, 2013, there were 100 rural cultural auditoriums; the development of elderly-friendly cities and the communities livable for the elderly was accelerated; the development of old-age care institutions was strengthened continuously; as of the first half of 2013, there were 964 private old-age care institutions and 66 nursing-oriented old-age care institutions; the number of private old-age care institutions increased by 32.8% compared with 2010; there were 258,000 old-age care beds, up 29.8% compared with 2010; the needs of the elderly people for institutional care had basically been met.

---

[42]The Party Committee of Zhejiang Province: The Decision of the Party Committee of Zhejiang Province on Comprehensively Improving the People's Well-being and Promoting Social Harmony, *Zhengce Liaowang*, 2008(5).

[43]Ke and Ye (2006).

## 5.4.2 Building an Appropriately Universal New Social Welfare System

Thanks to a strong economic foundation, Zhejiang has gradually developed a social welfare system from the one aimed at meeting the basic living needs to an appropriately universal one. Initially, Zhejiang's social welfare programs gave top priority to meeting the basic living needs of the people in difficulty and offered the last safety net for those people in urban and rural areas. With all-round economic and social development, at the beginning of the 21st century, Zhejiang became the first nationwide to build a new coordinated urban-rural social welfare system. The system starts with addressing the most pressing issues of the greatest concern to the people and has gradually become a new social welfare system which is integrated between urban and rural areas, features a network-based organization, socialized management and provision of security under the rule of law and is commensurate with the level of economic and social development and it also covers urban and rural areas.[44]

In this process, Zhejiang has constantly expanded community welfare services and enhanced the community service function. As of late 2008, there were more than 20,000 community workers, 13,000 community volunteer service organizations, 110,000 community service facilities and outlets and 2613 rural community service centers across the province.[45] In March, 2013, Zhejiang issued the *Circular of Zhejiang Province Concerning the Implementation Plan for Piloting the Establishment of the Universal Children's Welfare System*, identifying Wenzhou City (Cangnan County), Haining City and Jiangshan City as the areas for piloting an appropriately universal children's welfare system in the province.

## 5.4.3 Developing the Mid-and-Long-Term Social Welfare Developmental Plan

How to develop the social welfare programs on a step-by-step basis in a planned and methodical way is an important issue considered by the successive collective leadership of Zhejiang Province. According to the overall requirement of the Party Committee and the People's Government of Zhejiang Province for "Carrying out Concrete Work to Stay Ahead", with long-term explorations, discussions and pilot work, Zhejiang developed and issued the *Plan of Zhejiang Province for Social Welfare Development (2006–2010)* in 2005; this was the first five-year social welfare plan in China. Zhejiang has become the first nationwide to start the practice of building a new social welfare system with Chinese characteristics, era characteristics and Zhejiang's characteristics.

---

[44] Wang and Yan (2009).
[45] Wang and Yan (2009).

The plan presents long-term and short-term goals. The long-term goal consists in building a well-functioning social welfare system, with well-defined duties, encompassing old-age care, medical services, health, education, housing and other aspects, covering all members of the society. The short-term goal lies in exploring and building a new social welfare system which is led by the government and features departmental cooperation and social participation and mainly serves the elderly people, the handicapped and orphans, covers urban and rural areas and benefits migrant workers.

### 5.4.4 Advocating Popular Social Charity

The successive leaders of Zhejiang Province have attached importance to advocating and spreading charity culture, and have taken developing popular social charity as the government's pursuit. During each one of Zhejiang's Charity Conferences, they stressed that charity was a popular cause, it was an important sign of civic-mindedness and social harmony, it was an important embodiment of the socialist concept of honor and disgrace, and it was necessary to widely popularize the charity culture, carry forward the charity spirit, publicize charity models, arouse the enthusiasm of the people from various sectors of the society about participation in charity, foster a strong atmosphere in which everyone supports and participates in charity in the whole society and make due contributions to jointly building a harmonious socialist society.[46] The Party committees and governments at various levels and relevant departments have been required to practically strengthen, organize and lead relevant work, incorporate the development of charity into an economic and social plan for development and a working plan.

With guidance and impetus from this thought, charitable organizations have shown a good momentum of development, charitable activities and services have become increasingly active, more and more citizens and enterprises have participated in charitable donations in Zhejiang, Zhejiang has continued to stay ahead nationwide in the level of charity and has become one of the areas with the fastest charity development in China. First, charitable organizations have developed rapidly. Various types of charitable organizations, including chariy federations and red cross societies, have been established in all of the 101 cities, counties (county-level cities, districts) across the province, 4530 charity branches (workstations) and 261 enterprise branches have been set up in towns (subdistricts) and villages (communities), thus a charity network which involves a number of charitable fields, covers urban and rural areas and is rich in content has basically formed. Second, the work on charity fundraising has been promoted concretely. Subject to an economic downturn and great difficulties for enterprises, the network of charity federations across the province raised 2.15 billion yuan in 2012, up 7% compared with the previous year; the scale of the issued welfare lotteries across the province exceeded 10 billion yuan for the first time, raising 3.01 billion yuan in public welfare funds. The network of charity federations

---

[46]Zhou (2006).

across the province alone raised a total of 15.44 billion over the years, the scale of funds named after donors and with a principal retained reached 10.4 billion yuan, and various types of charitable organizations across the province raised more than 12.6 billion yuan in three years. Third, a number of brand charity programs have been developed. The charitable organizations across the province have, with great passion, explored and innovated various types of charity programs, Zhejiang has put charity donation and charity assistance under program-based operations, a number of representative and innovative excellent charity programs—including the Pick Up Pearls Program, the Charity New Year's Eve Dinner, the 1000-Village Charitable Fund, the Clear Eye Loving Care Program—have taken shape, better meeting the needs of the people from various sectors of the society for participating in charities. Fourth, the charity culture has been further spread. There are nearly 4 million registered volunteers across the province, they have taken actions to publicize the charity culture and convey the positive energy of a loving heart. In Zhejiang, the philosophy of charity has been deeply rooted among the people, the charitable activities have been carried out more widely, and the good stories of charity have been further spread throughout the society.

### 5.4.5 Promoting Professional and Standardized Development of Charity

Zhejiang has taken the lead nationwide in charity, while Zhejiang has also made down-to-earth experiments in making charitable work professional and standardized; Zhejiang started from scratch to pursue constant development in this regard through continuous innovations, thus making great achievements. When the Zhejiang Provincial Charity Federation was established in 1994, fundraising was promoted by the government; later, Zhejiang became the first to introduce funds under professional operations named after donors and with large-sum principals retained; so far, the Charity New Year's Eve Dinner under market-oriented operations, the most influential charity brand in China, was developed in Zhejiang; Zhejiang has incessantly advanced in promoting charity in a professional way. Zhejiang has been at the forefront nationwide in the overall level of charity development, the charity culture has been deeply rooted in the heart of the people, the charitable network has covered rural areas, and Zhejiang has preliminarily accomplished the leap from support-based development to self-development.[47]

For a long time, the leaders of Party committees and governments at various levels across the province have paid a great amount of attention to the charitable work; developing charity has been incorporated into the plan for economic and social development and taken as a significant way to doing substantive work for the people. Zhejiang has always regarded public credibility as the lifeline of charity, and Zhejiang has gradually established a well-functioning internal self-discipline mechanism and

---

[47] Wang (2009).

operating mechanism covering survey, planning, publicity, fundraising, assistance, evaluation and commendation; Zhejiang has introduced the systems involving the appointment of legal advisors, annual auditing and disclosure of management information, and it has established a feedback mechanism to implement the philosophy of "governing charity federations under the rule of law and practicing charity according to laws" in the work on various fronts.

## 5.5 The Improvement of the People's Well-Being and Economic Growth

"Both successfully solving the problems in economic development and addressing the issues relating to the people's well-being are officials' achievements",[48] this is a plain explanation made by the collective leadership of Zhejiang Province about the relations between economic development and the people's well-being. Therefore, Zhejiang has always understood the connotation of the building of a moderately prosperous society in all respects from the following six perspectives: a stronger economy, greater democracy, more advanced science and education, more prosperous culture, greater social harmony, and a better quality of life. Zhejiang has evaluated its officials' achievements from the perspective of the Party's commitment to serving the public good and exercising power in the interests of the people; Zhejiang has better combined promoting development with valuing the people's well-being. In governance, Zhejiang has placed equal emphasis on both income growth and social growth, both social policy and economic policy, and has ensured that the incremental financial resources are first allocated for improving the people's well-being.

### 5.5.1 Placing Equal Emphasis on Both Income Growth and Economic Growth

Economic growth is an important prerequisite for social development, but economic growth is merely the yardstick for measuring production, it neither fully mirrors the society's reality nor really reflects the actual living standard. Economic growth will not necessarily result in the improvement of the people's living standard.[49]

The successive collective leadership of Zhejiang Province has a clear understanding of this regard, so Zhejiang has always paid equal attention to both economic development and the increase in the people's income, sought the common development of the economy and society and it has endeavored to make the province strong and the people rich side by side; Zhejiang has also shifted more focus to making the people rich, so that the building of a strong province is promoted by making the

---

[48] Xi (2013), p. 30.
[49] Yang (2008).

people get rich, and the effect of making the people become rich is guaranteed by building a strong province. Therefore, as the economy has grown rapidly in Zhejiang, the people's income has basically increased at the same time; in particular, the income of urban residents has grown. For instance, during the period of the 10th Five-Year Plan, Zhejiang's per capita GDP grew annually by an average of 11.7%, while the income of urban residents increased annually by an average of 11.3%, basically equivalent to the economic growth rate.[50] In 2013, Zhejiang's per capita GDP grew by 7.9% compared with the previous year, while the per capita disposable income of urban residents and the per capita net income of rural residents grew by 9.6% and 10.7% compared with the previous year, the growth rate of incomes exceeded the economic growth rate.

## 5.5.2  Placing Equal Emphasis on Both Social Policy and Economic Policy

Social policy is the general term for the code of conduct, measures, decrees and regulations made mainly through state legislation and administrative intervention and aimed at solving social problems, ensuring public order, improving the social environment and enhancing social welfare; it is an institutional arrangement for ensuring that the entire population lives safely, improving the living standard and promoting social fairness.[51] As one of the coastal developed provinces for first-ever implementation of pilot programs in the economic field, Zhejiang has started to consider the concurrent introduction of a social policy after a period of rapid economic development. Since the beginning of the new century, under the leadership and support of the successive Party committees and people's governments of Zhejiang Province, Zhejiang has attached greater importance to achieving coordination between economic policy and social policy, and has valued the important role of social policy in improving residents' life and living standard; Zhejiang has given social policy a corresponding space and status, and has taken developing complete social policy and resolving social contradictions in economic development as an important effort for improving the capacity for governance of the Party and the government.[52] With the promulgation of the *Measures of Zhejiang Province for Subsistence Allowances* in 2001, Zhejiang started to be in the lead nationwide in policy innovation and developmental goal. This innovation to social policy broke the long-standing line of thought of urban-rural duality, and comprehensively introduced the subsistence allowances to urban and rural poor population, making Zhejiang the first nationwide to carry out the coordinated system of urban-rural subsistence allowances. In order to promote scientific development and social harmony, in 2004, the Party Committee of Zhejiang Province made the strategic decision of building a safe Zhejiang, pro-

---

[50] Yang (2008).

[51] Yang (2008).

[52] Yang (2008).

viding systematic arrangements for social development for the first time. In 2006, Zhejiang developed the first relatively complete 11th Five-Year Provincial Plan for Social Development, thus the development of Zhejiang's system of social policies entered the stage of overall planning and holistic promotion with clear goals. The *11th Five-Year Plan of Zhejiang Province for the Development of an Extensive Social Security System*, unveiled in 2007, presented the overall plan for employment, social insurance, social assistance and social welfare. In 2008, Zhejiang adopted the *Decision on Comprehensively Improving the People's Well-being and Promoting Social Harmony*, calling for following the requirement of establishing and improving the public financial system to further adjust and optimize the structure of fiscal expenditures and increase fiscal input in the field of the people's well-being. In September, 2008, Zhejiang became the first nationwide to develop and unveil the Action Plan for Ensuring Equal Access to Basic Public Services, arranging ten major projects involving employment promotion, social security, educational equality, Health for All and social welfare, and incorporating their implementation into the evaluation against annual targets and responsibilities of local governments and the evaluation of the achievements of leading groups and cadres. In May, 2009, the Party Committee of Zhejiang Province adopted the *Decision on Intensifying the Reform and Opening-Up and Promoting Scientific Development*, identifying "benefiting the people's well-being" and "guaranteeing growth" as two ways for Zhejiang to cope with the global financial crisis, and calling for focusing on improving the people's well-being in an all-round way to push forward the institutional reforms in education, employment, distribution, medical services and healthcare, social security and social management, and promoting equal access to basic public services. In the meantime, Zhejiang has actively responded to the requirement of the Central Government for piloting the new medical reform and the new rural social endowment insurance, and has more rapidly promoted innovations to the coordinated urban-rural social policy, thus making significant achievements in the development of the system of social policies.[53]

### 5.5.3  Making Sure that the Incremental Financial Resources are First Allocated for Improving the People's Well-Being

In parallel to the introduction and improvement of social policies, Zhejiang has also increased fiscal input in the field of people's well-being, with a rising proportion of annual incremental financial resources allocated to improve the people's well-being. During the period 2003–2007, in order to establish an extensive social security system covering both urban and rural areas, Zhejiang earmarked 70.3% of the annual incremental financial resources to improving the people's well-being by utilizing them in the fields of medical services, education, urban and rural employment and

---

[53]He (2012).

social security, so that the people can obtain more benefits from development.[54] The proportion of the expenditure on the people's well-being in Zhejiang's total fiscal expenditure of the current year increased from 64.3% in 2003 to 67.8% in 2007, while that in the incremental fiscal expenditure increased from 67.1% in 2003 to 70.3% in 2007. The fiscal expenditure on the people's well-being made up an increasing proportion, and more than 2/3 of the incremental financial resources were used to improve the people's well-being, marking a substantive change of Zhejiang's finance to the finance focusing on the people's well-being.

Since the beginning of the 21st century, Zhejiang has intensified fiscal support for social security. In 2013, Zhejiang's public financial budget expenditure was 473.1 billion yuan, with the key expenditure accounting for more than 70%; the expenditure on housing security, that on social security and employment, that on medical services and healthcare, that on culture, sports and media, that on public security, that on education and that on urban and rural communities grew by 25%, 14.9%, 14.7%, 12.6%, 9%, 8.2% and 8.2%, respectively. The number of the people covered by basic endowment insurance for enterprise workers, unemployment insurance, work-related injury insurance and maternity insurance increased by 1,892,000, 788,000, 944,000 and 883,000 respectively at the end of this year compared with the end of the previous year; there were 41,205,000 people covered by basic medical insurance, among whom 17,905,000 people were covered by medical insurance for urban workers, and both figures increased by 1,615,000 and 1,195,000 compared with the end of the previous year; there were 13,558,000 urban and rural residents covered by endowment insurance. Construction of government-subsidized housing was accelerated; in urban areas, new construction began with respect to 194,000 units of government-subsidized housing, while 111,000 units of government-subsidized housing were completed across the province.

# References

Wang Chengming, Yan Yongzhou, Building a New Social Welfare System, *Zhejiang Daily*, September 25, 2009, Page 2.
Wang Chun, Xu Yinghua, The Households with a Per Capita Net Income Slightly Lower Than the Minimum Living Security Line Are Incorporated into the Scope of Social Assistance for the First Time, *Legal Daily*, August 6, 2014, Page 3.
Chen Da, Zhejiang: Building a Rural Social Security System in Ten Years, *China Financial and Economic News*, June 4, 2005, Page 1.
Yue Deliang, Zhejiang: "3+1" Promotes Full Coverage of the Urban-Rural Resident Medical Security, *Chinese Society News*, September 12, 2008, Page 1.
Ye Hui, Putting the Improvement of the People's Well-being in a More Prominent Position, *Guang Ming Daily*, March 3, 2008, Page 6.
Xi Jinping, *Zhijiang Xinyu*, Zhejiang People's Publishing House, 2013.
Su Jing, Zhejiang Initiated the First Action Plan for Ensuring Equal Access to Basic Public Services in China, *Zhejiang Daily*, July 13, 2008, Page 1.

---

[54]Zhang (2008).

Xi Jinping, *Carrying out Solid Work to Stay Ahead – Line of Thought and Practice in Promoting New Development in Zhejiang*, The Party School of the CPC Central Committee Press, 2013.

Yang Jianhua, From a Safe Zhejiang to a Harmonious Zhejiang, *Zhejiang Today*, May 24, 2012, Page 4.

Yang Jianhua, Zhejiang's Practice in the Improvement of the People's Well-being in 30 Years of Reform and Opening-Up and Inspirations, *Journal of Zhejiang Party School of C.P.C*, 2008(6).

Zhang Le, More Than 70% of Zhejiang's Incremental Financial Resources Were Used to Improve the People's Well-being in the Past Five Years, *China Society News*, January 21, 2008, Page 1.

Liu Mingzhong, Removing the "Threshold" in Medical Assistance, *China Financial and Economic News*, August 2, 2007, Page 2.

Jiang Nan, Zhejiang Practices the Hierarchical and Classified Assistance, *People's Daily*. May 9, 2006, Page 10.

Zhang Ran, Zhejiang Makes a Legislative Amendment to Ensure Full Coverage of Endowment Insurance, *China Labor Security News*, April 10, 2008, Page 2.

Sun Shengmei, The Effectiveness of Zhejiang's Social Security System in Recent Years, Its Problems and Suggestions for Improvement, *Statistical Science and Practice*, 2011(7).

Liu Tianxi, Xia Xue, The Course of Evolution of Zhejiang's Policy of the People's Well-being since the Reform and Opening-Up, *Journal of Zhejiang Sci-Tech University*, 2012(2).

Zhong Wen, Xie Fangwen, From Zhejiang to Shanghai, Xi Jinping Always Pursued Substantive Achievements in the People's Well-being, *China Business News*, May 24, 2007, Page A4.

Liu Xiaoqing, Chen Guoqiang, More Rapidly Building a Social Assistance System with Zhejiang's Characteristics, *Zhengce Liaowang*, 2007(2).

Ke Xiaohan, Ye Hengshan, The Development of Zhejiang's Welfare System Focuses on the Elderly People, *China Old Man News*, February 23, 2006, Page 1.

Xu Yu, Zhejiang Establishes the First Provincial Assistance Management System in China, *China Social Welfare*, 2004(8).

Wang Yong, Zhejiang's Efforts in Charity for 15 Years Have Delivered Fruitful Outcomes, *The Chinese People's Political Consultative Conference News*, December 1, 2009, Page B01.

Zhou Yongnan, Making Concerted Efforts to Develop Charity, Working with One Mind to Build a Harmonious Society, *Zhejiang Daily*, December 13, 2006, Page 1.

Liu Zhijun, Chen Jiansheng, The Practice in the Assistance Management System and Social Response – Take Three Prefecture-level Cities in Zhejiang Province as an Example, *Journal of South-Central University for Nationalities* (Humanities and Social Sciences Edition), 2011(4).

Fu Zhiguo, A Survey on Zhejiang's Subsistence Allowances System for Farmers, *Farmers' Daily*, September 17, 2005, Page 3.

Liu Zhijun, Chen Jiaojiao, From "Duality" to "Two Low Standards": An Analysis of the Zhejiang Model for Social Security for Rural Migrant Workers, *Journal of South-Central University for Nationalities* (Humanities and Social Sciences Edition), 2010(3).

He Ziying, The Development of the Coordinated Urban-Rural Social Policy System – A Study of Zhejiang's Practice during the Period of the 11th Five-Year Plan, *Comparative Economic & Social Systems*, 2012(4).

Hu Zuohua, Zhejiang Overcomes the Security Difficulties in Policy-oriented Agricultural Insurance, *Economic Information Daily*, March 25, 2006, Page 2.

# Chapter 6
# Primary-Level Social Governance

**Youxing Lang**

Social governance refers to the process and mechanism in which, based on community identity, multiple players, including the Party, the government, residents and community-level social organizations, coordinate interest relations, provide excellent public services, work together to handle public affairs to achieve primary-level sustainable social development. In primary-level governance, the governing actors become diverse, the top-down administrative control is changed to a two-way interactive consultation from top to down and from down to top, and the vertical bureaucratic structure is changed to the horizontal grid structure.

Zhejiang made early innovative experiments in the primary-level social governance system and has acquired much experience. This experience is mainly embodied in social order, grid-based management and group-based service, primary-level democratic governance and community development. Social order is key and fundamental to primary-level social governance. In this regard, Zhejiang has made painstaking efforts to gain extensive experience. The grid-based management is a new means to innovate the primary-level social governance system, while the group-based service shifts the focus of primary-level social governance from management to service, and injects rich and concrete content into the building of a service-oriented government. Primary-level democracy is an effective mechanism for promoting primary-level social governance and also represents the main direction for future development. The most basic and important space for primary-level governance is the community, thus the community is the cornerstone for primary-level governance and the whole social governance system. The experiments made and the experience accumulated by Zhejiang, a forerunner in this regard, can serve as a reference for other areas.

Y. Lang (✉)
Zhejiang University, Hangzhou, China

© Social Sciences Academic Press and Springer Nature Singapore Pte Ltd. 2019    165
G. Chen and J. Yang (eds.), *Chinese Dream and Practice in Zhejiang—Society*,
Research Series on the Chinese Dream and China's Development Path,
https://doi.org/10.1007/978-981-13-7406-7_6

## 6.1 From the Fengqiao Experience to a Combination of the Rule of Virtue, the Rule of Law and Self-governance

For a modern country, primary-level governance is an important part of the national governance system. The building of a harmonious society focuses on the primary level. As mentioned by comrade Xi Jinping, the priority of governance lies in the primary level, work should place more emphasis on the primary level and loving care should be conveyed to the primary level.[1] The primary level is the cell of the society and is fundamental to building a harmonious society. Therefore, it is necessary to consolidate the frontline platform at the primary level for safeguarding social stability, better coordinate interest relations, rationalize thinking, mitigate social contradictions, resolve the destabilizing factors at the primary level and nip them in the bud. The Fengqiao Experience is a typical type of experience in resolving the primary-level social contradictions and coordinating interest relations. In the early 1960s, during the socialist educational campaign, the cadres and people in Fengqiao, Zhuji City, Zhejiang Province created a mode of relying on and mobilizing the people to properly address contradictions at the primary and local level, making sure that the number of people arrested became small and that public security was good, thus small matters were handled within villages, large matters were handled within the town, contradictions were not escalated to higher authorities and were resolved at the local level. Comrade Mao Zedong made written instructions to call on local authorities to draw upon Fengqiao's mode, make trials and widely promote it, so the Fengqiao Experience took shape.[2] However, it is necessary to keep the Fengqiao Experience in line with the times. Comrade Xi Jinping opportunely pointed out that it was necessary to foster a new outlook on stability,[3] and stressed that safeguarding social harmony and stability was also the achievement of the officials,[4] and that being peaceful and harmonious was essential to scientific development,[5] and he required the whole province to stay ahead in building a harmonious socialist society.[6] In recent years, Zhejiang has always upheld and developed the Fengqiao Experience; based on putting the people first, resolving contradictions and promoting development, Zhejiang has created a new experience of relying on primary-level organizations, integrating forces and resources to resolve contradictions at the local level, ensuring the well-being and security of the people; Zhejiang has built a new mechanism of making joint and coordinated efforts to improve public order, resolve contradictions, solve problems, handle matters and guarantee security; Zhejiang has also created a new pattern of arousing the initiative of the Party and the government, relying on

---

[1] Xi (2006), p. 432.
[2] Xi (2014).
[3] Xi (2013), p. 46.
[4] Xi (2013), p. 50.
[5] Xi (2013), p. 46.
[6] Xi (2006), p. 65.

the people, taking preventative measures at the source and governing under the rule of law to reduce contradictions and promote harmony, thus giving rise to a number of effective mechanisms and methods for resolving primary-level contradictions.[7] Afterwards, local authorities in Zhejiang drew upon the Fengqiao Experience and thus innovatively developed new experiences or modes in light of the local reality. The representative one is the new governance mode of integrating the rule of virtue, the rule of law and the self-governance adopted in Tongxiang City.

### 6.1.1 Establishing and Improving the Systems and Mechanisms for Resolving Contradictions

1. Creating a diversified pattern of extensive mediation

Zhejiang has stepped up efforts in early warning, identification, joint mediation and handling of contradictions and disputes, and has promoted routine management for identifying and resolving contradictions and disputes; Zhejiang has built a diversified pattern of extensive mediation which integrates the people's mediation, administrative mediation and judicial mediation. Zhejiang has developed professional and industrial mediation organizations, guided the people's mediation organizations, expert consultant committees, intermediary organizations, industry associations and other social forces to participate in the mediation of contradictions and disputes, Zhejiang has supported the development of the non-governmental mediation forces and "safety volunteers", and has established a crisscross, interconnected extensive system of the fusion of mediation which contains diverse players and means and is based on the adoption of legal, policy, economic and administrative means as well as integrating education, consultation and counseling. Zhejiang has strictly put into practice the systems involving the identification, mediation and handling of contradictions and disputes, Zhejiang has improved the mediation platforms at the county, town and village levels to solve problems at the primary and local level and nip them in the bud.

2. Deeply prompting the leading cadres to visit the primary-level units and receive the people who lodge complaints, carrying out mass work to lead the work on complaint-related letters and visits

The complaint-related letters and visits serve as important channels through which the people can express interest appeals. Comrade Xi Jinping pointed out, "Leaders should proactively visit the people so that the people do not need to lodge complaints to higher authorities; this is the fine tradition and style of our party, this is also the bounden duty of each leading cadre, all of the leading cadres at various levels are the servants of the people", and "the primary-level cadres should do a better job at the first post relating to the complaint-related letters and visits".[8] Since 2003,

---

[7]Zhao (2011).
[8]Xi (2013), p. 78.

Zhejiang has taken "urging the leading cadres to visit the primary-level units and receive the people who lodge complaints" as an important way to strengthen the work on the complaint-related letters and visits under the new situation; Zhejiang has incorporated this into the overall plans for economic and social development, into the important part of building a safe Zhejiang and into the long-term mechanism of the work on the complaint-related letters and visits, and has extended the work on the complaint-related letters and visits to the regular mass work.

3. Establishing and improving the mechanisms involving scientific decision-making and the assessment of social stability risks in great events

Zhejiang has continuously improved the systems concerning the survey, study and collective decision-making in great events, as well as expert consulting, public disclosure and solicitation of public opinions in major policies; Zhejiang has gradually improved the decision-making procedures to take into full account the people's interests and opinions and ensure democratic and law-based decision-making. In the key and sensitive fields vulnerable to social contradictions, including land expropriation, house demolition and relocation, environmental protection, project construction, law enforcement and judicature, it is necessary to fully consider possible social risks, environmental impacts, contradictions, disputes and destabilizing factors before major policies and measures are developed, and before major projects are approved and initiated; and it is necessary to follow the principle that "whosoever takes charge of the matter is responsible for it and whosoever makes decisions is responsible for them" to implement the evaluation, supervision, reverse investigation and accountability mechanism for social stability risks, and make sure that evaluation is fully, truly conducted where necessary. For the matters not understood and supported by most people, policies should be postponed or not be introduced, so as to prevent improper decision-making from causing social contradictions.

4. Building and improving an integrated information system for primary-level social management

Promoting IT applications and grid-based development is an effective way to achieve meticulous and substantive governance at the source. Based on the integrated information system for primary-level social management, Zhejiang has leveraged dense grids and grid information personnel to establish and improve the working mechanisms involving information collection, reporting on social conditions and public opinion and positioning management services. The "Zongzhi e Tong" mobile terminal has been promoted and applied throughout the province, while grid personnel can use this mobile terminal to pay a visit and make a record and report and record information, take pictures and upload them at any time, enable real-time collection and dynamic entry of the information on the people, places, matters, objects and organizations, discover problems at the earliest, deliver information to resolve contradictions and provide services, thus the information on the primary-level frontline can be accurately obtained on a real-time basis. In the meantime, Zhejiang has further strengthened the practical operation of the integrated information system for primary-level social management, so that grid personnel can promptly discover and report various kinds of information, relevant departments can promptly and quickly handle matters, resolve contradictions, solve problems, and respond to the people's appeals.

5. Carrying out the governance mode which integrates the rule of virtue, the rule of law and self-governance

It is necessary to combine the rule of law with the rule of virtue because only when laws are supported by virtue can they have an extensive social foundation to become good laws for sustaining good governance.[9] The rule of virtue is the foundation, while the rule of law serves as the guarantee and self-governance is the goal. These three elements complement and support each other, and they must be promoted in a coordinated way. In an era of a market economy, the rule of law and the rule of virtue constitute the order of life and play respective roles. Self-governance means that, subject to governance socialization led by the Party committee and the government, the people exercise self-management according to the daily norms, consisting of the rule of law and the rule of virtue under the normal, the members of the society are integrated and united to achieve a social identity. Tongxiang City has drawn upon and innovated the Fengqiao Experience to carry out social governance based on the rule of law, the rule of virtue and self-governance, establish a group of public participation in government and political affairs, a group for moral judgment and the service group for addressing diverse issues; as a result, the people work together to deal with important matters, judgment is made by everyone, and every matter is under management.

### 6.1.2  The Grid-Based Management and Group-Based Service in Zhoushan

As from the second half of 2007, the reform involving grid-based management and group-based service was piloted in Taohua Town and Goushan Subdistrict in Putuo District, Zhoushan City. Based on significant achievements from the pilot reform, it was promoted throughout Zhoushan City in August, 2008. In August, 2009, grid-based management was promoted throughout the province, and marked effects were produced in different areas.

Grid-based management and group-based service means that, under the condition that the administrative division of towns (sub-districts) and communities (villages) is unchanged, towns (sub-districts) are divided into a number of unit grids, various types of service resources at the primary level are integrated, a corresponding group of management services is established for each grid, the information management service platform is relied upon to offer active, efficient and targeted services

---

[9]Xi (2013), p. 206.

for the residents within the areas and to increase the level of primary-level social governance under the Party's leadership. Its experience mainly covers the following several aspects.[10]

1. Subdividing the network of primary-level social governance services, achieving full coverage

Under the principle of respecting the tradition, focusing on development, facilitating service provision and management, Zhoushan has divided 35 towns (sub-districts) throughout the city into 2395 management service grids by considering the scope of communities, the characteristics of village distribution, the size of the population, the degree of residential concentration, the people's habits in production and life, with 100–150 households as a unit in fishing and rural areas and 200–250 households as a unit in urban areas. In the areas in which the migrant population, the merchants and fishing boats are concentrated, new resident grids, merchant grids, offshore grids and other characteristic grids are rationally arranged to really turn the structure of the management service from a strip into a network. Each grid is provided with a fixed management service group for ensuring that every inch of land is under management and every task is carried out, thus a vertical and horizontal system for management services encompassing five levels including city, county (district), town (sub-district), community (village) and grid and covering both urban and rural areas is really built.

2. Improving the system of management services, building a group-based connection

In Zhoushan, grid service groups—with the cadres of towns (sub-districts) and communities (villages), local police and the leaders of Party groups as the backbone and consisting of Party representatives, deputies to the people's congress and CPPCC members, police, doctors, teachers, senior Party members in fishing and rural areas, veteran cadres, Party members engaging with particular households, volunteers—are established, group members are optimized and mixed according to their duties, expertise and characteristics, grid service groups take the form of routine service groups and professional service groups to provide the people within the grids with full services. In the meantime, the campaign of integrating departments into grids is carried out in a thorough and complete way, the working forces and resources of departments are fully mobilized to participate in grid service groups, assist the primary-level cadres in visiting households to conduct policy consulting, perform technical services, resolve contradictions, help the poor people and overcome difficulties, thus further broadening the connotation of serving the people. The system of stimulating the primary-level cadres to serve communities is actively implemented so that the cadres of state organs take the initiative to hold the grid service posts in communities, further enriching grid service groups. Experiments are made to set up the leader of the comprehensive governance group in each grid, cultivate such comprehensive

---

[10]Gong (2012).

governance volunteers as security-focused building keepers and shopkeepers among residents, at markets, business outlets and within units, and choose the personnel from them to serve as grid information personnel, grid security personnel, grid mediator and grid publicity personnel, who work with other service groups to carry out joint construction and management, enabling interaction and integration in services, and forming joint forces in work.

3.   Integrating management service resources to provide diverse services

Based on grid subdivision, Zhoushan has pioneered in the system of responsibility contracting for mass work—each management service group is responsible for management, service, education and improvement within its assigned grid, and has established the working rules for the grid-based management and group-based service, promoted 9 methods and 36 tips in the primary-level mass work; theme services are launched in each quarter, the service content is regularly determined, tasks are assigned to service groups, so that group members take actions according to their targets and in light of problems, and can receive feedback after actions are taken. In the meantime, contact cards are issued, relevant service personnel stay at households, and on-the-spot meetings are held to extensively collect opinions and suggestions from the people about entrepreneurship, children's education, medical security and family life. For the problems that are easy to solve, service groups make a reply on the spot; for the problems which are difficult to solve, information is delivered through the information platform to the higher authorities for a reply.

4.   Building an information service platform to exercise efficient management

Zhoushan has developed an integrated and shared information management system for grid-based management and group-based service, extending the information network to counties (districts), towns (sub-districts) and communities (villages); Zhoushan has also set up service management stations for grid information systems in towns (sub-districts) and communities (villages), which are provided with full-time information personnel for managing and maintaining the information platform, entering information and addressing feedback issues. The information management system contains five basic modules covering basic information on service targets, short message interaction, service work, work communication and system management; it also includes special modules relating to stability safeguarding, judicature, complaint-related letters and visits, fire protection and the work on young people.

5.   Putting in place the management service responsibilities to strengthen routine safeguards

As a systematic project, the grid-based management and group-based service involves extensive fields, so it is necessary to establish a corresponding mechanism for organizational coordination as well as a mechanism for evaluation and incentive-building for its sound and effective operation. Zhoushan has set up the leading municipal group for the grid-based management and group-based service, in which the head of the Party committee or the government serves as the leader; the leading group has an office staffed with full-time personnel for the daily work of the

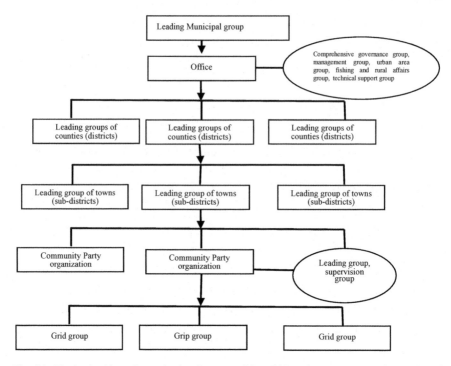

**Fig. 6.1** The leadership and organizational system of the grid-based management and group-based service in Zhoushan City

grids; Zhoushan has also established five special groups, including the comprehensive governance and security group (in the charge of the commission for political and legal affairs under the municipal Party committee), the group management group (in the charge of the department of organization under the municipal Party committee), the working group for urban areas (in the charge of the municipal department of civil affairs), the working group for fishing and rural affairs (in the charge of the municipal office for fishing and rural affairs) and the technical support group (in the charge of the office of the municipal government). The corresponding leading bodies are also set up in counties (districts), towns (sub-districts) and villages (communities); grid members are specially appointed to the leading groups of towns (sub-districts) to ensure that the matters which fall within the scope of the work of the grid groups are managed and handled by relevant personnel, so a system covering five levels including city, county (district), town (sub-district), village (community) and grid is built (see Fig. 6.1).[11]

Zhoushan has developed an evaluation system with well-defined powers and responsibilities, clear orientation and scientific standards. It mainly covers organization, engagement with the people who visit higher authorities for lodging complaints,

---

[11]Wu et al. (2009).

recording the people's conditions, service work, study and judgment of the people's conditions, coordination in key projects and the people's recognition. Evaluation is carried out through platform examination, secret survey, satisfaction test, project supervision and inspection. Platform examinations and secret surveys account for 70%, satisfaction tests 20%, project supervision and inspection 10%. One ballot veto is cast under the following two circumstances: First, problems can be solved within the limits of the functions and powers of towns (sub-districts) but are not promptly solved, causing mass visits of higher authorities for lodging complaints or mass incidents; problems cannot be solved within the limits of the functions and powers of towns (sub-districts), but relevant information is not promptly obtained and reported, causing mass visits of higher authorities for lodging complaints or mass incidents; second, matters are not handled earnestly, contradictions are not promptly resolved, causing deterioration and vicious incidents, exerting a great impact. In the meantime, Zhoushan has incorporated the work on the grid-based management and group-based service into the evaluation of the leading groups and leading cadres, while the results of the evaluation serve as an important basis for promoting and appointing the leading cadres; each year, Zhoushan organizes a series of evaluation and incentive-related activities, with the evaluation and incentive mechanism adopted to make sure that the departments at various levels and the members of the gird service groups have a stronger sense of responsibility for their work.

6.   The effects of the grid-based management and group-based service

The Party Committee and the People's Government of Zhejiang Province have attached great importance to the work on the grid-based management and group-based service, and have taken it as an important means for improving primary-level management and service, Party building, comprehensive governance and stability safeguarding at present and in a period of time to come; they have strengthened the organization, leadership and coordination of the work. With the experimentation and practice of recent years, significant effects have been produced. At present, there are 122,800 grids, 245,800 service groups and 402,400 full-time and part-time grid members throughout the province. This is mainly reflected in the following several aspects.

(1)  Integrating various types of social governance resources, reshaping the new modes of primary-level social governance. Based on public opinion, the grid-based management and group-based service put the people first and are performed to actively respond to and satisfy the reasonable interest appeals of the people in various effective ways, promptly overcome difficulties and problems for the people and reshape the people-oriented philosophy of governance. The primary-level autonomous forces are respected, full play is given to their basic roles in providing public services, maintaining social order, resolving contradictions and conflicts, and actions are taken to establish a Party committee-led, government-guided, market-driven cooperative joint governance mechanism with cooperation from social organizations and active public participation, thus achieving primary-level joint governance in which there is vertical and hori-

zontal interaction as well as interaction among multiple players. The grid-based management and group-based service incorporate the reasonable parts of various social governance modes and give birth to the primary-level governance mode in the new period, presenting the beneficial practical experiments in China's primary-level social governance mode during the period of transformation and offering vivid cases for theoretical research.

(2) Building a new system of resolving contradictions and disputes to effectively safeguard social harmony and stability. Each grid management service group is fully responsible for contacting the people within the assigned grid, learning about the people's conditions, improving the people's well-being, resolving contradictions, safeguarding stability and promoting development, following relevant requirements to visit households door-to-door with a view to gathering the basic information on residents and the special information on key groups in details, exercising classified service management, thus achieving a great success: (1) keeping closer ties with the people, making sure that visits and contacts cover all of the groups; (2) knowing the people's conditions in a more comprehensive way, timely summarizing and processing the information on various types of contradictions and disputes, relying on the grid information platform to establish the scientific and effective system of information collection, analysis, study, judgment, feedback and supervision involving the conditions of the people; (3) making analyses, studies and judgments more accurate—grid management service groups regularly convene in a meeting for the analysis of the conditions of the people and an affairs coordination meeting to enable direct, rapid and full communication regarding the conditions of the people and public opinion, smooth out and standardize the channels for expressing public appeals, coordinating interests, safeguarding rights and interests; (4) identifying and resolving contradictions more effectively. The departments at various levels fully share the information and resources gathered from the work on the grid-based management and group-based service, consider departmental functions to carry out the system of incorporating departments into grids and promptly take measures to serve the people and resolve contradictions.

(3) Building a new platform for enhancing the capability of cadres, broadening the channels through which cadres can engage with the people, promoting the change in the cadres' style. As the work on the grid-based management and group-based service is carried out, cadres are "driven" to the primary level and directly face varied contradictions and complicated problems, a mechanism arises and forces cadres to learn to better serve the people, so the capability of the primary-level cadres is improved significantly. The members of service groups regularly visit and contact the people, hold face-to-face talks with the people, really help them overcome their difficulties in production and life, thus cadres have built closer connections with the people, many primary-level cadres have experienced more and have become experts in their work regarding the people.

### 6.1.3   Integrating the Rule of Law, the Rule of Virtue and Self-governance in Tongxiang

With the operation of the Shanghai-Hangzhou High-speed Railway, Gaoqiao Town, Tongxiang City has ushered in a period of developmental opportunities and has also entered a period of painful adjustment; this is because the traditional social structure and governance mode have been subject to impact: the channels for public participation are not smooth, citizens lack a sense of responsibility, public service needs have become diverse. If the traditional line of thought and simple mode are still adopted to manage the society, the authorities will certainly be unable to cope with the situation and will lose the initiative. Therefore, Tongxiang has made experiments in integrating the rule of law, the rule of virtue and self-governance along with efforts to overcome the difficulties in primary-level social governance.

1.  Working together to deal with important matters, with the group of public participation in government and political affairs taking part in discussing developmental plans

Gaoqiao has established the town-level group of public participation in government and political affairs, fully guaranteeing stakeholders' rights to know, participate in and express their opinions on major issues, jointly making progress on major matters. In the group, 12 outstanding representatives selected throughout the town are stable members and 10–20 direct stakeholders are non-stable members, and a professional lawyer serves as the legal advisor. Since its inception, the group has played an active role in such projects as the high-rise settlement buildings in the Gaoqiao New Area, the comprehensive land improvement project in Sancun Village and heavy road repair in Tongxiexian. The group is an intermediary for making public affairs public; it is the experimentation and practice for the Party committee and the government of the town to regulate their power operations, identify the people's needs, understand the people's conditions and collect ideas from the people. It brings the government and the people closer together so that the people firmly advocate policies and become the best personnel to publicize those policies.

2.  Making sure that judgment is made by all, with the moral judgment group leading the cultural mainstream

In social life, some unhealthy tendencies are not governed by laws and regulations, and cannot be better governed by village rules; they are minor but affect the people's value judgment and value selection. Gaoqiao Town has set up a moral judgment group at the village level, making sure that matters are judged by the people; the people are educated, regulated and managed by themselves, and the moral judgment group can curb the bad and exalt the good, introduce righteousness and foster new healthy tendencies. In the moral judgment group, the secretary of the village Party branch serves as the coordinator, 10–15 model representatives are the members, and their identity is released on the village bulletin board. On the one hand, the moral judgment group develops the advanced models who are visible to and can be learnt by the people, so that the people can consciously practice the fundamental socialist values. On the other hand, the moral judgment group exercises supervision over and comments on the hot issues and major matters involving the immediate interests of villagers and those of concern to villagers; the moral judgment group participates in resolving the contradictions among households and disputes between neighbors, assists in the handling of the acts, people and matters running counter to morality, so that the people supervise each other and exercise self-management.

3.  Making sure that every matter is under management, with the service group for addressing diverse issues available for improving public services

Mobilizing the people to serve the people is one of the means by which Gaoqiao experiments with new modes of governance. Service conveys warmth, while warmth gives birth to harmony. In order to make sure that villagers can promptly enjoy the convenient services, Gaoqiao Town has established a village-level service group for addressing diverse issues, integrating the grid-based management and group-based service group, a volunteer service group for learning from role model Lei Feng, a red volunteer service group, a professional and technical service group in villages. The group has set up offices in villages, the village committees arrange for working personnel to coordinate and provide a liaison, and these offices provide 24 h service hotlines so as to be able to make an immediate response to the people's service needs. Generally, volunteer service is free of charge, while professional and technical services are made available by collecting fees based on low costs.

The rule of law, the rule of virtue and self-governance represent a sweeping, far-reaching reform involving social governance. The practice in the rule of law, the rule of virtue and self-governance sheds light on what should be done by the Party committee and the government and what should be done by fully delegating powers to the primary-level self-governing organizations and the people, thus achieving benign interaction between the top-down government force and down-top social forces. On the macro design, it stresses the diversity of actors, it leads and mobilizes more social forces and people to participate in relevant processes; it is people-oriented and ensures that the people have further rights to know, participate in and express themselves, and so decision-making becomes democratic and scientific; its characteristic is equitable interaction; it emphasizes more systematic and diverse means.[12] Promoting the rule of law, the rule of virtue and self-governance is of great significance for strengthening social governance at the present and plays an important role in improving primary-level social service management, promoting social harmony and stability and guaranteeing economic and social development. First, the moral level of the society has increased significantly; second, the pace of promoting the rule of law has been quickened noticeably; third, the harmonious environment has become sounder.

---

[12]Li et al. (2014).

## *6.1.4 The Routes for Primary-Level Social Governance*

1. Promoting governance at the source, preventing and resolving social contradictions

Given a great many contradictions and disputes in the new period, Zhejiang has actively explored a diversified dispute settlement mechanism based on the people's mediation, and has built an extensive mediation pattern, reinforced the connections among the people's mediation, administrative mediation and judicial mediation, integrated forces by giving overall considerations, thus effectively enhancing the capability for preventing and resolving major difficult and complicated contradictions and disputes. Zhejiang has established and promoted 7220 industrial specialized mediation organizations, increasing the overall effectiveness of coordination among the people's mediation, administrative mediation and judicial mediation.

2. Making decision-making scientific and democratic

As mentioned by comrade Xi Jinping in *Zhijiang Xinyu*, the primary-level contradictions should be resolved through primary-level democracy.[13] The risks to social stability involving major issues are assessed so that the Party committee and the government gain a more comprehensive understanding of major issues, the decision-making process becomes more transparent, the result of decision-making becomes more scientific, close attention is paid to the main contradictions affecting the stability, mistakes in decision-making, policies and projects can be effectively prevented from causing hidden troubles in social stability, contradictions can be prevented and reduced, thus carving out a new path for making decision-making scientific and democratic and strengthening the actual effect from safeguarding stability. The Department of Organization under the Party Committee of Zhoushan City has introduced social stability risk assessment into the village elections to ensure smooth elections. The municipal health and family planning commission conducted a risk assessment regarding Zhoushan's first-ever adoption of the selective two-child policy in Zhejiang to make sure that policies were introduced successfully. In 2013, 5113 items were assessed, and 163 were suspended or stopped in Zhejiang.[14]

3. Prompting leaders to visit the primary-level units to receive the people

Visiting the primary-level units to receive the people greatly tests the capability and level of the leading cadres, it ensures that the people are provided with satisfactory solutions and the goal of serving the people is truly achieved. More than ten years of practice fully proves that visiting the primary-level units is conducive to promoting the work at the primary level, fostering cadres' line of thought of governing for the people, bringing the Party and the people closer together and developing cadres' capability for grasping the overall situation and for pushing forward reform and

---

[13] Xi (2013), p. 226.
[14] Zhu (2014).

development. As of 2012, in Zhejiang, the provincial leaders visited the primary-level units for 180 person-times in order to receive the people in 4792 batches, the leading municipal and county cadres were present for 44,000 person-times to receive the people in more than 190,000 batches, dealing with a large number of tough cases; the number of complaint-related letters and visits across the province decreased from a peak of more than 500,000 in 2003 to 388,000 in 2011, the situation of complaint-related letters and visits has improved continually.[15]

4.  Pushing forward the building of the primary-level social service management platform

The departments of complaint-related letters and visits, education, civil affairs, public security, judicial administration, human resources and social security, health and family planning, industry and commerce, work safety supervision, quality supervision in counties (county-level cities, districts) have opened system accounts and established the mechanisms covering online information transmission, identification and reception of cases, transfer of the cases by the higher authorities to the departments at lower levels for handling at the latter's discretion, transfer of the cases by the higher authorities to the departments at lower levels for handling according to the instructions from the former, handling of cases under the supervision of the higher authorities and inter-departmental joint handling, and online operations are combined with offline handling to enhance the capability for dealing with matters at the primary level. At present, in many counties (county-level cities, districts), most information, delivered to the higher authorities by the people, involving conflicts, disputes, hidden dangers and appeals relating to the people's well-being, can be dealt with by the town (sub-district) social service management center, while the conflicts, disputes and matters involving multiple departments can also be effectively handled through online reporting, urging, supervised handling and evaluation. Zhejiang has launched 69,000 PC and mobile terminals in this regard, covering more than 1500 departments at the provincial, municipal and county levels, all of the towns (sub-districts), 86% of the villages (communities) and some enterprises.[16]

5.  Fully leveraging the big data-based advantages to solve problems

In the era of big data, the integrated, extensive, dynamic and vivid data entered into the primary-level social management information system are a huge wealth. As Zhejiang expands the building of the primary-level social management information system, Zhejiang is dedicated to exploring the solutions based on mass data, providing the basis for innovating social governance decision making. For instance, according to the system data analysis, the proportion of emancipists and community correction personnel who received help and education was generally not high in different areas, and with the philosophy of governing at the source, Zhejiang conducted security evaluation by considering not only the proportion of emancipists and community

---

[15]Lv (2011).
[16]Zhu (2014).

correction personnel who committed crimes again, but also the proportion of eman-cipists and community correction personnel who were resettled, received help and education, thus improving the work on resettlement, help and education in different areas, preventing and reducing the cases of committing crimes again at the source.

## 6.2 Primary-Level Democratic Development and Governance

For the current primary-level social conflicts, no matter how complicated and diverse they are, most of them are conflicts among the people, while primary-level con-flicts should be resolved through primary-level democracy. In this sense, promoting primary-level democracy is an important guarantee for achieving political stability and social harmony; when primary-level democracy becomes sounder, the society becomes more harmonious. Since the reform and opening-up, Zhejiang has carried out many bold reforms and innovations in the field of primary-level democracy, Zhe-jiang has innovated and improved the ways to institutionally practicing primary-level democratic development, making great achievements.

### 6.2.1 Experiments in Primary-Level Democratic Governance

1. Becoming the first to carry out direct elections of community neighborhood committees

Holding direct elections to generate the members of community neighborhood com-mittees is a great event in primary-level democratic political life; it is a fundamental task for improving resident self-governance and building harmonious communities; it is also a democratic practice for making sure that the members of neighborhood committees reflect the aspirations of residents and represent the residents' interests to the greatest extent. Ningbo started direct elections in urban communities early on. In 2003, Haishu District became the first nationwide to hold direct elections of neighborhood committees in 59 communities throughout the district, triggering strong reactions in China. In 2007, Ningbo City became the first nationwide to hold direct elections of neighborhood committees in 235 communities throughout the city. Direct elections in urban communities in Ningbo present several outstanding features: First, candidates were determined openly. Any person jointly recommended by more than 10 voters can be nominated as a candidate for becoming a member of a neighborhood committee; after a qualification examination was conducted under the leadership of the community's Party organization according to legal procedures, official candidates were determined and announced. Second, the election was com-petitive. Official candidates participated in competitive elections to the extent that two candidates competed for each of one position as director and one as deputy director of the neighborhood committee and five candidates competed for three positions as members of the committee. Third, the number of voters were extensive. Besides the permanent residents aged above 18 who enjoyed the ex officio right to vote, the migrant workers who had lived in communities for more than half year or one year also fell into the scope of voters. In 2013, Zhejiang became the first nationwide to establish election regulations for community neighborhood committees, direct elections were conducted for more than 80% of the community neighborhood committees across the province.

2. Wenling's practice in earnest democratic talk and participatory governance

In recent years, in Zhejiang, below the county level, mainly in towns, innovations have been made to develop consultative democracy. This is mainly embodied in earnest democratic talk represented by Wenling. Initially, earnest democratic talk was the meeting initiated by the town leaders to engage in open communication with the people to learn about public opinions; later, it became more mature, standardized and took its present shape. This form of a meeting is not only conducive to scientific decision–making, but it is also of great significance for reflecting public opinion, promoting civic awareness and preventing corruption. Currently, Wenling's earnest democratic talk is developing mainly in three directions: First, establishing the system of collective consultation on wages to hold consultations on labor relations; second, building the participatory public budget mechanism; third, establishing the participatory public decision-making mechanism. Participatory budget is a governance form for citizens to directly participate in decision-making; it is one form of participatory democracy. It means that citizens participate in discussing the government's annual budget plan mainly through earnest democratic talk, and the people's congress deliberates on the government's fiscal budget and decides on the budget revision and adjustment, resulting in budget review and supervision with substantive participation.[17] As from 2005, Wenling became the first nationwide to pilot the participatory budget. As from 2008, Wenling promoted earnest democratic talk on department budgets, one-to-one deliberation on department budgets by the delegations to the people's congress and budget disclosure, pushing forward the participatory budget in a profound and thorough way.

3. Hangzhou's working mechanism in which democracy promotes the people's well-being

The people's democracy is the life of socialism. The improvement of the people's well-being is the fundamental goal of social development; it is the essential requirement for putting the people first and achieving social harmony. Only when democracy is carried forward can the people's well-being be improved; only when the people's well-being is improved can democracy be embodied. As Hangzhou has carried out the strategy of democracy and the people's well-being, Hangzhou has established a working mechanism in which democracy promotes the people's well-being, which

---

[17]Zhang (2008).

works among the Party, the government, citizens and the media, to ensure that development is for and pursued by the people, the achievements of development are shared by the people and the effectiveness of development is tested by the people.

First, the mechanism includes making sure that the Party and the government make decisions in a scientific and democratic way. Making the Party and the government's affairs public, establishing and improving the system involving the primary-level Party representatives attending plenary sessions as non-voting delegates, the standing committee system and the system of collecting and handling the suggestions from the Party representatives, the system of inviting the delegates to the people's congress, CPPCC members and citizen representatives to attend major meetings of the government as non-voting delegates and carrying out the government's open decision-making, improving the mechanism of decision-making involving major issues and the projects relating to the people's well-being. Second, establishing the mechanism of democratic participation in the projects relating to the people's well-being is also included. For the execution of the projects relating to the people's well-being, the mechanism includes establishing the systems involving information disclosure, on-the-spot supervision, acceptance evaluation and return visit relating to quality, making sure that the people are the masters, promoting democracy to inject impetus for improving the people's well-being and to provide a guarantee for pushing forward scientific development and social harmony. Finally, also included in the mechanism is leveraging the media to build the platform for discussing issues to the extent that democracy promotes the people's well-being. This consists of taking advantage of newspapers, radio, television, the Internet and other media to launch a number of columns under the theme that democracy promotes the people's well-being, creating the platform for communication among the Party committee, the government and the citizens, offering interactive platforms for promoting consultative democracy among the different social groups, giving play to the role of the media as public platforms for ensuring that democracy promotes the people's well-being.

## 6.2.2   Particular Practical Case of Promoting the Committee for the Supervision of Village Affairs in Rural Areas

Zhejiang became the first nationwide to pilot and comprehensively promote the committee for the supervision of village affairs. With the improvement in village-level democratic management, Zhejiang has vigorously enhanced primary-level democratic management in rural areas under the new situation, providing an important guarantee for harmonious and stable development of rural areas and the construction of a new countryside.

In recent years, with sustained and rapid economic and social development and expanding construction of a socialist new countryside, in Zhejiang, the rural collective economy has continuously developed, and the "value" of village cadres' powers has been on the increase; however, with a lack of democratic supervision, village cadres have abused powers, making it difficult to make financial affairs public; in particular, the growing rural collective wealth has not made every villager happy for sharing the reform and development achievements; instead, it has led to disputes over village affairs. Subject to this grim reality, local authorities in Zhejiang have intensified experiments in democratic management. On June 18, 2004, the first committee for the supervision of village affairs in China was established at Houchen Village, Wuyi County, Zhejiang, with its members determined by direct election of the representatives of the villagers through voting. In the early days after its establishment, it drew much attention from the then main leaders of the Party Committee of Zhejiang Province.

The committee for the supervision of village affairs established at Houchen Village is essentially different from the groups for the supervision of village affairs and groups for the management of the wealth that had previously been set up in many areas. The committee has the following characteristics: It is in parallel to the villagers committee in institutional design, it is stipulated that the candidates for the committee for the supervision of village affairs should be the villagers' representatives who are not the members of the village Party branch committee and the villagers committee or their immediate relatives. The members of the committee for the supervision of village affairs are entitled to attend all of the meetings except the Party affairs meeting of the Party branch, and they are directly responsible for the meeting of villager representatives. Its main functions are as follows: examining, according to laws, the plan for making village affairs public as proposed by the villagers' committee, supervising the implementation of the systems for making village affairs public; supervising the execution of the decisions made in the villagers' meeting and the meeting of villagers' representatives, the democratic decision-making on major matters, democratic wealth management, the management and use of village funds, the contracting, leasing, guarantee and transfer of collective village assets, project bidding and the management and execution of other village affairs, supporting and cooperating with the villagers' committee and other village-level organizations to perform duties, assisting relevant work, collecting and handing the opinions and suggestions from villagers and timely reporting to relevant village-level organizations. The members of the committee for the supervision of village affairs are directly elected by villagers' representatives and independently exercise the right to supervise village affairs, making the first step in China's establishment of the village-level supervisory organization. Afterwards, the mode under which the committee for the supervision of village affairs is established to strengthen democratic supervision and promote democratic management received a positive response from other counties and cities in Zhejiang. At present, Zhejiang has witnessed the basic formation of the villager self-governing organization system in which the village Party organization serves as the core, the villagers' meeting and the meeting of villagers' representatives are the decision-making bodies, the villagers' committee is the management and executive body and the committee for the supervision of village affairs is the supervisory body.

## 6.2.3 Particular Practical Case in Which Democracy Promotes the People's Well-Being in Urban Areas

In late 2009, the Party Committee and the People's Government of Shangcheng District identified Hubin Subdistrict as the pilot area for establishing the Lakeside Barometer Studio, a non-profit social organization led by the Party and the government and based on coordination among citizens, the media and the society, initiating the innovative mechanism through which democracy promotes the people's well-being in Shangcheng District. With active promotion and improvement for more than four years, Shangcheng District has established a new social governance mechanism in which the government builds the platform, diverse actors are participants, various resources are integrated and problems are solved through consultation, which has produced marked effects, as follows: It can integrate social resources, collect public opinion and pool wisdom from the people to effectively address the issues relating to the people's well-being and improve the index of the people's happiness. Moreover, it helps arouse the people's capability for participation in and enthusiasm about innovation.

1. Basic structure

On December 28, 2009, given that the citizens had expressed their opinions in a random and disorderly way, Hubin Subdistrict set up the Lakeside Barometer Studio. The name of this studio comes from one of the ten views of the West Lake—Sunny and Rainy Views from the Lakeside; it means the barometer of the people's well-being; in this studio, the people express their opinions and the government conveys its purposes and serves the people's well-being. Regarding the structure of the platform, this studio features the basic structure consisting of one studio, six stations, two people and four reports.

"One studio": Lakeside Barometer Studio. The community worker with work experience is appointed as the director of this studio. This studio offers the mailboxes for online and offline collection of the information on social conditions and public opinion and one green channel for interaction between the upper and lower levels.

"Six stations": The "weather station" for the people's conditions in communities. This station is established in each of the 6 communities in the subdistrict and is headed by one community worker for community coordination.

"Two persons": The forecaster of the conditions of the people and the observer of those conditions determined through self-recommendation, residents' recommendation and organizations' recommendation. The people in charge of the functional departments at the municipal and district levels, experts, scholars and journalists serve as forecasters for publicizing policies, learning about the people's conditions, enhancing local residents' understanding of and support for government work, making the functional departments of the government work in a more scientific and efficient way. The Party representatives, deputies to the people's congress, CPPCC members, unit employees, new Hangzhou people and community residents serve as observers for collecting information on the people's conditions in response to social hot spots and difficulties and the concerns of the people, providing prompt, comprehensive and accurate information for the Party and the government's decision-making, publicizing policies to local residents and helping local residents express their opinions and offer suggestions.

"Four reports": A daily report on the people's conditions, a weekly report on focal points of the people's well-being, a monthly report on current politics concerning the people's well-being and an annual report on the quality of the people's well-being. The observers of the people's conditions observe the people's conditions each day, and deliver information to this studio for summarizing, processing, studying and judging. This studio conducts online and offline surveys on the focal points of the people's well-being to learn about public opinion in a week; it makes a monthly forecast about and delivers a monthly report on the political situation, great events and social hot spots relating to the people's well-being; it publicizes policies and dispels doubts with respect to the hot spots involving the people's conditions to which the people pay attention; it makes an annual summary and evaluation of the work on the people's well-being and commends the outstanding stations and observers on the people's conditions.

2.  Operational mechanism

As work is carried out, the Lakeside Barometer Studio has gradually explored and established four operational mechanisms.

(1)  The mechanism for collecting information on social conditions and public opinion. In light of the government's decision-making, social hot spots and the focal points of the people's well-being, each week, this studio determines the themes of the information collection so as to guide the observers in their collection of opinions and suggestions from the people, and makes sure that the collection of information covers both small and large matters.

(2)  The government communication and response mechanism. First, information delivery—with regard to common problems, the mechanism of delivering information on social conditions and public opinion is adopted or relevant departments are invited to hold earnest talk regarding the people's conditions in order to enhance mutual trust and resolve social contradictions. Second, tracking and feedback—actions are taken to enhance communication and coordination with the functional departments at the municipal and county levels, policy publicity and consultative analysis are conducted to make sure that the problems of concern to the people are solved effectively. Third, coordination among multiple parties—IT is applied to ensure coordination with the intelligent control platform for urban management, a safety 365 platform for social management, a worry-free domestic service online and other service platforms, giving a response to the people's conditions and addressing the issues relating to the people's well-being under the mode of one-stop acceptance for handling, whole-process entrustment with specialists acting as agents.

(3)  The consultation mechanism for public problems. A problem-focused consultation mechanism for public problems, which features public participation, departmental coordination and media supervision has been established to ensure that

specific problems are solved through consultation at the subdistrict, community and resident levels, and that public problems are solved through extensive consultation among the government, the media, experts and residents; a mechanism has been established to enable interaction with the media by achieving online and offline interaction at hwyst.hangzhou.com.cn and setting up special columns at www.zjol.com.cn; earnest talk is held to establish a mechanism of communication and consultation between the functional departments of the government and experts, scholars and citizens; such carriers as "Meet on Friday" are used to discuss community issues, generate collective views, opinions and suggestions, help the government better coordinate and deal with the interest relations among multiple parties and ensure that the decision–making is scientific.

(4) The mechanism of meeting the needs involving the people's well-being. This studio proceeds from the people's appeals relating to the people's well-being and focuses on addressing the issues relating to the people's well-being. In recent years, this studio has collected more than 5000 pieces of information on the people's well-being, producing special reports and delivering them to relevant departments at the municipal and county levels. For the specific issues relating to the people's well-being, this studio upholds the principle of duly acting in response to the people's appeals, and it strives to address the issues relating to the people's well-being and meet the people's needs by dealing with the complaint-related letters and visits, working with the county-level social management service center and handling the proposals put forward by the deputies to the people's congress and the CPPCC members. In more than four years, this studio has organized more than 40 large activities, including the Public Debate on the Development of Southern Song Imperial Street, the Earnest Talk on Public Transport (Service), How to Build a Beautiful Hangzhou, effectively solving the problems left over by history.

## *6.2.4  Practice in Primary-Level Democratic Governance*

1.  The committee for the supervision of village affairs strengthens supervision over the village-level public powers, ensuring the all-round, coordinated and healthy development of democratic elections, democratic decision-making, democratic management and democratic supervision.

After the pattern in which the people supervise financial resources, institutions govern matters and cadres do things took shape, primary-level conflicts and the tensions between cadres and the people eased, and there were improvements in the popularity of cadres, the people's enthusiasm about participation in democratic management and democratic supervision. In 2009, the organs for discipline inspection and supervision in Zhejiang handled 17,647 letters, visits and reports involving the problems of the Party members and cadres in rural areas, down 6.71% compared with the previous year; that figure further decreased by 15.5% in 2010. The effects are more apparent in some forerunner areas. In Houchen Village, since the establishment of the committee for the supervision of village affairs, with effective supervision, no cadre has violated discipline, no villager has visited higher authorities to lodge a complaint, no complaint has been raised against projects, and no irregular expenditure has been entered into the accounts.

2. The democratic consultation platform has been built to bring innovations to the democratic safeguard system for the issues relating to the people's well-being, so that the people enjoy more and better services

Local authorities in Zhejiang have, starting with public issues, held regular democratic consultations to address the issues relating to the people's well-being, and they have ensured that democracy becomes a lifestyle and consultation becomes a working mode, thus creating new spaces for the development of primary-level democracy. During the execution of the projects relating to the people's well-being, actions have been taken to try to understand the people's conditions, identify the people's needs, collect ideas from the people, work for the people, let the people decide whether to do something, what to do, how to do it and evaluate what has been done, as well as to fully safeguard the people's rights to know, participate in, choose and supervise. For instance, in response to the water supply issue which had troubled the residents at No. 213, Jiefang Road for more than 30 years, Hangzhou held coordinating meetings on many occasions, ultimately providing the residents with access to safe drinking water.

3. Supervision is exercised to effectively improve the actual effect from the work of government departments, earnestly promoting social harmony

As the people have actively participated in building a primary-level democratic platform and the issues relating to the people's well-being have been addressed effectively, the people no longer feel resentment and the government frequently engages in communication, thus greatly enhancing the people's understanding of, trust in and support for the government. As the government has carefully received criticism and opinions from the people, it has constantly improved its style of work and working mechanism, a large number of difficulties in the people's well-being have been overcome. For instance, the complaint-related letters and visits at the municipal and county levels received by Hubin Sub-district decreased by 49.9% and 30.6% in 2011 compared with 2009; this studio was rated as Hangzhou's Best Living Quality Experience Point of the Year 2011.

## 6.3 The Development of Communities and Social Organizations

In China, primary-level society refers to the social units and communities below the sub-district and town levels; it mainly takes the form of urban and rural communities. The most basic and important space in primary-level governance is the community, thus the community is the cornerstone for primary-level governance and the whole social governance system. As we know, with China's social development, social organizations, especially the community-level social organizations, will increasingly become important carriers in primary-level governance. With rapid economic and social development, the community-level social organizations have soared in number in China and have become important forces that are essential for building harmonious communities; they are of extensive and far-reaching significance for improving the structure of community governance. Therefore, the development of communities and community-level social organizations is an important field and one of the main parts of primary-level social governance.

### 6.3.1  Making Communities Better

As the "people of units" have been turned into "social people", communities have increasingly become the venues for supporting social life and bringing together the members of the society, as well as the focal points of various conflicts. Communities are the priorities for strengthening and innovating social governance; they are fundamental to safeguarding social stability, and they serve as the support for ensuring and improving the people's well-being. Therefore, it is necessary to reinforce primary-level basic work, carry out various measures at the primary level and give full play to the important role of communities in the national governance system.

In light of Zhejiang's reality, comrade Xi Jinping stressed, "Work should focus more on primary-level communities because they are the nodes connecting the upper and lower levels, the focal points of various conflicts and the priorities for carrying out work, thus emphasis should be placed on primary-level communities when it comes to governance and it is necessary to show more care for those communities".[18] Zhejiang is home to the first neighborhood committee in new China. Zhejiang started community development early; it has laid a good foundation in this regard and has actively promoted coordinated urban-rural community development. Zhejiang started the development of community services in the 1970s, initiated the reform of the community system in 2001 and coordinated urban-rural community development in 2008; Zhejiang has always stayed ahead nationwide in urban and rural community development. In particular, since the Party Committee of Zhejiang Province arranged for implementing the "Eight-Eight Strategies" in 2003, the mechanism and institutional system of urban and rural community development have improved constantly, community services and resident self-governance have flourished, laying a solid foundation for promoting the modernization of the system of primary-level social governance and governance capacity.

1.  Strengthening organizational leadership and improving top-level design

---

[18]Xi (2013), pp. 110–112.

The main leaders of the Party Committee of Zhejiang Province have conducted surveys, made arrangements and instructions on many occasions, established the leading group for urban and rural community development—it was the coordinating group for urban and rural community development before 2008—and improved the mechanism for leadership and coordination by which the Party committee and the government exercise unified leadership, the department of civil affairs leads and coordinates and relevant departments participate in the work concerned. In 2001, the Party Committee and the People's Government of Zhejiang Province decided to strengthen the development of urban communities, Zhejiang became the first to reform the community system, turn a number of neighborhood committees into a community neighborhood committee and set up the Party organization at the community level. In the meantime, Zhejiang promoted community building in the rural-urban fringe areas, the villages in cities, the areas where industrial and mining enterprises are located, newly built residential areas and the areas inhabited by the migrant population. Zhejiang successively introduced a series of policy documents, including the *Guiding Plan of Zhejiang Province for Urban Community Development (2003–2010)*, the *Opinions on Promoting the Development of Harmonious Communities* and the *Opinions on Promoting Rural Community Development*, ensuring the accelerated development of urban and rural communities in the right direction.

2.   Building community service centers for providing one-stop services

Since 2006, Zhejiang has, starting with addressing community housing, built a number of urban and rural community service centers by means of investments and new constructions, integration and renovation, resource sharing and comprehensive utilization. In the meantime, the community service centers have undertaken the functions delegated by the government to provide residents with one-stop public services covering living relief, social security, elderly welfare, integrated police services, health and family planning, culture, sports and education; Zhejiang has established a community service system which integrates market-oriented convenient services for the people, the government's public services, residents' self-help and mutual assistance among residents. Zhejiang has also, by establishing community-level social studios, made community services more professional, performed social work services to resolve social conflicts and promote social harmony.

3.   Attaching importance to cultivating competent personnel engaged in social work

Social workers are in charge of "alley affairs" and they are the leading forces in building harmonious communities. The Party Committee and the People's Government of Zhejiang Province have required that each urban community should be provided with no fewer than 5 full-time workers, every 400 households in the communities with more than 2000 households should be provided with 1 full-time worker, and every 2000 people in the case of temporary resident populations should be provided with 1 full-time worker. Local authorities have, according to the above requirement, made sure that community workers enjoy political status and security benefits and are respected in the society through open recruitment, improvement of remuneration packages, and education and training.

4.  Making scientific layout and plans, guiding diversified input

The development of the urban and rural communities is the important foundation for innovating primary-level social management and also the effective means for guiding the optimal allocation of public resources, so scientific and rational planning is very important. During the early stage of community development, Zhejiang combined community layout with urban and rural planning, gave full considerations to the needs of urban development and management at present and in the future. In an effort to push forward the development of rural communities, Zhejiang developed, in advance, the plans for all rural communities in counties (county-level cities, districts) to guide the development of rural communities and the allocation of public resources. In the meantime, Zhejiang increased fiscal input year by year for guiding such players as the village collective, the society and the market to put more resources into the development of urban and rural communities, and a diversified input mechanism dominated by finance at various levels and the public welfare fund from the welfare lottery was established to speed up community development.

5.  Expanding community participation, arousing vitality and impetus

The objective of community development is to turn communities into the social life communities which are managed in an orderly fashion, offer complete services, and are culturally advanced and peaceful. Only when there is extensive participation on the part of residents can endless vitality and impetus be generated for community development. In community development, Zhejiang has given prominence to the dominant position, aspirations and appeals of residents, and has established and improved the systems involving democratic elections, democratic decision-making, democratic management and democratic supervision; moreover, Zhejiang has continuously lowered the threshold for participation in community affairs, broadened the channels for participation, developed community-level social organizations and volunteer groups, guided residents to manage, educate and serve by themselves.

6.  Achieving the development of the community system and social services

New breakthroughs have been made in the community system. As of late 2013, there were 3266 communities throughout the province. The diversified input mechanism has gradually taken shape. In 2006, the Party Committee and the People's Government of Zhejiang Province decided to establish the sum of 35 million yuan for the construction of urban community housing. As from 2008, a special fund was allocated, for the purpose of financial aid, from the provincial-level public welfare fund from the welfare lottery; that special fund increased year by year, and reached 147 million yuan in 2013. Zhejiang has paid attention to guiding such players as the village collective, the society and the market to increase input in the development of urban and rural communities; Zhejiang's total expenditure on community work was 669 million yuan in 2007 and reached 4.12 billion yuan in 2013.

New progress has been made in the community service system. With concerted efforts across the province, the issues concerning community housing have been preliminarily addressed; based on the development of the community service centers, the urban and rural community service system has improved gradually and can, to varying degrees, meet the diverse and individual needs of the people. As of late 2013, there were 1334 town (sub-district) community service centers and 18,564 village community service centers covering 24,592 villages throughout the province.

A new leap has been achieved in developing competent personnel engaged in community services. In rural communities, there has been a work force consisting of full-time and part-time personnel including the cadres assigned to the lower levels, village cadres, college-graduate village officials and full-time workers. Significant improvement has been made in bringing about young, knowledgeable and professional community workers. At present, in Zhejiang, there are 24,322 full-time community workers at an average age of 38.5, among whom 19,959 people are above the junior college level and 6628 people have obtained the qualification of (assistant) social worker.

## 6.3.2  Guiding Social Organizations to Develop Healthily in the Right Direction

In an effort to promote the transformation of government functions, social change and the cultivation of the market system, it is impossible for the government to work on every aspect of social life, while social groups, social intermediary organizations and other social organizations have played an increasingly important role in social life. How to correctly improve the work on managing and serving social organizations and promote the orderly development of social organizations is a major issue for the Party committees and governments at various levels.

In response to the rapid development of social organizations in Zhejiang, comrade Xi Jinping promptly pointed out, "It is imperative to guide the healthy development of social organizations in the right direction". Zhejiang has always attached great importance to the development and management of social organizations. Since the beginning of the 21st century, Zhejiang has witnessed the steady growth of social organizations and has stayed ahead nationwide in the total number of social organizations, the number of increased social organizations and the extent of growth (see Table 6.1 and Fig. 6.2). As of late 2012, there were 31,880 social organizations registered with the department of civil affairs in Zhejiang, including 16,452 social groups, 15,163 private non-enterprise units and 265 foundations, placing Zhejiang at the forefront nationwide in number.

1.  Becoming the first to decouple industrial associations from administrative organs

Zhejiang is the province for early and earnestly separating industrial associations from administrative organs. In September, 2006, the People's Government of Zhejiang Province issued the *Several Opinions on Promoting the Reform and Development of Industrial Associations*. In 2007, the Department of Organization under the Party Committee of Zhejiang Province, the National Development and Reform

**Table 6.1**   The development of social organizations in Zhejiang, 2002–2012 Expressed in quantity

| Year | Social groups | Private non-enterprise units | Foundation | Total |
|------|---------------|------------------------------|------------|-------|
| 2002 | 10173 | 8192 | – | 18365 |
| 2003 | 10549 | 9279 | – | 19828 |
| 2004 | 10862 | 9760 | 95 | 20717 |
| 2005 | 11555 | 10189 | 109 | 21853 |
| 2006 | 12470 | 10810 | 125 | 23405 |
| 2007 | 12915 | 11290 | 140 | 24345 |
| 2008 | 13743 | 12383 | 151 | 26277 |
| 2009 | 14352 | 13061 | 167 | 27580 |
| 2010 | 14870 | 13878 | 189 | 28937 |
| 2011 | 15456 | 13770 | 222 | 29448 |
| 2012 | 16452 | 15163 | 265 | 31880 |

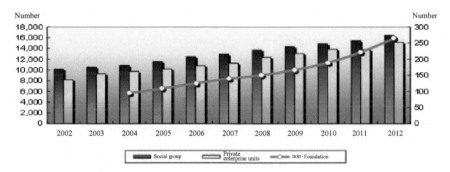

**Fig. 6.2**   The development of social organizations in Zhejiang, 2002–2012

Commission and the Department of Civil Affairs of Zhejiang Province jointly organized and carried out the work on separating industrial associations from administrative organs. According to statistics, in Zhejiang, 1346 industrial associations
which should be separated from administrative organs have fully undergone such
separation, the civil servants concurrently working at 1213 industrial associations
have been separated, 743 industrial associations working together with administrative organs as one office have been separately established, 203 industrial associations
sharing financial accounts with administrative organs have become financially independent, and a number of people from state organs at current posts—2703 people
(person-times)—have been dismissed.

2. Concretely developing private non-enterprise units in terms of self-discipline and
   integrity

In April, 2004, the People's Government of Zhejiang Province issued the *Administrative Measures of Zhejiang Province for Private Non-enterprise Units*, the first
local government regulation for the administration of private non-enterprise units in

China. In the meantime, Zhejiang became the first nationwide to carry out the theme campaign of stimulating private non-enterprise units to provide services in good faith and repay the society, initiating the development of private non-enterprise units in self-discipline and integrity nationwide. Private non-enterprise units have improved the committed service system and the information disclosure system, continuously carried out a large number of public benefit activities, have striven to serve the society without charge or with less compensation, thus consolidating the public service brand. A number of private non-enterprise units have been granted the title "National Advanced Unit in the Campaign for Promoting Self-discipline and Integrity in the Private Non-enterprise Units", providing experience and reference for a national campaign for developing private non-enterprise units in self-discipline and integrity.

3. Building the social organization development platforms

The platforms for the development of social organizations have played a prominent role in providing small and medium-sized organizations and grassroots organizations with funds, public benefit information, capacity training and policy consulting services. Zhejiang has extended the work of social organizations to primary-level communities by establishing social organization service centers and social organization promotion associations; Zhejiang has also provided funds, office premises and capacity training to build the bases for social organization cultivation and incubation so that the organizations which are industrially influential in the fields of social governance and social benefit affairs, enjoy developmental potential and are urgently needed in the society can become mature and grow as early as possible. At present, there are 102 associations for the promotion of social organizations, foundations, service centers and other hub- and support- type social organization service platforms in Zhejiang, and cities such as Ningbo, Wenzhou, Jiaxing, Shaoxing and Zhoushan have preliminarily achieved full coverage from the platforms for social organization services; in some areas, the platforms for social organization services have extended to towns and communities.

4. Innovating the mechanism for the registration of social organizations

With a pioneering spirit, Zhejiang has broken the original institutional barriers. In 2012, Wenzhou City issued the 1+7 series of documents including the *Opinions on Accelerating the Cultivation and Development of Social Organizations*. According to these documents, there is no requirement for initial funds in the case of applying for establishing and registering such social organizations as charity and social welfare-type social organizations. As from July 1, 2013, the Department of Civil Affairs of Zhejiang Province first delegated to the departments of civil affairs of all of the cities divided into districts and Yiwu City the administration authority involving the registration of non-public foundations in which the residents of the Chinese Mainland serve as the legal representatives, and the powers and responsibilities of the competent department for the non-public foundations in the field of civil affairs. Afterwards, the *Circular Concerning the Work on Direct Registration of Four Types of Social Organizations* was issued. According to the circular, as from September 18, 2013, four types of social organizations—including industrial associations and chambers of commerce, science and technology, charity, urban and rural community service-type social organizations—are directly registered throughout the province. The *Trial Opinions on the Reform of the Management System Involving the Registration of Social Groups* was issued, simplifying the registration procedure and abolishing the registration of preparations for establishing social groups.

5. Intensifying the management of daily supervision

Zhejiang has promoted the standardization of social organizations. Zhejiang has raised standardization requirements for the agenda and operating rules for social organization founding meetings and elections, the financial system, the seal system and archives management system. Zhejiang has constantly improved the work on and the way of annual inspection, combined the traditional written annual inspection with online annual inspection, enabled coordination with the building up of the Party, evaluation, daily management, law enforcement and supervision to ban, according to laws, the organizations which fail to pass the annual inspection. In order to increase the popularity among the general public, Zhejiang has energetically demonstrated and publicized the public benefit programs, charity and the construction of demonstration points through websites, brief reports, QQ, microblogs, WeChat and other platforms. Zhejiang has become the first to initiate the rating of social organizations, established the rating-based access system for social organizations, and incorporated the rating results into the social credit system, and provided the highly-rated social organizations with preferential treatment in the transfer of government functions, project bidding, entrustment of an agent, social services, and appraisal and commendation.

### 6.3.3   Jiaxing's Practice in the Interaction Among Communities, Social Groups and Social Workers

Communities, social groups and social workers are the basic elements for bringing innovations to social governance. Strengthening the development of communities, social groups and social workers is of important significance for bringing innovations to the social governance system, safeguarding the people's rights, promoting social fairness and justice, maintaining social stability and harmony. With a focus on enhancing and innovating social governance services, Jiaxing City has proceeded from the people's needs to fully integrate social resources, explore, according to local conditions, the mechanism for the operation of social work in which the Party committee and the government play the leading role, departments participate in promoting relevant work, communities, social groups and social workers develop in an interactive way. At present, Jiaxing is seeing the gradual formation of a crisscross, flat and networked management service mode in which communities serve as the foundation, social groups are carriers and social workers are the backbone and there is interaction among communities, social groups and social workers.[19]

Currently, there are 1969 standardized social organizations and 8981 community-level social organizations in this city. In 2013, this city was included by the Ministry of Civil Affairs in the first batch of national demonstration areas for social work services. In 2014, this city piloted interaction among communities, social groups and social workers in 25 communities throughout this city, with a view to promoting the building and interactive development of communities, social groups and social workers and thus ensuring that social public services are no longer provided solely by the government and are made available jointly by social forces, as well as upgrading social management to social governance. Jiaxing has mainly taken the following actions.

First, it has promoted the return of community functions and the expansion of services. In parallel to hardware renovation and upgrading at urban and rural community service centers, actions have also been taken to expand the functions of 96,345 community service centers, further improve the service network, increase its coverage and more rapidly enhance the capability for community service. In the meantime, the community service carriers have been actively nurtured and developed. At present, social work service bodies have been set up in all of the harmonious urban communities above the municipal level throughout the city, the goal of making sure that one village, one community is served by multiple social workers and one social work group has been achieved.

Second, it has stimulated social organizations to display vitality and play their roles. After the first municipal social organization development center in the province was established, this city stepped up its efforts to promote the development of platforms for the incubation of social organizations, and achieved full coverage at the municipal and county levels. This city has explored the development of social organization incubation centers at the sub-district level in Jiefang Sub-district and Nanhu Sub-district, Nanhu District, and has built a social organization cultivation and incubation system with different priorities and characteristics at the municipal, county (county-level city, district), town (sub-district) levels, injecting vigor into the development of social organizations. In the meantime, this city has also pushed forward the work on the government's purchase of services and the undertaking of government functions by social organizations, and has set up a committee for reviewing the projects involving the government's purchase of services from social organizations, and the committee is responsible for collecting and reviewing projects as well as arranging purchasing funds.

Third, it has boosted the development of professional social work and brought innovations to social governance. The units of the social work committee under the municipal Party committee and various types of social work bodies have been actively stimulated to carry out professional social work, apply the professional social work philosophy, skills and methods into traditional services, thus making social work services highly professional. In 2013, the social work bodies in this city

---

[19]Yang (2012).

adopted case work, group work, community work, other professional knowledge and methods to carry out 2035 professional social work service cases—including 1139 case service cases, 380 group service cases and 516 community service cases, up 134% compared with the previous year—and offer professional services for 48,000 person-times.

Under the new mode of interaction among communities, social groups and social workers, the communities serve as the platforms, various types of professional social work bodies act as the carriers and professional social workers represent the means; this manner gives rise to a mechanism for the operations of social work in which the government plays the leading role, social participation and non-governmental operations take place, social work guides the way, volunteers provide services and the people obtain benefits; under this mode, social workers guide volunteers, volunteers serve the people and the people participate in volunteer services; under this mode, the relations of social work among the government, communities, organizations, residents are rationalized, and there is a mechanism for work operations in which operations are smooth, resources are shared, and harmonious interaction is achieved.

## *6.3.4  Promoting Primary-Level Social Self-governance in Communities and in the Society*

The extensive and complete participation of social organizations is the basic direction for and important characteristic of diversified governance in a modern society. Zhejiang has gradually established a social organization cultivation and management system commensurate with the province's economic and social development needs, and it has preliminarily built an extensive distinctive organizational system covering a wide range of fields, different levels and with complementary functions; they have played important roles in boosting economic development, providing public services, meeting diverse needs, expressing interest appeals, standardizing social behaviors, promoting social fairness, expanding public participation and resolving social conflicts.

(1) Increasing the level of self-governance in primary-level society. The development of primary-level social organizations has offered the organizational platform through which community residents can participate in the management of community affairs and interact with each other; as residents participate in the management of public affairs and the community-level public benefit activities, social interaction is enhanced, they promote various cultural, sports and fitness activities and the level of self-governance in primary-level society is greatly increased.

(2) Shaping a pattern in which diverse players cooperate in joint governance. A basic direction for innovations to social governance is that the government's top-down governance is transformed into joint governance by diverse social players through cooperation. In recent years, Ningbo City has purchased 400

new non-profit service items from social organizations; as a result, such a purchase has enhanced the benign interaction between the government and social organizations, it has provided a large number of jobs to the society and has saved fiscal expenditure for the government.

(3) Improving the capability for serving the people and responding to the people's needs at the primary level. In fact, social organizations serve as the organizational platforms for sharing tasks and responsibilities with the primary-level cadres. As the primary-level social organizations are flexible in mechanism and close to the people, and they enjoy more professional advantages in medical service, education, old-age care and assistance, they are better positioned to meet the increasingly diverse and individual public service needs of the people. Social organizations have become important players in primary-level management services. According to statistics, the Zhejiang Charity Federation raised 15.44 billion yuan to assist the people with difficulties for 9.27 million person-times over the years. A total of 304 foundations in Zhejiang have annually donated an average of more than 2 billion yuan in income and public benefit expenditure, and they have carried out and assisted more than 1000 charity projects.

# References

Zhu Haibing, The Pilot Sample of Building a Safe China – A Review of the 10th Anniversary of Building a Safe Zhejiang, *Zhejiang Daily*, March 31, 2014, Page 1.

Zhao Hongzhu, Deepening the Building of a Safe Zhejiang, Strengthening and Innovating Social Management, Creating Good Social Conditions for Finishing the Building of a Moderately Prosperous Society in All Respects for the People across the Province – The Report Delivered during the 9th Plenary (Enlarged) Session of the 12th Party Committee of Zhejiang Province, June 14, 2011.

Yang Jianhua, The Interaction among Communities, Social Groups and Social Workers: the Building of a New Social Management System, *China Social Work*, 2012(27).

Xi Jinping, *Carrying out Solid Work to Stay Ahead – Line of Thought and Practice in Promoting New Development in Zhejiang*, The Party School of the CPC Central Committee Press, 2006.

Wu Jinliang, *Primary-level Social Governance*, China Renmin University Press, 2014, p. 41.

Xi Jinping, *Zhijiang Xinyu*, Zhejiang People's Publishing House, 2013.

Wu Jinliang, Sun Jianjun, Wang Lingyun, and Ding Youliang, Grid-based Governance: All-round Innovations in Primary-level Social Management, *Juece Canyue*, 2009(37).

Li Jie, Liang Xiao, and Yang Zhidong, Tongxiang: Integrating the Rule of Law, the Rule of Virtue and Self-governance to Reach a New Stage of Social Governance, *Zhejiang Legal News*, May 23, 2014, Page 1.

Zhu Xianliang, News release at the press conference on the 10th anniversary of building a safe Zhejiang, April 10, 2014.

Zhang Xueming, Deepening the Reform of Public Budget, Enhancing the Effect of Budget Supervision – Wenling's Practice and Thinking in Participatory Budget, *Wenling Theory and Practice*, 2008(2).

Gong Ying, *Innovations in the Social Management Mode – A Study of Zhoushan's Practice in the Grid-based Management and Group-based Service*, Intellectual Property Publishing House, 2012, pp. 162–166.

Lv Yue, Alleviating Poverty, Overcoming Difficulties and Relieving Anxieties –The Cadres at State Organs in Zhejiang Visit the Primary-level Units to Receive the People, *Zhejiang Daily*, December 6, 2011, Page 1.

# Chapter 7
# Migrant Population Services and Management

**Xiumei Zhang**

In more than 30 years since the reform and opening-up, Zhejiang has made tremendous achievements in economic and social development; Zhejiang has developed from an agricultural province only at the intermediate level nationwide into an economically large province which became the first to achieve development; in the meantime, Zhejiang has also attracted a massive migrant population. Since 2001, Zhejiang has ranked No. 2 nationwide in total migrant population, only second to Guangdong. In many parts of Zhejiang, the size of the migrant population has exceeded that of the population with local registered permanent residence, and the migrant population has become a crucial force in Zhejiang's economic and social development.

The migrant population has also become the social group to whom Zhejiang has to provide the corresponding public goods and services in labor employment, education and training, health services, social security, social management, family planning and information sharing. Zhejiang's philosophy of service for and management of the migrant population has shifted its focus from management to service; the content of migrant population services and management has gradually changed from single services, the services in single fields, to integrated and full services; the manner of providing services to the migrant population and the way to manage it have gradually changed from the unitary management mode dominated by public security management to the specialized body management mode dominated by integrated services. Zhejiang has introduced a number of management systems and policy measures for the services for and management of the migrant population, and based on the success made in pilot areas, Zhejiang has accelerated the institutional development at the provincial level, the services for and management of the migrant population have been institutionalized and standardized as well as put under the rule of law.

X. Zhang (✉)
Zhejiang Academy of Social Sciences, Hangzhou, China

© Social Sciences Academic Press and Springer Nature Singapore Pte Ltd. 2019
G. Chen and J. Yang (eds.), *Chinese Dream and Practice in Zhejiang—Society*,
Research Series on the Chinese Dream and China's Development Path,
https://doi.org/10.1007/978-981-13-7406-7_7

## 7.1  Valuing the Status and Role of the Migrant Population

As Zhejiang is a large province of private enterprises and a processing industry, Zhejiang has always attached importance to the role of the migrant population, including rural migrant workers. When working in Zhejiang, comrade Xi Jinping gave priority to addressing the issue of rural migrant workers, he took charge of special surveys, summarized the previous practices, analyzed the existing problems, made in-depth analyses regarding the next work, creatively put forward the philosophy of ensuring that farmers have land, newcomers are respected, workers receive remuneration and get access to housing, the people of no family are supported, the outstanding people enjoy glory, workers have their joy and newcomers have a sense of belonging.[1]

The above philosophy is defined in eight aspects as follows: farmers have land—safeguarding the land rights and interests of rural migrant workers to ensure that they can proceed or step back freely; newcomers are respected—fully integrating rural migrant workers into the local society, ensuring equality and harmonious coexistence; workers receive remuneration—ensuring that wages are promptly paid in full; workers get access to housing—actively carrying out affordable housing projects for rural migrant workers; the people of no family are supported—endeavoring to expand public services for rural migrant workers, universally providing identical treatment in the education of the children of rural migrant workers; regarding medical services, issuing the Love Card to rural migrant workers, providing medical assistance to rural migrant workers; with regard to old-age security, increasing the coverage in some economically developed areas; the outstanding people enjoy glory—fully ensuring that rural migrant workers enjoy democratic political rights; workers have their joy—paying attention to the cultural life of rural migrant workers; newcomers have a sense of belonging—trade unions in enterprises should make sure that rural migrant workers have a sense of belonging.

These eight aspects not only address the situation of the migrant population in Zhejiang, but they also take into full account the rights and interests of that population; these eight aspects take into account both material life and the cultural pursuit of the migrant population; they cover both their current welfare and their long-term interests. These eight aspects involve the most pressing and real issues of the greatest concern to the people. The above-mentioned philosophy represents a review and summary of Zhejiang's previous work on the migrant population and also identifies the direction and priorities for the future work. "The Party committees and governments at various levels and leading cadres should earnestly address the major issue—the issue of rural migrant workers—by strengthening leadership, conducting in-depth surveys, providing effective guidance, carrying out more analyses and research, further improving policies and putting measures into practice, carving out a new path for addressing the issue of rural migrant workers and making positive contributions to national endeavors".[2]

[1] Xi (2006), pp. 252–258.
[2] Xi (2006), p. 259.

When it comes to valuing the status and role of the migrant population, it is necessary to consider the issue of the migrant population from the perspective of consolidating the status of the Party as the governing party. "The issue of rural migrant workers is not only an economic issue and a social issue, but also a serious political issue having a vital bearing on consolidating the Party's class basis and expanding the Party's mass base".[3] Rural migrant workers are the group in transition from the farmer class to the working class, they have the identities of both a farmer and a worker and play an important role in consolidating the alliance of workers and farmers. The way of treating the group and the extent of the Party's integration of the group have a direct bearing on the foundation and resources for the Party's governance.

With regard to valuing the status and role of the migrant population, it is essential to approach the issue of the migrant population from the perspective of socialist fairness and justice. "When we treat rural migrant workers well, we are kind to ourselves; we should renew our mindsets, firmly uphold the philosophy of putting the people first, actively foster an atmosphere for getting along equally, we cannot have any discrimination against rural migrant workers; this is an issue of mindset and also an issue of affection as well as a major issue of learning the Important Thought of Three Represents and carrying out the Scientific Outlook on Development".[4] It is necessary to really safeguard the legitimate rights and interests of the migrant population, provide them with a guarantee of survival and opportunities for development, so that they can reasonably enjoy the fruits of their labor and the achievements in social development.

Only when we deeply understand the important status and indispensable role of the migrant population can we better serve and manage them. Thus "it is essential to put the people first, show greater care for rural migrant workers, actively provide a good working environment for them, create the necessary material and cultural living conditions, help them solve real problems concerning housing, their children's education and personal marriage".[5] "Overall, in this regard, only preliminary breakthroughs have been made a good start has been made; in some respects, there are good practices and excellent experience, while these practices and experience are being applied in a wider scope. The issue of rural migrant workers cannot be addressed unless progress is made in the economic and social fields, the capability of social development is further improved and the overall quality of rural migrant workers is further enhanced; it cannot be addressed in one stroke".[6] The successive leading cadres of Zhejiang Province have attached great importance to the rights and interests of rural migrant workers, including the migrant population, and have continuously explored new measures for the services for and the management of the migrant population.

---

[3] Xi (2006), p. 252.
[4] Xi (2006), p. 251.
[5] Xi (2006), p. 251.
[6] Xi (2006), p. 259.

## 7.2    Innovating the Systems and Mechanisms for the Migrant Population

As Zhejiang is one of the most economically developed provinces, thanks to its great advantages regarding institutions and mechanisms, the development of advanced manufacturing bases and the modern service industry, and due to the ageing of the labor force in Zhejiang, Zhejiang is highly attractive to various types of talents and other labor forces in other provinces, resulting in population agglomeration. The flow mechanism for the migrant population is very complicated because many factors affect that flow, and they affect and check each other. The theories which are used to explain the migration of the migrant population and are highly influential in China are mainly the Push and Pull Theory and the Dual Economy Theory. The Push and Pull Theory was developed by D.J. Bagne. In his view, the push for population flow is the unfavorable economic and social conditions in the areas from which the population flows, while the pull is the factors for improving the living conditions in the areas to which the population flows; according to this theory, population migration occurs under the combined action of the push and the pull. W. Arthur Lewis, the founder of the Dual Economy Theory, put forward the Two-sector Model of Structural Development, also called the Model of Development with Unlimited Surplus Labor. In his opinion, the national economic structure of the developing countries consists of the traditional self-sufficient agricultural economic system and the modern urban industrial system; it is called the dual economic structure. The limited land used by the traditional agricultural sector is nonrenewable, with sustained population growth, surplus population will occur, while the output value and marginal productivity of surplus farmers are close to "zero", and they even grow negatively, so the return on the agricultural economy is on the decline; the modern industrial sector has renewable production materials, the expansion of its scale of production and the increase in the speed of production may exceed population growth. Therefore, as long as the wage level in the industrial sector is slightly higher than that in the agricultural sector, the unlimited agricultural surplus labor from the agricultural sector will move to the industrial sector.

The migrant population in Zhejiang can also be explained by the Push and Pull Theory and the Dual Economy Theory. The following four factors mainly make Zhejiang attractive: sustained economic development, a relatively advantageous social policy, the Zhejiang Spirit characterized by openness and inclusiveness, and a diversified and rich lifestyle.

### 7.2.1    Sustained Economic Development is the Economic Factor for Attracting the Migrant Population

According to Levenshtein, the founder of the population migration theory, population migration is mainly driven by the economy; although exploitation, oppression, harsh duties, living conditions, weather and geographical environment are some important causes for population migration, the most important cause is the economic factor; population migration to improve living conditions accounts for most migration. This law has been recognized and applied by subsequent scholars.

Zhejiang's sustained rapid economic development is fundamental for attracting the migrant population. In 2013, Zhejiang's GDP, per capita GDP and local public fiscal budget revenue were 3,756.8 billion yuan, 68,462 yuan and 379.7 billion yuan, respectively. Zhejiang's development has not only been rapid but it has also delivered good benefits. In Zhejiang, the per capita disposable income of urban residents and the per capita net income of rural residents were 37,851 yuan and 16,106 yuan, up 9.6% and 10.7% compared with the previous year; Engel's Coefficient of urban households was 34.4%, down 0.7 percentage points compared with the previous year; Engel's Coefficient of rural households was 35.6%, down 2.1 percentage points compared with the previous year. The people have gradually become wealthy, and the building of a moderately prosperous society in all respects has basically been completed. According to the *Statistical Monitoring Evaluation of the Progress in Building a Moderately Prosperous Society in All Respects in Zhejiang Province* released by the Zhejiang Provincial Bureau of Statistics, Zhejiang's Well-off Index started from 62.7% in 2000 and increased year by year; it reached a new level in 3–4 years, and increased to 71.3% in 2004 and 81.4% in 2007, exceeded 90% in 2010, further increased to 95.8% in 2012, and it was higher than 90% for three consecutive years; it annually increased by 2.53 percentage points on average in nearly three years, the goal of building a moderately prosperous society in all respects has basically been achieved. The level of Zhejiang's urbanization was on the rise. In 2013, The urbanization rate of Zhejiang's permanent population reached 64%.

With respect to the per capita net income of rural residents, Zhejiang is greatly different from six provinces that are the main sources of the migrant population, including Hubei, Anhui, Henan, Sichuan, Jiangxi and Guizhou. In 2003, the per capita net income of rural residents in Hubei, where it was the highest among these six provinces, was 47.27% of that in Zhejiang, while that in Guizhou, where it was the lowest, was only 28.82% of that in Zhejiang. In 2013, the per capita net income of rural residents in these provinces was only 33.74–55.05% of that in Zhejiang. There was a greater difference between the per capita net income of rural residents in these provinces and the per capita disposable income of urban residents in Zhejiang.

As Zhejiang witnesses sustained economic growth, the difference between the resident income level and that in the main areas from which the population flows continues, Zhejiang enjoys comparative advantages in attracting the migrant population; as long as the difference in economic development continues, Zhejiang remains attractive for the population in these areas, and the migrant population will continue to flow into Zhejiang.

## 7.2.2   Superior Systems and Policies are the Political Factors for Attracting the Migrant Population

In response to long-term household-based population flow and sustained growth of the entire migrant population, the governments at various levels in Zhejiang have put the people first to create a good, harmonious and sustainable environment for the survival and development of the migrant population, and provide them with more and better public goods, legitimate rights and interests—including strengthening the construction of public facilities, developing public services involving employment, social security, education, science and technology, culture, health and sports and releasing public information—to meet the basic needs of the migrant population regarding public resources.

First, with regard to the employment environment, the governments at various levels in Zhejiang have provided good employment services to the migrant population. Zhejiang has abolished the restrictive regulations and unreasonable charges for the migrant population and it has provided the migrant population with free services of introduction to occupation and vocational training. Zhejiang has also paid special attention to the arrears of wages for the migrant population. Given the fields where the arrears of wages for rural migrant workers are severe, including construction, Zhejiang has specially introduced the measures for guaranteeing wage payment for those workers in the province's construction field, it has established the systems involving security deposits for enterprises' wage payment and the government's emergency revolving fund for the arrears of wages in order to make sure that rural migrant workers can receive wages in full on time. Given that the wages for rural migrant workers are low, Zhejiang has required that the wages for rural migrant workers must not be lower than the local minimum wage standard, overtime wage must be paid in the case of overtime work, thus effectively safeguarding the legitimate rights and interests of rural migrant workers.

Second, with respect to educational resources, Zhejiang has been at the forefront nationwide in teaching conditions, teachers and the quality of teaching. For some households among the migrant population with a certain economic foundation, ensuring children's access to better education is one of the driving forces for migration. More importantly, Zhejiang is especially inclusive towards the children of the migrant population, and has lowered the threshold for enrollment and actively taken measures to adapt migrant children to the new environment, make sure that migrant children receive the same social care as local children and that they share the same blue sky.

Moreover, Zhejiang has introduced a number of systems and policy measures for the services for and management of the migrant population, and it has speeded up the provincial institutional development for the migrant population, so Zhejiang's social environment enjoys comparative advantages. When Zhejiang's urban areas are compared with the rural areas from which the population flows, Zhejiang's advantages are more apparent. This is exactly the political factor for attracting the migrant population.

### 7.2.3  The Zhejiang Spirit Characterized by Inclusiveness is the Cultural Factor for Attracting the Migrant Population

Thanks to the Zhejiang Spirit characterized by openness, tolerance, recognition and harmonious coexistence, diverse lifestyles coexist in Zhejiang. The lifestyles of different classes, different occupational groups and different regional groups are in a state of fusion and coexistence in Zhejiang.

In 2000, the 4th Plenary (Enlarged) Session of the 10th Party Committee of Zhejiang Province preliminarily defined the Zhejiang Spirit as follows: constantly pursuing self-improvement, being firm and indomitable, making bold innovations, stressing actual effects. With a series of development, in 2006, comrade Xi Jinping, the then Secretary of the Party Committee of Zhejiang Province, summarized the Zhejiang Spirit which should be carried forward in line with the times as follows: being realistic and pragmatic, stressing integrity and harmony, being open-minded and striving to become stronger. The former is developed by summarizing and refining the existing spirit in Zhejiang, while the latter is identified and summarized as Zhejiang's market economy becomes mature. In the great debate "Our Values" in 2012, "being pragmatic, trustworthy, advocating learning and upholding goodwill" were identified as the shared values of the contemporary people of Zhejiang. Each expression shows the cultural factors of the people of Zhejiang—self-improvement and moderation—and their complexion and character—harmony, unity of man and nature, coexistence.

The Zhejiang Spirit of inclusiveness is embodied in accepting and recognizing the migrant population. As Zhejiang has been a socially stable area throughout history, the people of Zhejiang are sweet-tempered and adept in accepting external ethnic groups; they attach importance to the building of a social community. Zhejiang regards its migrant population as new residents. This recognizes the institutional identity and also shows recognition in mind and connectivity in thinking. That connectivity in thinking is a harmonious social environment which is more suitable for making it possible for the migrant population to work and live than having merely an institutional identity; it can make sure that the migrant population can cheerfully participate in economic and social development, and discover their social value through social development.

In institutional design, the Zhejiang Spirit of inclusiveness is that Zhejiang adopts the philosophy of "greater population" to remove the differences in rights and interests caused by the difference in registered permanent residence, and it recognizes a political identity. In many cities in Zhejiang, the children of the migrant population enjoy equal treatment in education as the local residents; new residents make up a certain proportion of the deputies to the people's congress and CPPCC members; new residents are governed by the mechanism of expressing rights, interests and appeals which combines government guidance with socialized safeguarding of rights. With these institutional designs, the migrant population is included into the local strategy for economic and social development; they enjoy a basically equal political status as local residents, demonstrating strong affinity and inclusiveness of Zhejiang's social systems.

The Zhejiang Spirit of inclusiveness is also embodied in co-building and sharing with the migrant population in economic and social development—the migrant population is regarded as part of the main players in social management and they share the responsibility for economic and social management with the local residents; for instance, the outstanding new residents are invited to participate in social governance; they are provided with identical treatment in sharing the achievements of economic and social development. With the introduction of various measures, Zhejiang has made the migrant population develop a stronger sense of identity and belonging regarding the areas where they work and live.

## 7.2.4  The Diverse Lifestyles Constitute the Social Factor for Attracting the Migrant Population

As the commodity economy is developed in urban areas, the available materials and services for life are more than what they are in rural areas in terms of quantity and variety; urban areas are characterized by a rich lifestyle, a high degree of socialization, convenient means of transportation, a heterogeneous population, adequate venues for social engagement and diverse ways to enjoy one's leisure time; these factors enhance the people's needs for self-realization and also provide the conditions for realizing those needs. As a coastal developed province, Zhejiang is very attractive to the migrant population thanks to the developed commodity economy and the diversified urban life.

In urban areas, there is a society, which is "anonymous" relative to rural areas, in which the people can be free from the inhibition and constraint caused by the network of acquaintances. In China's traditional rural areas, the people live in an acquaintance society which is highly stable. Such a stable network and monotonous lifestyle restrict the space and vitality for the people's activities while also protecting the people. One of the appealing factors in urban areas is that the migrant population can try to carry out some work originally thought to be impossible in new fields, making it possible for tapping their potential and seeking self-affirmation. When the people work in urban areas, many choices are available for them; as a dense population and intense needs bring about frequent repetitive operations, there are outstanding advantages for improving the capability of the service-oriented and technical rural migrant workers, thus their income has increased rapidly. As there are many opportunities, the migrant population is highly free to choose jobs.

## 7.3   The Contribution from the Migrant Population to Zhejiang's Economic and Social Development

The migrant population has made tremendous contributions to Zhejiang's economic and social development. As mentioned by comrade Xi Jinping, in recent years, with urbanization and the development of profitable agriculture in Zhejiang, millions of rural migrant workers have worked in towns across the province; as the friends of cities, rural migrant workers have become an important new force and essential human resource for Zhejiang's economic development.[7] First, the migrant population, as a labor force, contributed 26.84% to the GDP, and the migrant population contributed 2.04% to the GDP by saving enterprise costs, the combined rate of contribution was 28.88%. Second, the migrant population is dominated by the working-age population and can mitigate the structural contradictions in the labor supply. Third, as producer and consumer, the migrant population can stimulate the development of the consumer market and urbanization. Finally, as the migrant population flows among regions, it strives to improve its social status, thus arousing the enterprising spirit in the whole society and enhancing the government's capacity for social governance.

### 7.3.1   Quantitative Analysis of the Contribution from the Migrant Population to Zhejiang's Economic Development

The role of the migrant population in stimulating the economic and social development of the areas to which the migrant population flows has been fully proven. An analysis of the relations between the migrant population and the GDP shows the contribution from the migrant population to Zhejiang's economic and social development.

As shown in Table 7.1 and Fig. 7.1, Zhejiang's economic growth is closely associated with the changes in the migrant population, their relationship is approximately linear.

In order to further verify that relationship, we can analyze the distribution of the migrant population in Zhejiang and the economic development in various parts of Zhejiang in 2013. As shown in Fig. 7.2, the distribution of the migrant population was almost in sync with regional economic development, in other words, the economic aggregate was high in the areas where the migrant population was dense; the economic aggregate was low in the areas where the migrant population was less dense.

According to the dynamic analysis of the migrant population and economic development, the migrant population is positively correlated to Zhejiang's economic development in the longitudinal direction on the time axis; the regional distribution of the

---

[7] Xi (2004).

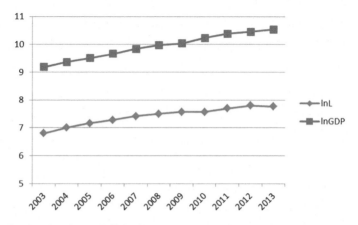

**Fig. 7.1** The logarithmic trend of the GDP and the migrant population in Zhejiang, 2003–2013. *Source* The data regarding the migrant population come from the Department of Public Security of Zhejiang Province, the data regarding the GDP come from the Zhejiang Statistical Yearbook (2004–2014)

migrant population is also positively correlated to economic development, so we can conclude that the migrant population and economic development show a trend of integration.

**Table 7.1** The changes in the migrant population and the GDP in Zhejiang, 2003–2013

| Year | The size of the migrant population (10,000 people) | GDP (100 million yuan) |
|---|---|---|
| 2003 | 898.2 | 9705.02 |
| 2004 | 1101.9 | 11648.7 |
| 2005 | 1291.0 | 13437.85 |
| 2006 | 1459.8 | 15742.51 |
| 2007 | 1670.7 | 18780.44 |
| 2008 | 1823.4 | 21486.92 |
| 2009 | 1944.1 | 22832.43 |
| 2010 | 1950.3 | 27722.31 |
| 2011 | 2215.1 | 32318.85 |
| 2012 | 2459.5 | 34665.33 |
| 2013 | 2362.5 | 37568.49 |

*Source* The data for the migrant population come from the Department of Public Security of Zhejiang Province, the data regarding the GDP come from the Zhejiang Statistical Yearbook (2004–2014)

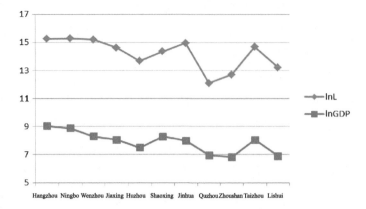

**Fig. 7.2** The logarithmic trend of the GDP and the migrant population in different areas in 2013. *Source* The data regarding the migrant population come from the Department of Public Security of Zhejiang Province, the data regarding the GDP come from the Zhejiang Statistical Yearbook (2014)

Based on the Cobb-Douglas production function, we can further calculate the rate of contribution from the migrant population to economic development.[8] According to the Cobb-Douglas production function, it is necessary to first calculate the values of a and b; it is widely acknowledged in the academic circles that $a = 0.6$, $b = 0.4$; this is because China is a developing country, its economy is almost a labor-intensive economy, so the elastic coefficient of the labor output is generally high, while the elastic coefficient of the capital output is generally low. As Zhejiang is a processing-oriented, outward-looking province dominated by small and medium-sized enterprises, Zhejiang's elastic coefficient of the labor output should be high, so $a = 0.6$ and $b = 0.4$ will be adopted here.

Therefore, $\ln GDP = \ln A + 0.6\ln L + 0.4\ln K$; when the labor input increases by 1%, the economy can grow by 0.6%,[9] and when the capital input increases by 1%, the economy can grow by 0.4%. We assume that the labor productivity of the migrant population is the same as that of the local population, so based on $L'/L*\ln L/\ln GDP*100\%$, we can calculate the rate of contribution from the migrant population to the GDP—that rate of contribution is equal to the proportion of the migrant population in the total labor force multiplied by the contribution from the total labor force.

---

[8]Its general form is $Q = ALaKb$, where $Q$ is output, $L$ and $K$ are labor input and capital input, $A$, $a$ and $b$ are three parameters, $A$ is the factor of impact from technical or management parameters on economic growth, $a$ and $b$ are the degrees of contribution from labor and capital to output. This production function is changed into another form by processing both sides with logarithm and replacing GDP with $Q$, so the formula is changed to $\ln GDP = \ln A + \ln L + \ln K$.

[9]The calculation process is as follows: $\ln GDP1 = \ln A + 0.6\ln(L*1.01) + 0.4\ln K$

namely, $\ln GDP1 = \ln A + 0.6\ln L + 0.6\ln(1.01) + 0.4\ln K$

$\ln GDP1 - \ln GDP = 0.6\ln(1.01) = \ln(GDP1/GDP)$

$GDP1/GDP = 1.01^{0.6} = 1.00598$.

**Table 7.2**  The contribution from the migrant population to the GDP, 2003–2013

|      | The number of the employed people in the whole society (10,000) | The rate of contribution from the labor force to the GDP (%) | The proportion of the working-age migrant population in the employed people in the whole society (%) | The rate of contribution from the working-age migrant population to the GDP (%) |
|------|------|------|------|------|
| 2003 | 2918.74 | 52.15 | 27.7  | 14.44 |
| 2004 | 2991.95 | 51.29 | 33.15 | 17    |
| 2005 | 3100.76 | 50.74 | 37.47 | 19.01 |
| 2006 | 3172.38 | 50.05 | 41.41 | 20.73 |
| 2007 | 3405.01 | 49.59 | 44.16 | 21.9  |
| 2008 | 3486.53 | 49.06 | 47.07 | 23.09 |
| 2009 | 3591.98 | 48.94 | 48.71 | 23.84 |
| 2010 | 3636.02 | 48.09 | 48.27 | 23.21 |
| 2011 | 3674.11 | 47.44 | 54.26 | 25.74 |
| 2012 | 3691.24 | 47.14 | 59.97 | 28.27 |
| 2013 | 3708.73 | 46.81 | 57.33 | 26.84 |

*Source* The data regarding the migrant population come from the Department of Public Security of Zhejiang Province, the data regarding the number of the employed people in the whole society and the GDP come from the Zhejiang Statistical Yearbook (2004–2014)

According to the data analysis from the Department of Public Security of Zhejiang Province, the population aged between 16 and 59 accounted for an average of 90.36% of the migrant population in the past five years, while that proportion was higher in the past; we conservatively take 90% of the migrant population as the labor force. For details, see Table 7.2.

According to Table 7.2, the rate of contribution from the labor force to the economy in Zhejiang decreased year by year, but the rate of contribution from the migrant population to the economy increased from 14.44% in 2003 to 26.84% in 2013. As indicated, the migrant population has played a huge role in Zhejiang's economic development.

Another line of thought of quantitative analysis is as follows: compare the average wage of the migrant population to that of Zhejiang's local population, convert the difference into monetary input, and then adopt the relationship between capital input and GDP growth to measure the contribution from the migrant population to Zhejiang's economic growth. In this case, we assume that if there is no migrant population, Zhejiang's local population can ensure a continued supply, the labor force necessary for Zhejiang's economic development can be obtained at the local level. However, the wages of the local labor force are high, so Zhejiang's enterprises need to bear more costs. At present, the additional cost does not need to be borne and is dealt with by the "contribution" from the migrant labor force. Of course, there is deviation in the assumption that the local labor force is the same as the migrant labor force. This is because the local labor force enjoys some advantages compared with the migrant labor force. In particular, some local individual businesses have an operating capacity which cannot be found among the migrant population. However, most people in the society are almost the same in quality and skills, so such a quantitative analysis can offer a certain basis for us.

In 2013, the average annual wage of on-post staff and workers in Zhejiang (the units in the whole society, including private economic units) was 44,513 yuan. According to the dynamic monitoring data on the migrant population in Zhejiang, the average wage of the migrant population in April, 2013 was 3311 yuan, thus the average annual wage was 39,732 yuan; we tentatively consider this figure as the average annual wage of the migrant population in Zhejiang. Thus, the difference in annual wages between the local labor force and the migrant labor force was about 44,513–39,732 = 4781 yuan. This means that as Zhejiang's enterprises employ the migrant labor force, the cost can be saved by 4781 yuan as compared with the local labor force. In 2013, the population of the labor force among the migrant population in Zhejiang was 21,262,200; thus, Zhejiang's enterprises saved costs by a total amount of 101.66 billion yuan.

### 7.3.2 The Migrant Population Provides Abundant Labor Resources, Mitigating the Conflicts between Supply and Demand

The growth in the regional migrant population results from the role of the laws of economics; it is an important sign of economic prosperity and social development. The improvement in social productive forces can promote population aggregation, while population aggregation can stimulate regional economic development. According to Adam Smith, continued population growth is the symbol of economic prosperity in a country or territory; it is the result of economic development and also the reason for economic development. The growing migrant population in Zhejiang has pushed forward economic and social development.

First, quantitatively, the migrant population has provided Zhejiang with abundant labor resources and eased the conflicts between labor supply and demand. Since the reform and opening-up, with rapid economic development in Zhejiang, labor demand has been on the rise, the migrant population serves as the supplement amidst a labor shortage in Zhejiang.

Historically, 40% of the additional employed population in Zhejiang was the migrant population. With more than 30 years of development, Zhejiang has been far ahead of the central and western regions in the level of industrialization; Zhejiang has become a large manufacturing province in China and has attracted a massive rural surplus labor force from the central and western regions to work in Zhejiang. According to the data from the bureau of statistics, the total number of the employed people in Zhejiang increased from 17,949,600 in 1978 to 37,087,300 in 2013, up 19,137,700, an average annual increase of 2.10%; the population with Zhejiang's registered permanent residence increased from 37,509,600 to 48,268,900, up 10,759,300, an average annual increase of 0.72%. The growth rate of the population with Zhejiang's registered permanent residence was noticeably lower than that of the employed people, and 43.80% of the new employed population was the migrant population.

Second, in terms of the age structure, the migrant population has mitigated the pressure from population ageing and injected vigor into Zhejiang. The average age of the working-age population and the proportion of the working-age population aged 45 and above in the total number of those within the working-age population increased year by year in Zhejiang. According to the communiqué on the sample survey of the population released by the Zhejiang Provincial Bureau of Statistics, in late 2013, the population below the age of 14 accounted for 13.23% of the total permanent population in Zhejiang, while the population aged between 15 and 64 and that aged 65 and above accounted for 76.52% and 10.26%. As shown by the data on the population with registered permanent residence, the population below the age of 18 accounted for 16.62%, while that aged between 18 and 60 and that aged 60 and above accounted for 64.70% and 18.68%. Obviously, the population with registered permanent residence showed a higher degree of ageing. Population ageing will certainly affect the vitality of economic development and the ability to carry out innovations, while the young migrant population has grown rapidly, playing a certain role in mitigating the ageing of the permanent or actual population in Zhejiang.

Third, from the perspective of employment level, the migrant population has filled the employment gap caused by the economic structural adjustment in urban areas and is conducive to a rational allocation of labor resources in Zhejiang. On the one hand, the migrant population has provided abundant labor resources for the development of the secondary industry. Zhejiang's industrialization mainly features a labor-intensive industrial structure in which the labor force is the main factor contributing to industrial development. The employed population flowing into Zhejiang is concentrated in the secondary industry, providing ample labor resources for the development of the secondary industry, thus offering a labor guarantee for speeding up industrialization and modernization in Zhejiang. On the other hand, the migrant population has provided a guarantee for the development of the tertiary industry in Zhejiang. As the tertiary industry contains labor-intensive, technology-intensive and capital-intensive sectors covering a wide range of categories and fields, the tertiary industry needs a lot of labor. As a massive labor force at different levels flows into Zhejiang, at the macro level, that flow is conducive to matching supply with demand on the labor market and rationally allocating labor resources in Zhejiang.

### 7.3.3 The Migrant Population Stimulates the Consumer Market and Boosts Urban Development

Urbanization is a historical process in which the human production mode and lifestyle change from rural ones to urban ones, as evidenced by the change of the rural population into an urban population, continued urban development and improvement. The level of urbanization is a quantitative indicator for measuring the degree of urban development; generally, it is expressed in the proportion of the urban population in the total population in a certain area. For a long time, the level of urbanization was measured by the proportion of the population with urban registered permanent residence in the proportion with regional registered permanent residence; with an accelerated migration of the population, such a measurement deviated increasingly from the reality; later, the permanent population was gradually adopted. In fact, this change indicates that population migration has exerted a far-reaching impact on urbanization.

The migrant population has promoted the development of urban businesses. First, the massive migrant population brings an enormous consumption power; they push forward the development of agriculture, animal husbandry and fishery and sidelines in the areas surrounding cities, and they play a very big role in driving economic development forward. Second, as the massive migrant population engages in business, catering and service industries in urban areas, they generate more revenue to urban areas while increasing their income.

### 7.3.4 The Migrant Population Accelerates Social Mobility and Promotes Modern Change in Social Governance

Social mobility refers to the changes in the people's particular social status. Social mobility is divided into vertical mobility and horizontal mobility. Vertical mobility means the rise and fall of the people's status, while horizontal mobility mainly refers to regional and spatial mobility of the population. Based on horizontal mobility among regions, the migrant population seeks to achieve upward mobility. Many of them have improved in identity and status through their unremitting efforts. That improvement brings about progress in the whole society.

The attitude towards the migrant population in an area reflects, to a certain extent, the level of civility, harmony and social management in that area. This is because under the market economy, it is impossible for an area to reject personnel flow, and the economic development in an area depends upon the mass flow of talents and materials. As a province into which a massive migrant population flows, Zhejiang has made attempts at and experiments on introducing new management methods; this is the intrinsic need of the social management of the migrant population; for instance, in 2005, Jiashan established the Bureau of New Resident Affairs; in 2006, Zhejiang became the first to develop the national coordinated service management mechanism for family planning; in 2008, a system for the management of information regarding the migrant population covering the provincial, municipal, county and town levels across the province was built; in 2009, Zhejiang became the first to introduce a system for the management of migrant population residence permits throughout the province. Moreover, Zhejiang has also explored and established the mechanisms involving cross-regional collaborative management of the migrant population, such as the Yangtze River Delta regional cooperation mechanism and the mechanism of cooperation with the provinces as the main sources of migrant population. The migrant population is complicated and dynamic, so it can continuously promote innovation and improvement in the mechanism for social management and propel the modern transformation of social governance.

## 7.4   The Establishment of the System for Services for and Management of the Migrant Population

The integrated service management of the migrant population covers many fields and is a major complicated and systematic project, thus it is particularly important for building a system of services for the migrant population. With the development of the market economy and social transformation, the social issues involved in the current services for the migrant population have become increasingly complicated, so it is necessary to value the services for and management of the migrant population in terms of philosophy, holistically design framework of services for the migrant population, open-mindedly deal with the problems in the services for and management of the migrant population and continuously innovate that system.

### 7.4.1   Developing a Relevant Philosophy as a Guide, Giving Priority to the Services for and the Management of the Migrant Population

The Party Committee and the People's Government of Zhejiang Province have attached great importance to the services for and the management of the migrant population, and have studied those aspects by taking them as a major issue for strengthening and innovating social management and promoting sustainable economic and social development. The main leaders of the successive Party Committees and the People's Governments of Zhejiang Province have often followed the work on the services for and management of the migrant population, conducted surveys and arranged for relevant work to be carried out.

In 2005, comrade Xi Jinping pointed out that rural migrant workers were important forces for promoting economic development and building a harmonious society; rural migrant workers were part of the farmers and the working class; rural migrant workers had made great contributions to urban and social development, so we must show that we take care of them; rural migrant workers were the main part of the migrant population, so the way of treating rural migrant workers reflected the way of dealing with the migrant population.

Zhejiang has always paid a great deal of attention to the services for and the management of the migrant population. The successive Party committees and the people's governments in Zhejiang have carried through one blueprint to pursue development year after year, and have actively built a system of services for and management of the migrant population by putting the people first. Comrade Zhao Hongzhu stated that we should establish and improve a system for the management of the migrant population in which the government exercises the unified leadership, departments engage in cooperation based on a division of the work, various parties participate in relevant work and resources are effectively integrated, and we should make local people show more inclusiveness and a stronger sense of identity towards the migrant population; moreover, we should further integrate the migrant population into the areas where they live and make sure that they develop a stronger sense of belonging to these areas. Comrade Xia Baolong stressed that it was essential to put the people first and give priority to services, firmly uphold the philosophy of giving fair treatment, giving paramount consideration to services and exercising management according to laws, and to provide services through management and perform management in services, achieve a transformation from preventive and control-based management into individual and service-oriented management so as to increase the level of the services for and the management of the migrant population in an all-round way.

## 7.4.2  Making Institutional Arrangements First, Intensifying the Reform of the System of Services for and Management of the Migrant Population

The specific attributes of the institutional structure determine the pattern of distributing social resources, opportunities and powers and the direction of their allocation. The design innovations in institutions are not made on a single segment; instead, they involve correlation among multiple institutions and represent a set of institutional designs and arrangements. In essence, an institutional system is an institutional network. Good institutions can create a fair and harmonious working and living environment for the migrant population, and they address the pressing issues regarding their employment income, social security, protection of rights and interests and living environment, so that they can enjoy fair opportunities for survival and development, get equal access to public resources and social welfare, and so that they are able to live in an inclusive and friendly social environment.

First, top-level design of institutions, namely, a management system. In 2006, Zhejiang established the system of joint meeting on the work relating to rural migrant workers with a view to strengthening coordination in safeguarding the rights and interests of rural migrant workers. In 2006, the Department of Public Security of Zhejiang Province set up the office for the services for and the management of the migrant population as a provincial-level body for carrying out daily work on those services and that management. In 2009, the Party Committee and the People's Government of Zhejiang Province established the provincial group of leaders for the services for and the management of the migrant population, which consists of the people in charge of 17 relevant functional departments and is responsible for daily work, with its office set up at the Department of Public Security of Zhejiang Province. Eleven cities established the comprehensive coordination bodies for the services for and the management of the migrant population, which are headed by the leaders in charge from the Party committee and the government with the participation of the people in charge of relevant functional departments, among which 8 cities and 96 county-level units established the bodies of services for and management of the migrant population or standing bodies at the level of the Party committee or the government.

Second, concrete institutional innovations. Zhejiang made bold innovations in reforming the household registration system. Against the background that fundamental change had not yet been made in the system of management of national household registration, Zhejiang made active experiments, took continuous practical actions, and piloted the reform of the household registration system. Based on summing up successful experience and drawing lessons from failures, as from October 1, 2009, Zhejiang has carried out the *Regulations of Zhejiang Province on Residence Registration of the Migrant Population* throughout the province, making breakthroughs in the institutional development involving the migrant population; this indicated that Zhejiang's management of the migrant population had entered the stage of residence permit management from the stage of temporary residence permit management.

Regarding the institutional development involving the migrant population, besides the regulations on residence registration of the migrant population, Zhejiang has also issued a number of documents for services for and management of the migrant population: in January, 2006, the Party Committee and the People's Government of Zhejiang Province issued the *Several Opinions on Further Strengthening and Improving the Services for and the Management of Rural Migrant Workers*; in August, 2006, the People's Government of Zhejiang Province issued the *Implementation Opinions on Addressing the Issue of Rural Migrant Workers*; in September, 2009, the People's Government of Zhejiang Province developed the *Implementation Opinions on Establishing the Social Endowment Insurance System for Urban and Rural Residents*; in August, 2009 and October, 2010, the General Office of the People's Government of Zhejiang Province issued the *Opinions on the Implementation of the Regulations of Zhejiang Province on Residence Registration of the Migrant Population* and the *Circular Concerning Issuing the Plan of Zhejiang Province for the Building of the Integrated Information Platform for the Migrant Population*, specifying institutional norms for the employment security for the migrant population, public services, legitimate rights and interests, social management and information-sharing concerning the migrant population. Furthermore, since 2009, Zhejiang has held a provincial working conference on the migrant population in the name of the Party Committee and the People's Government of Zhejiang Province four consecutive times, arranging the measures for promoting the work on the migrant population.

### 7.4.3 Engaging in Open Communication, Innovating the Cooperation Mechanism for the Services for and the Management of the Migrant Population

The services for and the management of the migrant population are not merely based on administrative division. This is because the migrant population comes from the areas from which the migrant population flows, and it may flow among different regions, thus when it comes to the services for and the management of the migrant population, Zhejiang has always engaged in open communication and brought innovations to the mechanism for cooperation.

Zhejiang has engaged in cooperation in various forms and at various levels with the governments in the main areas from which the migrant population flows. For instance, since 2007, the department of population and family planning of Zhejiang Province has signed the agreements with Henan Province and Shandong Province with respect to joint efforts in strengthening cooperation on population and family planning; the two sides have jointly established the Association of Family Planning for New Residents to engage in cross-provincial and cross-regional cooperation, and have worked together to build a platform for the management of the information on the total population-related individualized tracking service.

Zhejiang has also engaged in regional cooperation with the pan-Yangtze River Delta region regarding the services for and the management of the migrant population. In 2007, the departments of family planning of Jiangsu Province, Zhejiang Province and Shanghai reached the *Opinions on the Issues Concerning Strengthening Regional Coordinated Cooperation on Family Planning Services and on the Management of the Migrant Population*, specifying the basic principles for regional cooperation, the administrative procedure for family planning, the duties of childbearing-related technical service management, the reporting of information about pregnancy and childbearing of the migrant population, and cooperation on the collection of social compensation fees relating to illegal childbearing.

In 2010, Zhejiang, as the rotating province for the pan-Yangtze River Delta region, held a meeting on regional cooperation, in which Shanghai, six provinces, Jiangsu, Zhejiang, Anhui, Jiangxi, Henan and Hubei, signed a regional cooperation agreement, and vowed to jointly carry out the *Implementation Plan for Regional Coordinated Work on Migrant Population Family Planning in the Pan-Yangtze River Delta Region*, the *Action Plan for Network Cooperation on the Services for and the Management of the Migrant Population in the Pan-Yangtze River Delta Region*, the *Guiding Opinions on Public Services for Migrant Population Family Planning in the Pan-Yangtze River Delta Region*, the *Regulations on the Registration of the Migrant Population for the One-Child Childbearing Service in the Pan-Yangtze River Delta*

*Region*, and the *Agreement on the* collection of social compensation fees *Involving the Migrant Population in the Pan-Yangtze River Delta Region*, strengthening internal regional integration, cooperation and coordination, building the regional cooperation framework for information exchange, equal access to services and policy research and other respects, more rapidly shaping the work pattern for the exchange of regional information, service complementation, management interaction and the sharing of responsibilities, ultimately laying a foundation for national coordinated development. Moreover, since 2013, the People's Government of Zhejiang Province has worked with the people's governments of five provinces including Anhui, Guizhou, Jiangxi, Henan and Sichuan to establish the mechanism of two-way cooperation on the migrant population; the two sides signed the agreements on regional cooperation on the services for and the management of the migrant population, enhancing communication and cooperation between the governments and departments in the areas from which and to which the migrant population flows.

### 7.4.4  Upholding Inheritance and Innovation, Safeguarding and Improving the Public Service System for the Migrant Population

**The labor employment system.** Zhejiang has earnestly carried out the *Law of the People's Republic of China on Employment Promotion*, the *Law of the People's Republic of China on Labor Contracts*, the *Regulations of the People's Republic of China on the Implementation of Labor Contracts* and relevant national laws and regulations, promptly made and issued local regulations fit for different areas, providing an institutional guarantee for the labor rights of the migrant population.

First, guaranteeing the right of the migrant population to labor remuneration. Wage is the main source of income for the migrant population, so arrears of wages will directly affect their life and social stability. At present, Zhejiang has comprehensively implemented the systems involving security deposits for the payment of wages, the government's emergency revolving fund for the arrears of wages and time cards for rural migrant workers, while the foundation for building the brand of Zhejiang as a province without arrears of wages was laid in 2003. In 2003, local authorities in Zhejiang explored and established the system involving security deposits for the payment of wages for rural migrant workers in construction enterprises, standardizing the behavior of construction enterprises in labor employment and solving the problem concerning the arrears of wages caused by construction enterprises for rural migrant workers; in 2004, Zhejiang initiated the emergency revolving fund for the arrears of wages; in 2007, the People's Government of Zhejiang Province required that the enterprises engaged in construction, decoration, the construction of transportation, leasing of operating premises and other enterprises in which arrears of wages occurred once must put in place security deposits in advance, and security deposits must be managed under special accounts and specially used to pay the wages not yet paid by the enterprises; in 2008, the system involving the emergency revolving fund for the arrears of wages was established in all cities, counties (county-level cities, districts) in Zhejiang, under the system, thus ensuring advance payment through the government's public finances and enhancing the government's capability for handling the emergencies involving the arrears of wages; in 2011, the People's Government of Zhejiang Province signed agreements on objective responsibility for work with the governments of 11 cities divided into districts to prevent and handle the arrears of wages caused by enterprises.

Second, guaranteeing the ability of the migrant population to obtain employment. As from 2004, Zhejiang carried out the project for quality training concerning the rural labor force of 10 million people; in 2006, Zhejiang developed the training plan for improving the occupational skills of rural migrant workers in Zhejiang; on-the-job training and skills training have accelerated the integration of the migrant population in urban areas.

**The social security system.** Given the characteristics of the migrant population, Zhejiang has started with the work-related injury and medical insurances most needed for the migrant population to gradually incorporate the migrant population into the social security system. In 2007, Zhejiang identified rural migrant workers in construction enterprises as the priority for increasing the coverage of the work-related injury insurance and worked out the policy for making sure that rural migrant workers in construction enterprises are covered by the work-related injury insurance. Regarding medical security, in 2004, Zhejiang issued the *Several Opinions on Further Intensifying the Reform of the Medicine and Health Care System*, stressing continued efforts to actively and steadily make sure that more of the migrant population is covered by medical insurance.

**The housing security system.** A stable residence not only addresses the housing issue for the migrant population but it is also the foundation for the migrant population to integrate themselves into cities and develop a sense of belonging. At present, housing security is provided to the migrant population mainly in the following three ways in the prefecture-level cities in Zhejiang: First, encouraging the purchase of commercial housing—local governments have actively explored and established the housing fund system for the migrant population to help them with stable work and certain savings so as to be able to obtain a housing loan; second, encouraging enterprises and local governments to build special houses for the migrant population, for instance, large enterprises or economic development zones provide dormitory-type housing or low-rent housing for the migrant population through self-construction, co-construction with local governments, joint construction between local governments and village committees; third, properly serving and managing the migrant population in living in private houses through renting; the *Administrative Measures of Zhejiang Province for Residential House Renting Registration* became effective as from 2011. Zhejiang has actively encouraged local governments and enterprises to improve the living conditions for the migrant population through multiple channels, gradually address, in stages, the issue of housing security for the migrant population who have worked and lived in cities for a long time, and solidly promote the building of the housing security system for the migrant population.

**The childbearing health care system.** In 2006, Zhejiang became the first to put forward the national coordinated mechanism for the management of the service of family planning, vigorously promoted localized management and citizen services, adopted the mode of ensuring the same publicity, management and services for the migrant population and the population with registered permanent residence. In 2008, the migrant population information management system covering the provincial, municipal, county and town levels was applied across the province; the system extended to villages (communities) in some counties; it incorporated most of the migrant population into the framework for the management of the system of family planning services, continuously enhancing the administrative efficiency and service capability for public health service relating to the migrant population in Zhejiang.

**The educational system for the children of the migrant population.** Besides earnestly carrying out the *Law of Compulsory Education* and the *Transmittal by the General Office of the State Council of the Circular of the Ministry of Education and Other Departments on Further Improving the Work on Education Concerning the Children of Rural Migrant Workers*, the governments at various levels in Zhejiang also promptly made local regulations and implementation opinions, providing an institutional guarantee for ensuring that migrant children have equal access to education and basically incorporating the children of the migrant population into the local compulsory education system. In late 2009, the People's Government of Zhejiang Province issued the *Implementation Opinions on Carrying out the Guiding Opinions of the State Council on Further Promoting Reform, Opening-Up, Economic and Social Development in the Yangtze River Delta Region*, stating that Zhejiang would gradually ensure that the children of the migrant population enjoy the same rights in education as the children in cities. In March, 2010, Zhejiang carried out the *Regulations of Zhejiang Province on Compulsory Education*, stipulating that where the people with the province's residence permit and their children living with them need to receive compulsory education in their place of residence, the competent department for education of the people's government at the county level must provide a guarantee accordingly. More than 95% of the migrant children in the cities and counties in Zhejiang attend schools, basically addressing the issue of education concerning the school-age children of the migrant population.

## 7.5 The Practice of Expanding the Social Integration of the Migrant Population[10]

As the size of the migrant population continues to be large, the migrant population lives in the areas to which the migrant population flows for a longer time and

---

[10]See Yang (2008).

household-based flow has become increasingly prevalent; in fact, a large part of the migrant population is in the state of "staying" rather than "migrating", they hope to integrate themselves into the society in the areas to which they flow and get equal access to basic public services and welfare benefits.

Zhejiang is a large province with a migrant population and also a province where the work on the services for and the management of the migrant population is carried out better than in other provinces. Regarding accelerating the social integration of the migrant population, Zhejiang has made many experiments and has made a lot of practical actions: Zhejiang regards the migrant population as new people of Zhejiang, Zhejiang has become the first to carry out the residence permit system for its migrant population; Zhejiang has made continuous experiments in ensuring that the migrant population enjoys the same treatment as the urban population. Being open-minded and inclusive, Zhejiang has created a great deal of excellent experience in serving the new people of Zhejiang and promoting social integration.

### 7.5.1 Jiaxing City Became the First to Experiment the Residence Permit System

As from October 1, 2009, Zhejiang carried out the *Administrative Regulations of Zhejiang Province on Residence Registration of the Migrant Population* across the province, while Jiaxing City, as a pilot area, carried out experiments in this regard earlier. In November, 2006, Jiaxing issued the *Several Opinions on Strengthening the Work on the Services for and the Management of New Residents in Jiaxing*. In April, 2007, Jiaxing was designated by Zhejiang as the pilot prefecture-level city for the reform of the services for and the management of the migrant population. In November, 2007, a batch of residence permits were issued on a piloted basis in Pinghu, Jiaxing. As from January 1, 2008, Jiaxing comprehensively promoted the residence permit system. The new residence permit is divided into three types of permit under two categories, including the red temporary residence permit, the green residence permit and the residence permit for professional employees. These three types of permits are different in the conditions of their application. The conditions for applying for a temporary residence permit are basically the same as that for the original temporary residence permit: the new residents who are at the age of 16 and plan to live in the areas of temporary residence for more than 30 days can apply for a temporary residence permit. The residence permit holders can hold Jiaxing's temporary residence permit for more than one year; applicants must have received education above the junior middle school level; the period from the application date to the statutory time for receiving the basic pension must be at least 15 years. For the residence permit for professional employees, applicants are subject to relatively high requirements: they must have received education above the level of technical secondary school including senior middle school, or have mastered a professional skill, and they must have held a residence permit for two years (a temporary residence permit for three years). In the meantime, applicants are subject to point-based evaluation on whether there is a legal fixed domicile, a stable source of income and whether laws and discipline are observed.

Although Jiaxing was not the first to introduce a residence permit, previously Shanghai and Shenzhen introduced a residence permit, Jiaxing's innovation lies in promoting the reform of welfare benefits attached to the residence permit. The residence permit will be linked to social security, employment, residence, children's education and family planning; the residence permit holders can enjoy certain benefits and preferential policies as Jiaxing citizens. As calculated, after the reform of introducing the residence permit, each year Jiaxing allocates about 100 million yuan and 30 million yuan in fiscal funds for the education of the children of the new residents and family planning, respectively, there is also a fiscal expenditure on medical insurance.

Jiaxing's reform in the household registration management of the migrant population is of important demonstration significance for Zhejiang to initiate the household registration reform in an all-round way across the province. In June, 2009, Zhejiang issued the *Regulations of Zhejiang Province on Residence Registration of the Migrant Population*, which became effective across the province as from October 1, 2009; the *Administrative Regulations of Zhejiang Province for the Temporary Resident Population*, implemented for 14 years, were abolished at the same time. According to the regulations, all of the migrant population satisfying certain conditions can apply for Zhejiang's temporary residence permit or residence permit, the holders of either a temporary residence permit or a residence permit can enjoy social security, public services and other benefits; where the holders of Zhejiang's residence permit satisfy the conditions required by the people's governments above the county level, the holders can apply for registered permanent residence in the place of their residence.

This suggests that Zhejiang's management of its migrant population has entered the stage of the management of the temporary residence permit and it has left the stage of management of the residence permit. This is a great institutional breakthrough. Its significance is that it is universal and changes the previous practice of only rewarding a small part of the migrant population. Literally, "temporary residence" contains an additional word compared with "residence"; however, as the residence permit is introduced, the migrant population becomes the local population, has a sense of being respected and a sense of belonging; the residence permit vigorously promotes the rapid development of Zhejiang's new-type urbanization, and boosts social integration between the migrant population and the local population, and the building of a harmonious society in Zhejiang.

## 7.5.2 Hangzhou City Ensures that Rural Migrant Workers Enjoy the Same Benefits as Urban Residents

Hangzhou City has actively explored the institutional arrangement for ensuring that rural migrant workers get access to the same benefits as urban residents, gradually overcome the difficulty that rural migrant workers cannot enjoy residents' welfare benefits due to registered permanent residence. The urban public welfare system has gradually covered all social groups in urban areas in Hangzhou. In January, 2006, Hangzhou issued the *Several Opinions on Improving the Work on the Employment and Life of Rural Migrant Workers*, ensuring that rural migrant workers enjoy benefits just like urban residents in the following six aspects: ensuring an income for rural migrant workers by establishing and improving the wage payment guarantee system to ensure the wages of rural migrant workers are paid in full and on time; providing rural migrant workers with access to housing by enabling coordination among cities, districts, sub-districts (communities), enterprises and individuals and gradually establishing a multiform, multi-actor, multi-channel and multilevel housing security system for rural migrant workers; providing rural migrant workers with access to education by expanding enrollment in compulsory education to make sure that the children of rural migrant workers who satisfy the relevant conditions can receive education; ensuring rural migrant workers' access to medical service by improving the basic medical service system to mitigate the difficulties that rural migrant workers encounter in receiving medical services; making sure that rural migrant workers enjoy social security by basically establishing a social security system fit for the characteristics of rural migrant workers; providing organization for rural migrant workers by further increasing the degree of organization to make sure that more than 70% of the rural migrant workers who satisfy the conditions can join trade unions, and incorporating rural migrant workers who are the Party members into the Party organization of enterprises or communities for management.

Since Hangzhou introduced measures for making sure that rural migrant workers enjoy the same benefits as urban residents, the work in various respects has been carried out in an orderly fashion. With regard to ensuring an income, rural migrant workers receive the same pay as ordinary industrial workers doing the same work; the minimum wage system is strictly enforced so as to make sure that the minimum labor remuneration for rural migrant workers is not lower than the local minimum wage standard; the wage payment guarantee system for the employees in construction enterprises has been established and improved, the wage payment guarantee system is established in small and medium-sized leasing enterprises and the enterprises under contracted operations, the system of collective consultation on wages is actively carried out; intensified efforts are made to monitor the payment of wages for rural migrant workers, enterprises are urged to pay wages on a monthly basis; the system of an emergency revolving fund for living security for rural migrant workers subject to arrears in wages in enterprises has been established and improved; measures are being taken to prevent vicious cases in which business owners abscond after arrears of wages occurs. With regard to ensuring access to housing, enterprises are encouraged to build dormitories for rural migrant workers in Hangzhou; the urban areas, sub-districts (towns), communities (villages) in which rural migrant workers are concentrated are encouraged to build a number of low-rent apartments for rural migrant workers, the government provides the necessary infrastructure, improves the public transportation system, environmental and health conditions, and raises the living standard and the quality of dwellings of rural migrant workers in Hangzhou. Regarding the guarantee of access to education, the children of rural migrant workers are incorporated into the local plan for educational development; public schools play the leading role, supplemented by schools of the children of rural migrant workers, so that the children of rural migrant workers can enjoy urban benefits by relying on the resources of public schools. In September, 2009, the Bureau of Education of Hangzhou City issued the *Implementation Opinions on Better Carrying out the Work on Compulsory Education Involving the Children of Rural Migrant Workers*, specifying eight measures for making sure that the children of rural migrant workers really enjoy the same benefits as local children. With regard to ensuring access to medical service, the services of community-level health service bodies are extended from the population with registered permanent residence to the permanent service population within the areas involved. With regard to ensuring access to medical security, the work-related injury insurance basically provides full coverage across the city; the issue of the most basic medical security for rural migrant workers has been addressed in light of the fundraising burden on enterprises and the bearing capacity of rural migrant workers; given the high mobility of rural migrant workers and the low level of their income, the endowment insurance policy of making insurance contributions at a low standard and enjoying benefits at a low standard is being studied and developed. Regarding ensuring organization for rural migrant workers, rural migrant workers who are the Party members are incorporated into the Party organization of enterprises or communities, improving the work on developing the Party members among rural migrant workers and further guaranteeing the right of rural migrant workers to participate in trade unions.

### 7.5.3 Yiwu City More Rapidly "Localizes" Rural Migrant Workers

Yiwu is a city which has developed rapidly, while that development is largely attributable to the participation of rural migrant workers in Yiwu's economic, social and cultural development. For the size of its population, Yiwu has become a multi-ethnic immigrant city where rural migrant workers outnumber local people. According to the sixth population census in 2010, Yiwu's permanent population reached 1,234,000, while the migrant population was 585,800, accounting for 32.2%. As Yiwu has witnessed rapid economic development in recent years, more and more people have come to Yiwu to work and do business. Yiwu has carried out work on the following aspects: First, actively introducing the policy of localizing the migrant population, gradually making sure that rural migrant workers enjoy the same benefits as citizens regarding social security, medical services, housing, employment, children's education, employment introduction and labor protection, enhancing their sense of belonging and sense of ownership, really integrating them into their second hometown, changing their status from marginalized people in urban areas to the new force for urban development. Second, integrating services into the whole process of management, optimizing services to promote management, offering excellent services to enhance cohesion. Yiwu has established an organization of management covering the municipal, town (sub-district) and community (rural area) levels, and exercises management with full-time management personnel, a coordinator and liaison personnel, it promotes socialized management, warmhearted services and individualized law enforcement. Given that there are many resident foreign merchants, Yiwu is actively experimenting with a new mechanism of foreign-related police affairs, it has established a system of foreign-related specialist and foreign-related liaison personnel. Third, enhancing identity recognition. Yiwu regards rural migrant workers as external builders and treats them equally in an open and inclusive way. The outstanding example is that Yiwu has become the first nationwide to invite rural migrant workers to participate in the election of the deputies to the people's congress and the CPPCC members and to serve as the people's assessors.

### 7.5.4  Ningbo City Provides a Package of Social Insurances for Rural Migrant Workers

As a southeastern coastal developed area, Ningbo City has achieved rapid economic and social development and enjoys a good employment situation, and it has become one of the preferred cities for rural migrant workers to work and live in. Ningbo has attached great importance to and has strengthened the services for and management of rural migrant workers, has earnestly safeguarded the rights and interests of rural migrant workers, promoted the social integration of rural migrant workers and it has made constant efforts to optimize the employment environment. Since 2004, Ningbo has, under the principle of giving priority to social insurances, energetically stimulated rural migrant workers to first seek the coverage of work-related injury insurance, made a series of relevant policies; for instance, allowing the employers to provide insurance coverage for rural migrant workers on production and operation sites; stating that in case rural migrant workers are injured due to accidents or suffer from occupational diseases, the work-related injury is identified and the ability to work is appraised in the areas where the insurance coverage is provided. On May 1, 2006, the *Interim Measures of Ningbo City for Low-standard Endowment Insurance for Workers* and the *Interim Measures of Ningbo City for Hospitalization-related Medical Insurance* officially became effective, incorporating low-income groups, including rural migrant workers, into the scope of insurance coverage. Subject to appropriately reducing the burden on enterprises with respect to insurance contributions, based on application, rural migrant workers are not obliged to make any insurance contributions, and insurance contributions and the assistance fund for serious diseases are fully borne by the employers.

In October, 2007, the People's Government of Ningbo City officially issued the *Interim Measures of Ningbo City for Social Insurance for Rural Migrant Workers*, which officially became effective as from January 1, 2008. These interim measures present a package of social insurances covering the work-related injury insurance, medical insurance for serious diseases, endowment insurance, unemployment insurance and maternity insurance urgently needed for rural migrant workers; these interim measures specially provide a composite package of social insurances for more than 3 million rural migrant workers. This social insurance package policy for rural migrant workers is better suited to the reality of enterprises and the insured; it ensures a connection between old and new policies, communication between low and high-standard social insurances, the transfer of social insurances between the inside and the outside, among regions, high compatibility and connectivity. This feasible new social insurance system is expected to change the current situation in which most rural migrant workers are not covered by the social insurance system; undoubtedly, it is of important significance for improving and implementing the national policy for rural migrant workers.

Social security is a right given by the state to every worker. Establishing the social security system for rural migrant workers is essential for safeguarding the basic civil rights of those workers. The social insurance package for rural migrant workers, introduced by Ningbo, has been well received throughout the entire society; this system offers active experimentations and beneficial experience for establishing and improving the social security system for rural migrant workers in Zhejiang, and even nationwide.

### 7.5.5  Diankou, Zhuji Creatively Leverages the Resources of Fellow-Townsmen

Diankou, Zhuji has introduced three policemen who are fellow-townsmen from Guizhou and Jiangxi on the basis of consultation since 2004, and has established the mode under which external police assist with the management of the migrant population. External police do not participate in law enforcement and case handling by local public security organs, but they are responsible for managing the migrant population, providing clues, mediating conflicts and disputes, conducting publicity and education involving legal affairs. The cadres who are fellow-townsmen are utilized to overcome the management difficulties caused by different regional cultures; the mode under which fellow-townsmen manage fellow-townsmen is conducive to communication and understanding between local governments and rural migrant workers.

Fellow-townsmen represent a network of interpersonal relationships which congenitally arise out of regional characteristics; after the migrant population goes outside their hometown, they often accumulate their social capital, find jobs and start businesses through the relationship of fellow-townsmen; where necessary, they also seek help from fellow-townsmen. In the Diankou Experience, Diankou has tapped the traditional interpersonal resources—fellow-townsmen—better to serve modern social management, and has integrated the interpersonal elements peculiar to fellow-townsmen in the traditional mindset of the Chinese people—trust, kindness, friendliness and mutual assistance—into the management of the migrant population. This management mode is beneficial to save management costs, improve the efficiency of social management and maintain social harmony and stability.

The greatest significance of the Diankou Experience consists in building the bridge of communication among the governments of the areas from which the migrant population flows, the governments of the areas to which the migrant population flows and the migrant population, and basing social management on communication and trust. Since its inception, the Diankou Experience has been widely learnt; it has been promoted throughout Zhejiang and also serves as reference for the rest of the country. So far, the Diankou Experience has been applied for ten years, the mode under which external police assist with the management of the migrant population has gradually become mature. During the period from January to August, 2014 alone, the police coming from other provinces to Diankou mediated and handled 76 disputes, resolved and controlled 2 mass incidents, assisted in solving 29 criminal cases, cracked down on and dealt with 21 people.

# References

Xi Jinping, The speech delivered when meeting with rural migrant workers on the construction site of the West Lake Culture Square on August 6, 2004.

Xi Jinping, *Carrying out Solid Work to Stay Ahead—Line of Thought and Practice in Promoting New Development in Zhejiang*, The Party School of the CPC Central Committee Press, 2006.

Yang Jianhua, The Title, Migration of Rural Migrant Workers and Its Sociological Significance, *Journal of the Party School of CPC Ningbo*, 2008(5).

# Chapter 8
# The Building of a Safe Zhejiang

Jianhua Yang

Safety is a blessing; this is a plain creed in the life of the Chinese people. Safety is a blessing; this is a plain creed in the life of the Chinese people. When social development enables the people to go beyond the state of seeking survival, adequate food and clothing, the people have higher expectations about safety. When safety has increasingly become the people's important need, the fundamental significance of safety, which is an important part of the people's well-being, has become more prominent. Zhejiang officially vowed to build a safe Zhejiang in 2004. Now, more than ten years have elapsed. How does the development towards greater safety promote the building of a harmonious Zhejiang? What are the good practices and experience in building a safe Zhejiang? What inspirations from the building of a safe Zhejiang are available for our current social governance and modernization? These questions are discussed in this chapter.

## 8.1 The Development Towards Greater Safety and the Building of a Harmonious Zhejiang

### 8.1.1 The Development Towards Greater Safety is the Prerequisite for a Harmonious Society

Social harmony is an essential attribute of socialism with Chinese characteristics; it is an ideal pursuit in social development. Taking social harmony as an essential attribute of socialism with Chinese characteristics means that the building of a harmonious society in China embodies the essential requirement of socialism in terms of the relationship among the people, between the people and nature: neither poverty nor

J. Yang (✉)
Zhejiang Academy of Social Sciences, Hangzhou, China

© Social Sciences Academic Press and Springer Nature Singapore Pte Ltd. 2019    229
G. Chen and J. Yang (eds.), *Chinese Dream and Practice in Zhejiang—Society*,
Research Series on the Chinese Dream and China's Development Path,
https://doi.org/10.1007/978-981-13-7406-7_8

disharmony can define socialism. From the perspective of sociology, we hold that social harmony has three basic targets: social equilibrium, social sharing and social justice. It mainly covers economic and social development, a rational social structure, a fairly comfortable life, abundant public goods in the society, social fairness and justice, a safe social environment. How to build a harmonious society? It is a classic theoretical and practical issue which the people have painstakingly pondered and explored for thousands of years.

Social harmony and stability is the core element of a safe Zhejiang. Social harmony and stability is an orderly state of social and political development; it is an organic unity of the law of social development, of the effectiveness of social control and of harmony in social life. A good social order and a safe living environment are the basic preconditions for human continuity and social development. As mentioned by comrade Xi Jinping, a harmonious lute and bell sound represents harmony in rhyme; clean, clear water and lush mountains, peaks and valleys give expression to harmony in nature; good governance and the best use by people of the heavens with seasonal changes and the earth with abundant resources, a unity of the heaven and the people represent harmony between the people and nature; respect for the old and love for the young, conjugal harmony, neighborhood solidarity, understanding and tolerance and benevolence mirror harmony among the people; equality and interdependence among social classes, various sectors, good fusion without conflict, cooperation without opposition, checks and balances without impedance, orderliness without chaos among organizations in the society reflect harmony in social division of labor and in the society.[1]

### 8.1.1.1  Growing Pains

Since the beginning of the new century, as the forefront of reform and opening-up and the forerunner of the market economy, Zhejiang suffered growing pains amidst rapid economic growth earlier than other areas. These pains are mainly reflected in the following aspects.

First, accelerated economic structural adjustments have generated a new situation. With more than 30 year of development since the reform and opening-up, Zhejiang has entered a stage of rapid economic growth, it has accelerated industrial structural adjustment, resource factor bottlenecks and social change. This has put heavy pressure and a reverse force on Zhejiang's economic development. The original extensive growth mode has become unsustainable, the problem that manufacturing activities are at the low end of the industrial chain is salient, there has been increasing external pressure on industrial upgrading. A daunting task in Zhejiang's social development lies in coping with the new situation and the new problems caused by economic structural adjustments to the social structure and social governance to promote harmonious and sound social operations.

---

[1] Xi (2006), pp. 237–238.

Second, increasingly diverse social needs have raised new requirements for social development. Since the beginning of the new century, in Zhejiang, the level of resident income has increased rapidly, the consumption ability of its residents has improved significantly, the people's needs have upgraded from daily necessities to consumer durables, from private products to public goods, a stage of equal access to public products and mass consumption has come, the people have more expectations about the provision of public services. These needs cover basic public services including compulsory education, public health, basic medical services and social security, and public safety including the quality of the ecological environment, food safety and health safety. The people's needs have upgraded from the economic level to the political, cultural and ethical levels.

Third, the increasing diversity in the interest pattern has brought new challenges in social development. With the intensification of market-oriented reform and rapid social transformation, great changes have taken place in social relations, stakeholders and interest requirements have become diverse, the interest relations have become complicated. As the development is unbalanced and there are unreasonable factors in systems, mechanisms and policies, the degree of access to the achievements of reform and development varies with different groups, and in particular, the people at the primary level get insufficient access to those achievements; the developmental gap between urban and rural areas and among regions, the wealth gap among the members of the society have further widened; some people have borne more costs for reform and development, they have suffered loss in interests, and the resulting problems in social fairness and justice have greatly affected social development.

Fourth, frequent social conflicts have posed new tests to social development. Since the beginning of the new century, Zhejiang's society has been generally stable, but frequent, intensive occurrence and superposition of various conflicts and disputes have become increasingly apparent, contradictions and disputes involve diverse stakeholders, contents, appeals and forms. Social conflicts and disputes have loomed large; they involve property rights, the right to work and economic activities as well as the sharing of the achievements of reform and development. The disputes involving the people's immediate interests—enterprise relocation and restructuring, expropriation of rural land, demolition and relocation of urban houses, environmental pollution, traffic accidents, the relations between patients and doctors, wages and welfare, labor services and private lending—have emerged one after another. There are increasingly prominent tasks to be handled correctly, and these increasingly complicated social conflicts, safeguarding social stability and solidarity and building a harmonious and stable society need to be resolved.

### 8.1.1.2    Safety is the Prerequisite for Harmony

In the new century, Zhejiang is in the period of opportunities for development and acute social contradictions, while actively preventing and effectively overcoming these contradictions and problems is the realistic need for safeguarding social stability and also the fundamental aspiration of the people. In May, 2004, based on in-depth surveys, in response to some problems in Zhejiang's economic and social development, the Party Committee of Zhejiang Province made a great decision and arranged to build a safe Zhejiang and promote social harmony and stability. This is another great decision and arrangement that have a vital bearing on Zhejiang's overall development, and it was made by the Party Committee of Zhejiang Province after the "Eight-Eight Strategies" were developed since the 16th National Congress of the Communist Party of China. Elevating the building of a safe Zhejiang to the level of provincial governance reflects a new stage for Zhejiang and new requirements for Zhejiang's development.

When it comes to the building of a safe Zhejiang, under the guidance of the scientific outlook on development, according to the overall requirement of promoting democracy and the rule of law, making progress in fairness and justice, keeping integrity and friendliness, great vitality, high stability and good order as well as harmonious coexistence of the people and nature, based on the overall goal of building a moderately prosperous society—which benefits the people across the province—in all respects, in response to the new changes and new trends in the domestic and foreign situation, the new stage and new characteristics of Zhejiang's economic and social transformation and development, the new expectations of the people of the province about living a fairer, happier and more beautiful life, governance at the source and in key fields, systematic and comprehensive governance, governance under the rule of law are conducted to more rapidly ensure that social elements are integrated, social resources are compatible, social development is coordinated, social interests are balanced, social structure is rational, social management is effective, social operation is orderly, social relations are harmonious, social security is vigorous and the society is vibrant; thus, building a harmonious Zhejiang with coordinated development in the economic, political, cultural, social and ecological fields and overall harmony among the people, between the people and the society, between the people and nature will be achieved.

A harmonious socialist society should first of all be a safe society. Only when the society is stable and safe can the people live and work in peace and contentment. The building of a safe Zhejiang is a great decision and arrangement made when comrade Xi Jinping worked in Zhejiang. The building of a safe Zhejiang is the concrete practice of the scientific outlook on development; it is an important carrier for building a harmonious society; it is a major project which conforms to the will of the people, safeguards safety, makes the people rich and brings benefits to the people. It puts the people first and focuses on the well-rounded development of the people, love for life, care for health and safety; it vigorously offers a harmonious and stable social environment in which the people can develop on an equal footing, live and work in peace and contentment, and it really makes it possible for the achievements of reform and development to be shared by the overwhelming majority of the people. Comrade Xi Jinping said, "Only when the society is harmonious and stable can the country enjoy enduring stability and the people live and work in peace and contentment; the people look forward to living a happy life, while social harmony and stability must be first of all guaranteed in order to ensure a happy life".[2]

Safety is the prerequisite for harmony, while harmony intensifies safety. If there is not a safe society, there is not a harmonious society. Comrade Xi Jinping profoundly expounded the rich connotation of a safe Zhejiang as follows: safety in a safe Zhejiang is not safety in a narrow sense, it is safety in a broad sense involving the economic, political, cultural and social fields and many other fields, a wide scope and multiple levels, it is a systematic project involving the economic, political and cultural fields; it covers the safeguarding of social and political stability, sound economic development and the safety in the lives of the people. He also earnestly put forward the overall goal of building a safe Zhejiang: ensuring that Zhejiang's economy further develops, politics become more stable, culture more prosperous, the society more harmonious and the people's lives happier; ensuring that the society and politics are stable, public order is good, economic operations are sound, the state of work safety is stable and better, public security is in a good condition and the people live and work in peace and contentment. A safe Zhejiang embodies the philosophy of governance characterized by the scientific outlook on development; it contains the new line of thought of making the people rich and the province strong; it fully conforms to the requirement, put forward by the Central Committee of the Communist Party of China, of building a harmonious socialist society; it completely tallies with the fundamental interest and aspirations of the people of Zhejiang; it presents the distinctive characteristics of Zhejiang.

### 8.1.1.3   The Mechanism of Building a Safe Zhejiang

A harmonious society contains three organic unities, including the unity of democracy and the rule of law, the unity of vitality and orderliness and the unity of diversity and justice. With the building of a safe Zhejiang, Zhejiang has consolidated the foundation for maintaining social harmony. In the building of a safe Zhejiang, Zhejiang has always upheld the philosophy of achieving extensive safety, developed planning from the perspective of coordinated economic and social development and promoted relevant work under the overall layout of promoting balanced economic, political, cultural, social, and ecological progress. The essence of a safe Zhejiang does not lie in safety itself; instead, its essence is sound, orderly, rational and harmonious operations and development in the economic, political, cultural, social and ecological fields. In an effort to build a harmonious society, it is necessary to take the development towards greater safety as the foundation and means and put into place the development towards greater safety through institutionalized, scientific and standardized mechanisms. In this regard, Zhejiang has made huge efforts and painstaking explorations to establish some scientific and standardized mechanisms for promoting and guaranteeing the building of a safe Zhejiang.

---

[2]Xi (2006), p. 235.

First, the mechanism for a guarantee of leadership. To build a safe Zhejiang, it is essential to strengthen leadership and produce a strong synergy, improve and carry out various systems of work responsibility. In May, 2004, when the strategy of building a safe Zhejiang was put forward, the Party Committee of Zhejiang Province established the leading group for building a safe Zhejiang in which the Secretary of the Party Committee of Zhejiang Province serves as the head, the Vice-governor of Zhejiang Province and the Deputy Secretary of the Party Committee of Zhejiang Province serve as the deputy heads and 5 members of the Standing Committee of the Party Committee of Zhejiang Province serve as the members. The leading group for the development towards greater safety in which the chiefs of the Party and the government serve as the head and the deputy head is established at the municipal and county levels accordingly. In a decade, with the spirit of focusing on practical actions and perseverance, the successive Party committees and the people's governments of Zhejiang Province unremittingly carried through one blueprint regarding safety year after year, they always took the work on maintaining a safe and stable society as the first responsibility and equated the work with economic development, gave overall considerations, addressed both the symptoms and the root cause, carried out concrete work to meet the new expectations of the people about safety, thus making significant achievements in building a safe Zhejiang.

Second, the two-report mechanism. In January, 2004, the Central Group of Theoretical Learning under the Party Committee of Zhejiang Province held a learning meeting, putting forward the building of a safe Zhejiang for the first time and thoroughly pointing out that prosperity and stability serve the fundamental interests of the people, making the people rich and keeping good public order is the political responsibility of the leading cadres. Since the building of a safe Zhejiang was initiated in 2004, the leading cadres at various levels in Zhejiang have two reports at hand each month, the economic report and the safety report, to promote economic development and maintain social stability at the same time. The Party committees at various levels in Zhejiang Province have established the system involving an analysis of the state of social stability to regularly analyze the state of social stability like analyzing the economic situation, and promptly study and address the major issues in work.

Third, the mechanism of scientific evaluation. Zhejiang has established a complete mechanism of safety evaluation. The evaluation of the safe cities and counties covers more than 100 indicators under 6 categories. There are 15 items subject to one ballot veto, involving the economic, social and ecological fields, including food and drug safety accidents. In other words, if food and drug safety accidents with a great impact occur in an area, that area will be dealt with by one ballot veto and cannot participate in the current year's appraisal of safe cities, counties (county-level cities, districts).

Fourth, the mechanism of a need-driven response. In the development towards greater safety, the Party committees and the governments at various levels in Zhejiang have carefully listened to the people, actively responded to the people's expectations, stayed realistic and pragmatic, carried out concrete work to safeguard public security and make the people safe in clothing, food, housing and transportation. In a decade, Zhejiang took pains to address the safety issues in the economic, political, cultural, social and ecological fields, ensure that the building of a safe Zhejiang and the work in other respects promote and improve each other. In recent years, Zhejiang has made great efforts in governing water, addressing congestion, renovating old residential areas, old factory areas in urban areas and the villages in cities, demolishing illegal buildings, building an ecological Zhejiang, carrying out realistic, pragmatic and concrete work as well as dealing with governance priorities, while each of these efforts involves safety and the people's well-being, and provides a guarantee for the safety of people's clothing, food, housing and transportation.

## 8.1.2  Marked Effects Have Been Produced in Building a Safe Zhejiang

The 3rd Plenary Session of the 18th Central Committee of the Party Committee of Zhejiang Province vowed to enhance the national capacity for governance and establish a modern national governance system. The building of a safe Zhejiang, put forward by comrade Xi Jinping when serving as the Secretary of the Party Committee of Zhejiang Province ten years ago, is a good practice and experiment in enhancing the national capacity for governance. The efforts in building a safe Zhejiang have brought about new changes and a new look: Zhejiang's politics are stable, the society is secure, the economy has developed, ecology is beautiful, life is affluent and the people live and work in peace and contentment. In a decade, tremendous achievements were made in building a safe Zhejiang.

### 8.1.2.1  Smooth progress Has Been Made in Building a Moderately Prosperous Society in All Respects

Zhejiang has actively pushed forward six major action plans for building a moderately prosperous society in all respects, and speeded up the building of a moderately prosperous society in all respects. According to the evaluation based on the *Explanatory Notes for the Evaluation of Zhejiang Province's Progress in Building a Moderately Prosperous Society in All Respects*, the composite evaluation index concerning Zhejiang's building of a moderately prosperous society in all respects was 98% and the society in Zhejiang had basically become moderately prosperous in all respects (90%) in 2012. One of the important criteria for judging whether it is moderately prosperous is the income of urban and rural residents. In 2013, the per capita disposable income of urban residents and the per capita net income of rural residents were 37,851 yuan and 16,106 yuan in Zhejiang, ranking Zhejiang No.1 among the provinces and autonomous regions across the country for 11 and 27 consecutive years, which exceeded the corresponding criteria among the indicators concerning a moderately prosperous society in all respects developed by the National Bureau of Statistics. The ratio of urban residents' income to rural residents' income across the province decreased from 2.49:1 in 2007 to 2.35:1 in 2013, making Zhejiang one of the provinces with the smallest urban-rural gap in China. Another main indicator is the Engel's Coefficient. In 2013, the Engel's Coefficient of urban and rural residents in Zhejiang was 34.4% and 35.6%. According to the criteria of the Engel's Coefficient of the Food and Agriculture Organization of the United Nations, Zhejiang is currently at the stage of transition from being well-off to being affluent.

A social security system covering urban and rural residents has been basically established. Zhejiang has promoted the building of a social security system mainly covering old-age care, unemployment, medical services, work-related injury and maternity security according to laws; it has actively built a new assistance system based on the subsistence allowances, supported by special assistance including old-age, medical, educational and housing assistance and supplemented by other assistance, relief and social help; Zhejiang has comprehensively carried out a new rural cooperative system of medical care focusing on fund pooling for serious diseases and the basic medical security system for urban residents, basically extended medical security to both urban and rural areas; it has steadily promoted the basic living security system for the farmers whose land has been expropriated, the system involving centralized support of the rural people enjoying five guarantees and the urban people without identification papers, a normal residence permit, and a source of income to address the issue of social security for special groups; it has issued a number of policy documents including the implementation plan for provincial fund pooling for basic old-age security for enterprise employees to improve the social security system.

The social programs have developed rapidly in an all-round way. Concrete work has been promoted in building a culturally large province, a strong province in science, technology, education, health and sports. The building of a pilot province for national technical innovation projects has been accelerated, the proportion of the R&D fund expenditure in the GDP has reached 2.4%, and Zhejiang has ranked No.5 nationwide in regional comprehensive innovation ability. Zhejiang has become the first to conduct free compulsory education in urban and rural areas, the popularization rate of 15-year education and the gross enrollment ratio of higher education have reached 97% and 50%, ranking Zhejiang No.1 among the provinces and autonomous regions across the country. A network of cultural and sports services covering the whole province has preliminarily taken shape. The capability for medical and health services has improved significantly. The number of practicing (assistant) physicians has reached 2.41 and the per capita life expectancy has reached 76.9.

### 8.1.2.2 Primary-Level Social Development Has Been Pushed Forward Rapidly

The development of communities and social organizations has been promoted rapidly. In a decade, the Party Committee and the People's Government of Zhejiang Province issued the *Opinions on Further Strengthening the Building of Neighborhood Committees in Urban Communities*, the *Guiding Opinions on the Preparation of the Plan for the Layout of Rural Communities*, the *Key Points of Guidance for the Work on the Building of Urban and Rural Communities across the Province*, the measures for stimulating college graduates to serve as full-time community workers in urban and rural communities, the *Circular Concerning Standardizing the Registration and Management of Non-local Chambers of Commerce* and the *Implementation Measures for the Evaluation of Provincial Social Organizations* and the *Implementation Plan of Zhejiang Province for the Development of Industrial Associations*. Zhejiang has become the first to pilot the building of urban and rural communities, it has strengthened the development of community workers and the building of the organizational system of urban and rural communities as well as the building of the community service centers and the Party member service stations (points); Zhejiang has established and improved the urban and rural community service system and service facilities, promoted primary-level social governance and community service capacity according to the requirement of covering all the members of communities, diversifying service providers, developing complete service functions, making improvements in the quality and level of services. The development of social organizations has been supported and standardized. Zhejiang has introduced the preferential fiscal and tax policies including pre-tax deduction in donations, and it has actively supported social organizations through the government's purchase of services, thus promoting the development of social organizations. As of late 2013, there were 35,021 social organizations approved by and registered with the departments of civil affairs at various levels across the province, and more than 100,000 grassroots social organizations filed with the primary-level departments of civil affairs, ranking Zhejiang no.4 nationwide in the number of social organizations.

Significant achievements have been made in primary-level democratic development. Zhejiang has actively made new progress in primary-level democracy while energetically promoting Zhejiang's practice of the system of a people's congress and the system of multi-party cooperation and political consultation led by the Communist Party of China. With the philosophy of promoting the people's well-being through democracy, based on further improving primary-level democratic elections, Zhejiang has actively explored primary-level consultative democracy. The earnest democratic talk, public communication day, democratic hearings and villagers' talks are held to fully solicit the people's opinions and delegate the decision-making power to the people; such practices as industrial collective consultation on wages have been adopted to promote harmony between employees and enterprises; the participatory budget reform in towns and the participation of community residents in the management of community affairs are promoted to experience with and establish a new mode of primary-level social governance characterized by two-way interaction and democratic management. All of these experiments and innovations offer channels for promoting primary-level election democracy and consultative democracy, and boost the interaction between intraparty democracy and primary-level democracy, thus further putting into practice the rights of the people at the primary level to elect, participate in, manage and supervise.

### 8.1.2.3    All-Round Improvements Have Been Made in the Capacity and Level of Social Governance

In a decade, the Party committees and the governments at various levels in Zhejiang laid great importance on the development towards greater safety and they took the building of a safe Zhejiang as the important duty of the Party committees and the governments; they also brought continuous social governance innovations to major policies in response to the new situation and new changes in social development, thoroughly carried out the activities of promoting the development towards greater safety, upheld and developed the Fengqiao Experience, improved the working mechanism of complaint-related letters and visits, innovated the services for and management of the migrant population and promoted the social governance mode of grid-based management and group-based service in an all-round way. The prevention and control system for public security has been improved, emergency management has been intensified comprehensively and the emergency response system has basically taken shape. The building of urban and rural communities has been promoted in a thorough and complete way; Zhejiang has become the first nationwide to build an institutional framework for the building of rural communities; the network of primary-level social management and services has gradually achieved a state of good functioning and the primary-level democratic self-governance mechanism has been further improved; Huzhou City has become the first nationwide to bring innovations to the manner of supervising primary-level public security, and has established town-level centers for the supervision and management of public security which share one leading group and six stations with the town-level comprehensive supervisory bodies on the basis of each body maintaining its separate identity, thus promoting social security and stability. Zhejiang has also universally established a mechanism for the management of responses to public crisis emergencies so as to effectively safeguard the safety of the people's lives.

According to a sample survey conducted by the National Bureau of Statistics, in 2005, a year immediately after the building of a safe Zhejiang was initiated, 96% of the people believed that Zhejiang was safe. In the past ten years, the proportion of the people of Zhejiang who recognized the building of a safe Zhejiang increased from less than 20% in 2005 to 79.2% in 2012. Eleven cities and 90 counties (county-level cities, districts) in Zhejiang were granted the tile of "safe", among which 3 cities and 64 counties (county-level cities, districts) were rated as safe cities, counties (county-level cities, districts) for 8 consecutive years. The development towards extensive safety in Zhejiang has become the conscious pursuit and point of action of cadres and of the people.

## 8.2 The Systematic Nature of the Development Towards Greater Safety

As mentioned by comrade Xi Jinping, safety in a safe Zhejiang is not safety in a narrow sense, it is safety in a broad sense, involving the economic, political, cultural and social fields and many other fields, a wide scope and multiple levels, it is a systematic project involving the economic, political and cultural fields; it covers the safeguarding of social and political stability, sound economic development and safety in the daily lives of the people. Since the major strategic arrangement of building a safe Zhejiang was made in 2004, the Party Committees of Zhejiang Province have always upheld this major strategy, promoting the systematic project of building a safe Zhejiang in the economic, political, cultural, social and other fields and at multiple levels. This is mainly reflected in the following several aspects.

### 8.2.1 Scientific Development Guarantees Safety

Economic and social development is the foundation and prerequisite for achieving social harmony. Development is the prerequisite for the society to become harmonious. Development must be fostered in a scientific way; it is essential to transform the growth mode, improve the quality of development, ensure that development is for and pursued by the people, development achievements are shared by the people and promote well-rounded development of the people.

Scientific development is the foundation for building a safe Zhejiang; it is also the basic part and goal of building a safe Zhejiang. According to comrade Xi Jinping, making sure that everyone is safe and that the society is harmonious is the essential part of a scientific outlook on development; it is an important goal of building a moderately prosperous society in all respects.[3] In the process of building a safe Zhejiang, Zhejiang attaches great importance to pursuing people-oriented development and making development achievements universal, enabling development achievements to be more sufficiently reflected in guaranteeing and improving the people's well-being, better embodied in making sure that everyone enjoys the economic, political, cultural, social and ecological rights and interests, thus promoting social harmony to the greatest extent.

Zhejiang has put great attention on coordinated development and has combined current development with long-term development, placed equal emphasis on current and long-term interests, endeavored to promote coordinated economic development led by investments and consumption and driven by export and domestic demand, while developing the troika—investment, consumption and export—at the same time; Zhejiang has followed both economic law and natural law, combined economic and social benefits with ecological environmental benefits to shape a regional

---

[3]Xi (2007).

industrial structure with a rational division of work, distinctive characteristics and complementary advantages, promoting the common development of different areas; Zhejiang has intensified support for the underdeveloped areas and the areas in difficulty, it has increased fiscal transfer payment to the poverty-stricken areas and the areas subject to heavy tasks in ecological protection; with a focus on overcoming the environmental problems doing harm to the people's health and affecting sustainable development, Zhejiang has moved faster to build a resource-conserving and environmentally-friendly society, carrying out major projects for ecological and environmental improvement, thus effectively curbing ecological environmental deterioration.

Zhejiang has given importance to balanced development by combining new-type urbanization with the construction of a new countryside, overcoming the acute social contradictions and problems in industrialization and urbanization, further breaking the dual urban-rural structure, more rapidly promoting equal access to the basic public services in urban and rural areas, pushing forward urban-rural and regional development in a coordinated way across the province, extending urban civilization to rural areas and introducing rural civilization to urban areas, so that the life in urban and rural areas becomes better, and urban and rural residents enjoy a higher quality of life. Local authorities in Zhejiang have shifted their focus in the construction of infrastructures and the development of social programs to rural areas, and have gradually increased the proportion of the government's land transfer fees used in rural areas; they have also integrated urban and rural medical and health resources, established the system of offering assistance between urban and rural hospitals through pairing programs, intensified the development of rural medical and health personnel, increased the level of rural teachers, given prominence to the projects for extending radio and television coverage to all of the villages in rural areas and they have taken measures to safeguard the legitimate rights and interests of workers, especially rural migrant workers; moreover, they have drawn profound lessons from Latin American countries and other countries falling into the Middle Income Trap, made great efforts to promote balanced economic, political, cultural, social and ecological progress, to ensure reciprocal adaptation, mutual and holistic promotion and benign interaction in the economic, political, cultural, social and ecological fields.

Zhejiang has placed emphasis on sustainable development by combining current development with long-term development, focusing on both current and long-term interests, following both economic law and natural law, valuing economic and social benefits and ecological environmental benefits at the same time, taking the path of building up the province through ecological development, further increasing the potential for development, concurrently improving the quality of economic development, the quality of the ecological environment and the quality of the people's lives, laying a solid foundation for building a safe Zhejiang, making the people rich and the society harmonious.

## 8.2.2 Emphasis is Placed on the People's Well-Being to Promote Safety

The people's well-being covers the people's livelihood, their welfare and their rights. The people's livelihood involves daily necessities, food, clothing, housing, transportation, births, deaths, illnesses and old age. The people's welfare covers social security, social welfare, access to social public goods and public services. The people's rights refer to civil rights, namely the social rights which citizens enjoy, mainly including social justice and the power for appropriate resource allocation, the rights to work, receive medical service, property rights, the right to housing, the right to be promoted, the right to migrate, the right of reputation, rights to receive education, enjoy entertainment and be supported and equal gender rights. Improving the people's well-being, bringing more benefits to the people and safeguarding civil rights is the intrinsic requirement of putting the people first and also the basic requirement of scientific development and social harmony. To address the issue of the people's well-being, it is necessary to follow the people's requirements and aspirations, start from the most pressing, most immediate issues that concern them the most to sincerely do substantive work for them, promptly and proactively dispel anxieties and overcome difficulties for them. It is essential to make sure that everyone gets access to education, labor remuneration, medical services, old-age care, and housing. Only when actions are taken to meet the people's needs, realize the people's aspirations, enhance the people's welfare, and safeguard the people's interests and rights can the people-oriented nature of development really be seen and appreciated. With the gradual improvement in the market economic system, the governments at various levels in Zhejiang have shifted more energy and public resources to the social field and have allocated more than 70% of the government's financial resources to improving the people's well-being; each year they handle a series of concrete affairs in a down-to-earth manner for the people as planned, taking social security as the basic work in building a safe Zhejiang; Zhejiang has ranked no.1 nationwide in many aspects regarding ensuring and improving the people's well-being.

Employment is the basis of people's well-being. In an effort to build a safe Zhejiang, local authorities have worked hard to strengthen macro control, promote the formation of a flexible, uniform and fair labor market, create a loose environment for a rational flow of urban and rural population, especially talents and remove the discrimination due to identity, which is caused by the urban-rural division in the whole society. The distribution of income is the source of the people's well-being. Economic growth does not necessarily bring about improvement, commensurate with it, in the living standing of the ordinary people. In parallel to rapid economic growth, Zhejiang has developed an action plan for increasing the income of the low-income groups, and has endeavored to make the achievements of social development shared by the people; the level of the people's incomes has increased generally, Zhejiang has ranked no.1 among the provinces and autonomous regions across the country in resident income for many consecutive years; the income gap between urban and rural residents is smaller than the national average. Social security is the safety net for the people. Zhejiang has more rapidly established the legal system for social security, and has taken measures to comprehensively and correctly carry out the labor security laws and regulations, continuously increase the coverage of social insurances, move towards the developmental goal of making it possible for more people to enjoy security. Zhejiang has increased public financial transfer payments and has put social security funds in place. Zhejiang has concretely promoted equal access to basic public services and has become the first to develop and implement the action plan for ensuring equal access to basic public services; Zhejiang has developed an institutional framework for ensuring equal access to basic public services with a focus on social security, social programs and public facilities. Zhejiang has rapidly developed social programs in an all-round way. Concrete progress has been made in building a culturally large province, a strong province in science, technology, education, health and sports. The building of a pilot province for a national technical innovation project has been accelerated, the R&D fund expenditure has accounted for 1.82% of the GDP, and Zhejiang has ranked no.5 nationwide in ability for comprehensive regional innovation. Zhejiang has become the first to conduct free compulsory education in urban and rural areas, and the popularization rate of 15-year education has reached 97%; the capability for medical and health services has improved significantly, the per capita life expectancy has increased to 76.9. Zhejiang has attached importance to quality and fairness in the development of social programs, and has transformed social programs from quantitative expansion to qualitative improvement and diversified development and it has increased the degree of social fairness.

### 8.2.3 Consolidating Safety Through Democracy and the Rule of Law

Promoting democracy and the rule of law is essential for a safe society. A safe and harmonious society is essentially a democratic society under the rule of law. Only when democracy is expanded, the legal system is improved, the people's legitimate rights and interests are safeguarded and social fairness and justice are safeguarded can the vitality of the Party and the country be enhanced, can the enthusiasm of the people from various sectors of the society be aroused and can a vibrant, harmonious, orderly and safe society be built. In the development towards greater safety, Zhejiang has always upheld the people's leading position, expanded primary-level democracy, promoted the rule of law in governing the province, ensured the people's rights to participate and develop on an equal footing, safeguarded social fairness and justice, thus laying a solid foundation for enduring stability.

As Zhejiang has actively promoted the practice of the system of a people's congress and the system of multi-party cooperation and political consultation led by the Communist Party of China, local authorities, especially the primary-level units, have made many creations in democratic management, democratic participation, democratic elections and democratic supervision, such as socialized safeguarding of rights by trade unions and the election of rural migrant workers as the deputies to the people's congress in Yiwu City, the establishment of a committee for the supervision of village affairs for promoting the building of a system of rural primary-level punishment and prevention in Wuyi County, earnest democratic talk first initiated in Wenling and the practice in making government affairs public to build a sunshine government in Jinhua City; all of these efforts are active experiments in safeguarding civil rights and expanding democratic participation.

Zhejiang's decision-makers have upheld scientific legislation, strict law enforcement, impartial administration of justice, consciously applied the line of thought and way of the rule of law to promote development, deepen reforms, resolve contradictions and maintain stability. The action plan for safeguarding citizens' rights and interests has been pushed forward smoothly. Zhejiang has developed a number of regulations and policies for safeguarding civil rights and interests and the system of indicators for evaluation involving the safeguarding of citizens' legitimate rights and interests; Zhejiang regularly organizes a survey on social satisfaction and promptly announces the survey results before the general public. Zhejiang has intensified efforts in handling labor disputes, and has carried out a project for making it possible for the handicapped to share in a fairly comfortable life. Zhejiang has vigorously promoted the rule of law in government administration, and has made sure that the government takes actions in a fair, open and just way. Zhejiang has institutionalized the government's information disclosure, and has gradually improved the administrative decision-making procedure, carried out a system of making major administrative decisions public to solicit public opinions and the system of making feedback about the adoption of opinions, Zhejiang has openly collected government projects from the society. Zhejiang has introduced the decision-making hearing system in key fields involving planning, enterprise restructuring, expropriation, demolition and relocation. Zhejiang has really standardized the discretionary power over administrative punishment. Zhejiang has taken special actions to deal with lax enforcement of administrative laws and weak law enforcement which has triggered strong reactions from the people; Zhejiang has strengthened and improved administrative review, and has put in place the responsibility for responding to administrative litigations; 100% of the effective judgments and rulings in administrative litigations have been executed.

## 8.2.4 Strengthening Governance to Safeguard Safety

(1) Intensifying the development of primary-level communities and social organizations. In recent years, Zhejiang has vigorously reinforced social management, improved the mechanism for social governance and it has given importance to the development of social organizations and communities; Zhejiang has unremittingly improved the work at the primary level to lay the foundation for building a safe Zhejiang. As of late 2012, there were 31,448 social organizations approved and registered with the departments of civil affairs in the province,

ranking Zhejiang no.4 nationwide in the number of social organizations. Zhejiang has given importance to community management. A total of 244 town (sub-district) community service centers and 3000 village community service centers have been newly built, and the village service centers have basically provided full coverage across the province. Zhejiang has actively guided and given full play to the roles of the urban and rural primary-level self-governing organizations and social groups and organizations in coordinating interests, resolving conflicts and maintaining stability; Zhejiang has carried out popular activities aimed at promoting harmony. Zhejiang has extensively conducted the activities of ensuring greater harmony and safety at the primary level, thus further making the philosophy of safety and harmony deeply rooted among the people and vigorously boosting the building of a safe Zhejiang.

(2) Applying and developing the Fengqiao Experience in the new period, continuously improving the system of resolving social conflicts. Zhejiang has improved the system involving extensive medication of conflicts and disputes, and has worked on preventing and resolving social conflicts and establishing an extensive pattern of mediation with full scope given to and the coordination of the people's mediation, administrative mediation and judicial mediation. Actions have been taken to promote the development of regional mediation and arbitration organizations and professional mediation organizations and to actively cultivate and support the non-governmental forces for promoting harmony. Hangzhou City has introduced the five-chain mechanism for resolving social conflicts, in which peacemakers and the people's mediation promote reconciliation, comprehensive governance centers keep peace, the people's tribunal seeks settlement and special measures guarantee reconciliation. Ningbo City has established associations for the promotion of harmony, Jinqing Town, Luqiao District, Taizhou City has set up people mediation centers to ensure socialized mediation, multi-department coordination and one-stop mediation. The Fengqiao Experience is being upheld and developed, such practices as grid-based management and group-based services and the harmony promotion program have been promoted; 304,000 grids have been jointly built, 96,000 service groups have been established, covering 217,000 enterprises and primary-level units and consolidating a primary-level foundation.

(3) Establishing and improving the mechanism for the prevention of social risks. Zhejiang has organized the leading cadres to approach conflicts for overcoming difficulties, stay in particular areas to conduct surveys, keep diaries on the people's conditions and visit the primary-level units to receive the people, further developing open and regular channels for communication between the leading cadres and the people at the primary level and urging relevant departments to address the issues which have aroused strong reactions from the people. The local departments have given importance to preventing problems at the source, improving the people's well-being, and they have really dealt with the issues relating to the people's immediate interests. The leaders at various levels have extensively received the people who lodge complaints, they have visited the primary-level units and people, cleared up the long-pending cases involving

complaint-related letters and visits, actively explored the mechanism for the conclusion of the cases concerning complaint-related letters and visits involving law violations and lawsuits; moreover, they have solved the prominent problems in complaint-related letters and visits in a centralized way and specially coped with repeated letters and visits relating to complaints and coordinated efforts to solve the difficult and complicated problems. During their activities, the provincial leaders received 40 batches of people for 124 person-times, the municipal, county (county-level city, district) and town (sub-district) leaders received 9350 batches of people for 24,750 person-times in a coordinated way, handling 4721 cases on the spot. The mass incidents, complaint-related letters and visits have decreased across the province year by year. Zhejiang has solidly carried out major projects of social management, and has developed the *12th Five-Year Plan of Zhejiang Province for Major Projects of Social Management*, making new breakthroughs in the development towards greater safety. The decision-making bodies at various levels have established and improved the rules and procedures for major decisions, improved the systems concerning meetings for feasibility study, hearings, public disclosures and expert consulting to ensure the people's rights to know about and participate in making major decisions.

### 8.2.5 *Carrying Out Reforms and Innovations to Promote Safety*

Reforms and innovations are the sources of impetus for building a safe Zhejiang. Good social systems and mechanisms are the foundation for building a safe Zhejiang. There are a great many social conflicts and a great deal of disharmony during social transformation, while the underlying cause lies in inadaptation of systems and mechanisms. To build a safe Zhejiang, it is necessary to intensify reforms to generate impetus, innovate systems and mechanisms to solve the source-induced, fundamental and basic problems affecting social harmony and stability, remove the disharmonious barriers to institutions and mechanisms, establish rational relations among the government, the market and the society, let the market regulate what should be regulated by the market, make sure that the government regulates what should be regulated by the government better and transfers what should be regulated by the society to the society.

The reform of the system of administrative management has been intensified. In the development towards greater safety, Zhejiang has addressed the needs of developing a socialist market economy and transforming the society from a survival-oriented society to a development-oriented society, it has intensified the reform of government institutions, streamlined administration and delegated power to the lower levels, rationalized the relations between the government and the society, transferred the affairs which should not be regulated by and cannot be regulated well by the government to market players and social organizations; Zhejiang has identified the governments at various levels as the direct managers and providers of public services, and has stepped up efforts to improve the capability for providing public services and for ensuring the people's well-being; Zhejiang has transformed the government from an omnipotent, regulated and power-oriented government into a limited, service-oriented and responsibility-focused government. Zhejiang has continuously improved the system in which the provincial government directly takes charge of counties and has intensified the reform involving the expansion of the powers of strong counties and towns to arouse the developmental vitality of counties; Zhejiang has taken measures to encourage counties (county-level cities) to draw on each other's resource strengths and enable co-building and sharing, and to explore and build the system and mechanism of cross-regional development. Zhejiang has intensified the reform of the administrative examinations and approval system, standardized and cleared up the items subject to examination and approval and streamlined the examination and approval procedure. Zhejiang has endeavored to improve the quality of the government's public services, standardize public policies and power operations, establish the public fiscal system and allocate more financial resources and materials and other public resources to the fields of social management and public services.

The reform of the economic system has been expanded. Zhejiang has unswervingly worked on two fronts, further expanded the reform of state-owned enterprises, earnestly carried out two 36-article regulations of the State Council on encouraging the development of the non-public economy, further relaxed restrictions on the capital's access to the non-public sectors, broadened the financing channels for non-public enterprises, protected the private property rights, the rights and interests of non-public enterprises according to laws, actively improved the government's services for and supervision over the non-public enterprises, supported private enterprises to strengthen institutional, management, cultural and industrial innovations, moved faster to achieve a transformation towards modern enterprises. Zhejiang has actively supported fusion and interaction among state-owned, private and foreign economies, vigorously developed the economy of mixed ownership and supported enterprises to leverage international market resources to "go global" in order to become strong and excellent. Zhejiang has deepened comprehensive reform for changing the economic developmental mode, focused on promoting the pilot efforts in national reforms, and it has comprehensively pushed forward the pilot work on multi-level and multi-theme reforms in the departments directly under the provincial government, cities and counties (county-level cities, districts). Zhejiang has deepened the market-oriented reform involving the allocation of resource factors, improved the mechanism of land resource allocation, established and improved the water rights system, the system of paid use and trading of emission rights. Zhejiang has expanded local financial innovations and development, actively cultivated and developed the capital market and optimized the financial environment.

The reform of urban and rural systems has been intensified. Zhejiang has upheld and improved the rural basic operational system, orderly pushed forward the circulation of the right to the contracted management of land, energetically promoted the reforms of the land expropriation system and the land use system. Zhejiang has improved the exchange of factors on an equal footing in urban and rural areas, and has made sure that the land appreciation income and rural deposits are mainly used in agriculture and rural areas. Zhejiang has established a social system conducive to removing the dual urban-rural structure and conducted reforms to break through the institutional barriers; Zhejiang will make relevant laws and regulations as early as possible to eliminate the costs for farmers to enter cities, remove the restrictions on farmers' employment in cities in terms of region, identity, registered permanent residence and industry, fundamentally address the issues relating to rural migrant workers in social security, housing and children's education; Zhejiang has actively promoted the exchange of rural homesteads, encouraged and guided farmers in building houses and obtaining urban registered permanent residence in urban areas, and thus it has further promoted urban-rural coordinated development and urbanization.

The reform of the system of social management has been intensified. Zhejiang has continuously improved and consolidated the pattern of social management in which the Party committee plays the leading role, the government assumes the responsibility, there is social coordination and public participation; Zhejiang has established a social management network in which the mechanism for government regulation is interconnected with the mechanism for social coordination, so the government's administrative functions and communities' self-governance functions reinforce each other and the government's administration forces and social regulation forces interact with each other. Zhejiang has constantly brought innovations to and improved the mechanism of the rule of law for regulating social conflicts. Zhejiang has pushed forward innovations to social management, and it has given importance to guiding the healthy development of social organizations, has given full play to the roles of the people's organizations and social organizations.

### 8.2.6  Protecting Ecology to Enhance Safety

A harmonious society stresses harmony between the people and nature. Protecting the quality of the ecological environment is equal to guaranteeing the basic well-being of the people and the survival conditions and the home of life for the people. Protecting the ecological environment is the foundation for building a safe Zhejiang. As mentioned by comrade Xi Jinping, if ecological development is achieved, progress will be made; if ecological degradation occurs, retrogression will come about. The harmony between the economy and the environment and between the society and the environment are essential parts of a harmonious society. Based on the requirement of carrying out a scientific outlook on development, Zhejiang has made and implemented a strategic decision on and arrangement of leveraging the "Eight Advantages" and pushing forward the "Eight Measures", an important aspect of which consists in further leveraging Zhejiang's ecological advantages, building an ecological province and a green Zhejiang. Turning Zhejiang into an ecological province is an important part of the "Eight-Eight Strategies" and also an important facet of building a safe Zhejiang.

Zhejiang has thoroughly carried out the *Decision on Promoting Ecological Progress* made by the Party Committee of Zhejiang Province, calling for the further development of the ecological economy and the ecological culture and improving the ecological environment and making new progress in the ecological field in Zhejiang by taking the building of an ecological province as the carrier, relying on ecological sectors as the important foundation, considering the saving of ecological resources as the intrinsic requirement, seeking a fundamental guarantee from improving the ecological system, with a view to building an ecological Zhejiang which is affluent, beautiful, harmonious and peaceful.

Zhejiang has upheld the path towards the development of an ecological economy of making the high-carbon industries low-carbon and moving the low-carbon industries to the high end. Zhejiang has promoted economic ecologization and ecological economization; subject to the pressure from environmental constraints, based on the goal of low-carbon and environmentally friendly development, with a focus on energy conservation, energy consumption and emission reduction, Zhejiang has actively developed a circular economy, resolutely shut down outdated production facilities, strictly controlled the market access for the industries, enterprises and products which consume too much energy and cause serious pollution, accelerated the transformation of the high-carbon economy into the low-carbon economy; it started with production and life to really achieve low consumption and low emissions; it has moved faster to make the environment green and colorful and adopt rare and valuable materials and plants for environmental improvement; it has further increased the rate of forest coverage and carbon sequestration in forests, and it has expanded the environmental capacity. As a basic task for making ecological progress, Zhejiang has taken the special action of making the areas beside highways, railways, rivers and mountains clean, green and beautiful, and has identified the action as an important part of the evaluation involving the building of an ecological province. Zhejiang has actively developed a green industry, built a natural ecological environmental system with clear, clean waters and a blue sky; Zhejiang has intensified efforts in coping with the water environment and air pollution, disposing of solid wastes and protecting the soil. Zhejiang has strengthened supervision, resolutely curbed the acts of harming the people's interests due to ecological environmental problems and strictly prevented mass incidents caused by ecological environmental problems.

## 8.3   Local Practice in the Development Towards Greater Safety

The building of a safe Zhejiang is an experiment and a practice in building the national governance system and modernizing the governance capacity. In the past decade, Zhejiang has actively carried forward the Zhejiang Spirit of stressing actual effects and making bold innovations to the practice, highly valued and encouraged the creative practice of cadres and the people in building a safe Zhejiang, earnestly summed up and actively publicized and promoted the successful experience from innovations to the building of a safe Zhejiang, and incorporated the innovations in the building of a safe Zhejiang into the "Eight-Eight Strategies" and the overall strategy of making the people rich by starting a business and of building a strong province through innovation.

### 8.3.1 The System of the Committee for the Supervision of Village Affairs at Wuyi Village

On June 18, 2004, the committee for the supervision of village affairs was first initiated at Houchen Village, Wuyi County. In 2005, this system was promoted comprehensively in 546 villages throughout the county; the system was later regarded as the Houchen Experience. The Houchen Experience centers on standardizing the power source, operating rules and governance mode of the committee for the supervision of village affairs, and establishing the incentive and restraint mechanism to ensure that the committee for the supervision of village affairs exercises its powers within the specified institutional framework. It mainly covers the following three aspects.

First, two systems have been developed to specify the power source and operating rules of the committee for the supervision of village affairs. The basic institutional framework for this committee features one body and two systems, including the committee for the supervision of village affairs, the *Village Affairs Management System* and the *Village Affairs Supervision System*.

Second, a relatively independent establishment of one body is guaranteed for enhancing its supervisory status. The committee for the supervision of village affairs is directly elected by the meeting of villager representatives. There are 1 chairman and 2 members in the committee for the supervision of village affairs. The assignment avoidance system has been adopted, and the members of the Party branch, the village committee and their close relatives cannot concurrently serve as or serve as the members of the committee for the supervision of village affairs. The committee for the supervision of village affairs independently supervises the management of village affairs by the Party branch committee and the village committee and the execution of the financial system according to the *Village Affairs Management System* and the *Village Affairs Supervision System*, and reports the work to the meeting of villager representatives.

Third, the procedures for governing the supervision exercised by the committee for the supervision of village affairs ensure the quality of supervision. When village cadres are found to violate regulations through supervision or after whistle-blowing from villagers, the committee for the supervision of village affairs initiates the error correction procedure and expresses the error correction opinions to the Party branch committee and village committee; if the village cadres adopt the opinions and make corrections, the error correction procedure ends; if the village cadres disagree with the opinions, village cadres request a meeting of the village representatives to deliberate and decide on the matter, and their resolution will govern. If the village cadres neither adopt the opinions nor hold the meeting of village representatives for deliberation, the committee for the supervision of village affairs can handle the matter through remedy, in other words, the committee for the supervision of village affairs, the villagers can apply to the county and town-level leading groups for open and democratic management for a remedy, while the remedy body shall, within 15 days after receiving that application, handle the matter, so that the committee for the supervision of village affairs can rely on external forces to overcome barriers and continue their sound operations.

The system of the committee for the supervision of village affairs is conducive to promptly discovering errors and initiating the error correction procedure, making sure that village cadres cannot and do not dare to commit corruption through institutions and mechanisms, thus greatly reducing the number of the incidents involving the people's visit to higher authorities for lodging complaints, thus creating a good political ecological environment for the village-level governance. After the system of the committee for the supervision of village affairs is established, a good communication mechanism is built between villagers and village cadres, and a relationship of trust between village cadres and villagers is rebuilt. The system of the committee for the supervision of village affairs offers an organizational carrier for villagers' participation in village affairs, especially financial management, and enables supervision over village affairs during the entire process; it ensures farmers' rights to know, make decisions, participate and supervise.

## 8.3.2 The System of Industrial Collective Consultation on Wages in Wenling City

In recent years, the shortage of rural migrant workers has become acute; labor disputes have caused frequent collective work stoppage and incidents involving the people's visits to higher authorities to lodge complaints, severely affecting the development of enterprises and social stability. In order to solve problems at their source and reduce labor disputes, in 2003, Wenling City piloted a collective consultation on wages in the woollen sweater industry in Xinhe Town. Specifically, the trade union committee of the woollen sweater industry was established in Xinhe Town, in which 9 representatives, recommended and elected by workers, serve as the members. The trade union committee organized the woollen sweater industry association, an industrial trade union, where business owners and worker representatives hold earnest democratic talks on the collective consultation regarding wages in the woollen sweater industry. The specific procedure is as follows: First, identifying work types and processes, determining the unit prices of piece wages in the industry, choosing the representative workers, conducting tests organized by the labor department, determining the labor quota during each process and finally determining the unit prices of piece wages.

Second, organizing several rounds of collective consultation, signing an industrial wage agreement. Given that the woollen sweater industry is vulnerable to various factors including the market, prices and costs, collective consultation on adjusting the wages of industrial workers is held once a year to make sure that workers' wages are aligned with the growth of enterprise performance.

After the pilot work on collective consultation on wages was carried out in the woollen sweater industry in Xinhe, marked effects were produced in the same year. The cases involving the people's visits to higher authorities to lodge complaints arising out of labor disputes in the woollen sweater industry in Changyu decreased by 70% in 2003 compared with 2002. Wenling City promptly summed up the successful experience in wage consultation on the woollen sweater industry and gradually promoted it throughout the city. At present, the system has been promoted nationwide.

### 8.3.3 "81890" Primary-Level Public Service Platform in Haishu District, Ningbo City

The 81890 Service Center was established by the Party Committee and the People's Government of Haishu District, Ningbo City on August 18, 2001. The center has, via the telephone and the Internet, built an integrity information platform with interaction between the supply and demand sides, bringing together the planner, the provider and the user of public services, thus addressing the inadequacy of the planner's organization and production capacity and the supply and demand information asymmetry for the service provider and delivering tangible benefits to the government, enterprises and citizens; it has become a new mode for the primary-level government to provide services. The 81890 service platform has been well received by citizens. The center has received more than 90 laurels, including the 8th National Top 10 Units for Professional Ethics Development of Workers, the National May 1 Labor Medal, the National Advanced Unit for Cultural and Ethical Development. At present, the 81890 service mode has been applied in more than 100 cities nationwide.

The 81890 Service Center mainly covers the following work.

First, establishing a large integrated platform for public services. Currently, the 81890 Service Center has 50 employees and 18 24 h hotlines, it handles about 3000 services per day on average; there is the China 81890 service website, with an average of daily clicks being more than 20,000 person-times; more than 800 enterprises have joined it, with 189 service items under 19 categories; it interacts with 56 Party and government departments, with 868 service items under 14 categories. In 2009, the 81890 Service Center extended across the city, 8 subcenters were set up in Yinzhou, Zhenhai, Beilun, Fenghua, Ninghai, Xiangshan, Yuyao and Cixi, with Jiangdong District and Jiangbei District still served by Haishu 81890, thus further enhancing its service capacity. In the meantime, the 81890 Service Center has continuously expanded its service functions in response to the changes in social needs, based on the 81890 call platform and the 81890 service website, and it has built, year by year,

40 service platforms, including the 81890 lost and found center, the 81890 loving-care supermarket, the 81890 elderly emergency call system, the 81890 Guangming Cinema, the 81890 Party member service center and the 81890 cultural and ethical development platform.

Second, integrating resources to improve the service capacity. With the integration of the government's resources, 81890 promptly delivers citizens' voices, opinions and suggestions about urban public management to relevant government departments, it coordinates and supervises efforts to address relevant issues, so that the citizens' needs, opinions and suggestions concerning public services can be promptly dealt with. In order to further strengthen the connection between the government's resources and the information on enterprises' needs, 81890 established the 81890 enterprise service platform to incorporate the service functions of 56 Party and government departments throughout the district and provide enterprises with all-weather, multidimensional tracking supervision services covering the whole process. With the integration of market resources, based on more than 800 service enterprises which have joined 81890 and more than 27,000 employees, 81890 offers 189 service items under 19 categories and provides enterprises with all-weather full life services, while a large number of enterprises which have joined it have found a vast service market.

Third, establishing a system of credit management and building an integrity image in the service industry. Based on the 81890 credit platform, 81890 has established a system of restraint on service enterprises, education and training systems and a system for the guarantee of quality service, so as to provide the basic guarantees for quality service and to better safeguard the people's interests; for instance, 81890 signs the quality guarantee agreement with the enterprises which have joined it, 81890 carries out a system for serious quality follow-up for service targets, and exercises strict supervision over service enterprises; it set up the national community service training center to conduct standardized training among the service personnel in the service industry; it appointed legal advisors and consumer service quality inspectors in the 81890 service system to specially deal with the disputes relating to the quality of services and prices.

### 8.3.4   Socialized Safeguarding of Rights by Trade Unions in Yiwu

Under the new situation in which labor conflicts involving rural migrant workers have become increasingly complicated, government departments are defective in their functions and services; in response to the profound changes in the labor relations in the new period, the Yiwu Federation of Trade Unions has made active experiments and innovations to introduce a new mechanism for the trade unions led by the Party to safeguard rights according to laws. In October, 2000, Yiwu became the first nationwide to establish the Yiwu Association for Legal Safeguarding of Workers' Rights, a special body for the safeguarding of rights by trade unions, giving rise to the Yiwu Model under which legal means are adopted to safeguard workers' rights. Specific actions are as follows.

Becoming the first to establish the body for socialized safeguarding of rights—the Yiwu Association for Legal Safeguarding of Workers' Rights, later called the Yiwu Center for Legal Safeguarding of Workers' Rights. It actively participates in collective consultation on workers' wages and the arbitration of labor disputes, it takes charge of mediating labor disputes and provides legal aid to workers. It adopts the following operating mechanism: its working personnel are appointed through open recruitment by the Yiwu Federation of Trade Unions in the society, they enjoy the same political status and economic benefits as the cadres at state organs; the funds for its safeguarding of rights come from trade unions, the government and the society; it is in the charge of the Yiwu Federation of Trade Unions and is subject to service guidance from the public security, procuratorial and judicial organs and courts.

Improving the network for socialized safeguarding of rights. Horizontally, there is cross-regional coordination; it works with the trade unions in Kaihua in Zhejiang and more than ten cities in other provinces, including Chengdu City in Sichuan Province, to achieve coordinated intercity safeguarding of rights by trade unions; vertically, the Yiwu Federation of Trade Unions establishes the center for legal safeguarding of workers' rights, the workstations for safeguarding rights are set up in towns and sub-districts, the committees for the mediation of labor disputes are established in enterprises; an information network for socialized safeguarding of rights has also been built.

Expanding the forces for socialized safeguarding of rights and giving play to the roles of departments in leading the work and of judicial organs, law firms, public media, research institutions and colleges in providing coordination. Actions are being taken to improve the mechanism for the socialized safeguarding of rights in mediation on labor disputes, arbitration of labor disputes, response to lawsuits on behalf of employees, labor contracts, collective contracts, labor protection for work safety; the Yiwu Federation of Trade Unions has actively attempted to advocate enterprises' assumption of social responsibility as the means for safeguarding rights and thus incorporate employees' rights and interest appeals and trade unions' position on safeguarding rights into the standard of enterprises' social responsibility.

The mode of socialized safeguarding of rights by trade unions in Yiwu has effectively safeguarded the legitimate rights and interests of more than 1.30 million rural migrant workers and has promoted social stability and harmony in Yiwu.

### 8.3.5   The Mechanism for Open Decision-Making Operations in Hangzhou City

With the philosophy of letting public opinions lead the government, Hangzhou City has actively made beneficial experiments in expanding citizens' orderly political participation and making decisions democratic and scientific; this has become a typical case of institutionalizing and standardizing the decision-making innovations of local governments in the era of networks; this was granted the China Local Government Innovation Award, an award presented for the fifth time. Its main efforts are shown below.

First, making the government's decision-making democratic and open. According to the requirement of ensuring open decision-making, Hangzhou has become the first nationwide to launch the 12345 mayor hotline, it established the mechanism for making it possible for citizens to appraise the work of the government, it worked on collecting proposals from the general public with respect to the projects for improving the people's well-being, it improved the system of experts' feasibility studies, technical consulting and decision evaluation involving decisions on major issues and it energetically broadened the channels for civic participation, thus fostering a good atmosphere in which there is extensive civic participation and the decision-making is open, democratic and scientific.

Second, diversifying and institutionalizing the government's decision-making. Hangzhou has established a system involving advance disclosure of the matters involved in the municipal government's decision-making and the hearing system; Hangzhou has built the system of inviting the deputies to the people's congress and CPPCC members to attend, as non-voting delegates, and citizen and expert representatives to participate in the executive meeting of the municipal government; Hangzhou has broadened the ways for public participation in the government's decision-making by inviting media to attend meetings as non-voting delegates, and through online live coverage, BBS, video connection and mobile phone's interaction function; Hangzhou has established a system for engagement among the members of the municipal leading group and entrepreneurs, scientific and technical personnel and the people of literary and artistic circles to ensure the normal development of the activities in which the ordinary people participate in the municipal city's decision-making.

Third, making the government's decision-making standardized and procedure-based. Hangzhou has issued 9 local regulations including the *Regulations of the People's Government of Hangzhou City on the Procedure for Open Decision-Making Involving Major Administrative Matters*, specifying the rules concerning major matters for open decision-making, the non-voting delegates, opinions and suggestions and initiation procedures, the particulars to be disclosed, the disclosure mode, public participation and the mode for it; Hangzhou has promoted open decision-making in 13 districts and counties (county-level cities). This is conducive to achieving regional coordination in open decision-making and enhancing the overall decision-making performance.

### 8.3.6 The Three People-Oriented Programs in Quzhou City

Based on improving the operational mechanism for villagers' self-governance, promoting the handling of matters based on laws and regulations and transforming the work style of rural cadres, Quzhou City has established the archives concerning the people's conditions, deepened communication with the people and carried out a system of handling matters for the people and offering services during the whole process ("Three People-oriented Programs") in rural areas throughout the city, which has been well received by the people. The main actions are as follows.

First, establishing the archives concerning the people's conditions, building the platform for learning about the situation and engaging with the people. With villages as units, the town cadres staying in villages and village cadres in Quzhou City have comprehensively established the archives concerning the people's conditions under three categories—the conditions of the village, the conditions and issues of the households– according to the requirement of one volume for one village, one archive for one household and one form for one issue. The archives concerning the conditions of the village involve village overview, near-term and long-term development plans, village affairs and disclosure, village-level collective assets and key personnel. The archives concerning the conditions of the households mainly contain family members and social relations, living conditions, entrepreneurship and employment, main difficulties and the causes of poverty. The archives concerning issues mainly cover the construction of major programs and projects, decisions on major matters and their execution, villagers' interest appeals, opinions and suggestions. Furthermore, Quzhou City has also built an online information system for the archives concerning the conditions of the people to enable hierarchical management, electronic processing and network-based operations; Quzhou City has ensured that targeted measures are promptly taken according to the management authority to deal with the problems found in surveys in light of four levels: common aspects, concerns, emergency handling, extraordinarily significant issues.

Second, deepening communication with the people, providing open channels for soliciting opinions and solving problems. With villages as the units, Quzhou City carries out the activity of communicating with the people at least once a month. The activity is in the charge of the village Party organization and is attended by the secretary of the village Party branch committee and the chairman of the village committee. Its main agenda lies in publicizing the decisions and arrangements made and the work tasks assigned by the Party committees and the governments at higher levels, reporting the handling of the matters for which commitments are made in the previous communication, giving explanations about relevant issues and soliciting opinions and suggestions from the people. Based on communication, the village Party branch committee and the village committee study and develop a work plan to be carried out by the village committee under the supervision of the village Party branch committee during the whole process.

Third, handling matters for the people and offering services throughout the whole process. Quzhou has developed new ways to handle matters according to laws and serve the people; with towns as the units, service centers and service halls have been established in 106 towns (sub-districts) across the city, provided with more than 400 people as full-time working personnel, for working in a centralized way. Service points have been set up at 1238 villages (communities) where conditions permit. According to the requirement of offering convenient services for the people, the departments of planning, construction, land, family planning and health, civil affairs, agriculture, forestry, water conservation authorize the town service centers to directly handle, on their behalf during the whole process, the applications filed by the village-level organizations and the people and the matters subject to examination and approval, while the stations of these departments in towns are responsible for verification.

These innovations at the primary-level units in Zhejiang highlight the requirements advocated in building a safe Zhejiang—giving play to the leading role of the people, strengthening primary-level social governance, guaranteeing citizens' basic rights, ensuring and improving the people's well-being, and promoting social harmony and progress.

## References

Xi Jinping, *Carrying out Solid Work to Stay Ahead—Line of Thought and Practice in Promoting New Development in Zhejiang*, The Party School of the CPC Central Committee Press, 2006.
Xi Jinping, *Zhijiang Xinyu*, Zhejiang People's Publishing House, 2007, p. 119.

# Chapter 9
# Zhejiang's Experience in Social Development and Inspirations

**Jianhua Yang**

Social development is closely associated with the people's happiness and well-being. The objective of social development is to mobilize social forces, integrate social resources, ensure and improve the people's well-being, develop social programs, optimize the social structure, improve the functions of social services to build an environment for social development in which all of the people play their proper roles, enjoy due benefits and get along with each other in a harmonious way.

Social development is, relative to economic development, mainly the development of production relations. Economic development is the foundation and prerequisite for social development. Only when economic development is achieved can strong material force be provided to the society for improving the people's material and cultural life. However, economic development cannot be separately promoted for a long time without social development, and economic development cannot naturally enhance everyone's well-being. To achieve sustained, rapid and healthy economic development, it is essential to improve labor productivity, optimize the industrial structure and enhance the overall economic quality. This calls for making progress in the scientific, technological, educational and cultural fields and improving the quality of the people. Social development is the guarantee for economic development. To achieve rapid and healthy economic development, it is also necessary to foster a safe, orderly and stable social environment, including a rational social structure, good market order and an impartial institutional guarantee. Social development is also an important goal of economic development. The people's production and other economic activities are, in the final analysis, aimed at meeting the people's diverse needs, improving the people's living environment and the quality of the people's life, promoting the well-rounded development of the people. Obviously, economic development is the foundation and prerequisite for social development, while social development is one of the driving forces and goals for economic development and is the support and guarantee for economic development. Therefore, strengthening

J. Yang (✉)
Zhejiang Academy of Social Sciences, Hangzhou, China

© Social Sciences Academic Press and Springer Nature Singapore Pte Ltd. 2019
G. Chen and J. Yang (eds.), *Chinese Dream and Practice in Zhejiang—Society*,
Research Series on the Chinese Dream and China's Development Path,
https://doi.org/10.1007/978-981-13-7406-7_9

and comprehensively promoting social development is of great strategic significance for and exerts a far-reaching impact on safeguarding the fundamental interests of the people, becoming the first to realize the ambitious social goal of building a moderately prosperous society in all respects and basically achieving modernization, and maintaining enduring stability.

## 9.1 Promoting Social Development, Solving the Problems in Social Development

Social development covers a wide range of fields; it mainly includes ensuring and improving the people's well-being, developing social programs, optimizing the social structure, improving social services, strengthening community development and innovating social governance. Zhejiang is the province where the market economy first developed, and Zhejiang started to witness rapid economic growth in the 1980s; however, Zhejiang was socially undeveloped in the 1990s as compared with rapid economic growth. According to the comprehensive calculation, from the National Bureau of Statistics, of the level of social development over the years during the periods of the 8th Five-Year Plan and the 9th Five-Year Plan, the overall level of social development was 3–4 places lower than the economic development in Zhejiang. Public goods and public service resources were inadequate; in many fields, the scale and quality of provision for the people hardly satisfied the growing needs of the people; for instance, the employment situation was grim, social security failed to meet the basic needs of the people, the systems of public services were fragmented and not integrated. Communities and social organizations were underdeveloped, urbanization was slow, income distribution was unreasonable, regional economic and social development was unbalanced, the contradictions between economic and social development and the resource environment tended to be acute. The manner of social governance was relatively backward, and the government was severely absent and overstepped its functions and powers in managing social affairs.

Since the beginning of the new century, the Party Committee and the People's Government of Zhejiang Province have given great importance to social development and have taken social development as the concrete practice in carrying out the Important Thought of Three Represents, the scientific outlook on development and the philosophy of building the Party to serve the public good and exercising power in the interests of the people; moreover, they have given priority to social development in the work of the Party committee and the government; the leading groups for social development headed by provincial leaders have been established, there is a pattern in which the Party committee leads and the government is responsible for social development and management with social coordination and public participation, laying a good foundation for Zhejiang's social development. Social development is promoted to overcome the difficulties in that development; Zhejiang has endeavored to ensure and improve the people's well-being by promoting entrepreneurship and thus making the people rich, and to optimize the social structure by pushing forward social mobility and urban-rural integration, and to propel the development of social programs by building a strong province in four respects, as well as to increase the level of social governance by building a safe Zhejiang, thus producing marked effects.

### 9.1.1 Residents Have Become Well-Off in All Respects

Zhejiang has actively pushed forward six action plans for building a moderately prosperous society in all respects, and has speeded up the building of a moderately prosperous society in all respects in Zhejiang. According to the *Explanatory Notes for the Evaluation of Zhejiang Province's Progress in Building a Moderately Prosperous Society in All Respects*, the composite evaluation index concerning Zhejiang's building of a moderately prosperous society in all respects was 93% and the society in Zhejiang had basically become moderately prosperous in all respects (90%) in 2010, only 7% points lower than the index suggesting that the society is moderately prosperous in all respects (100%). One of the important criteria for judging whether the society has become moderately prosperous is the income of urban and rural residents. In 2011, the per capita disposable income of urban residents and the per capita net income of rural residents in Zhejiang reached about 30,971 yuan and 13,071 yuan, respectively. Zhejiang has ranked no. 1 among the provinces and autonomous regions across the country for 11 and 27 consecutive years in the per capita disposable income of urban residents and the per capita net income of rural residents. The ratio of the income of urban residents to that of rural residents in Zhejiang decreased from 2.49:1 in 2007 to 2.35:1 in 2013, making Zhejiang one of the provinces with the smallest urban-rural gap in China. Another important indicator is the Engel's Coefficient. In 2013, the Engel's Coefficient of urban and rural residents in Zhejiang was 34.4% and 35.6%. According to the criteria for the Engel's Coefficient established by the Food and Agriculture Organization of the United Nations, Zhejiang is currently at the stage of transition from being well-off to being affluent.

### 9.1.2 Social Programs Have Developed Rapidly in a Balanced Way

Solid progress has been made in building a strong province in education, science and technology, health, culture and sports. In 2014, the rate of popularization of 15-year education reached 98.9%, and the main working-age population (16–59 years old) received education for an average of 10 years in Zhejiang. The gross enrollment ratio of higher education reached 52%, up 14% points compared with 2007. The layout of higher education has tended to be rational, there have been one university and one junior college or one university and multiple junior colleges in the cities divided into districts across the province. The building of a pilot province for national technical innovation projects has been accelerated, the proportion of the R&D fund expenditure in the GDP has reached 1.95%, Zhejiang has ranked no. 5 nationwide in the ability for regional comprehensive innovation; the people who often take physical exercise have accounted for 31.1% of the province's total population. The capacity for medical and health services has improved significantly, and the per capita life expectancy has reached 78.09.

### 9.1.3   The Institutional System for Ensuring Equal Access to Basic Public Services Has Been Built

Since 2008, Zhejiang has carried out an action plan for ensuring equal access to basic public services with a view to expanding the coverage of basic public services and increasing the degree of equal access to basic public services, Zhejiang has focused on developing social security, social programs and public facilities to build a regionally balanced basic public service system covering both urban and rural areas and that is shared by everyone. Since 2008, Zhejiang has annually organized and carried out more than 80 projects for ensuring equal access to basic public services; as of 2011, Zhejiang invested 310 billion yuan in projects for ensuring equal access, the gap in basic public services between urban and rural areas, among regions and among different groups gradually narrowed. In 2012, Zhejiang developed a new poverty alleviation standard by identifying the people with an annual income of 4600 yuan (constant price in 2010) as the targets of poverty alleviation. The standard is 100% higher than the new national poverty alleviation standard of 2300 yuan (constant price in 2010). In the new round of poverty alleviation through development, Zhejiang will carry out three programs, including the Program for Doubling the Income of the Low-income Rural Households, the Special Program for Helping the Key Underdeveloped Counties and the Program for Boosting Development through Mountain-Sea Cooperation.

Balanced educational development has been achieved between urban and rural areas. More educational resources have been allocated to the economically underdeveloped areas, rural schools and weak schools; Zhejiang has carried out four projects for rural primary and middle schools, the project for adjustment and renovation of small schools in rural areas and the project for paired educational assistance; the mechanism for guaranteeing compulsory education funds has been established, the educational gap between urban and rural areas, among regions and among schools has continuously narrowed. Special education, the education of the children of rural migrant workers, education for nationalities and continuing education have been intensified. The system for helping the students from families in difficulty has been established; Zhejiang has introduced a number of policies for financially aiding the education of the children of rural migrant workers, handicapped children and adolescents and the students from families in difficulty; compulsory education has become totally free, financial aid now covers 100% of the students in vocational education.

The system of medical and health care services covering both urban and rural areas has been basically built. In 2014, there were 7314 community health service centers including health centers and 12,400 village clinics across the province; there were 0.79 community doctors for every 1000 residents, 20 min medical and health service circles had been preliminarily established, and a multilevel and multiform system of urban and rural health services covering the whole province had taken shape. Smooth progress has been made in building a medical and health system covering disease control, health supervision, medical treatment, emergency command and information reports.

The urban-rural integration of public employment services has preliminarily taken shape. In 2014, the platforms for human resources and social security services were built in 990, 352, 3131 and 26,273 out of 1001 towns, 368 sub-districts, 3212 urban communities and 28,273 administrative villages, respectively, across the province, accounting for 98.9%, 95.65%, 97.48% and 92.93%, respectively. Zhejiang has put in place bodies, the size of bodies, staffing, venue, funds and systems to develop a well-functioning urban-rural network of management services. Zhejiang has carried out the Project for Quality Training Concerning the Rural Labor Force of 10 Million People and the Sunshine Project for Training Concerning Rural Labor Transfer.

## 9.1.4  The Institutional Framework for Social Security Has Been Preliminarily Established

Universal coverage of medical insurance has been preliminarily achieved. With regard to medical insurance, the "3 + 1" medical security system covering basic medical insurance for urban workers, basic medical insurance for urban residents and new rural cooperative medical care and the system for urban and rural medical assistance have been basically established and promoted in an orderly fashion. The coverage of work-related injury, unemployment and maternity insurance has been greatly expanded. Given the characteristics of rural migrant workers, Zhejiang has started with the work-related injury and medical insurance most needed for rural migrant workers to gradually incorporate rural migrant workers into the social security system. Breakthroughs have been made in the new rural cooperative medical care system. The new rural cooperative medical care system has covered all counties (county-level cities, districts) across the province, more than 95% of the people have been covered by the system, the per capita raised funds under the new rural cooperative medical care system has increased from 185 yuan to more than 285 yuan.

The urban and rural old-age security system is in the making. In 2009, Zhejiang issued the *Implementation Opinions on Establishing the Social Endowment Insurance System for Urban and Rural Residents*, achieving full coverage of endowment insurance at the institutional level. In 2011, Zhejiang issued a number of policy opinions on addressing the issues concerning some group benefits in the field of endowment insurance. As of late 2011, throughout the province, 17.90 million people were covered by basic endowment insurance for enterprise workers, including 15.80 million on-the-job people and 2.10 million retirees; 12.85 million people were covered by social endowment insurance for urban and rural residents, including 11.45 million people in rural areas and 1.40 million people in urban areas; 5.98 million people received a basic pension, more than 90% of the people below the age of 60 who were eligible for seeking insurance coverage made insurance contributions across the province.

The new social assistance and social welfare system is taking shape. Zhejiang has improved the mechanism for dynamic adjustment of the subsistence allowances standard, and has provided not less than 60 yuan in monthly assistance per person to the targets of subsistence allowances, and it has incorporated all rural households with a per capita annual net income lower than 2500 yuan and satisfying the conditions of subsistence allowances into the scope of subsistence allowances. Zhejiang has further intensified the medical assistance, continuously increased the level of assistance and has comprehensively carried out real-time settlement and reimbursement of medical assistance. Zhejiang has executed five projects for legal aid, giving prominence to safeguarding the legal rights and interests of rural migrant workers, the elderly, juveniles, women and forest workers. Zhejiang has actively promoted pilot work on building up the national system for basic old-age services in Zhejiang, and strengthened the construction of old-age infrastructures; Zhejiang has newly increased 15,000 beds at old-age service institutions; Zhejiang has built 300 town (sub-district) old-age service centers and 3000 rural Starlight Homes for the Elderly. Zhejiang has thoroughly carried out the project for making a fairly comfortable life shared by the handicapped, providing 20,000 handicapped people with rehabilitation services for aiding hearing, sight and walking and finishing the task of raising (foster) service for 36,000 people with severe disabilities; moreover, Zhejiang has built 42 Well-off Sunshine Shelter Centers; 75% of the handicapped have become well-off across the province, placing Zhejiang at the forefront nationwide in this regard.

## 9.1.5 *The Social Structure Has Been Transformed More Rapidly*

The employment structure has been continuously optimized. In the past decade, in coordination with the strategic adjustment of the economic structure, Zhejiang has vigorously promoted industrial transformation and upgrading, and has energetically pushed forward employment transfer from the primary industry, stabilized the employment share in the secondary industry, and made great efforts to develop the employment channels for the tertiary industry. The proportion of the employed people in the primary industry has been on the decrease, while that of the employed people in the secondary and tertiary industries increased from 75.5% in 2005 to 85.86% in 2012.

Zhejiang has changed from an urban-rural type of division into coordinated and common development of urban and rural areas. Urban-rural integration has developed rapidly. With a focus on making improvements in the level of farmers' incomes and the quality of the life of farmers, Zhejiang has carried out a lot of effective work on holistically promoting development regarding six aspects,[1] it has endeavored to develop a new system for coordinated urban-rural development, pushed forward the Village Broad Road Project and the project of "1000-village demonstrations and 10,000-village improvements", directly benefiting numerous rural households and making the rural environment cleaner and more beautiful. Through pilot work and experiments, local authorities in Zhejiang have, in light of local conditions and the people's needs, actively explored the effective ways to develop rural communities, so that the distance between the quality of life for urban and rural residents has gradually become "zero".

The level of urbanization has been on the rise. In the past decade, Zhejiang has speeded up urbanization, and fostered diversified development with promotion at lower and upper levels and internal and external coordination; a massive rural surplus labor force transferred to the non-agricultural industries, stimulating the movement of the rural labor force to cities and further boosting the urbanization of the population. In 2013, Zhejiang's level of urbanization reached 63.5%.

The middle-income group has taken shape more rapidly. With the current per capita annual disposable income of urban residents in Zhejiang as the reference standard, we identify the group with the per capita annual disposable income between the reference standard and the level of 2.5 times the reference standard as the middle-income group in Zhejiang. According to statistics, in 2010, the per capita disposable income of urban residents in Zhejiang was 27,359 yuan, so the annual income of the middle-income group in Zhejiang was between 27,000 yuan and 68,000 yuan. That group accounted for about 31% in Zhejiang.

---

[1]It means that Zhejiang has holistically promoted the strategic adjustment of the urban-rural industrial structure and the urban-rural employment structure; urban-rural planning construction and ecological environmental development; the development of new communities in rural areas; accelerated development of the developed areas and the leapfrog development of the underdeveloped areas; the building of a moderately prosperous society in the underdeveloped towns; the building of the urban-rural social security and public service system.

### 9.1.6 The Development of Urban and Rural Communities Has Been Deepened

Zhejiang has become the first nationwide to establish an institutional framework for the development of rural communities; the primary-level network of social management and services has gradually become complete, and the building of urban and rural community service centers has been promoted steadily. Local authorities have actively explored the long-term operational mechanism of rural community service centers; 244 town (sub-district) community service centers and 3000 village-level community service centers have been newly built; now the service centers at the village level have basically covered the whole province. The community service network has been continuously improved across the province. The primary-level democratic self-governance mechanism has been further improved; 97.5% of the villages have carried out the activity of building villages under democracy and the rule of law; more than 95% of the villages have reached the standard of making village affairs public and standardizing democratic management. Social organizations have increasingly played an important role. As of late 2013, there were 34,481 social organizations approved by and registered with the departments of civil affairs at various levels and more than 50,000 grassroots social groups filed with the primary-level departments of civil affairs in the province, ranking Zhejiang no. 4 nationwide in the number of social organizations.

### 9.1.7 Intensified Efforts and Innovations Have Been Made in Social Governance

A new pattern of social governance has preliminarily taken shape. The Party committees and the governments at various levels have placed great importance on social governance and institutional innovations, and have regarded strengthening and improving social governance as an important duty of theirs; in response to the new situation and new changes in social development, the Party committees and the governments at various levels have intensified social governance innovations in policies, and marked effects have been produced in building a safe Zhejiang: innovating and developing the Fengqiao Experience, continuously improving the system for resolving social contradictions, establishing an extensive mediation system for resolving conflicts and disputes through the people's mediation, administrative mediation and judicial mediation, promoting the development of regional organizations for mediation arbitration and professional mediation organizations, actively cultivating and supporting the non-governmental forces for the promotion of harmony. In recent years, the Party Committee of Zhejiang Province has issued a series of documents, supporting the people's congress, the CPPCC and the people's groups to perform respective functions in promoting democracy, supporting the people in expressing their interest appeals through these channels. Zhejiang has organized the leading cadres to approach contradictions for overcoming difficulties, stay at particular areas to conduct surveys, keep diaries on the people's conditions, visit the primary-level units to receive the people; Zhejiang has further developed open and regular channels for communication between the leading cadres and the people at the primary level and urged the leading cadres to address the issues which have aroused strong reactions from the people. Zhejiang has improved the working mechanism for complaint-related letters and visits, completely cleared up the long-pending cases involving the complaint-related letters and visits, actively explored the mechanism for the conclusion of the cases concerning complaint-related letters and visits involving law violations and lawsuits. The total number of mass incidents, complaint-related letters and visits across the province has decreased year by year. With regard to primary-level social governance, Zhejiang has created experience in comprehensive governance centers, comprehensive governance in private enterprises, the evaluation of the risks to stability of major projects, the people's mediation with subsidies replaced by rewards, the concurrent handling, at three organs, of the issues involved in complaint-related letters and visits. Regarding the services for and the management of the migrant population, Zhejiang has established the Bureau of New Resident Affairs and the Harmony Promotion Association. Zhejiang has promoted and carried out the system of collective consultation on wages to mitigate labor-capital conflicts.

The state of public security has tended to improve. The overall level of safety at work has increased significantly; the upward trend of accidents has fundamentally been reversed; the state of safety at work has become stable and better; the number of work-related accidents, death toll and direct economic loss have maintained zero growth for many consecutive years, so Zhejiang has been commended by the Safety at Work Commission of the State Council. The state of food and drug safety has been generally stable. Zhejiang is the first to have established a network of market circulation, a network of supervisory responsibility and a network of people's supervision relating to food safety in rural areas, a network of rural drug supplies and a network of rural drug supervision as well as rural integrated service specifications, thus achieving full coverage of food safety demonstration stores and a drug supervision network.

## 9.2 Zhejiang's Ten-Year Basic Experience in Social Development

With ten years of practice and experiments in social development, Zhejiang has accumulated rich and valuable experience. That experience is mainly summarized as maintaining "equal importance on three fronts" and "persistence in five respects" in social development.

## 9.2.1  "Equal Importance on Three Fronts" in Social Development

1. Popular entrepreneurship and transformation of government functions are equally important
(1) Popular entrepreneurship is the solid foundation for focusing on the people's well-being

The people are the main actors in social development; they are the leading players and motive force for creating wealth. Popular entrepreneurship is aimed at letting the people become emancipated and benefit themselves, and at developing an economy owned, run, managed and shared by the people, so that the people really become the main actors in entrepreneurship, operations, property rights, management and wealth. The continuous improvement in the people's well-being and steady enhancement of the quality of the people's life in Zhejiang mainly come from the people's entrepreneurship and innovations, and the development and prosperity of the popular economy.

During the initial stage of reform and opening-up, the people of Zhejiang carried out the spirit of taking a long and arduous journey, speaking various languages, making every effort and overcoming numerous difficulties and dangers, triggering an epic wave of economic development with thousands upon thousands of households starting businesses and a large number of people developing the market. One distinctive feature of Zhejiang's economic and social development is that there are numerous small enterprises and small bosses. In Zhejiang, a great many farmers have actively developed a household industry and family enterprises; with ceaseless self-improvement, keen market insight and emphasis on practical results, they have started from the sectors only delivering meager profits in which others were unwilling to engage in, they have worked hard, leveraged the intensive social capital advantage to earnestly mobilize and organize social resources. As numerous people have striven to start businesses, bosses and entrepreneurs have emerged in large numbers. At present, Zhejiang is home to more than 6 million small and large bosses out of 54 million people and a great many famous entrepreneurs who are adept at operations and have stayed innovative. According to statistical data, there is an average of one boss among every 25 people of Zhejiang; on average, every 4 households have one enterprise in Wenzhou and Taizhou.

As the people have become rich by starting businesses, the income of urban and rural residents has increased steadily and rapidly, ranking Zhejiang no. 1 among the provinces and autonomous regions across the country in this regard. Popular entrepreneurship has also generated more fiscal revenue, laying a solid economic foundation for implementing the policies focusing on the people's well-being. Popular entrepreneurship has helped rapidly reduce the poverty-stricken population and quickly expand the middle-income group; it is conducive to a sustained and steady increase in the level of consumption of urban and rural residents and to sustained and healthy economic and social development in Zhejiang.

(2)  Government transformation is the fundamental way to focus on the people's
     well-being

Government transformation means transformation from a construction-focused,
omnipotent and regulation-oriented government into a service-oriented, limited and
responsibility-focused government, a public service-oriented government. A public service-oriented government has undergone a change in functions, it puts the
people first, is aimed at making the people rich and creates a good, harmonious and
sustainable environment for the people's survival and development; moreover, it provides the people with more and better public goods, legitimate rights and interests,
including strengthening the construction of urban and rural public facilities, developing social employment and social security services and public programs involving
the educational, scientific, technological, cultural, health and sports fields, releasing
pubic information, meeting the people's basic needs for public resources, leveling the
playing field for market players, offering excellent public services to market players,
so that all of the sources for creating social wealth fully flow and the people become
rich.

In more than 30 years since the reform and opening-up, especially during the past
ten years, the Party committees and the governments at various levels in Zhejiang
have paid a great deal of importance to government transformation, the building
of a public service-oriented government and to the improvement and development
of the people's well-being; they have developed a slew of important policies, major
project plans and introduced a raft of proactive and vigorous measures for promoting
the development of the programs relating to the people's well-being. Actions have
been taken to build a culturally large province and a strong province in science and
technology, education, health and sports, to carry out the strategies for the construction of a new countryside and urban-rural integration, five 10-billion-yuan projects
and six action plans for building a moderately prosperous society in all respects, the
"Eight-Eight Strategies" and the strategies of building a safe Zhejiang, of promoting
the rule of law in Zhejiang and of building the province through ecological development, thus practically promoting all-round development of the programs relating to
the people's well-being in Zhejiang.

During the period of a decade, the governments at various levels in Zhejiang continuously enhanced the function of providing social public goods. The Party committees and the governments at various levels carefully built up the service network
and a safety net. The establishment and improvement of the government's service
network covering the departments above the county level across the province is an
important achievement in changing the functions of the governments at various levels
in Zhejiang. Local authorities have generally set up service centers and economic
environmental complaint centers in various forms, greatly enhancing the efficiency
of the work.

2.  The improvement in the people's well-being and economic growth are equally
    important

(1) The growth of the people's income is in sync with economic growth. Economic growth is an important prerequisite for social development, but economic growth is merely the yardstick for measuring production, it neither fully mirrors the society's real situation nor really reflects the actual living standard of the people. Economic growth will not necessarily result in the improvement of the people's living standard. As Zhejiang has witnessed rapid economic growth, the people's income, especially the income of urban residents, has grown basically at the same time. For instance, during the period of the 11th Five-Year Plan, the per capita GDP grew annually by an average of 11.7%, while the income of urban residents grew annually by an average of 11.3% in Zhejiang, which was basically in sync with economic growth.

(2) Giving priority to making the people rich is essential for building a strong province. Making the people rich is an important prerequisite for improving the people's well-being; the greatest aspiration of the people lies in becoming rich. The path for making them rich consists in promoting the common prosperity of the entire population on the basis of letting some of the people get rich first. Giving priority to making the people rich and making it possible for the wealth to be shared by all of the people is the important experience to be learned from Zhejiang's development. Zhejiang's prosperity is mainly the prosperity in Zhejiang's rural areas and that of the people. Making the people rich is the foundation for building an economically and socially strong province. According to Zhejiang's path for developing a strong province by making the people rich, giving priority to making the people rich and making it possible for the wealth to be shared by all the people is the endless source and fundamental guarantee for building a strong province. Only when the government creates the environment and conditions favorable for the people to get rich by starting businesses, and it makes sure that the vigor of labor, knowledge, technology, managerial expertise and capital keeps bursting forth and all the wealth-creating sources fully flow can the people's entrepreneurial wisdom be fully tapped and can social wealth grow rapidly. Therefore, the government's tax revenue will certainly grow steadily.

Making the people rich is the path for dependence in expanding the middle-income group. The middle-income group is the leading force for economic development and is the main consumer on the market; with a strong purchasing power, the middle-income group is the main driving force for sustained growth of consumer demand. Making the people rich is a process of continuously expanding the middle-income group. It is necessary to make it possible for the wealth to be shared by all of the people and to let every citizen have the opportunity to become the main part of an entrepreneurial endeavor and a market player, so that every citizen has the opportunity to become part of the middle-income group or the wealthy group and a majority of the people move towards common prosperity. This way can make the social structure more rational, help solve social conflicts, safeguard social justice and achieve balanced development.

(3) Social policy goes in tandem with economic policy. Social policy refers to the general term of the code of conduct, measures, decrees and regulations developed mainly through national legislation and administrative intervention and mainly aimed at solving social problems, guaranteeing public security, improving the social environment and enhancing social welfare. Social policy plays the role of making compensation in a certain form for the disadvantaged groups in the society, meeting social needs and enhancing public interests. Social policy is an institutional arrangement for promoting social fairness.

Since the beginning of the new century, Zhejiang has given great importance to ensuring coordination between economic policy and social policy, and has valued the important role of social policy in improving residents' living conditions and the quality of the life of its residents; Zhejiang has given the corresponding space and status to social policy; Zhejiang has regarded developing a sound social policy and solving social conflicts in economic development as an important effort in enhancing the governance capacity of the Party and the government. Zhejiang has established the social security system for the farmers whose land has been expropriated and a new social assistance system covering both urban and rural areas; moreover, it has improved the extensive social security system; Zhejiang has developed public education in a balanced way, providing every member of the society with equal opportunities for development; Zhejiang has improved the housing security system to make sure that the people have access to housing; Zhejiang has promoted the reform of the income distribution system to achieve social justice; Zhejiang has adopted a more proactive employment policy to ensure the people's well-being, safeguard the social rights of rural migrant workers and promote overall upward mobility in the society.

3. Reform of the social system and that of the economic system are equally important
We have intensified the reform of the economic system and preliminarily established a socialist market economic system, but the reform of the social system that is commensurate with a market economic system is far from being put in place. At present, some problems in the people's well-being—such as difficulties in getting access to medical services, education, employment, housing and old-age care—have loomed large, and they are associated with the lag in the reform of the social system. In the past decade, Zhejiang has accelerated the reform of the social system to promote all-round development of the society.

(1) Zhejiang has removed the institutional barriers to the development of the middle-income group in order to make it possible for the middle-income group to grow more rapidly. Given the institutional barriers to the middle-income group in entrepreneurship, distribution and other fields, Zhejiang has intensified reforms in these fields. Zhejiang has encouraged small and medium-sized enterprises and individual workers, including university grad-

uates, to start businesses, and has fostered the development of the rural household industry; Zhejiang has promoted entrepreneurship to stimulate employment and improve the system of entrepreneurial services, and it has waived the administrative charges relating to entrepreneurial registration of university graduates and the unemployed people. Zhejiang has created conditions to let farmers earn property income. In recent years, Zhejiang has fully leveraged the favorable conditions created by Zhejiang's determination, by the Office of the Central Leading Group for Rural Work, as the contact point for the experiment of the rural comprehensive reform to further ascertain the key fields and segments for promoting the reform experiment and institutional development, place equal emphasis on non-point reform innovations and the experiment of reform at points, and build the mechanism and institutional system for urban-rural integration. Zhejiang has intensified the comprehensive reform for coordinated urban-rural development, including intensifying the reform of the rural property rights system, confirming and registering the right to the contracted management of rural collective land, the right to use homesteads and house property ownership and issuing rights and ownership certificates as well as guiding the trading and circulation of the land and mountain forests, rural collective construction land and the reserved rural collective land whose rights have been confirmed. Zhejiang has actively explored the modes of circulating the right to contracted management, such as cooperation based on land as shares; Zhejiang has built the mechanism for ensuring that the ordinary farmers participate in agricultural modernization on an equal footing and get equal access to the achievements of agricultural modernization.

(2) Zhejiang has improved the mechanism for the rational allocation of public resources to ensure the people at the primary level enjoy more social public goods and public resources. In a decade, Zhejiang has introduced the policies for promoting coordinated urban-rural employment, stimulating employment through entrepreneurship and strengthening the employment of university graduates; a system and mechanism for full employment have basically taken shape; Zhejiang has become the first to establish the social endowment insurance system for urban and rural residents, and it has continuously increased the coverage of the urban and rural medical insurance system, reformed the system of low-rent housing and economically affordable housing and endeavored to build an extensive social security system; it has also intensified the reform of the medical and health system, comprehensively pushed forward the key reforms in the system of basic medical security, that of basic medicine, that of primary-level medical and health services, and it has provided equal access to basic public health services and public hospitals; moreover, Zhejiang has kept intensifying the reforms of the educational system and the compulsory education fund guarantee system as well as the reform in performance-based wages for compulsory education teachers, thoroughly carried out four projects for rural middle and primary schools and six action plans for vocational education; it has

intensified the reform of public institutions, further built the pilot province for the reform of the cultural system, it has become the first to finish the reform of for-profit cultural institutions and the reform involving the system of comprehensive law enforcement within the cultural market, it has stayed ahead nationwide in the development of the public cultural service system and the private cultural industry and it has actively innovated the mode of public service provision, encouraged social organizations to provide public goods and public services, relaxed restrictions on investment access to the field of basic public services, provided classified guidance for public benefit programs and for-profit industries, and vigorously developed the social service industry.

(3)  Effects have been produced in the reform of the urban system and the development of social organizations. Zhejiang has been at the forefront nationwide in urbanization. In 2013, the urban population accounted for 63.5% in Zhejiang. Zhejiang's path towards urbanization is different from that in Jiangsu, Guangdong and Shandong; as the number of large cities is relatively small in Zhejiang, Zhejiang has energetically carried out an action plan for pilot development of small cities and made great efforts to improve the function of a platform for public services of small cities. In the pilot towns, actions have been taken to actively promote comprehensive management and the building of the public service platform, energetically introduced new systems and mechanisms to boost intensive use of land and population agglomeration according to the goals of urban-rural integration, rural urbanization, agricultural modernization and farmer urbanization; a new residence permit system has been adopted to extend the residence permit to all rural migrant workers and grant the civil rights which rural migrant workers should enjoy, which is the effort in removing regional restrictions, narrowing the urban-rural gap and ensuring equal access to interests. The development of social organizations should be the core of the current new round of institutional reform and also one of the priorities in social development. In the past decade, Zhejiang has vigorously cultivated and developed various types of social organizations, strengthened the division of work and cooperation between the government and social organizations, given full play to the active role of social organizations in providing services, coordinating interests, resolving conflicts and expressing appeals, so a multidimensional public self-organization network has taken shape beyond the government.

### 9.2.2 *"Persistence in Five Respects" in Social Development*

1. Upholding scientific development to elevate the strategic position of social development in an all-round way

   Zhejiang has always upheld the philosophy of scientific development and given prominence to the strategic requirement of "giving more value to social development on the basis of economic development" to actively improve the system of policies for social development and greatly speed up Zhejiang's coordinated economic and social development. Zhejiang has stayed ahead nationwide in economic development and the level of social development. For instance, with the overall index of the level of Zhejiang's social development in 2007 as the base value 100, that in 2010 was 114.76, up 14.76 points compared with 2007, suggesting a significant increase in the level of development.

2. Giving priority to the people's well-being to improve the quality of the people's life in an all-round way

   Zhejiang has endeavored to let the people share the achievements of social development amidst rapid economic growth. The level of the people's income has increased generally and the system for guaranteeing the people's well-being has improved gradually. When developing and implementing the action plans for ensuring equal access to basic public services and increasing the income of the low-income groups, Zhejiang has given higher priority to doing substantive work for the people. During the period of the 11th Five-Year Plan, Zhejiang's fiscal expenditure on the people's well-being grew annually by an average of 21.1%, and more than 2/3 of the incremental fiscal expenditure was used to improve the people's well-being for five consecutive years. Zhejiang has paid a great deal of attention to ensuring coordination between economic policy and social policy, and has valued the important role of social policy in improving residents' living conditions and the quality of the residents' life; Zhejiang has given the corresponding space and status to social policy; Zhejiang has regarded developing a sound social policy and resolving social conflicts in economic development as an important effort in enhancing the governance capacity of the Party and the government. As stressed by comrade Xi Jinping, it is necessary to provide special legal and policy protection for the groups in difficulty in the society, including accelerating the building of the vocational training service system, the social security system and the system of subsistence allowances, making sure that the groups in difficulty obtain the opportunities for engaging in market competition in the society.[2] Zhejiang has established the social security system for the farmers whose land has been expropriated and the new social assistance system covering both urban and rural areas; it has improved the extensive social security system and the housing security system, promoted the reform of the income distribution system and adopted a more proactive employment policy to ensure the social rights of rural migrant workers.

---

[2]Xi (2006), p. 250.

3. Upholding the Party's leadership, the government's assumption of responsibilities, social coordination and public participation to comprehensively increase the level of social development

   In a decade, the Party Committee and the People's Government of Zhejiang Province have given great importance to social development, ensured that the Party plays its role as the leadership core in exercising overall leadership and coordinating all efforts, it has continuously made improvements in the capacity and level of social management of the Party organizations at various levels; it has strengthened the government's social management functions, made sure that the government does not go beyond the specified limits, and is not in the wrong position and is not absent in discharging duties, so that the government really assumes its bounden social management responsibility; it has given full play to the roles of various types of social organizations, reinforced the cooperation between the government and social organizations, built and improved a network of social organizations dedicated to providing services, expressing appeals and standardizing behaviors; it has actively cultivated public awareness about participation, continually broadened the channels for public participation and standardized public participation behavior, and relied on the people to bring about innovations to social management. The Party committees at various levels have, according to the arrangements made by the Central Committee of the Communist Party of China and the Party Committee of Zhejiang Province, built and improved a pattern of social development and management in which the Party committee plays the leading role, the government assumes the responsibility, there is social coordination and public participation; they have reached a common understanding, identified goals and enhanced mechanisms, continuously improved the system of goal responsibility to establish a working mechanism in which unified leadership is exercised, division of work and cooperation are enabled, joint management is performed and responsibilities are assigned to individuals. The governments at various levels have given importance to building a public service-oriented government, improving and developing the people's well-being; they have developed a slew of important policies and major project plans, and have taken a number of active and vigorous measures to promote social development. Zhejiang has increased government input, actively established and improved a long-term mechanism for social development, greatly helping achieve the goal of ensuring access to education, labor remuneration, medical service, old-age care and housing.

4. Proceeding from the province's conditions to carry out reforms and innovations, improving the quality of social development across the board

   As Zhejiang started the market-oriented reform early, the private economy has been developed in Zhejiang; with drastic changes in the structure of the social classes and increasingly diverse economic sectors, organizational forms and employment modes in the society, social development and management have been subject to huge challenges. In five years, in light of the province's conditions, the Party Committee of Zhejiang Province earnestly conducted institutional innovations on social development and management, strengthened the building of a sound social operational mechanism and made many beneficial experiments and much institutional improvement in social organization, social management, public security, social integration and the mechanism for different groups' expression of interests.

Zhejiang has carried out reforms in coordinated allocation of educational, health, cultural, urban and rural public resources, the public financial system and the income distribution system; Zhejiang has overcome developmental difficulties through reforms and strengthened social management through innovative measures to ensure that the society is harmonious and orderly, continuously injecting vigor for social development; Zhejiang has started with key fields and segments to deepen the mechanism and institutional innovations in the social field so as to provide a strong institutional guarantee for the development of change. In the meantime, Zhejiang has speeded up the reform of the social management mode to integrate the respective management functions and services of the government's functional departments, thus upgrading decentralized management to integrated management; Zhejiang has accelerated the reform of the main actors in social management to build a new pattern of social management in which the Party plays the leading role, the government assumes the responsibility and there is social coordination and civic participation; Zhejiang has energetically cultivated primary-level self-governance and actively developed social organizations, so that the non-governmental and non-market forces grow in a good environment.

5.  Innovating and developing the Fengqiao Experience to carry out the basic projects for ensuring the security of the society

    Stability is the prerequisite and foundation for harmony. To promote the building of a harmonious society, it is essential to ensure that the society is safe, stable and orderly. In a decade, Zhejiang has brought innovations to and developed the Fengqiao Experience to consolidate the foundation for maintaining a safe and orderly society. The Party Committee of Zhejiang Province made the decision about and arrangement of building a safe Zhejiang in 2004, setting the goals for harmonious and stable development in the economic, political and social life. A safe Zhejiang, envisioned by the Party Committee and the People's Government of Zhejiang Province, features harmonious development between the economy and the society, between urban and rural areas and between the people and nature. As mentioned by comrade Xi Jinping, the "safe" in a safe Zhejiang is not "safe" in a narrow sense; instead, it is a wide-ranging kind of "safe" in a broad sense with a wide scope and at multiple levels in the economic, political, cultural and social fields.[3]

Zhejiang has given overall considerations to the economic, political, cultural and social factors, adopted the administrative, legal and educational means to correctly handle the relations between economic development and social development, and intensified the building of a working mechanism to solve problems at their source. Zhejiang has established and improved various mechanisms including forecast and

---

[3]Xi (2006), p. 235.

early warning about mass incidents, their identification and settlement, emergency response, accountability and work guarantee to institutionalize and standardize the work on maintaining stability. Zhejiang has reinforced the building of a social security mechanism, it has always focused on the primary level, continuously consolidated the foundation for work, with a focus on pushing forward the development of comprehensive governance centers and promoting comprehensive governance in private enterprises, so Zhejiang's comprehensive governance network has further extended to the primary level. Zhejiang has earnestly improved the work in organizing efforts to identify, mediate and resolve conflicts, exercising supervision and providing guidance. Zhejiang has combined regular identification with centralized identification, integrated the people's mediation, administrative mediation and judicial mediation, promoted the leaders to take charge of efforts to handle major conflicts and called for resolving major conflicts within the specified time, thus fostering a holistic synergy for preventing and resolving conflicts and disputes. Zhejiang has summed up the Fengqiao Experience, the Lucheng Practice and the Yiwu Model for prevention and control in public security, and incessantly improved the multidimensional social prevention and control network.

## 9.3 The Inspirations from Zhejiang's Experience in Social Development for National Modernization

### 9.3.1 Giving Priority to Improving the People's Well-Being is the Focus of Social Development

The people's well-being refers to the people's livelihood and the guarantee for livelihood, covering the way of making a living, the matters in life, the guarantee of social public goods and services. Giving priority to improving the people's well-being is an effort at moving towards the goal of social development and is the fundamental part of social development. Giving priority to improving the people's well-being highlights three main features of social development: a people-oriented nature, inclusiveness and justice. Giving priority to improving the people's well-being is the focus of Zhejiang's social development during the period of a decade.

1. Giving priority to improving the people's well-being highlights the people-oriented nature of development
   The people-oriented nature is the highest yardstick for measuring social development. The people-oriented nature first means continuous improvement in the people's livelihood, well-being and rights. Our society is people-centered; in other words, it is a society in which the people are the masters. The people participate in and are also served by social modernization. Therefore, it is essential to ensure and improve the people's well-being, and to the greatest extent reduce the costs and price for the people in reforms, let the people participate in the whole

process of development as much as possible, and enjoy as many opportunities for development and achievements of development as possible and meet the people's basic needs; only in this way can the people-oriented nature be embodied. This is the solid foundation for ensuring and improving the people's well-being and gives the best expression to the people-oriented nature of development.

Ensuring and improving the people's well-being is the intrinsic requirement of putting the people first; it is also the basic requirement of scientific development and social harmony. To address the issue of the people's well-being, it is necessary to follow the demands and aspirations of the people and start with the most pressing, most immediate issues that concern the people the most to wholeheartedly do substantive work for the people, promptly and actively dispel anxieties and overcome difficulties for the people. It is essential to ensure the people's access to education, labor remuneration, medical services, old-age care and housing. Meeting the people's needs, realizing the people's aspirations and enhancing the people's well-being really embody the people-oriented nature of development.

2. Giving priority to improving the people's well-being highlights the inclusiveness of development

   Inclusiveness is the most fundamental philosophy of social development. Inclusiveness means that the people enjoy the resources and achievements of development as much as possible. The government and the society should endeavor to provide more public goods and public services for meeting the ever-growing social public needs of the people. This also involves the transformation of government functions and the transformation from the original omnipotent and regulation-oriented government into a government which carries out the effective public provision strategy and provides public goods. Giving priority to improving the people's well-being provides a guide and a goal for social development: letting everyone live a happier life and enjoy more social public goods and more opportunities for development.

   Inclusiveness stresses full coverage from the achievements of social development. Giving priority to improving the people's well-being calls for enabling co-building and sharing, breaking the dual urban-rural social system, boosting urban-rural integration, removing the unreasonable restrictions and rules on labor flow and employment of rural migrant workers by urban enterprises, establishing a fair, orderly and competitive employment mechanism, turning rural migrant workers into citizens and making sure that everyone enjoys the basic public services and public goods.

3. Giving priority to improving the people's well-being highlights the justice of development

   Justice is a fundamental goal of social development. Social justice means equality at the starting point, rules and opportunities and a certain equality in outcomes. To make sure that the people enjoy the resources and achievements of development as much as possible, it is necessary to ensure social fairness and justice. Given China's socialist nature, China cannot embody social justice only in a small scope like the capitalist society during the early stage; China must, from the beginning, to the greatest extent embody social justice in every member of the society. This is the core and essence of China's strategy for social development; this is also the ultimate goal and pursuit of China's modernization. Giving priority to improving the people's well-being is governed by the basic principle—maintaining social justice—and calls for reducing, to the greatest extent, the costs and price that the people must bear in development and reform, increasing input in social public goods and public services to continuously improve the people's well-being.

## 9.3.2  Optimizing the Social Structure is the Central Task of Social Development

In the drive towards modernization, besides state regulation and market regulation, the transformation of the social structure is another invisible hand which exerts an impact on resource allocation and economic development; it is the result of economic growth, the driving force for social change and the important force for promoting economic development.

A rational social structure plays a crucial role in economic and social development. This is because the social structure restricts the social actions of social actors by means of path dependence; it determines social stability, harmony and development. In other words, social structure more or less builds and shapes social actions. The state of the social structure is one of the essential characteristics of the society; the change in social structure is a process of social transformation and development. Like the economic structure, the social structure is one of the important dimensions for observing and understanding the development of a country or territory. The change in economic structure boosts the change in social structure, while the change in social structure acts on the economic structure.

The core of the social structure is the structure of social classes; it directly reflects the state of social relations. A rational structure of social classes is the foundation for social stability, harmony and development, while an irrational structure of social classes is a cause for social conflicts, disputes and social disorganization. The transformation from a pyramid-shaped structure of social classes into a social structure dominated by the middle-income class is the important sign of high social quality. Zhejiang has paid attention to making the people rich by starting businesses and to promoting a more rapid growth of the middle-income group. In 2010, the middle-income group accounted for about 31.6% of the total population, placing Zhejiang at the forefront nationwide in this regard. Based on making the people rich by starting businesses, Zhejiang strives to increase the proportion of the middle-income group to 40–45% and make the middle-income group the main part of the society and thus shape a modern class structure by 2020.

Optimizing the social structure is also embodied in the coordinated development among different residents. This calls for improving the social ecology in which the groups in difficulty live. An important experience from Zhejiang's decade-long social development is that continuous benefits are brought to the majority of the people through reform and development. Zhejiang has kept intensifying social security for the groups in difficulty and has introduced a number of plans for increasing the income of the low-income groups; Zhejiang has also taken practical measures to improve their situation and status within the market, provided them with more opportunities in policy, institution and mechanism and further improved the environment in which these groups can survive.

A rational social structure is also embodied in the coordinated development between urban and rural areas and among different regions. Breaking the dual system to promote rapid development of new-type urbanization and urban-rural integration is an important part of Zhejiang's social development. Urbanization is a great engine for expanding the middle-income group and is conducive to improving the class structure. In a decade, the level of Zhejiang's urbanization increased rapidly, it surged from 41% in 2001 to 63.5%, the proportion of the employed people in the primary industry decreased to 13.8%.

### 9.3.3 The Balanced and Coordinated Development is a Significant Characteristic of Zhejiang's Experience

Balance in development is an important guarantee for steady social development in Zhejiang. Balance in development means that there is coordination in the society and harmony among the people, the social structure in a sociological sense is rational, social operations are coordinated, the development between urban and rural areas, between developed and underdeveloped areas, between the economy and the society is promoted in a balanced way, social wealth is distributed rationally, poverty is eliminated and polarization is prevented. Balance in development is the intrinsic requirement of sustainable social development. If a developmental mode leads to imbalance in regional structure, urban-rural structure and wealth structure, polarization and poverty, and makes the poor people unable to rationally enjoy the achievements of economic and social development, that developmental mode cannot achieve the social goals in the minds of the people and will certainly cause many social problems, making development unsustainable. Zhejiang's balanced social development is mainly embodied in the following several aspects.

1. Social development and economic development are promoted in a balanced way
   The all-round social development covers development in the economic and social fields. The development of social programs covering science, education, culture, health, sports and environmental protection should be commensurate with the level of economic development. As the economic level increases, social programs develop accordingly, so it is necessary to build a system of social programs which can fully meet the needs of economic and social development and the residents' living needs. Besides attention paid to economic development, Zhejiang has also increasingly given importance to the development of social

programs, the composite evaluation index concerning Zhejiang's social development has gradually kept up with economic development and has increasingly been coordinated with that development. The improvement in the overall quality of the society and the all-round development of social programs constitute a solid foundation for lasting economic development. Social development is also consistent with the improvement in the people's living standard and the quality of the people's life. In a sense, attention to social development is attention to improving the people's living standard and the people's well-being. According to the comprehensive evaluation of the levels of social development in various parts of the country conducted by the National Bureau of Statistics in 2011 and 2012, Zhejiang ranked no. 4 nationwide in the composite evaluation index concerning the level of social development, following Shanghai, Beijing and Tianjin, which basically corresponds to the ranking of the provinces across the country regarding the level of economic development.

2. Balanced development is promoted between urban and rural areas
   Cities are the result of social change and the sign of social development. The level of urbanization is the yardstick for measuring the level of socialization and it is also the standard for measuring the degree of social civilization. As of late 2013, the level of Zhejiang's urbanization reached 63.5%. Rural development is the foundation for urban development and the priority in Zhejiang's modernization; rural development is also an important part of the improvement in and development of the people's well-being; it is the key to building a harmonious society. Amidst rapid urban development, Zhejiang has become the first nationwide to promote urban-rural integration, and has increased input in rural public goods and speeded up the building of new communities in rural areas. With concerted efforts of the people across the province, great progress has been made in the construction of a new countryside and the people's income has increased significantly in Zhejiang.

3. Balanced development is promoted between underdeveloped and developed areas
   Quzhou City and Lishui City in Zhejiang are currently underdeveloped compared with northeastern Zhejiang due to natural factors, including geographical location. If Zhejiang is considered to be in transition from the middle period of industrialization to the later period of industrialization, both cities generally remain in transition from the early period of industrialization to the middle period of industrialization. Since the 16th National Congress of the Communist Party of China, in light of Zhejiang's reality, the Party Committee of Zhejiang Province has put forward a new line of thought of leveraging the advantages of mountain and sea resources and coordinated regional development, and has comprehensively carried out the Mountain-Sea Cooperation Project, the Project for Making the Underdeveloped Towns Become Well-to-do and the Project with Ten-Billion Assistance and Support for Achieving Prosperity; further, Zhejiang has trained the rural labor force in the underdeveloped areas, provided multi-field paired assistance in an all-round way and promoted coordinated regional development. As the developed areas develop rapidly, industrial gradient transfer and rational allocation of factors are carried out in the developed areas through inter-regional

project cooperation, and coordinated development is fostered between the coastal developed areas and the underdeveloped areas in the west and south of Zhejiang.

4. Coordinated development is promoted between the low-income group and the middle-high-income group

   The development of the disadvantaged groups has a vital bearing on the optimization of the social structure and social harmony. Paying attention to and supporting the development of the disadvantaged groups and providing opportunities for development to the disadvantaged groups are the government's responsibilities and duties and also embody social morality, justice and conscience. In a decade, Zhejiang has intensified support for the underdeveloped areas, including rural areas, and such disadvantaged groups as farmers, the coverage from social security has been further increased and the socialized assistance system has preliminarily taken shape. Zhejiang has become the first nationwide to establish a system of subsistence allowances for farmers; Zhejiang has finished, in advance, the work on centralized support of the rural people enjoying five guarantees and the urban people without identification papers, a normal residence permit, and a source of income. The social assistance system covering medical services, education and housing has been built in an all-round way, basic public services have covered all farmers across the province, the goal of letting no student fail to attend schools due to poverty has basically been achieved; the *Measures of Zhejiang Province for Urban Low-rent Housing Security* have been issued to provide low-income groups and rural migrant workers with much economically affordable housing and low-rent housing.

5. Balanced development is promoted between rural migrant workers and local people

   The rights of the migrant population have been duly protected. Zhejiang is a province with a large number of migrant population. As of 2013, there was a migrant population of about 23 million in Zhejiang. When it comes to dealing with rural migrant workers, Zhejiang has changed from the initial management to one of sharing in mindset, service in mode, and integration in title. As mentioned by comrade Xi Jinping, as the friends of cities, rural migrant workers have become important new forces and essential human resources for Zhejiang's economic development,[4] they have made tremendous contributions to local industrialization, marketization and urbanization; the leaders of the Party committees and the governments at various levels have profoundly realized that rural migrant workers, as important human resources, should be part of the local population, rural migrant workers should be treated on an equal footing, services should be strengthened and management should be improved for them. To protect their legitimate rights, really integrate them into cities and local life and improve the quality of their life, Zhejiang has carried out the new resident system to improve the employment environment for rural migrant workers and provide basic social security for them; Zhejiang has incorporated the training of rural migrant workers into the plan for social development and has given great importance to the

---

[4] Xi (2006), p. 250.

education of their children. In Zhejiang, th migrant population enjoys social and political rights; they are called the new people of Zhejiang. Local authorities in Zhejiang have realized that the growth of the new people of Zhejiang is an important sign of regional economic vitality and prosperity. The new people of Zhejiang have promoted social mobility, enhanced the awareness of the whole society about development, carved out more paths for rural migrant workers to become urban residents.

6. Balanced development is promoted between the people and nature

In 2003, the Party Committee of Zhejiang Province made the decision to build an ecological province. Comrade Xi Jinping, the then Secretary of the Party Committee of Zhejiang Province pointed out, "Clean, clear waters and lush mountains are the gold and silver mountain",[5] shedding light on the relations between ecological protection and economic and social development. In 2010, the Party Committee of Zhejiang Province made the great decision to promote ecological development, put forward the strategy of building an ecological province, and vowed to achieve the goal of ecological development characterized by sustainable economic and social development. In 2014, the Party Committee of Zhejiang Province made the decision to turn Zhejiang into a beautiful province for living a good life, elevating ecological development to a new level. In a decade, Zhejiang has made significant achievements in the control of environmental pollution and has made comprehensive arrangements to carry out the "811" action for the control of environmental pollution focusing on eight major water systems and provincial-level key environmental supervision areas; Zhejiang has set the goal of basically finishing the work on two fronts and becoming the first to make progress in two respects, and it has put forward the policy of governing the old and controlling the new, placing equal emphasis on supervision and construction; it has concretely controlled the pollution in key river basins, key areas, key industries and key enterprises, made significant achievements in improving such water systems as the Qiantang River, the Yong River and the Tiaoxi River; it has strengthened environmental access in construction projects, comprehensively pushed forward structural adjustment, "vacated the cage to change birds", vetoed or required the re-selection of sites for more than 4000 construction projects inconsistent with national industrial policies and ecological environmental requirements. The environmental quality has remained basically stable. Since the period of the 10th Five-Year Plan, Zhejiang has noticeably increased the input in ecological development and environmental governance, higher than the average national level of input in environmental protection. The total emissions of the main pollutants has been basically controlled in an effective way, the intensity of pollutant emissions from industrial products has decreased year by year and the work on improving the environment in key river basins and areas has been promoted in an orderly fashion; moreover, ecological protection and development have been strengthened. The plans for ecological development and environmental protection of three main industrial belts have been developed. Local authorities and various departments have

---

[5]Xi (2006), p. 198.

developed and implemented the plans for ecological development. In a decade, Zhejiang's forest coverage has reached 60.5%, Zhejiang has ranked no. 4 among the provinces across the country in the overall energy consumption level per 10,000-yuan GDP (from low to high), and has been at the forefront nationwide in this regard. According to the annual report on China's strategy for sustainable development which was released by the Chinese Academy of Sciences, Zhejiang has ranked no. 3 nationwide for many consecutive years in the capacity for environmental support, following Tibet and Hainan. According to the *National Ecological Environmental Assessment Report* released by the China National Environmental Monitoring Center, Zhejiang has stayed ahead nationwide in the ecological environmental index and the capacity for ecological environmental support, Zhejiang has been generally at the advanced national level in the quality of its ecological environment.

### 9.3.4  Joint Governance by the Government and the Society is an Important Mode of Social Development

Theoretically, a healthy society depends upon the balance among the government, the market and the society. As an important part of China's drive towards modernization, actions are being taken to gradually rationalize the relations among the country, the market and the society, ensure that the government generally does not intervene in the issues which can be addressed by the market and the society, that the government manages the matters which should be managed by the government vigorously and better, and that the government performs its functions better in employment, basic education, basic medical services, public health, housing, income distribution, social security, social relief, safety at work, environmental protection and public security.

The people are the fundamental driving force for social development and the cornerstone of the governing party. The people have enormous forces for maintaining stability and promoting development. Only when there is sincere trust in the people and the people are unswervingly relied upon can a good pattern of social development take shape. This calls for giving great importance to the people's participation in social development and the people's pioneering spirit, broadening the channels for the people's participation, providing the people with various opportunities for participating in social development and social governance and establishing the mechanism for public participation in making public social policies; this calls for improving the systems for collective decision-making, expert consulting, social disclosure and hearings and the evaluation of decisions concerning major matters; sufficiently valuing and utilizing the Internet as the new channel for the people's participation in social development and governance, providing the people with the rights and opportunities for knowing, participating in and supervising public social affairs. In the meantime, Zhejiang has enhanced cooperation between the government and the society and it has established a modern social public governance structure to meet diverse social needs. Zhejiang has leveraged social organizations and social forces to provide public goods and public services for covering the shortage of public goods and public services from the government, increase the rate of resource utilization and to the greatest extent meet the public needs of various classes and the people, keep order and social fairness and promote social stability and development.

### 9.3.5   The Development Towards Greater Safety is an Important Way to Make Improvements in the National Capacity and Level of Modern Governance

The modernization of social governance is an important part of national modernization, while the modernization of national governance is mainly embodied in promoting social governance under the rule of law and in a democratic and scientific way. "Safe" is the ideal of those governing the country and the aspiration of the people; it is the basic requirement for the people's happiness and well-being; it is also the basic prerequisite for reform and development. The modernization of national governance stresses equal importance of enhancing public interests and maintaining public order, while the capacity for achieving both goals is the most important embodiment of the national governance capacity.

The building of a safe Zhejiang presents a large platform for Zhejiang to adopt new ways of social governance and promote the modernization of the national governance system and governance capacity. In January, 2004, the Central Group of Theoretical Learning under the Party Committee of Zhejiang Province held a meeting for learning, putting forward the building of a safe Zhejiang for the first time, in which comrade Xi Jinping profoundly pointed out, "Prosperity and stability serve the fundamental interests of the people, making the people rich and keeping a good public order is the political responsibility of the leading cadres".[6] Since the building of a safe Zhejiang was initiated in 2004, the leading cadres at various levels in Zhejiang have two reports at hand each month, including an economic report and a safety report, to promote economic development and maintain social stability at the same time. The Party committees at various levels in Zhejiang Province have established the system involving analysis of the state of social stability to regularly analyze the state of social stability, and promptly study and address the major issues in work. In an effort to promote rapid and sound economic and social development in Zhejiang, both reports reflect the philosophy of extensive safety under the leadership of the Party committees and the governments at various levels. Under the guidance of the philosophy, the people across the province have made concerted efforts to actively push forward stable and coordinated development in the economic, political, social, cultural and ecological fields in Zhejiang.

---

[6]Xi (2006), p. 235.

Zhejiang has promoted the development towards greater safety by incorporating it into the overall pattern of economic and social development and the five-sphere integrated plan, and has thus ensured that the development toward greater safety is commensurate with economic and social development. Zhejiang has opportunely adjusted the particulars concerning safety under evaluation so that the development towards greater safety extends to the areas where the problems affecting safety occur. Zhejiang has explored effective systems and mechanisms in practice, correctly handled the relations between maintaining stability and safeguarding rights, between vitality and order, between democracy and the rule of law and it has adopted new ways of social governance; with a focus on continuously improving the people's well-being, Zhejiang has promoted the work on developing social programs, innovating social governance and maintaining social harmony and stability in a coordinated way, making sure that the people live and work in peace and contentment and that the society is stable and orderly.

Intensifying the building of a safe Zhejiang is essential to bring about innovations to social governance, modernize the governance system and governance capacity, and to maintain the overall situation of reform, development and stability and to ensure that Zhejiang comprehensively intensifies reforms in a smooth way; it is also essential to address the new expectations of the people about a good life and write Zhejiang's chapter for the Chinese Dream. As Zhejiang intensifies the building of a safe Zhejiang, it is necessary to focus on the overall goal of improving the socialist system with Chinese characteristics and modernizing the national governance system and governance capacity, earnestly push forward the modernization of the social governance system with Chinese characteristics, establish and improve the system of maintaining national security and social stability, the system of preventing social conflicts at their source, the system of mediating and resolving social conflicts, the system of guaranteeing public security and the system of guaranteeing economic security, build a safe Zhejiang with a stronger economy, greater political stability, more prosperous culture, greater social harmony and a better quality of life. It is necessary to earnestly strengthen the building of the capacity for social governance, make improvements in the capacity and level of the Party committee to lead, of departments to perform duties and of the people to conduct self-governance, to make sure that the social governance system is under orderly and efficient operations and to provide effective guarantees and support for continuously intensifying the building of a safe Zhejiang. It is essential to build and improve the system of safeguarding national security and social stability, to reinforce IP applications, to scientifically predict possible situations and problems so as to make preparations for them; it is necessary to build and improve the system of preventing social conflicts at their source, make efforts in protecting and benefiting the people, devote great energy to scientific and democratic decision-making, strict law enforcement and impartial administration of justice; moreover, it is necessary to establish and improve the system of mediating and resolving social conflicts, uphold and develop the Fengqiao Experience, institutionally erect a firewall for mediating and resolving social contradictions and strive to resolve conflicts at the local level in a diversified way according to laws, establish and improve the system of guaranteeing public security to strengthen prevention, control and supervision in public security, network-based integrated prevention and control as well as to build and improve the system of a guarantee of security in the economic field, give play to the role of development towards greater safety in coordinating the economic interest relations, regulating the economic order and creating a good environment for development and carve out a new developmental path based on the philosophy that "clean, clear waters and lush mountains are the gold and silver mountain".

## Reference

Xi Jinping, *Carrying out Solid Work to Stay Ahead – Line of Thought and Practice in Promoting New Development in Zhejiang*, The Party School of the CPC Central Committee Press, 2006.

# Postscript

The research and writing relating to the major issue "The Chinese Dream and Zhejiang's Practice" (Society Volume), jointly conducted by the Party Committee of Zhejiang Province and the Chinese Academy of Social Sciences, has lasted for more than half a year since April when it was officially initiated. In the Research Group, Chen Guangjin, the Director of the Institute of Sociology of the Chinese Academy of Social Sciences, serves as the leader, and Yang Jianhua, the Director and research fellow of the Institute of Public Policy of the Zhejiang Academy of Social Sciences, a member of the Advisory Committee of the Zhejiang Provincial People's Government, serves as the deputy leader. Under the careful guidance of the leaders from the Chinese Academy of Social Sciences, the Party Committee of Zhejiang Province, the Department of Publicity under the Party Committee of Zhejiang Province and the Zhejiang Academy of Social Sciences, with great efforts of all the members of the group, the Research Group ultimately finished the task of research and writing on schedule.

In the research project, we resolutely followed the overall requirements of the leaders at various levels, especially the specific requirements raised by Hu Jian, the Executive Deputy Director of the Department of Publicity under the Party Committee of Zhejiang Province, about the research and writing relating to the Society Volume; we earnestly learnt the thoughts and theories concerning social development developed by General Secretary Xi Jinping and his two works *Carrying out Solid Work to Stay Ahead*, *Zhijiang Xinyu*, summarized the thoughts, experiments and the practical experience of comrade Xi Jinping, the practical experience of the subsequent successive Party Committees of Zhejiang Province in inheritance and carrying through one blueprint, and presented the great significance of these practices and experience for Zhejiang's modernization, inspirations and significance for reference for national development.

During the research, the members of the Research Group conducted in-depth surveys and proceeded from practice and facts rather than analysis and debates and they developed ideas through rethinking and refining on the basis of surveys. The Research Group carried out intensive surveys in June, and later conducted scattered

© Social Sciences Academic Press and Springer Nature Singapore Pte Ltd. 2019
G. Chen and J. Yang (eds.), *Chinese Dream and Practice in Zhejiang—Society*,
Research Series on the Chinese Dream and China's Development Path,
https://doi.org/10.1007/978-981-13-7406-7

and small surveys. The Research Group visited a number of departments including the Department of Civil Affairs of Zhejiang Province, the Commission for Political and Legal Affairs of Zhejiang Province, such prefecture-level cities as Jiaxing and Zhoushan, and gathered a great deal of first-hand materials through visits, talks and on-the-spot surveys. At the Department of Civil Affairs of Zhejiang Province, the Research Group listened to the introduction of the overall situation made by comrade Yu Zhizhuang, the Deputy Director-General of the Department of Civil Affairs of Zhejiang Province, a member of the Party Group at the Department of Civil Affairs of Zhejiang Province; they conducted surveys and held talks at relevant functional divisions and offices of the Department of Civil Affairs of Zhejiang Province to learn more about Zhejiang's social security, social assistance, development of urban and rural communities, development and social organizations, old-age care and charity, social welfare, social affairs, benefits for the entitled groups, while the leaders of 11 divisions of the Department of Civil Affairs of Zhejiang Province in charge of the management of social organizations, the benefits for the entitled groups and other affairs attended the talks. At the Commission for Political and Legal Affairs of Zhejiang Province, Zhu Yijun, the Deputy Director-general of the Comprehensive Governance Office of Zhejiang Province, led the heads of the Division of Comprehensive Coordination, the Division of Primary-level Guidance and the Division of Supervision and Evaluation at the Commission for Political and Legal Affairs to communicate with the members of the Research Group with respect to the building of a safe Zhejiang, social governance, social management innovations and the management of and services for the migrant population. The Research Group visited Lakeside Barometer Studio in Shangcheng District, Hangzhou City, Nanxiaobu Community in Kaixuan Sub-district, Jianggan District to hold talks with community cadres and social workers in order to get a profound understanding of the characteristic experience in the governance of primary-level communities and public services.

During surveys in Jiaxing and Zhoushan, the Research Group listened to the work reports delivered by nearly ten departments of both cities, including the commission for political and legal affairs and the development and reform commission, about the overall state of social development, urbanization, social governance, social programs and public services, and conducted on-the-spot surveys on Jiaxing's practice of the scientific outlook on development, the construction of a new countryside at Yaozhuang Town, Jiashan County, local urbanization in Haiyan, and the grid-based management and group-based service in Zhanmao Sub-district, Putuo District, Zhoushan City. Cao Xuegen, the Deputy Secretary of the Commission for Political and Legal Affairs of Jiaxing City, Zhang Junda, the Deputy Director of the Department of Publicity under the Party Committee of Zhoushan City, Yang Hongwei, full-time Deputy Director of the Comprehensive Governance Office of Zhoushan City, Teng Genlin, the Deputy Secretary of the Party Committee of Jiashan County, the Secretary of the Commission for Political and Legal Affairs of Jiashan County, and Guo Tenghui, a member of the Standing Committee of the Party Committee of Haiyan County made introductions to the Research Group.

The Volume focuses its research on the practice in the period from 2002 to 2007 during which General Secretary Xi Jinping worked in Zhejiang and that in the period during which the subsequent successive Party Committees of Zhejiang Province acted in the same endeavor and carried through one blueprint; it presents the line of thought from the perspectives of ensuring and improving the people's well-being and maintaining sustained healthy development and keeping balance between development and stability in an area; it shows the line of thought of social development, Zhejiang's path and experience in social development during the period when comrade Xi Jinping worked in Zhejiang, as well as the inspirations. Therefore, the structure of each chapter is generally a thinking exploration—practice (measures, ways, methods)—cases—effects.

The authors of the Volume's chapters are as follows:

Chapter 1, Guangjin Chen (Chinese Academy of Social Sciences);
Chapter 2, Feng Tian (Chinese Academy of Social Sciences);
Chapter 3, Chunguang Wang (Chinese Academy of Social Sciences);
Chapter 4, Jinjun Wang (Party School of the Party Committee of Zhejiang Province);
Chapter 5, Zhijun Liu, Ying Huanhong (Zhejiang University, Zhejiang Academy of Social Sciences);
Chapter 6, Youxing Lang (Zhejiang University);
Chapter 7, Xiumei Zhang (Zhejiang Academy of Social Sciences);
Chapter 8, Jianhua Yang (Zhejiang Academy of Social Sciences);
Chapter 9, Jianhua Yang (Zhejiang Academy of Social Sciences).

Wang Chunguang, Yang Jianhua, Liu Zhijun and Wang Jinjun participated in reading and proofreading the whole book. Wang Chunguang and Yang Jianhua conducted the final compilation and editing of the whole book; Chen Guangjin and Yang Jianhua finalized the book.

The successful completion of the research and writing relating to the book is attributable to the care, support and guidance of the leaders at various levels from the Chinese Academy of Social Sciences, the Party Committee of Zhejiang Province, the Department of Publicity under the Party Committee of Zhejiang Province and the Zhejiang Academy of Social Sciences, the support and help from the leaders of relevant provincial departments, bureaus and offices, municipal and county leaders, the coordination, help and guidance of the leaders from the Bureau of Scientific Research Management of the Chinese Academy of Social Sciences, the Theory Division of the Department of Publicity under the Party Committee of Zhejiang Province, the Division of Scientific Research and the offices of the Zhejiang Academy of Social Sciences. Hu Jian, the Executive Deputy Director of the Department of Publicity under the Party Committee of Zhejiang Province, Jin Yanfeng, the Director and research fellow of the Party History Research Office under the Party Committee of Zhejiang Province, Lan Weiqing, former Vice Chairman and research fellow of the Zhejiang Federation of Humanities and Social

Sciences Circles, Chen Xianchun, the Vice Chairman of the Zhejiang Federation of Humanities and Social Sciences Circles, and other leaders read and proofread the manuscript of the book, gave many pertinent and constructive opinions, and provided good guidance and help for revision of the book.

We hereby express heartfelt thanks to Li Peilin, the Vice President of the Chinese Academy of Social Sciences, Wang Xiaoxi, the Secretary of the Party Committee at the Institute of Sociology of the Chinese Academy of Social Sciences, Hu Jian, the Executive Deputy Director of the Department of Publicity under the Party Committee of Zhejiang Province, Zhang Weibin, the Secretary of the Party Committee at the Zhejiang Academy of Social Sciences, Chi Quanhua, the President of the Zhejiang Academy of Social Sciences, Ge Licheng, the Vice President of the Zhejiang Academy of Social Sciences, Chen Xianchun, the Vice Chairman of the Zhejiang Federation of Humanities and Social Sciences Circles, Lan Weiqing, former Vice Chairman of the Zhejiang Federation of Humanities and Social Sciences Circles, Yu Zhizhuang, the Deputy Director-General of the Department of Civil Affairs of Zhejiang Province and a member of the Party Group at the Department of Civil Affairs of Zhejiang Province, and Zhu Yijun, the Deputy Director-general of the Comprehensive Governance Office of Zhejiang Province, for their guidance and support.

We also express heartfelt thanks to Yu Guojuan, researcher, Deputy Director of the Theory Division of the Department of Publicity under the Party Committee of Zhejiang Province, Hua Zhonglin, the Director of the Office of the Zhejiang Academy of Social Sciences, Yu Jun, the Deputy Director of the Office of the Zhejiang Academy of Social Sciences, Lu Dunji, the Director of the Division of Scientific Research of the Zhejiang Academy of Social Sciences, Li Dong, the Deputy Director of the Division of Scientific Research of the Zhejiang Academy of Social Sciences, Cao Xuegen, the Deputy Secretary of the Commission for Political and Legal Affairs of Jiaxing City, Zhang Junda, the Deputy Director of the Department of Publicity under the Party Committee of Zhoushan City, Yang Hongwei, full-time Deputy Director of the Comprehensive Governance Office of Zhoushan City, Teng Genlin, the Deputy Secretary of the Party Committee of Jiashan County, the Secretary of the Commission for Political and Legal Affairs of Jiashan County, Guo Tenghui, a member of the Standing Committee of the Party Committee of Haiyan County, Xu Yuntai, a member of the Party Working Committee of Hubin Sub-district, Xihu District, Hangzhou City, Xu Limin, the Director of Lakeside Barometer Studio, Shi Haiyan, a member of the Party Working Committee of Kaixuan Sub-district, Jianggan District, Hangzhou City, and Liang Xuzhen, the Secretary of Nanxiaobu Community, Kaixuan Sub-district, Jianggan District, Hangzhou City for their support and help.

Special thanks goes to comrade Lu Yuqun, a staff member of the Office of the Zhejiang Academy of Social Sciences, since she served as the liaison officer for the Research Group of the Volume and carried out a lot of careful and meticulous work on the research and writing relating to the Volume. We thank comrade Mo

Yanqing, assistant research fellow of the Institute of Public Policy of the Zhejiang Academy of Social Sciences, for doing much administrative and technical work for the surveys and writing relating to the Volume. We thank all leaders and personnel who made efforts in the surveys and writing relating to the Volume.

The Research Group of The Chinese Dream
and Zhejiang's Practice·Society Volume
December 10, 2014

# Bibliography

The Division of Social Development of Zhejiang Provincial Development and Reform Commission, A Survey on the Status Quo of Zhejiang's Industrial Structure and Talent Structure Matching, *Zhejiang Economy*, 2005(21).

The Survey Group of the Provincial and Ministerial Class for Advanced Studies at the Party School of the Central Committee of the CPC, There Is No Harmonious Society If There Is No Social Security – Survey Report on Zhejiang's Accelerated Efforts in Building an Extensive Social Security System, *Zhejiang Today*, 2005(7).

Wang Chengming, Yan Yongzhou, Building a New Social Welfare System, *Zhejiang Daily*, September 25, 2009, Page 2.

Wang Chunguang, *The Changes in China's Rural Society*, Yunnan People's Publishing House, 1995.

Wang Chunguang et al, *Social Modernization: Taicang's Practice (Vol. II)*, Social Sciences Academic Press (China), 2012.

Zhang Congqun, A Study of the Transformation Mode of Zhejiang's Small and Medium-sized Enterprises Based on Industrial Cluster, *Economic Review*, 2009(12).

Hu Danyang, From Segmentation to Pooling: A Study of Provincial Social Security Integration – Take Zhejiang as an Example, *Zhejiang Social Sciences*, 2011(5).

Ye Hui, Putting the Improvement of the People's Well-being in a More Prominent Position, *Guang Ming Daily*, March 3, 2008, Page 6.

Yang Jianhua, Zhang Xiumei,Survey Report on Zhejiang's Social Mobility, *Zhejiang Social Sciences*, 2012(7).

Li Jianzhong, Several Issues Concerning Zhejiang's Industrial Transformation and Upgrading, *Zhejiang Economy*, 2009(4).

Wu Jinliang, *Primary-level Social Governance*, China Renmin University Press, 2014.

Han Jun, *Survey Report on China's Rural Policy II*, Shanghai Far East Publishers, 2008.

Duan Juan, Lu Qi, and Wen Yuyuan, Comprehensive Evaluation of Regional and Urban-Rural Interactive and Associated Development, *China Population Resources and Environment*, 2005 (1).

Tian Kai, The Survey Analysis and Thinking of the Urban Adaptability of Rural Migrant Workers, *Social Science Research*, 1995(5).

Huang Kunming, *A Study of the Evolution of Urban-Rural Integration Path*, Science Press, 2010.

Zhu Li, On the Urban Adaptability of the Farmer Class, *Jianghai Academic Journal*, 2002(6).

Zhang Li, Good Governance of Counties Ensures National Stability – Pujiang Sample: the Leading Cadres Visit and Receive the People, *Zhejiang Daily*, March 19, 2014.

© Social Sciences Academic Press and Springer Nature Singapore Pte Ltd. 2019            293
G. Chen and J. Yang (eds.), *Chinese Dream and Practice in Zhejiang—Society*,
Research Series on the Chinese Dream and China's Development Path,
https://doi.org/10.1007/978-981-13-7406-7

Zhang Qingxia, A Study of the Evolution of Zhejiang's Rural Relative Poverty and Its Strategy, *Economic Affairs*, 2011(5).

Guo Shutian, Liu Chunbin, *Unbalanced China*, Hebei Peoples Publishing House, 1990.

Pang Shuqi, Qiu Liping, Preliminary Explorations of the Class and Stratum Structure at the Present Stage of the Chinese Society, *Sociological Study*, 1989(4).

Chen Shida, Ying Jianmin, and Wu Wei, A Study of the Talent Development Strategy of Zhejiang Province for Non-public Enterprises, *The First Resource*, 2012(2).

Luo Weihong, Zhejiang: Exploration and Establishment of the Moderately Universal Child Welfare System, *China Social Welfare*, 2014(3).

Bu Xiaojun, The Institutional Change in the Provision of Rural Public Services in the New China, *Journal of Northwest University (Philosophy and Social Sciences Edition)*, 2010(1).

Lu Xueyi, Wang Chunguang, and Zhang Qizi, *A Study of China's Rural Modernization Path*, Guangxi People's Publishing House, 1998.

Gong Ying, *Innovations in the Social Management Mode – A Study of Zhoushan's Practice in the Grid-based Management and Group-based Service*, Intellectual Property Publishing House, 2012.

Yao Yinmei, The Opportunities and Challenges in Zhejiang's Talent Resource Development after Accession to the WTO, *Human Resources Development of China*, 2001(12).

Fu Yunsheng, The Constraint Conditions for Industrial Transformation and Upgrading, Development Trends in Zhejiang, *Zhejiang Academic Journal*, 2010(5).

Printed by Printforce, the Netherlands